FINANCING SOVEREIGNTY

Financing Sovereignty

THE POYAIS SCANDAL
IN THE EARLY
NINETEENTH-CENTURY ATLANTIC WORLD

Damian Clavel

Translated by
Anthony Bulger
and
George Fowler

STANFORD UNIVERSITY PRESS
Stanford, California

Stanford University Press
Stanford, California

English translation ©2025 by the Board of Trustees of the Leland Stanford Jr. University. All rights reserved.

Translated by Anthony Bulger and George Fowler with support from the Howard Marks Chair in Economic History at the University of Pennsylvania.

A version of this work was originally published in French in 2022 under the title *Créer un pays, le royaume de Poyais: Gregor MacGregor, emprunts d'État et fraude financière 1820–1824* [Creating a Country, the Kingdom of Poyais: Gregor MacGregor, State Loans and Financial Fraud 1820–1824]. ©2022, Éditions Livreo-Alphil, Neuchâtel, Switzerland.

No part of this book may be reproduced or transmitted in any form or by any means, electronic or mechanical, including photocopying and recording, or in any information storage or retrieval system, without the prior written permission of Stanford University Press.

Library of Congress Cataloging-in-Publication Data
Names: Clavel, Damian, author.
Title: Financing sovereignty : the Poyais scandal in the early nineteenth-century Atlantic world / Damian Clavel ; translated by Anthony Bulger and George Fowler.
Other titles: Créer un pays, le royaume de Poyais. English
Description: Stanford, California : Stanford University Press, 2025. | "A version of this work was originally published in French in 2022 under the title Créer un pays, le royaume de Poyais: Gregor MacGregor, emprunts d'État et fraude financière 1820-1824." | Includes bibliographical references and index.
Identifiers: LCCN 2024049949 (print) | LCCN 2024049950 (ebook) | ISBN 9781503641730 (cloth) | ISBN 9781503643215 (paperback) | ISBN 9781503643222 (ebook)
Subjects: LCSH: MacGregor, Gregor, 1786-1845. | Bank fraud—England—London—History—19th century. | Swindlers and swindling—Great Britain—History—19th century. | Investments, British—Central America—History—19th century. | Mosquitia (Nicaragua and Honduras)—History—19th century. | Central America—Colonization—History—19th century.
Classification: LCC HV6692.M32 C53 2025 (print) | LCC HV6692.M32 (ebook) | DDC 364.16/309421—dc23/eng/20250121
LC record available at https://lccn.loc.gov/2024049949
LC ebook record available at https://lccn.loc.gov/2024049950

Cover design: Ann Weinstock
Cover art: William Home Lizars, "View of the Port of Black River in the Territory of Poyais," engraving in *Sketch of the Mosquito Shore, Including the Territory of Poyais*, by Thomas Strangeways (Edinburgh: W. Blackwood, 1822). Courtesy of the John Carter Brown Library, Brown University.

The authorized representative in the EU for product safety and compliance is: Mare Nostrum Group B.V. | Mauritskade 21D | 1091 GC Amsterdam | The Netherlands | Email address: gpsr@mare-nostrum.co.uk | KVK chamber of commerce number: 96249943

With gratitude to the Howard Marks Chair in Economic History at the University of Pennsylvania for supporting this translation.

Contents

Preface		vii
	Introduction	1
ONE	Once upon a Time, Moskitia	21
TWO	A Miskitu Land Grant	52
THREE	A Protean Plan	73
FOUR	A Foreign Loan	102
FIVE	Saving Poyais	137
SIX	Shadow Government	176
	Conclusion	192
Notes		209
Bibliography		245
Index		269

Preface

The idea of writing this book emerged from the aftermath of the 2008 financial crisis. I was struck at the time by how the media and scientific community had treated different financial scams that came to light following the meltdown—the most emblematic being the scheme devised by Bernard Madoff. I was especially intrigued by the way in which history was employed as a scholarly discipline to draw questionable connections between the most recent debacle and past crises. Leading newspapers, works of fiction, and even scientific papers explored great frauds from history perpetrated by the likes of Victor Lustig, Charles Ponzi, and Nick Leeson, passing them off as tragicomic one-offs in order to put the damage into perspective or to reassure investors undone by the scams. But these episodes were not given due scientific attention, except to dwell on their humorous side. The historical research on financial fraud appeared to rely, at best, on a scant selection of sources, many of which could be discounted as they were attributable to the con artists in question. To my mind, many historical cases of financial fraud were sealed in a kind of analytical black box that prevented their internal complexities from being examined as anything other than examples of extraordinary deeds by supposedly inveterate fraudsters.

My initial research goal was to revisit and unpick the many threads making up one specific case of financial fraud. So why not choose the biggest of all time: Gregor MacGregor's "fake" country of Poyais? In accounts of multifaceted financial frauds from the past, MacGregor is often put in a category of his own. Nicknamed the "King of Con-Men," he traveled in the 1820s to the City of London, then the world's largest financial center, styling himself as the cacique, or ruler, of Poyais, a state in Central American Moskitia, between present-day Honduras and Nicaragua. To finance his country's improvement, MacGregor issued loans worth several hundred thousand pounds sterling—equivalent to millions today—on the City's booming market in South American sovereign debt. But he did not have full sovereignty over the territory, and public opinion soon came to view him as a swindler who had managed to dupe the British financial community into believing in a made-up country.

By offering a fresh perspective on the history of Poyais, this book offers several contributions. The first is historiographic. In opening up the Poyais black box, it delves into the previously overlooked specifics of MacGregor's venture. Rather than simply telling the story of a huge, unprecedented fraud in a way that disconnects the events from their era, by compiling many hitherto unseen archive documents from England, Scotland, France, and Belize, and analyzing them through the prism of the individual, regional, and transcontinental factors at play, we reveal a complex and multilayered political, financial, and commercial enterprise. This is not the tale of a compulsive con man, but of a Scottish mercenary, a former soldier in the revolutionary armies of South America who was trying desperately to establish a colony and a military base that would benefit not just the local Indigenous Miskitu but also the new Latin American republicans and British transatlantic trade. Exploiting the lack of clarity within the British government and the City's financial institutions about recognizing the recently decolonized South American territories, MacGregor sought to raise money for his commercial and political enterprise on the London sovereign debt market. Seen in this light, the notion of issuing a loan on London's capital markets in the opening decades of the nineteenth century seems less like financial fraud and more like an ultimately unsuccessful attempt to finance the establishment of a politically and commercially independent territory in Central America. MacGregor was hired to help build a Miskitu country: Poyais. This book places Gregor MacGregor back in his own time, an era marked by a proliferation of private British trade and financial schemes aiming to exploit the natural resources of the hazily defined American territories emerging from Spain's crumbling empire. The sad story of Poyais, so often held up as an exception, is shown to be almost banal, with strong resemblances to those of other new American republics, including Colombia, Chile, and Peru, that likewise sought to bankroll their independence on England's financial market.

This book's second contribution is methodological and concerns the study of social sciences more generally. Rather than reinterpret an amusing historical fable, we assume that a close analysis of one seemingly outlying case study can open the way to broader conjectures. This novel examination of MacGregor's Poyais thus opens a portal that reveals numerous new fields—or "worlds"—of investigation, and highlights the political, economic, legal, and social dynamics of the financial and imperial transformations sweeping across the Atlantic space in the early nineteenth century. Through the story of a failed sovereign loan, this reinterpretation of Poyais contributes to the research on the nascent transatlantic credit market and imperial relations between the loosely defined new political entities in the Americas and the City of London. However, instead of focusing, as some historians have done, on the prominent figures and players who dominated this era of change, such as Rothschild and Barings, probably the two most influential merchant banks of the day, we propose to examine another case that may seem less important or appears to be a failure at first glance, in order to uncover some of the peculiarities and complexities of a time that the historian Eric Hobsbawm famously called the "Age of Revolution."[1] In pursuit of this goal, this book identifies the political and legal frameworks governing issuance processes for new sovereign loans, their recognition, and sustainable access to international capital markets. Seen through the Poyais lens, the principle of sovereignty is shown to be a malleable concept that was manipulated by individuals and groups—not just in London but also in Central America—to support commercial, financial, and political schemes amid a fast-changing imperial environment.

This study, like those of many other historians, owes much to the work of Carlo Ginzburg, and in particular *The Cheese and the Worms*.[2] First published in 1976, Ginzburg's book explores the world of Domenico "Menocchio" Scandella, an insignificant Italian miller tried at the end of the sixteenth century by the Roman Inquisition and executed as a heretic for daring to invent his own cosmogony. Scandella believed that creation began with an original rotten mass, like a piece of cheese, riddled with worms, which were angels. His unorthodox understanding of the divine stemmed essentially from his conflation of the printed works that he had read, such as the Bible in vernacular translation, Giovanni Boccaccio's *The Decameron*, and Sir John Mandeville's *Travels*, with the oral tradition that he had grown up with. Through his study of this single person, Ginzburg reveals far more than the cultural underpinnings of Menocchio's individual and unique belief system. He sheds light on the miller's capacity to allow the different worlds that he had encountered—the Reformation, the Counter-Reformation, an ancient agrarian oral culture—to coexist in his individual reality. Similarly, our close analysis of MacGregor and his deeds—repeated or one-off interactions, successes, travels, victories, losses, military grandeur, and financial downfall—not only exposes significant and hitherto unsuspected trade and financial connections linking a fast-changing Atlantic world. By reinterpreting the history of Poyais and resetting it in its various contexts—London, Europe, Atlantic, Latin America, financial, military, imperial, colonial, Indigenous—we demonstrate how these interconnections were able to exist and be maintained, albeit briefly, through MacGregor himself.

I would like to express my deepest gratitude to all the people and institutions that supported the research that provided the foundation for this book. I must first express my profound gratitude to those closest to me. Words cannot adequately capture the depth of appreciation and love I hold for these individuals. I will nevertheless try to convey to each of them, heart to heart, how their presence, unwavering support, patience, and inspiration have been the bedrock upon which this book was built. Their contributions are woven into the very fabric of this work.

While the personal support I received was invaluable, this book really owes its existence to a wide array of academic colleagues and institutions. Their guidance, resources, and expertise were instrumental in bringing this project to fruition. The intellectual foundations of this book owe first and foremost to Marc Flandreau, whom I thank for believing in my project from its infancy. This undertaking would never have come about without his invaluable support, enthusiasm, and the enormous kindness with which he constantly pushed me out of my intellectual comfort zone. I equally thank Pilar Nogues-Marco for her precious advice, encouragement, and support, as well as the careful initial readers—Susanna Hecht, Jean-Laurent Rosenthal, and Richard White—for their thoughts and feedback.

I would like to extend my deepest gratitude to the Howard Marks Chair in Economic History at the University of Pennsylvania for its most generous support in funding the translation of this book from French to English. The translation of this work also owes much to the work of Anthony Bulger and George Fowler. Their skillful renditions have not only bridged the language gap but have also enriched the text in unexpected ways. Anthony Bulger's contribution deserves special mention: his illuminating notes in the manuscript's margins offered fresh perspectives and occasionally challenged my own language, ultimately enhancing the clarity and depth of the final text. My sincere thanks also go to the Haiti Seminar for organizing a book panel discussing an early version of the translated manuscript, and especially to the commentators Maria Christina Chatziioannou, Anna Gelpern, Trevor Jackson, and Nathaniel Millett for their invaluable and encouraging comments. I am grateful to the editorial team at Stanford University Press—Margo Irvin, Kate Wahl, Natalie Gabriela Rovero, Amy J. Schneider, and Emily Smith—for their guidance and support throughout the publication process. I would also like to express my appreciation to Alain Cortat and Rachel Maeder of Alphil, whose enthusiasm was instrumental in bringing this English edition to fruition.

The genesis of this work also owes a debt of gratitude to two individuals who played pivotal roles in its early stages. My thanks go to Youssef Cassis, whose introduction to Poyais sparked the initial flame of curiosity that would eventually become this book. Equally deserving of recognition is Matthew Dziennik, whose unwavering support from the very outset of this Poyaisian adventure provided both encouragement and valuable insights.

This research drew upon a vast array of scattered sources, made accessible through the infrastructure and assistance of numerous institutions. I am grateful for the warm welcome and excellent resources provided by several institutions where I conducted research: the California Institute of Technology, the Huntington Library, the University of Pennsylvania, and Oxford University. These institutions not only granted me access to their collections but also provided me with the support and setting to transform my research into this book. Patricia Arnold, Laurel Auchampaugh, Dominic Eggel, Jeanne Ruch, Valérie Von Daeniken, and Ghislaine Ann Wharton provided invaluable assistance and advice in navigating some of these institutions.

I am also deeply indebted to the myriad archives that granted access to their collections. From the departmental archives of Dordogne to the National Archives in Kew, each institution contributed vital pieces to unraveling the story of Poyais. I am particularly indebted to Mary Alpuche (Belize

State Records and Archives Service in Belmopan), Justin Cavernelis-Frost (Rothschild Archive in London), and Siân Yates (Lloyds Banking Group Archives in Edinburgh), for their assistance in unearthing crucial documents. I am also grateful to Martine Basset and Yves Corpataux from the Graduate Institute of International and Development Studies at Geneva, for answering innumerable calls for bibliographic assistance.

Finally, I would like to express my gratitude to the Graduate Institute of International and Development Studies in Geneva, the Swiss National Science Foundation, the Howard Marks Chair in Economic History of the University of Pennsylvania, and the Economic History Society for the financial assistance provided throughout this research.

FINANCING SOVEREIGNTY

Introduction

ON MAY 1, 1824, the *Newcastle Courant* reported on a trial that had taken place a few days earlier at the Court of King's Bench in London in which one Sir Gregor MacGregor sued his financial agent, Mr. Lowe, for £10,000. This amount, which MacGregor claimed his agent had failed to pay him, was allegedly part of a much bigger, "famous" Poyais sovereign loan. However, much to MacGregor's dismay, the court dismissed the case: The judges found that there was no "State of Poyais" and that the entire affair was nothing more than a "bubble."[1]

On November 9 of the same year, the committee in charge of the Foreign Stock Market in the City of London—a specialized market trading in foreign securities that opened in 1823—formally announced that it no longer recognized bonds issued against the Poyais loan.[2] In doing so, the market's committee confirmed the rumor that had made headlines for some time in the London papers and done the rounds of the City's coffeehouses—hubs of trade and finance to which traders flocked after the markets closed—that the country did not actually exist. Yet hundreds of bonds from a loan worth hundreds of thousands of pounds sterling had been trading on London's financial markets for more than a year. Launched to great fanfare in October 1822, the debt issue was initially earmarked to develop the bountiful Central American lands allegedly controlled by MacGregor, who presented himself as Cazique and Prince of Poyais.[3]

By 1824, the bonds were trading for pennies and had been pulled from the official market, for want of buyers. By the time the Foreign Stock Market Committee made its announcement, MacGregor was no longer seen as the dashing Scottish mercenary who had bravely signed up alongside thousands

1

of other British volunteers a decade earlier to join the Creole revolutionaries in toppling the American bastions of Spain's faltering empire. Rather than the charming leader of a new American state in need of capital to consolidate its independence, MacGregor would, from then on, be portrayed by caricaturists and other wits as a wicked con artist, a shamefaced fraudster crowned with the straw and smoke of his own disillusionment who had tricked his fellow countrymen into believing in an imaginary country (Fig. 1).[4]

In the early 1820s, London went wild for Latin American securities.[5] In the aftermath of the Napoleonic Wars and revolutionary uprisings in South America, there was growing enthusiasm within the London financial community for transatlantic trade and financial opportunities of all kinds. A speculative bubble formed in the City as investors plunged into a market whose primary purpose was to exploit the perceived wealth of the New World, which was gradually being freed from the Spanish yoke and suddenly opened up to British business. Investors rushed to buy shares in companies created to harness American resources. They also flocked to buy sovereign loans, interest-bearing instruments representing government debt that were split into bonds, for the new states of South America. As a global financial powerhouse, the City was a key talking partner for agents of the new governments formed following the fall of Spain's empire, who came to England to negotiate and issue the loans needed to fund their war efforts and develop novel economic and political systems. Between 1822 and 1825, new states such as Colombia, Peru, Mexico, and Chile each issued one or more loans, worth tens of millions of pounds on the London market. Information gleaned from merchants' letters or countries' newspapers concerning their political, commercial, or fiscal situation was slow to cross the Atlantic, so investing in their bonds was considered a risky business, but one for which investors were nonetheless rewarded with a premium compared with British funds and other European bonds. This created an environment in which it was hard to distinguish between new borrowers seeking financing in London and to separate the wheat from the chaff.[6]

Legend has it that Poyais was worse than just a lower-quality sovereign borrower: It was the imaginary brainchild of Gregor MacGregor. The narrative that has persisted until today goes something like this: Born in 1786 in Scotland, MacGregor led a colorful life as a military officer and mercenary in Europe and South America (Fig. 2) before embarking on his most notorious

Figure 1. Poyais royalty in quad, with a crown of straw and smoke. Source: John Fairburn, *Poyais Royalty in Quad, or the Cacique Waiting for Bail*, 1827, paper, 350x248, 1868,0808.8817, British Museum, London. © The Trustees of the British Museum.

Figure 2. Gregor MacGregor. Source: George Watson, *Gregor MacGregor*, 1804, National Gallery of Scotland, Edinburgh. Purchased 1972.

endeavor: the Poyais scheme. After claiming to have acquired land rights in Central America, MacGregor invented the fictional country of Poyais and presented himself as its cazique, or ruler. He leveraged his reputation as a decorated military officer, as well as his connections to South American revolutionaries, to gain credibility in London society. The financial aspect of MacGregor's fraud was extensive. He issued a £200,000 sovereign loan for Poyais on the London Stock Exchange in 1822, which was hungry for anything relating to Spanish American investments. Floated alongside the loans of other new states such as Colombia, Peru, or Chile, MacGregor's loan was quick to find takers and was soon fully subscribed. His scheme, which was elaborate and impossible to verify, attracted hordes of investors, and the bonds quickly traded above their issue price. In other words, MacGregor had become rich by making people believe in a country that never existed, thus pulling off perhaps one of the most audacious frauds in history. However, when reports reached London from Central America, they revealed that Poyais did not exist. The exposure of MacGregor's fraud had immediate repercussions. As knowledge of the deception proliferated, Poyais bonds rapidly depreciated on the Foreign Stock Market, resulting in significant financial losses for those investors who were credulous enough to have believed the cacique's tales.

At the height of the Poyais scandal, one commentator wrote in the *Times* in October 1824 that Poyais was a "medley of knavery and credulity—[an] extraordinary mixture of impudent imposture and confiding folly."[7] By then, it had become the scandalous synonym for financial fraud, greed, and even the absurdity of certain financial practices. Further, MacGregor's loan was seen as an obvious folly that met its seemingly inevitable fate. For later writers and caricaturists, Poyais remained a byword for credulousness, fraud, and scandal in financial circles and far beyond, not just in the mid-1820s but for years to come. An anonymous handbill written in 1827 about investments considered shady warned British investors about other "Poyais humbug[s]."[8] Poyais was also believed to share dubious qualities with other financial projects of the period. Shortly after the project was officially denounced by the Foreign Stock Market, the London-based caricaturist Charles Williams depicted Poyais as a financial soap bubble emitting a thick cloud of black smoke as it bursts (Fig. 3). Although one of the few to have actually popped, the Poyais bubble floats alongside many others, each bearing the name of an obscure and presumably speculative enterprise.[9] A crowd of investors of vastly disparate backgrounds, driven by urgency, jostles below the burst or soon-to-pop bubbles, eager to acquire shares.

The story of Poyais also spread beyond the City of London. In a novel first published in 1839, Alexandre Dumas told the adventures of a French sailor, Captain Pamphile, who introduces himself to London high society as Don Gusman y Pamphilos, Cazique of Poyais, and convinces his audience to take out a loan for an obscure Central American territory. Here, Dumas used MacGregor's story to portray international finance in the aftermath of the 1837 panics as the vicious, malignant tormentor of the innocent victims standing in its way (whom Dumas portrays as exotic animals).[10] As a testament to the effectiveness of this Poyais story, Dumas's novel was reprinted shortly after the May 1873 banking crisis in a lavishly illustrated edition by Charles Albert d'Arnoux, also known as Bertall, a famous caricaturist (Fig. 4).[11]

Accounts such as Dumas's have been woven into a tale of credulity and

Figure 3. Bubbles for 1825. Source: Charles Williams, *Bubbles for 1825- or- Fortunes Made by Steam*, 1824, paper, 250mm x 353mm, 1868,0808.8629, British Museum London. © The Trustees of the British Museum.

Figure 4. Captain Pamphile, after Bertall. Source: Alexandre Dumas, *Le capitaine Pamphile* (Paris: Calmann-Lévy, 1877). Bibliothèque de France.

greed that has since been told again and again. Its outlines have become legendary, even mythical, and are invoked almost ritually whenever financial speculation or fraud are in question. The Poyais scandal has spawned novels, plays, and even paintings.[12] Yet aside from their comical appeal, MacGregor's deeds tend to be viewed, contradictorily, as a footnote of history. And because of the scandal's brief time span, it tends to be discounted as worthless "noise," its existence anchored in a fleeting, haphazard, or accidental reality. The number of people affected by the actions of the self-styled cazique relegates the story to the ranks of a minor event. At a total face value of £200,000, the Poyais loan issued in London in October 1822 was small compared with other contemporary foreign borrowings. That same year, Prussia had plans to borrow £3.5 million on the London capital market, while Russia was proposing to issue bonds worth £5 million.[13] Bereft of interest beyond its supposedly singular aspect, the Poyais story could have happened anytime, anywhere. Its tragicomic qualities are such a compelling conversation topic that the economic historical underpinnings often seem irrelevant. Yet the tale's exceptional qualities alone suffice to account for the very existence of the imaginary land.

An analysis of historical treatments of the Poyais affair nevertheless offers valuable insights and reveals recurrent themes that emerge frequently, if not consistently. Most scholars have characterized it as an anomalous historical occurrence, generally fraudulent, often citing it briefly before dismissing it as a mere curiosity. MacGregor's actions apparently have been deemed unworthy of serious historical inquiry beyond their anecdotal value. Consequently, instead of providing contextual analysis, accounts of the Poyais affair tend to present it as an isolated incident, stemming solely from MacGregor's pathological motivations.

The narratives surrounding the Poyais scheme find their place within a more expansive discourse on financial malfeasance, both contemporary and historical. In the wake of the 2008 financial crisis, a frenzied quest ensued to identify culpable parties, with particular emphasis on supposed confidence tricksters whose actions catalyzed widespread economic ruin.[14] Figures such as Kweku Adoboli and Jérôme Kerviel, responsible for staggering losses at UBS and Société Générale respectively, emerged as emblematic of this tumultuous period.[15] Yet it was Bernie Madoff, architect of a breathtakingly vast Ponzi scheme, who was revealed as the quintessential figure of financial treachery.[16] All these individuals, portrayed as manipulating the inherent flaws of the financial system, are often cast as social deviants with underlying pathological conditions.[17] The fervent media attention lavished upon them betrayed a collective moral panic, yet offered scant critique of the very structures they exploited. In seeking historical antecedents, commentators drew parallels with notorious figures like Charles Ponzi and Victor Lustig, thereby weaving a continuous narrative of pecuniary avarice and deception across time.[18] Such historical analogies serve a dual purpose: They stand as cautionary tales, portending future financial calamities, while simultaneously offering a peculiar form of reassurance.[19] By excavating tales of past malfeasance, these narratives implicitly suggest that—despite contemporary woes—modern financial systems have actually progressed. The egregious nature of historical swindles, when juxtaposed against present-day scandals, tacitly argues for the relative sophistication and security of current financial institutions. This comparative exercise casts a rather flattering light on the present, implying—however unintentionally—that while imperfect, our financial systems have evolved beyond the vulnerabilities of a past that was much worse in terms of the boldness of the perpetrators or the credulity of their victims.[20] Regularly given mythical status as the supreme figure in this pantheon of crooks, MacGregor stands apart in such stories. He is systematically portrayed as a cheeky fraudster who succeeded in conning gullible investors into believing in a puppet state about which they knew absolutely nothing.[21] Compared with Poyais, the infamous Madoff fraud pales into insignificance. Worse still, presenting the Poyais scam in this way and calling its perpetrator a "champion of fraud" almost fulfills the quest for original evil. The Christmas 2012 issue of *The Economist* announced the end of that quest, calling MacGregor the worthy "King of Con-Men."[22]

Most of the modern-day images of the Poyais scheme come from the biography of MacGregor by David Sinclair.[23] Giving ample details of his subject's military career and the Poyais venture, Sinclair portrays the scheme as the culmination of a swindler's ambitions. While certainly offering interesting insights into MacGregor's background, the book fails to provide a comprehensive account of the Poyais project: It presents the affair as an isolated incident stemming from MacGregor's personal motives, without considering the broader historical context. Sinclair's main source draws from two key articles by Alfred Hasbrouck and Victor Allan, which together form the questionable basis of contemporary historical understanding of the Poyais affair.[24] Hasbrouck describes it as a huge fraud organized solely so that MacGregor could lead a life of luxury in London using money raised on the sovereign debt market. Above all, the author portrays this so-called crook as a protagonist with values intrinsically distant from what he himself defines as "British morality." Briefly put, the article makes a ferocious attack on Scottish identity and attributes the failure of the cazique's plan less to the turmoil affecting the newly emerging independent territories of Central and South America, and more to a form of social unsuitability affecting the Scots, who are depicted as greedy and incapable. Victor Allan's interpretation of the Poyais affair is based on similar assumptions. It portrays MacGregor as a lucky villain who managed to build a "monstrous fabrication" without being held to account. Although Allan mentions the difficulty of sending news across the Atlantic as a plausible cause for the naïveté of British investors, his argument is nonetheless moralistic. MacGregor's Poyais project is described as "highly mischievous product of human nature," explained by a lack of scruples. Accordingly, Allan's text, filled with moralistic Christian imagery that transforms the Poyais story into a parable of amorality, differs little from Hasbrouck's. Both authors depict Poyais with little to no empirical evidence as a con man's scheme to get rich by duping gullible investors. Their studies seem preachy, their analysis based on Manichean concepts of natural or identity-based righteousness. MacGregor thus personifies the perfect expression of human greed during a period when, according to both authors, British values were being eroded.

In sum, the vast majority of studies on Poyais offer "exceptionalist" biographies in which MacGregor is detached from the environment of his time. This view exemplifies what Roland Barthes calls a myth—a linguistic element given a socially defined function and meaning different from its original signification.[25] Yet, much like Barthes's analysis of Greta Garbo's face as more than just that of an actress, MacGregor's portrayal as the ultimate fraudster overshadows any meaningful study of Poyais itself. This does not mean, however, that the historiography of the case has been completely neglected. Some of the authors who have dealt with MacGregor provide essential tools for historical understanding, particularly with regard to the military careers of adventurers engaged under foreign flags in the aftermath of the Napoleonic Wars. Research by Matthew Brown and Moises Enrique Rodríguez, for example, illustrates beautifully the often conflicting issues that arose throughout the career of a former British serviceman who joined the Bolivarian armies as a mercenary.[26] Their analysis contextualizes MacGregor's actions within Latin American independence movements, viewing practices such as self-assumption of noble titles as commonplace among New World caudillos. Brown also challenges the portrayal of MacGregor as an opportunistic coward who saved his own life at the expense of those of his subordinates by fleeing the combat zone (a trait too often portrayed as a foretaste of his monumental fraud), suggesting instead that the Scotsman's military defeats were simply due to superior opponents. In the histories that mention Poyais, however, Brown's analysis, and those similar to it, are largely in the minority.[27] As soon as the financial aspects of Poyais are addressed, the research seems to take the consensus view that the foreign loan was fraudulent. At best, some studies show Poyais as part of the spirit of the times, epitomized by the excesses of the speculative bubble caused by trading in Latin American bonds.[28] At worst, these writers hold up Poyais as a historical anecdote, merely embodying MacGregor's fraudulent dreams of grandeur and personal gain.[29]

We are thus left with a picture of Poyais in which the underlying assumption is that intrinsic and independent malice informed most, if not all, of MacGregor's actions. Yet historical research on Poyais has relied, at best, on a narrow selection of printed sources, generally discarded as inherently fraudulent because they are considered to have been penned by MacGregor himself. Consequently, the strategies, validations, and justifications he puts forward are systematically discarded as the lies of a deviant. More importantly, such research also denies any agency on the part of investors, financiers, settlers, or indeed anyone else involved in the Poyais project. If acknowledged, they are implicitly portrayed as infantile, dull, or lackluster, and bewitched by the cazique's almost supernatural charisma. For most observers, Poyais appears as the absurd but brilliant project designed by a swindler to ensnare gullible investors, an analysis that reinforces the image of the con artist as a scapegoat for the failures or flaws of financial systems. In consequence, any economic, social, or political considerations concerning the foundations of the Poyais project are treated as superfluous historical issues, and MacGregor himself as a mere financial criminal, albeit a supremely talented one.

This book takes a different approach. It revisits the story of Poyais by lifting the veil of blame that has been laid too often and too hastily over Gregor

MacGregor's actions—about which little is truly known—as he issued new sovereign debt on London's booming capital market. Briefly put, we take fraud and accusations of fraud as serious objects of historical inquiry. This involves considering the sources stemming from the Poyais case not as exceptionally fraudulent but for what they actually are, namely historical sources that perhaps tell us something about the political and economic contexts in which MacGregor evolved.[30] In doing so, we set ourselves apart from the many studies that pigeonhole the Poyaisian project as a quasi-mythical example of human greed at its worst.

The book also recognizes that archival records of and about Poyais exist. Considering MacGregor's story as void of any interest other than its humorous features, authors writing about his financial project deem it unnecessary to base their understanding of the scheme on an extensive collection of sources. By overlooking a wealth of British and foreign sources, researchers have often given themselves the dubious right to choose, judge, and discredit any evidence or testimony that clashes with their primary assumptions. This book, by contrast, follows a trail of clues through a diverse and fragmented body of archive material, tracking the elusive traces left by MacGregor not only in the City of London—an obvious destination when researching foreign loans in the early nineteenth century—but also in other parts of the world to which MacGregor traveled as he sought to turn Poyais into reality.[31] We assume that the best sources for studying these twists and turns are those of the Poyais project themselves.

Wherever possible, we draw on documents connected with MacGregor's (mis)adventures. Although Poyais has no national archive in the true sense of the term, European and American archives, both physical and digital, yield an extensive collection of hitherto unseen correspondence and other documentation.[32] Often using investigative tools that were nonexistent just a few years ago, we found various historical clues, previously hard to identify, in England, Scotland, Belize (formerly British Honduras), Venezuela, and, rather unexpectedly, the Périgord region of France.[33] The sources themselves take various forms, including published documents such as reports, newspaper articles, obituaries, and brochures, as well as originals and reproductions of handwritten documents. These include letters between people involved directly or indirectly in the promotion and eventual collapse of MacGregor's project; minutes of meetings by financial and business organizations caught up in the case, such as the Rothschild Archive and the committee of the Foreign Stock Market; and the registers of several English courts, including the Court of Chancery and the Court of King's Bench. The trail left by MacGregor and other protagonists in the Poyais story also crops up in a broad swathe of secondary literature across a range of seemingly unconnected topics, from the military history of Latin America to the colonial history of Central America and the history of global capital markets.

When we move beyond sensationalized accounts and examine Poyais more critically, a nuanced narrative emerges—one that nevertheless remains captivating.[34] Historians have well shown how closely studying the life of a single, marginal individual or institution can reveal the often unsuspected interweaving of local, regional, or even global dynamics in which they were embedded.[35] Rather than a simple story of deception, there emerges from the Poyais story a complex mix of early nineteenth-century finance, state-making, imperialism, and ultimately, failure. The Poyais affair serves as a lens through which we can examine the intricate and often precarious workings of the emerging international bond markets at a time when new states were not only being created, but their very creditworthiness was being constructed and, in the case of Poyais, dismantled. We must consider this within the broader context of the era. Alexander Hamilton, in his influential 1790 "First Report on the Public Debt," had already articulated the critical importance of establishing—or more accurately, reestablishing—the credit of the United States. As the first Secretary of the Treasury of a newly formed country emerging from revolutionary turmoil, he recognized that financing its continued existence would be impossible without sound credit.[36] However, Hamilton's efforts were not unique. Nascent states such as Colombia, Peru, Chile, and indeed Poyais all occupied a similar, nebulous position in international finance. These entities existed in a liminal space, their political legitimacy and financial credit often recognized only by a trifecta of interested parties: the states' representatives themselves, their hopeful bondholders, and those members of the London capital market willing to trade in their securities. But this book also reveals a forgotten story, one that reaches far beyond the confines of the City of London, across the Atlantic into the Caribbean.[37] By broadening the picture, we reveal a global picture containing a large group of actors in different areas of inquiry not considered to be traditionally linked to that of the London-based South American foreign loan market. The cast of characters includes Latin American revolutionaries, British Honduran slavers, Jamaican planters, senior officials of the Colonial Office, and, more importantly, American Indigenous peoples.

In sum, this fresh examination of the Poyais scandal reveals a narrative that is strikingly different from the one commonly told. Upon closer inspection, many of the assumptions and key details that have long underpinned the traditional story prove to be inaccurate. For example, Poyais was not merely a fictional construct designed to facilitate a fraudulent loan; it was a tangible place with real geographical and political dimensions. Taking MacGregor's story seriously reveals how the Poyais loan was actually the financial side of a political independence enterprise led by a Central American Indigenous leader, the Miskitu king George Frederic.[38] It also reveals how the latter's ambitions would have echoes within the English capital market, as well as repercussions on the shaping of the London Foreign Stock Market's regulations governing the recognition of new sovereigns. A few years before the first Poyais loan was floated in London, MacGregor received a substantial land grant from the Miskitu king. This territory, christened Poyais, was envisioned as a commercial and political venture that would materially benefit Central American Indigenous peoples, as well as Caribbean and American trade interests. To support this Central American Indigenous effort, MacGregor was hired to raise funds for Poyais in London. However, he did not just sell bonds from a single Poyais loan but from at least three between 1822 and 1824, amounting to between £200,000 and £725,000 and bearing interest of between 2 and 6 percent, for the "Service of the State of Poyais." Rather than serving solely to enrich MacGregor, these London-based fundraising efforts were intended to support the ambitious Miskitu project. The funds they raised were spent on sending English, Scottish, and even French workers aboard five ships to support the economic and political improvement of the Miskitu leader's polity. In this light, MacGregor's role changes significantly. Rather than being the mastermind behind an elaborate fraudulent scheme, he becomes a financial intermediary, an instrument in a larger, eventually failed enterprise—a crucial cog in a Central American Indigenous leader's state-building aspirations.

The process of decolonization in Spanish America, particularly its political aspects, has been extensively studied by historians.[39] The chain of events began in 1808 when Napoleon Bonaparte invaded the Iberian Peninsula and replaced Ferdinand VII with his brother Joseph on the Spanish throne.[40] This led Spanish American elites, who initially remained loyal to the Bourbon dynasty, to take local political control in the absence of their legitimate ruler. These actions eventually evolved into movements that were more independent and republican. Yet historians have shown how this was no straightforward march to independence. Instead, as figures like Simón Bolívar, Francisco de Paula Santander, and José de San Martín took up arms against Spanish royalists, they embarked on a "labyrinthine" quest to forge new social foundations amid the crumbling edifice of colonial norms.[41] The process was as much about reimagining society as it was about military victory.

This political reimagining and reshaping of Latin America drew from a far deeper well of influence than traditional accounts suggest.[42] European veterans, particularly British soldiers cast adrift after Napoleon's fall, saw a chance to ply their military skills as mercenaries or privateers in these conflicts.[43] More critically, recent scholarship has unearthed the pivotal role played by free people of color, whose contributions to both resistance movements and political restructuring have long been overshadowed.[44] The rich tapestry of actors involved in these upheavals—revolutionaries, privateers, mercenaries, and political thinkers alike—gave birth to a kaleidoscope of political visions. The nation-state in itself was not an inevitable endpoint but merely one possibility among a swirling array of competing ideals. Their imaginations, forged in the crucible of Spanish imperial collapse, ranged far beyond the borders of modern nationhood, encompassing a spectrum of potential futures as varied as the individuals who fought to bring them into being.[45] These more recent historiographical developments have just started to unveil the rich variety of political visions and, more crucially, the diverse forms of agency that were fundamental to shaping American independence. This new perspective paints these revolutionary and decolonial processes as consisting of myriad alternative paths to state-making.

The formation of new states and their projection into uncertain futures is not merely a political narrative but a deeply financial one as well. This intertwining of politics and finance has been well documented by historians, particularly in relation to the necessity for fledgling nations to finance both their decolonization and the subsequent longevity of their independence. Broadly, scholars have demonstrated the critical role of credit and financing in the development of state capacities.[46] The case of Latin American and

Caribbean decolonization is a particularly illustrative example of how these independence movements were not confined financially to the Spanish Main or the West Indies but extended across the Atlantic to the heart of European financial centers.[47] The initial uprisings against Spanish rule in the 1810s were often financed by private credit, frequently allocated by British merchants eager to secure potential commercial privileges in the event of republican victories.[48] This financial involvement only deepened in the subsequent decade. In the 1820s, several sovereign loans were issued on the London Stock Exchange to benefit the newly independent American countries. Colombia, Peru, and Chile each issued bonds in 1822, totaling a substantial £4.2 million. These new borrowers paved the way for other emerging countries in Latin America, which hastened to raise funds to finance the consolidation of their independence. This burgeoning American debt market was fueled not only by lower yields on British national debt but also by public enthusiasm for American independence movements, which promised more direct transatlantic trade with Latin America and thus captured the imagination of investors and speculators alike.[49] The wealth of historical studies of this period has helped us to understand the formation of transatlantic credit relations and to describe more clearly the microstructures of the burgeoning international finance market.[50] But these studies of early financial history appear to suffer from selection bias. Many historians tend to focus on the winners in these moments of seismic economic and political change, namely the Latin American political experiments that have survived to this day despite their turbulent history.[51] There existed, however, other less well-known attempts that failed to establish lasting independent states.[52] When they are recognized, they tend to be discounted as crooked schemes or comic inspiration for entertaining works of fiction.

Latin American decolonization, with its myriad financial and political threads, has been woven by historians into a broader narrative of Britain's imperial expansion into the American continent. As economic activities intensified in the early nineteenth century, foreign merchants, especially from Britain, poured into South America. The region's opening-up to trade and finance had effects at an individual level, as revolutions threw open the door to many smaller and medium-sized traders hoping to enter new markets. However, historians paint a portrait of a harsh, grasping world in which efforts by British merchants to enter Latin American territories were neither coordinated nor concerted. Flooding into South and Central America as ports began opening from the 1800s, hundreds of Britons seeking to carve out business positions on the continent found themselves competing bitterly to secure the best channels to market British industrial products.[53] While undeniably impressive in scale, these commercial endeavors—which allowed some astute or particularly fortunate merchants to prosper amid the tumult of emerging markets—were inextricably bound to their historical moment.[54] In fact, historians have considered these dimensions within a more finely drawn context of the early dynamics of Britain's imperial expansion into Latin America. Following the publication of John Gallagher and Ronald Robinson's seminal 1953 study, which identified an "informal empire" policy supporting sustained British trade expansion in South America, if need be through government intervention, the authors were widely criticized for exaggerating the scale of Britain's influence in the early years of the American republics.[55] This debate is still topical. According to Matthew Brown, many historians are "increasingly revealing, through painstaking archival searches, the extent to which imperial expansion in South America *was* on the British horizon in this period."[56] Furthermore, by investigating the daily lives of those who took part in Britain's expansion, recent empirical research has shed light on the peculiar forms taken by the colonial, trade, and financial campaigns of the nineteenth century, and shown how these embodied the development of British interests in the world. These studies reveal often paradoxical links that blur the lines between territories, people, and interests over time.[57]

The reassessment of the Poyais story undertaken in this book fits into these historiographies on Latin American decolonization and financing and British global expansion. By shedding light on the oft-overlooked centrality of Miskitu agency in MacGregor's Poyaisian enterprise, we illuminate the interplay between Central American Indigenous political aspirations and the broader currents of New World decolonization. This research serves to further unravel the manifold, and frequently unanticipated, actors embroiled in the formation of American states. Central America, a region often relegated to the margins of imperial studies and the histories of Latin American independence—with the Bay of Honduras and the broader Moskitia traditionally dismissed as mere appendages of British influence—here is shown to be an arena of complex political and legal maneuvering and massive economic ambition.[58]

Further, shedding light on the financial reverberations of the Poyais venture, reaching from the shores of Moskitia to the London-based foreign loan market, underscores the economic interconnectedness of seemingly disparate geographical spheres in the early nineteenth century. By unearthing the forgotten story of a Miskitu-driven project of independence and commercial improvement—hitherto obscured beneath layers of sensationalized accounts of the Poyais scandal—this book reveals a narrative that is, at its core, one in which American Indigenous peoples navigate the labyrinthine paths of global finance and American state-building. The reexamination of the Poyais loan, which, it turns out, was an attempt to secure funding for a Central American independence project, offers nuanced insights into the history of the first wave of Latin American loans. Since the project to sell Poyaisian bonds on the English capital market proved to be less a phenomenal fraud than a failed American Indigenous enterprise denounced (wrongly) as a deception, we can take an off-center view to better understand and identify the political and legal frameworks underpinning the bonds' issuance processes, their recognition, and their sustainable access to capital markets.[59]

In essence, this close examination, grounded in empirical evidence, of MacGregor and his failed attempt to fund the establishment of a country in Moskitia highlights the many and sometimes surprising spaces and players involved in a British financial and imperial undertaking in Central America. We see how Poyais stemmed simultaneously and successively from "worlds" located in different parts of an Atlantic region undergoing political, social, and economic transformation, and how the story was shaped by multifaceted American and British trade, financial and political imperatives, all of which were briefly brought together by, and (badly) mediated through, MacGregor.[60] By shifting the center of the narrative away from MacGregor, this book unveils the cast of actors who participated, whether intimately or tangentially, in the Poyais venture. This shift in perspective reveals the extent to which the story was also part of broader British imperial considerations. Although never prominent in the foreground, high-ranking officials of the British government were, in fact, systematically scrutinizing MacGregor's moves. Their watchful eyes were constantly assessing the colonial or economic potential of either encouraging or discouraging a British presence in Central America.

The Poyais story told in this book begins with the signature in April 1820 of a land grant by the Miskitu king, George Frederic, giving MacGregor the right to establish himself in Moskitia. It ends with the denunciation of the Poyais sovereign loan in London in 1824 by the Foreign Stock Market Committee, which sealed the fate and future disrepute of MacGregor's project. From then onward, Poyais would forever be known only as a monumental scam, a financial scandal cooked up by the "King of Con-Men," who managed to dupe an entire world—in this case the English financial sphere—into believing in a fictitious country. In a sense, this book treats the accusation of fraud as marking the end rather than the beginning of the Poyais story. Our investigation dives into the underlying causes of each milestone event—whether a success or a failure—marking the gradual evolution of MacGregor's financial project within a transatlantic space linking Moskitia and the British financial center. It goes further by placing the attempted formation of a potentially viable financial, commercial, and political entity into a global context. In doing so, it explores the potential trajectories of a Central American Indigenous sovereign and financial project that, despite its ultimate failure to materialize, offers insights into the efforts of a Miskitu leader to secure international recognition and financial autonomy amid challenges posed by Latin American revolutions and shifting European foreign loan markets. Through this new lens, the book uncovers an alternative path to state-making that was not taken but that nevertheless offers insights into the processes of state-building, financial development, and British imperialism in the early nineteenth century.

Following this timeline, the book is divided as follows. The first two chapters revisit the birth of Poyais in a bid to understand the reasons that led King George Frederic to make the Poyais land grant to Gregor MacGregor in 1820. By analyzing the ecology and political economy of Moskitia that had both linked but also divided Indigenous peoples and the settlers of British Honduras since the eighteenth century, we show George Frederic's decision to be an act of individual political resistance designed to position the monarch within the fast-changing imperial environment of Central America. Rather than suggest that MacGregor won the Poyais land grant by exploiting the ruler's weakness for alcohol, as is often described, this section shows that MacGregor's acquisition formed part of a deliberate strategy by the Miskitu ruler himself. The chapters aim to demonstrate that the king's granting of a concession not only signaled the beginning of MacGregor's Poyais project but was also—and more importantly—part of a process taking place independently of the man himself.

Chapter Three offers a genealogy of the Poyais project. By tracking MacGregor's Caribbean travels following his acquisition of the Miskitu concession, we see more clearly how his plans to develop the new territory evolved and shifted as he sought the capital needed to bring the project to fruition. At its inception, MacGregor's plan was built along the lines of a particular kind of military, financial, and political enterprise aimed at establishing colonial positions within disputed sovereign interstices. Modeled on the approach taken by eighteenth-century privateers, this method had been adopted by some of MacGregor's fellow foreign mercenaries. But a series of military setbacks and the successive losses of financial and business support in the Caribbean forced him to think again and to turn his business model into a singular commercial enterprise. Poyais was thus shaped by interactions with a diverse cast of Caribbean and London-based actors who tried to mold MacGregor's opportunistic aspirations to their own advantage. This chapter posits that the choice to fund his project on the London capital market was a last resort and represented the culmination of MacGregor's interactions with many and varied business figures in London and the West Indies between 1820, when the Poyais concession was obtained, and 1821, when he set sail for Britain.

Chapters Four and Five follow the construction of the Poyais loans. These sections show that MacGregor was essentially steered by British merchant bankers into issuing a first loan in 1822. Playing on legal ambiguities surrounding the formal recognition of sovereign entities on the London capital market, the Poyais financiers saw the issuance of a foreign loan as an alternative means to finance a private transatlantic business enterprise. With funding provided by holders of the initial Poyais securities, new waves of English and Scottish settlers were dispatched aboard two ships. The chapters also highlight the factors behind the political and financial downfall of the Poyais project and the birth of MacGregor's reputation as a con man. In short, the project failed because those involved in Poyais were unable to counter the informational and legal challenges mounted by settlers in British Honduras, who viewed the project as direct competition to their own commercial activities in the Bay of Honduras. Despite an incessant barrage of news accusing MacGregor of being a crook, the costs of chartering further ships bearing future Poyaisians were financed by issuing two new loans. But MacGregor's project was ultimately undone after the Foreign Stock Market Committee introduced internal amendments that rewrote the terms for the issuance of sovereign bonds.

The sixth and final chapter details the reasons why the British government did not get involved in any way or intervene in the Poyais affair. As shown over the course of the book, all the interactions that directly or indirectly made up the Poyais adventure were essentially based on relations between private protagonists. Despite being repeatedly contacted, the British government seemed completely uninterested in Poyais. Yet sources reveal that His Majesty's Government was aware of MacGregor's colonial undertaking from its infancy but opted not to intervene on the Shore, despite news in dispatches about the dramatic events unfolding as waves of colonial settlers arrived in Poyais. The choice of noninvolvement appears to have been an individual decision by Robert Wilmot-Horton, Under-Secretary of State for War and the Colonies, based primarily on hopes of personal political gain and the development of Britain's global emigration policies.

ONE

Once upon a Time, Moskitia

GEORGE FREDERIC, KING OF THE MISKITU, granted a plot of land to Gregor MacGregor on April 29, 1820. The terms of the deed stated:

> We grant unto the said Sir Gregor MacGregor full power and authority to enact laws, establish customs, and in a word to take and adopt all measures that he may deem fit and necessary for the protection, defence, better government and prosperity of the [. . .] District of land, commonly called Black River, Polayas or Poyais. But let it be clearly understood, that there is nothing contained in this Deed, which shall be construed into a Cession of the Sovereignty of the Country as now held by His Mosquito Majesty.[1]

This acquisition set in motion a story that some have dubbed the boldest fraud in history, as MacGregor suddenly found himself the owner of a vast territory spanning just over thirteen thousand square miles (Map 1), then inhabited by a few Indigenous polities represented by George Frederic. Over the ensuing years, MacGregor would come to be portrayed as a man whose egotistical, grasping, even pathological conceits caused him to style himself as Prince Gregor, Cazique of Poyais, openly flouting the king's orders.

Yet, as the next two chapters show, the way in which MacGregor came to own the vast territory of Poyais in early 1820 was dictated by a chain of events that had transformed Moskitia in less than a generation from an isolated backwater, visited by a handful of British adventurers, to a region that was opening up under its king's leadership to the wider world and to foreign colonial enterprises, many from Europe. In fact, George Frederic emerges as the figure that started the whole process, as he took advantage of the ever-shifting reality of South America's fast-evolving sovereign states. But these dynamics can be brought to light only if the focus of interest is placed firstly and squarely on the trade, political, and colonial relations then shaping the Shore and the wider Bay of Honduras area. By delving into the Poyais story's Central American origins, rather than beginning it in London, we gain a clear understanding of the motivations driving the players from the outset. We also spotlight a political and economic turning point in Central American and Atlantic history, one driven by Miskitu claims for political and economic independence.

This chapter thus sets the stage. It provides contextual background on the history of Moskitia, focusing on the political, economic, and environmental dynamics that characterized the region's political economy up to the signing

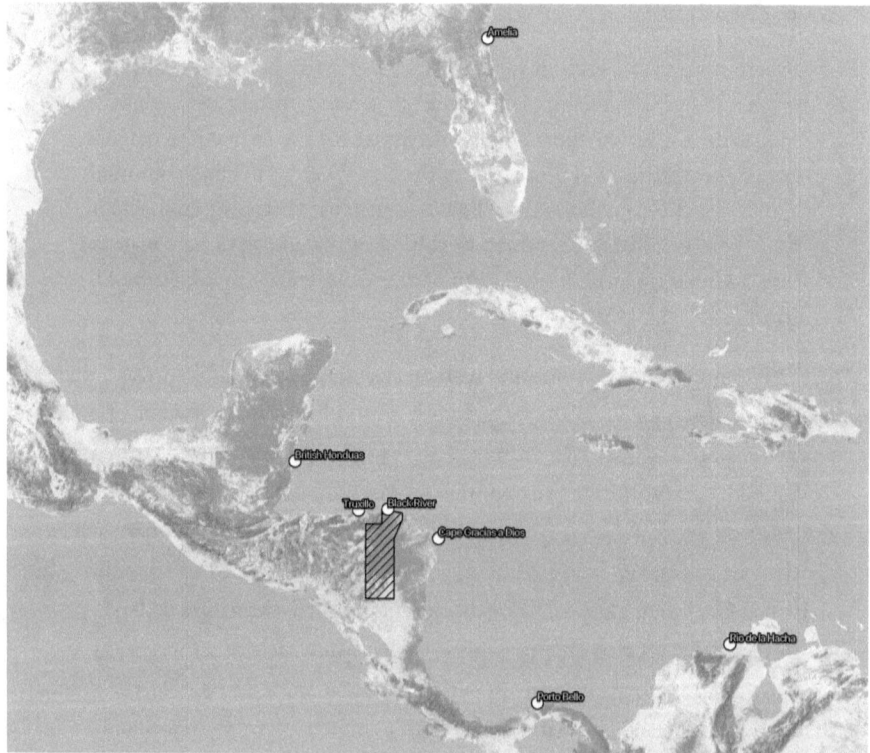

Map 1. Land of Poyais. Source: Coordinates transcribed from LBGA, "Grant of Land by George Frederic," NRAS945/20/19/72, April 29, 1820. Stamen Terrain Background by Stamen Design licensed under CC BY 3.0. Data from OpenStreetMap licensed under ODbL. The striped area shows the territory granted by George Frederic.

of the Poyais concession by Gregor MacGregor. It illuminates the relationships binding Indigenous polities and foreign colonial settlements initially established in Moskitia, and then, by the end of the eighteenth century, in nearby British Honduras. These were primarily centered on the extraction of mahogany resources from the Shore. In doing so, this chapter provides a better understanding of the historical foundations on which the interactions that bonded and opposed the Miskitu and British colonial enterprises in the region rested, as they were based on specific political, social, and environmental dynamics specific to Central America.

George Frederic's decision to grant Poyais to MacGregor has often been put down to the king's weakness for alcohol. Accounts often tell how the deal was sealed after a night of drinking, which enabled the scheming MacGregor to manipulate the inebriated Miskitu king.[2] Seen from this perspective, the Poyais grant appears to show a European exerting political, relational, and cultural dominance over the representative of an Indigenous polity. In turn, depicting George Frederic as inherently inferior and unable to control his alcoholic vices reflects physical but also civilizational degeneracy. Meanwhile, the description of MacGregor as an unscrupulous scoundrel who hoodwinked the Miskitu leader undone by his inability to control his own flaws was a dog whistle for the supposedly benign intervention and involvement of Western empires and colonial enterprises as the true guardians of moral and upstanding behavior.

Opinions of this nature and such descriptions of the Indigenous king abound in documents by historians writing about European colonial ventures on the Shore. The region was the scene of European incursions, notably by Britain, from the seventeenth century onwards. Writing after World War II, authors such as Troy Floyd, William Sorsby, and Victor von Hagen published research that hailed the ability of British settlers to improve the region, perhaps in a nostalgic tribute to their fading empire.[3] They felt that the settlers' ability to maintain good relations with the Miskitu as well as a relatively long-standing presence in the region—in contrast with their Spanish peers—pointed to a superior British ability to cope with difficult environments, a harsh climate, and local populations made up of violent, alcohol-soaked barbarians.

These perceptions of the Miskitu temperament are largely based on the same source. The narrative that pigeonholes George Frederic and his subjects as violent savages, unable to resist drunken excess, is rooted in *Waikna*, a travelogue written in 1855 by one "Samuel Bard," which relates the author's journey along the Miskitu Shore. Describing the local Miskitu, he says: "Their besetting vice is drunkenness, which has obliterated all of their better traits."[4]

But Samuel Bard never existed. The name was a pseudonym of Ephraim G. Squier, an American archaeologist known for his expertise in the architecture of pre-Columbian societies in the Mississippi Valley.[5] At the time, he was a chargé d'affaires of the American government who had been dispatched to Moskitia in 1849. The United States, backed by domestic financiers, saw the region as a potential site for infrastructure projects, including a transoceanic canal. Seeking to undermine Britain's presence in the region and aid Nicaragua, then a U.S. ally, to claim full sovereignty of the area, the United States sent Squier as a diplomatic representative. Once there, his task was to produce anthropological scholarship that would discredit the Miskitu, Britain's main allies in the region.[6] While writing *Waikna* under an alias, Squier also published a glowing review of his own book as well as articles and scientific discussion papers under his own name.[7] In his writing, he depicted the Miskitu as a people of inferior moral caliber, while stressing Britain's role in their lamentable moral state. Basically, Squier's unflattering portrait, originating in a U.S. diplomatic strategy geared to establish political and economic positions in Central America, sought to symbolically weaken Britain's presence and authority in the region.[8]

Although Squier's work was riddled with anti-British observations, his grotesque depiction of the Miskitu nevertheless acted as the inspiration and model for many subsequent publications and papers, which held up his descriptions as a trusted reference.[9] Worse, such arguments chimed somewhat with Eurocentric views deriving indirectly from the classical environmental deterministic arguments of American geographer Ellsworth Huntington, who saw regional climates as critical to understanding differences in the levels of civilization attained by population groups.[10] In this view, the moral corruption of the Miskitu could be chiefly attributable to their life in a hostile, hot, and humid environment. Writers using Squier as the starting point for their own analyses therefore placed the Miskitu at the bottom of a global civilizational pecking order, leaving Europeans to rightfully dominate all dealings, as their interactions were destined to lift up an inherently weak people.

In the wake of the Sandinista uprising and subsequent Contra rebellion between 1981 and 1984, national aspirations among a section of the Miskitu holding counterrevolutionary beliefs revived academic interest in Moskitia.[11] Rather than treat the region as a battleground fought over by European empires, the literature from this period sought to understand the development of the Miskitu community in its own right. In addition to exploring claims to independent nationhood against the backdrop of the Sandinista, research on the Shore underwent a major shift in perspective with the rise and spread of innovative contemporary historical approaches.[12]

In these readings, the region was no longer solely a zone of influence fought over by two rival foreign imperial powers. Rather, it became the native environment of an independent and autonomous community. As the work of Michael Olien in particular seeks to demonstrate, this community was legitimately composed of Indigenous polities with genuine agency that had hitherto been marginalized, ignored, or misrepresented by research primarily intended to validate imperial incursions in the region.[13] Yet this research in particular reveals the efforts at historical legitimization undertaken by some authors under the influence of Cold War tensions. Olien's writings on the Miskitu's historically documented ability to govern their own political fate were widely criticized. His critics implicitly sought to downplay the role of Miskitu, especially since some became fighters in the Contra rebellion. Historians such as Mary Helms and Linda Newson saw the longevity and relative stability of Moskitia's specific cultural and political structures as rooted in the turmoil caused by European incursions in the region.[14] The organization of the Miskitu community as a kingdom was interpreted as a necessity arising from colonial contact with the Spanish and especially British powers. As such, Indigenous kings were seen less as political rulers than as the colonized representatives of a community divided into ethnic factions, each governed by its own leaders. Nevertheless, contributions from the work from this period provided a foundation to better understand and rethink the political position occupied by Indigenous peoples in historical processes. Even so, there is a tendency to single out specific figures. The close attention paid to the Miskitu and the focus on rehabilitating their history as part of an independent and enduring community leave the Shore somewhat disconnected from its environment. To some extent, the consequences of European incursions into the region are pushed into the background.

Yet Moskitia was deeply transatlantic. It had been characterized by ongoing contact with European colonial empires, including Spain and Britain. From the seventeenth century onward, these Indigenous peoples interacted continually with European colonial enterprises, as Barbara Potthast illustrates in a longitudinal study tracing the history of the Miskitu Shore from Christopher Columbus's landing at Cape Gracias a Dios in 1502 to Nicaragua's declaration of independence in 1821. Considering that previous writing on the Shore had repeatedly taken political aspects out of their local context due to the primary focus on the Anglo-Spanish conflict in the region, Potthast conducts a study over a long period to gain a better understanding of how Miskitu society evolved. In her view, as contact was gradually established with the trading practices of foreign actors (introduction of rum, weapons, and metal tools), deep societal changes began to take place through a process of acculturation within the Indigenous communities, which gradually began to adopt an "English gentleman" lifestyle.[15]

While Potthast provides an essential tool to understand the transformations endured by the Miskitu over the course of multiple European contacts, she concentrates primarily on one facet of an inherently dual and even dialectical process involving the Miskitu and settler populations. But in her recollection, she depicts the external component of this acculturation process, namely British colonial ventures, as unaffected by contact with local populations. It is as if British campaigns in Moskitia are seen to be conducted by a monolithic, uniform imperial block with an established, defined, and opportunistic plan for gaining control of a resource-rich region.

However, as Robert Naylor shows, London did not view the Miskitu Shore as a region of great importance. Rather than stage an organized campaign, the British government preferred to concentrate on its military objectives and diplomatic interests in the Caribbean sugar colonies. But precisely because London discounted it as a minor territory, the Shore became a prime draw for individuals with limited capital and resources but aspirations of social and economic advancement. Most attempts to build British settlements on the territory were led by individuals who sought to found private colonies with little or no formal support from the British government.[16]

In a sense, Naylor's contributions offer the perfect counterweight to Potthast's analyses. He considers the effects that Moskitia's economics, national and international politics, and ecology had on British private colonial activities in the region. His history of the Shore covers an extended period (1600–1914) and describes the social and political changes undergone by English settlements in the area and neighboring British Honduras as essentially dictated by the ability of these colonies to maintain access to the region's plentiful reserves of natural resources, including mahogany, sarsaparilla, and turtle shell. Naylor's analysis thus helps to unpick the monolithic and widely held image of British colonial campaigns. However, it has its limitations. In addition to directing some rather racist remarks toward the Miskitu, Naylor tends to reduce the relationship between Indigenous communities and British colonial enterprises on the Shore to unilateral political interactions designed to maintain the settlers' grip on the region.[17]

Rather than focus on the specific characteristics of each class of player, namely settlers and Miskitu, this chapter aims to show the importance of their economic and political interdependence, and, critically, how this relationship changed over time. In this sense, the situation in Moskitia is akin to that described in Richard White's seminal *Middle Ground*.[18] The region is understood to be a theater for specific interactions both linking and opposing the Miskitu and British settlers. When viewed through the prism of trade, political, and social factors, these interactions are revealed to be structured both positively and negatively by a combination of local, regional, and imperial dynamics. Specifically, in response to local mahogany-related environmental constraints resulting from imperial imperatives, which in turn arose from international treaties signed in Europe, British settlers and the Miskitu were forced to continually adjust their political structures through specific interactions as they sought to exploit the wood as effectively as possible while bettering their own respective and mutual social and economic conditions.[19]

The topic of this chapter is not Poyais as such. Rather, it looks at the region's specific economic, political, environmental, and social dynamics that prompted a figure usually overlooked by the literature—Miskitu ruler George Frederic—to allow the foundations for the Poyais project to be laid. By understanding how the scope of what was possible for Indigenous peoples and colonialists operating on the Shore changed at the start of the nineteenth century, we can place them more effectively within a shared environment. An analysis of Indigenous/settler interactions before and during the land grant to

MacGregor shows how the decision to offer Poyais to the Scotsman resulted from disruptions to the middle ground established by both parties.

The Miskitu Shore extends from the southeast coast of present-day Nicaragua to the eastern shore of Honduras, forming a crude triangle linking the San Juan River, Cape Camarón, and Cape Gracias a Dios (Fig. 5). Behind a 310-mile strip of white-sand beaches and mangrove swamps, dotted with lagoons protected by sandbanks, vast savannas and marshland gradually give way to dense jungle filled with cedars and occasional towering mahoganies. Mountains, some more than three thousand feet tall, rear up in the far distance.[20]

In the early nineteenth century, at the time of George Frederic's reign, Moskitia was home to many Indigenous peoples living throughout the region. The four main polities, subdivided into numerous smaller communities, were primarily differentiated by language, geographical distribution, and ethnic affiliation. The Sumu (Mayangna) people lived mainly inland. Occupying the lands to the north around Black River, near Cape Camarón, the Paya formed a linguistically separate group and composed of both zambo and Indigenous peoples.[21] The Rama, who had a similar ethnic background, occupied the south. The Miskitu, who were by far the largest and most dominant group, were of mixed Indigenous, African, and European descent. After originally occupying the area around Cape Gracias a Dios, they had expanded to cover much of the coastline. The Miskitu reportedly took in survivors of shipwrecked slaving vessels on several occasions, and its distinctive ethnic heritage was the result of mixing between the locals and shipwrecked Africans over a period of time. The Miskitu were further divided ethnically and culturally into the Sambo-Miskitu, based in the north and identifying as Afro-Indigenous, and the Tawira-Miskitu, identifying as Indigenous and concentrated in the south.[22]

The Miskitu's demographic and geographical dominance chiefly reflected the Shore's particular political economy, which had been shaped by events dating back to the seventeenth century. After being visited for the first time by Christopher Columbus in 1502 during his fourth and final voyage, Moskitia was the subject of many European incursions.[23] The Miskitu had essentially traded for years with European colonists, particularly with British settlers based in the region, whose presence was technically tolerated by the

Figure 5. Map of Moskitia and the Bay of Honduras. Source: Thomas Jefferys, "A Complete Chart of the West Indies," in *The West-India Atlas, or, A Compendious Description of the West-Indies* (London: Robert Sayer and John Bennett, 1771). Geography and Map Division, Library of Congress.

Spanish empire. Although the region was officially under Spanish control following the signature of the Treaty of Tordesillas (1494), various attempts were made to set up English settlements, mostly in defiance of Spain's sovereignty. However, the Spanish and English crowns showed little interest in establishing permanent colonies in the area, deeming it unattractive because of the apparent lack of mineral resources.

So Moskitia attracted private enterprise. In 1632, Puritans led by Robert Rich, Duke of Warwick, established a base on tiny Providence Island off the coast of Bluefields. The venture was led by the Providence Island Company, which hoped to follow in the footsteps of the Massachusetts Bay Company. Unfortunately for its sponsors, the undertaking failed to recruit enough candidates for emigration, as many English Puritans saw New England as a more appealing place of refuge.[24]

In 1732, William Pitt established a settlement at Black River, at the mouth of the river of the same name, also known as Rio Tinto. The colony then spread gradually to cover most of the Miskitu Shore, which by 1757 had over 150 white settlers, owning a total of more than 800 slaves. Following the War of Jenkins' Ear (1739–1748), during which British and Spanish fleets battled for control of Caribbean trade, the British government forced Pitt's colony to appoint a superintendency between 1749 and 1787, as it sought to leverage the existing British settlement in the region to gain a military and political edge and thwart Spain's ambitions.[25]

The venture led by Pitt, a former logwood merchant who had made his first fortune in British Honduras (now Belize), was essentially based on three industries: turtle hunting, sarsaparilla harvesting, and mahogany logging. Turtles were prized for their shells, which were used in luxury European marquetry and cabinetmaking. Sarsaparilla, a type of vine then known as a treatment for syphilis, was Black River's second most-exported product by export value in 1769. By the second half of the eighteenth century, the mahogany trade was becoming increasingly important in the region, and by 1760 exports of the wood represented the colony's largest source of income.[26]

And the trend continued. From the second half of the eighteenth century onward, mahogany became a sought-after commodity in London, where it was held in high regard by shipbuilders as well as makers of fine furniture.[27] Admired for its durability, mahogany also offered aesthetic and structural qualities that allowed complex motifs and shapes to be carved. Over time it became a highly prized material, achieving the status of a luxury commodity when it began to be used in the workshops of Thomas Chippendale, a famed London cabinetmaker. In 1754, Chippendale published a book of furniture patterns showing how the London furniture market was dominated by Gothic, Chinese, and Rococo styles. The introduction of these fashions, which featured extremely ornate styles, was made possible mainly by the density and hardness of the exotic woods used, as they could support the extravagant designs and engravings involved.[28] Although the models and sketches proposed by Chippendale do not mention the specific woods used in his workshops, these designs could not have been executed without materials such as mahogany. It alone had the cosmetic and especially the structural qualities needed to execute the carvings and sculptures planned by the artist.

To keep up with demand, predatory exploitation of mahogany resources began on a significant scale in the West Indies, and particularly in Jamaica, which was considered to have the finest-quality trees. Systematic plundering led to overexploitation, and as local resources were depleted, Pitt's settlement gradually took on an important place in the transatlantic trade in mahogany, of which the Shore and the Bay of Honduras boasted extensive resources.[29]

In fact, mahogany extraction would go on to play a central role in shaping the political economy of the Bay of Honduras and Moskitia, possibly since the first colonial incursions into the region. Much of the historiography dealing with the Shore assumes that initial colonial incursions in the region were essentially focused on logwood, a type of redwood used by the London textile industry to produce red dyes. As logwood's popularity waned following the discovery of aniline in the first half of the nineteenth century, operations were assumed to have simply switched to mahogany. Yet as Karl Offen showed in a biogeographic study, logwood does not grow on the Miskitu Shore, preferring the marshy, chalky soils of Belize or the Yucatán Peninsula. With a logwood industry impossible in Moskitia's semi-arid climate, colonial activities in the region seem to have been driven by enterprises set up to extract local mahogany resources.[30]

These British colonial ventures in Moskitia were fundamentally private and thus could not count on official support from the Colonial Office or the British government more generally, although the Crown did intervene locally from time to time in different ways. Decision-making practices and approaches within the British Foreign and Colonial Offices at the end of the eighteenth century were essentially built around informal networks and working relationships, with the individual personalities of appointees playing a pivotal role. As a result, decisions taken in London on whether to intervene formally in the Shore varied not only in terms of the action that was actually taken—intervene militarily, appoint a superintendent, do nothing—but also as a function of the plans and motivations of the individuals heading these governmental agencies.[31]

In this environment, the Miskitu appear to have played a crucial part in building, maintaining, and disrupting the trade and colonial balance. Following the colonial ventures of the seventeenth century, the Miskitu actively positioned themselves as preferred partners to successive waves of English private enterprises. As political, economic, and cultural synergies were unlocked, interethnic relations and business ties were forged with the British settlers (and their African slaves) based in Black River from 1732 onward. Pitt's colony owed its relative stability and continued survival to a system of accommodation and interdependency linking the settler and Miskitu communities. In exchange for firearms and other valued European products, such as textiles and iron wares, the Miskitu essentially granted the British settlers safe access to their territory and natural resources, including turtle shell and sarsaparilla, which at the time were chiefly traded with Jamaica.

In particular, an extractive economy centered on the logging of precious timber—cedar and, especially, mahogany—emerged during the eighteenth century. The labor required for an economy based on the extraction of precious timber resources contributed to the creation of a significant system of Indigenous slavery, which was run by the Miskitu. Through preferred access to European markets, technologies, and know-how (both British and African), the Miskitu in turn gained an economic and military edge over the region's other ethnic groups. By redistributing non-native products on local markets or using the firearms obtained through these trades with foreigners—including muskets, from which their name is derived—to attack and take over neighboring groups, the Miskitu gradually overwhelmed the Rama, Sumu, and Paya peoples. They then sold the Indigenous slaves needed to exploit the Shore's mahogany resources to British settlers, while retaining others for their own farming needs.

In this sense, the situation on the Miskitu Shore is akin to that described by Richard White in his study of France's colonial campaign in the Pays d'en Haut, the North American Great Lakes region. White argues that the French settlers' initial success in maintaining a sustainable and secure colonial presence between 1650 and 1815 was down to effective management of the relationships of accommodation, negotiation, and understanding that existed between the local Algonquians and settlers, within a conceptual space that the author calls the "middle ground." In this system, Europeans and North American Indigenous peoples needed to act reciprocally, adjusting their differences and persuading their talking partners to accommodate the other party's practices and values. Within this specific social and political environment, in which the settlers could neither command nor sideline the Algonquians, new practices and relationships emerged, based on a balance of power rather than dominance.[32]

This unique form of coexistence found on the Shore did not come about through deliberate choices by those involved. Its system of negotiation was forced on the protagonists by environmental imperatives and structural changes to their individual and shared political, social, and, above all, economic realities. Since their ventures were essentially driven by private entrepreneurial goals, British settlers had to establish a secure framework based on peaceful relations with Indigenous communities that would provide a platform to build and maintain their economic activities in the region. With formal military support against the potential threat of Indigenous incursions both sporadic and dependent on political calculations made in London, the settlers had to make sure that they cohabitated peacefully with the local polities.

The Miskitu, meanwhile, operated in a social and economic environment that had changed radically since the first Europeans arrived in the sixteenth century. Initial waves of colonizers brought disease to the region.[33] A string of epidemics, including smallpox, had a devastating sociodemographic impact on the Caribbean region and Central America. These effects were further compounded by the encomienda system, a form of economic exploitation introduced by early Spanish colonial enterprises that undermined living conditions and disrupted family and clan networks.[34]

As relationships formed with settlers, particularly from the Pitt colony, the Miskitu saw an opportunity to better their own social and economic situation. Consistent with the dynamics identified by White, negotiations on the Shore were basically undertaken, conducted, and sealed through the exchange of gifts that benefited the other party. In addition to being mentioned in the travel journals of several contemporary witnesses, this practice was also described by Robert Hodgson, one of the British superintendents of the Black River settlement. In a memorandum written in 1774, Hodgson details a significant shipment of gifts sent to then Miskitu king George I.[35] Worth a total value of £45, which he called the most costly set of gifts ever presented to an Indigenous ruler, the shipment comprised salt (one barrel), millstones, rum (120 gallons), and miscellaneous British manufactured products, including hats of various sorts, pocket handkerchiefs (just over fifty yards of Scottish handkerchiefs and several linen handkerchiefs), and ribbons. The shipment additionally contained many metal products, including eight iron pots, sixty-five cutlasses, twelve woodcutting axes, and one hundred or so knives. Hodgson also sent George I gunpowder, ammunition, and several rifles.

As Indigenous peoples had not yet mastered ironwork when European colonists arrived on the American continent, this type of metal gift was undoubtedly of significant value for the representative of these Indigenous polities.[36] Recurring contact with a European colonial presence may also have gradually encouraged the Miskitu to adopt consumer habits modelled on those of the "English gentleman," further explaining the interest in British manufactured products.[37] As for firearms, the Miskitu used them to gain military superiority over the region's other ethnic groups, both effectively through armed raids and symbolically through the threat of such raids.

By regularly offering tributes similar to that delivered by Hodgson in 1774, the Pitt colony settlers gained security against potential attacks by the Miskitu or other Indigenous peoples under their command. Sometimes the Miskitu and Black River militias even formed temporary military alliances. For example, a joint battalion of British and Indigenous volunteers won a crushing victory at the Battle of San Juan in 1780 as they sought to push back the Spanish presence around Lake Nicaragua.[38]

The alliance with the Miskitu was also critical to the smooth operation of the slaving economy on which Black River's commercial activities were based. Members of the colony's large African and Indigenous slave population were forced to gather sarsaparilla, hunt turtles, and, most importantly, do the punishing work of cutting mahogany (Fig. 6). The seasonal business of mahogany logging was usually led by a British settler, who commanded a

Figure 6. Cutting and trucking mahogany in British Honduras. Source: Chaloner and Fleming, *The Mahogany Tree* (Liverpool: Rockliff and Son, 1850). Courtesy of HathiTrust.

gang of around fifty slaves.[39] Yet at the time, slaves made regular escape attempts, hoping to reach a nearby Spanish stronghold, since Spain had promised to free anyone who was taken in. In keeping with the ties established with the Black River settlers, Miskitu patrols agreed to track down and bring back any runaways on their lands.[40]

Maintaining, developing, and cultivating the middle ground resulted in the formation of a particular system of economic intelligence. Mahogany's ecological characteristics are such that logging the trees in the wild is subject to highly specific material constraints. Mahogany naturally grows across a dispersed range in often extremely dense forests.[41] It can take several decades for a specimen to reach adult size, at which point it can be cut down.[42] Keenly attuned to their environment, the Miskitu became prime providers of intelligence about where mahogany resources were located on their territory, as shown by the accounts of explorers in the region.[43] Furthermore, they appear to have had experience in cutting mahogany, which they used to build canoes.[44]

Rather than forming a homogenous group that was strengthened politically and militarily by prolonged contact with the British colonial presence, the Miskitu actually owed their existence as a politically and culturally structured social community to repeated interactions with the British in the region. As Mary Helms and Linda Newson show, demographic, economic, and social structures were undermined by the first contact with Europeans, which, combined with the initial forms of collaboration established with British settlers, led some previously nomadic groups to settle more permanently near the sites of trade and symbolic exchanges resulting from the gradual formation of the middle ground.[45] These interactions drove the formation of a specific social organization. As a politically, socially, and culturally organized group, the Miskitu formed what Helms calls a "colonial tribe," defined and structured by their relationship of codependence with the British settlers.

Shaped by the demographic, social, and cultural upheaval inflicted on many Indigenous groups following initial European incursions in the region, even the Miskitu's political hierarchy emerges as the product of Indigenous/colonial relations. The expansion of raids to capture Indigenous slaves, coupled with polygamous matrimonial alliances, played a part in shaping the region's political dynamics in favor of the Miskitu. At the start of the nineteenth century, Moskitia was divided into several districts, each led by a noble of Miskitu descent. A Sambo general controlled the north, commanding the Paya and, to some extent, the Sumu; a governor of Tawira descent had charge of the Rama in the south; and a Tawira admiral was responsible for the Miskitu near Cape Gracias a Dios (Map 2). A king of Sambo-Miskitu descent was responsible for the cohabitation of these different Indigenous polities across the entire Shore.[46] Gifts from European settlers enabled these distinct nobilities and their subjects to benefit economically and socially from trade with the outsiders.[47] Presents offered to the Miskitu king did not stay with him but were shared among the representatives of the main Miskitu groups, which in turn enabled the regional Indigenous elites to assume and affirm their hierarchical position by further sharing the tributes within their own communities.

The Miskitu king was at the heart of this territorial division and these political and ethnic structures. Although the king's role evolved as a result of contacts with Spanish, British, and African populations, and also civil wars between the Tawira and Sambo Miskitu during the seventeenth and eighteenth centuries, he eventually became a liaison between the Shore's leading

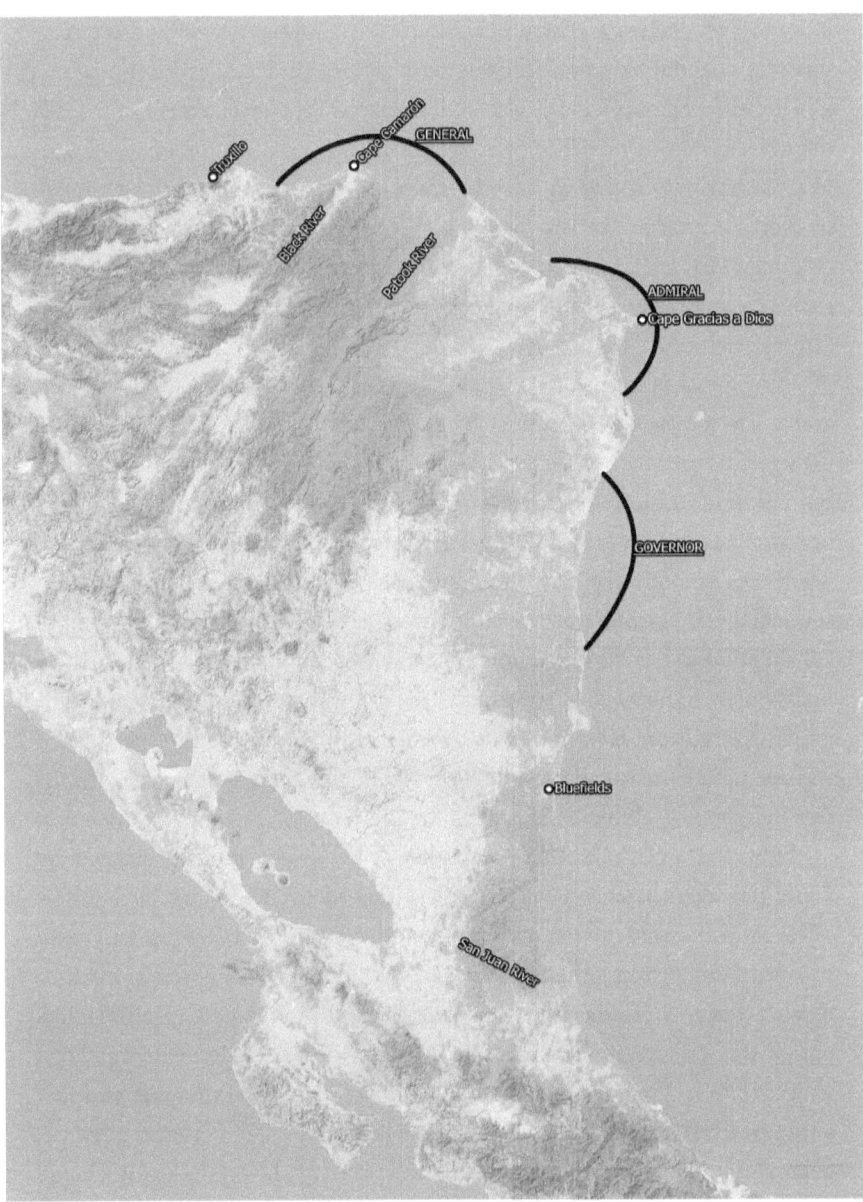

Map 2. Political map of the Miskitu Shore around 1820. Source: Map derived from Olien, Michael D., "The Miskito Kings and the Line of Succession," *Journal of Anthropological Research* 39(2), July 1983, p. 217. Stamen Terrain Background by Stamen Design licensed under CC BY 3.0. Data from OpenStreetMap licensed under OdbL.

polities. From his seat in Cape Gracias a Dios, he presented himself as a leader descended from a long royal line.[48] Yet in essence, he provided a platform for negotiation among local leaders and legitimized decisions made by and between Sambo-Tawira Miskitu aristocrats. The involvement of a headman or another principal in such situations was not uncommon. As James Warren Springer shows in a study exploring the malleable approach taken by North American settlers to applying European real property law in their relations with local populations, Indigenous polities often picked a leader, such as a sachem, to act as a single representative when dealing with foreign talking partners.[49]

The powers of a Miskitu ruler also differed from those of European monarchs. To borrow the term used by Alida Metcalf, Miskitu kings such as George I (1755–1776) and George II (1777–1800) often acted as "go-betweens," serving as a cultural intermediary recognized by two supposedly opposing groups and a single talking partner who facilitated the communication needed for smooth negotiations. Translating not only the language but also the social and cultural practices of parties seeking to build a relationship of cohabitation, Miskitu kings bore a certain resemblance to figures such as Pocahontas, Sacagawea (Lewis and Clark's interpreter and guide), and Malitzin/La Malinche (Hernán Cortés's slave and consort) as they performed the role of key intermediaries, who were appointed and authorized to facilitate Indigenous/colonial relations.[50]

However, unlike in these examples, the middle ground reached by Moskitia's British settlers and the Miskitu had the effect not of regularly selecting individuals to act as intermediaries but of establishing a dynasty of cultural mediators. The Shore's successive kings were chosen at birth to take on the role. Young princes from the royal family were given English names to facilitate cultural intermediation with British interlocutors (e.g., Edward, Peter, George) and were taken in by the settlers, who offered them a European education in Black River, Jamaica, or England, often at great expense.[51] For example, the young Luttrell Tempest, who was taken in charge by Colonel James Lawrie, Black River's last British superintendent, was sent to London in 1787 to complete his education. An expense note reveals that the young prince's costs for clothing alone (that is, not including the bill for the sea crossing or accommodation) exceeded £9 after only a few months and were apparently met by the colony's mahogany loggers.[52] The arrangement paid for Tempest to learn English and arithmetic, as well as Greek, Roman, and English history. Primarily, however, it ensured that the future monarch acquired a thorough understanding of the cultural and social codes of the British settler communities.

When one king died, the prince succeeded him, returning to Indigenous society and becoming the new go-between for the Miskitu and the British. And so, as a coalition of several ethnic groups coordinated and further organized into different subgroups, each with its own political leader, the Miskitu entered into dialogue with the British settlers, acting with one voice through a single official intermediary. In this sense, the Miskitu king was less a true sovereign than a symbolic figurehead representing the political elites of different local ethnic subgroups. His social, political, and material position—the royal court, a comfortable lifestyle, polygamy—thus depended critically on the good negotiating practices linking the local inhabitants and settlers.[53]

The middle ground established by the Miskitu and the Pitt colony managed to survive more or less throughout the eighteenth century. But international factors in the wake of North America's wars of independence disrupted the parties' codified interactions. In 1783, in addition to signing the Treaty of Paris formally recognizing the independence of the United States, Britain and Spain signed the Treaty of Versailles. While dividing up colonial possessions between the two empires (Minorca and eastern Florida for Spain, Gibraltar and several sugar-producing islands in the Caribbean for Britain), the treaty also stipulated that Britain's presence in British Honduras would be tolerated, provided that no British settler exploited resources other than logwood on the Shore within a duly prescribed area. Meanwhile, British possessions "whether on the Spanish continent, or in any of the islands dependent on the aforesaid Spanish continent," were required to be evacuated.[54] This wording, which was open to interpretation, led to an ongoing dispute between the two powers over Black River. Since the settlement was not considered as formally belonging to the Spanish continent, Britain took no steps to dismantle Black River, seeing potential geostrategic value in a continued private presence in the region of the river and Belize, the main port of the settlement of British Honduras.[55]

Fearful that Spain might align itself with the alliance forged by France and the Dutch Republic in 1785, Britain nevertheless agreed, in signing the Treaty of London in 1786, to recognize Spain's full sovereignty over Moskitia. Under the terms of this agreement, London undertook to evacuate the Pitt settlement. In return, not only were the woodcutting areas around British Honduras extended, but mahogany cutting was allowed.[56] To the dismay of the Shore's settlers, the British government's intervention, which forced the evacuation of Black River in 1787, upended the political economy governing relations between settlers and the Miskitu. More than 430 white settlers, owning a total of some 1,800 slaves, were forced to leave Moskitia. While some considered returning to London, Jamaica, or the Bahamas, the vast majority of the evacuees, accompanied by more than 1,670 slaves, headed for Belize.[57]

The evacuation caused the settler and slave population of British Honduras to suddenly triple.[58] Barring a few disputes, the Belize colony managed to accommodate its new citizens, more or less. Crucially, it managed to retain the know-how built up over long years by the Black River settlers about the rules of negotiating with the Miskitu.[59] Initially, mahogany logging abided by the limits set by the 1786 agreement. But the boundaries were soon broken as operations ramped up with the arrival of so many Black River loggers. A 1796 report by Spanish authorities in the Yucatán complained about the illegal expansion of Belizean woodcutting outside the areas established by the Treaty of London.[60]

Illegal logging raids were not confined to the northern border of British Honduras. They also took place on the Shore. Whereas a formal, permanent large-scale settlement could no longer be maintained in Moskitia, the region was nevertheless still home to valuable mahogany resources. Harvesting incursions now took place seasonally, following the mahogany life cycle.[61] Yet this illegal expansion of British mahogany logging on the Shore was complicated because the territory was still officially under Spanish control. Following the British evacuation in 1787, Spain tried to reassert and consolidate its sovereignty in the region by encouraging the establishment of new colonies.

However, it never made this a priority, and its attempts were largely unsuccessful, as Spanish settlers were seemingly unable to establish good relations with the Miskitu, a prerequisite for the survival of any colonial venture in the region. After failing to build a sustainable presence on the Shore, Spain eventually evacuated its final positions there in 1800, leaving the field open to loggers from British Honduras.[62] From the early nineteenth century, Moskitia thus constituted a "hollow frontier" for Belizeans, to borrow Preston James's term.[63] Many Belizean loggers, with support from the Miskitu, gradually encroached into the Shore's forests without setting up permanent bases. The Dos de Mayo Uprising in Madrid in 1808 against the Joseph Bonaparte–led French occupation finally convinced the settlers of British Honduras that any threat from Spain in the region was over. Belize's loggers then made plans to formally reestablish the secret ties that they had maintained with the Miskitu.[64]

———

British Honduras was founded in the seventeenth century by British buccaneers turned logwood cutters. Like the Pitt settlement on the Shore, it was essentially driven by economic activities that shifted over time from cutting logwood to exploiting the area's rich mahogany resources. Although its inhabitants did not answer formally to any of the European imperial powers, the settlement was often at the heart of disputes between Britain and Spain over diplomatic recognition of sovereignty in the region. After the Treaty of Paris was signed in 1763, British Honduras became a private settlement whose presence was formally tolerated on Spanish soil on certain conditions. This state of affairs was further confirmed by the treaties of Versailles (1783) and London (1786). However, the London agreement required the settlement to have a resident superintendent who would represent the British Crown's interests.

Following the signing of the Peace of Basel in 1795 between revolutionary France and the Spanish empire, which effectively split the first European coalition opposed to the creation of the French Republic, in 1798 Spain launched an attack on the small Belizean island of St. George's Caye, in retaliation for the failure by British loggers to keep to the boundaries set by previous treaties. With the support—willing or otherwise—of their slaves, Belizean militias successfully repelled the Spanish forces. From then on, safe from Spanish attack, British Honduras operated within a gray area, being on Spanish soil legally speaking, while actually being politically run by private British settlers. This situation lasted for much of the nineteenth century, as London balked at imposing formal British sovereignty because of the diplomatic relationship with Spain. British Honduras was eventually incorporated into the British empire as an official Crown colony in 1871.[65]

British Honduras was run by an oligarchy made up essentially of wealthy mahogany loggers and merchants based in the small city of Belize.[66] Studying the way in which the oligarchy survived after slavery was abolished locally in 1838, Nigel Bolland describes how the elite maintained its political and economic grip by setting up a system of social control for newly freed laborers of color, based around loans and a barter system. Rather than control the local economy's means of production by restricting access to land—the approach typically adopted in relatively large colonies such as Jamaica—the Belizean commercial and political elite used lending as a means to virtually enslave its labor force and stifle any political protest. As a result, the powerful mahogany merchants and loggers at the head of the colony enjoyed de facto control over the executive, legislative, and judicial branches of power. This elite group managed to obtain exclusive control not just of mahogany exports to London but also of imports connected with British Honduras's transatlantic and West Indian trade.[67] Bolland paints a fascinating picture, highlighting the financial strategies used post-abolition by a local elite seeking to hold on to its political status. However, he claims, without going into detail, that this system of control was rooted in pre-existing practices.[68]

By delving into the specific characteristics of the British Honduras settlement following slavery's abolition in 1838, we gain a clearer understanding of the social, political, legal, and financial organization that not only anchored the settlement's economic structure but also accounted for the central position that British Honduras's mahogany loggers swiftly came to occupy in Moskitia's political economy in the early decades of the nineteenth century. Above all, taking the time to carefully detail the structures and dynamics governing British Honduras reveals some of the historical contingencies that prompted George Frederic to grant Poyais to MacGregor, who was at the time an unknown foreigner on the Shore.

As this chapter argues, the oligarchy running British Honduras in the early nineteenth century held on to its position by appropriating and exerting social and political control over the local and transatlantic financing networks that underpinned the mahogany trade. The hold exerted by the settlement's wealthiest loggers and merchants over the three main branches of power, namely the magistracy (executive), the public assembly (legislative) and the grand court (judicial), stemmed basically from their ability to control the movement of local capital, backed by a system of political clientelism based around the purchase of individual legal protections. The influence brought to bear on the settlement's political structures and social hierarchies by this commercial, financial, and political elite enabled the oligarchy to take control of the production system supporting the region's mahogany trade. As a political and economic body, the British Honduras oligarchy controlled not only trade opportunities but also the channels of inbound capital needed to support international trade financing. Critically, the magistrates had sole control of all relations beyond the borders of British Honduras, which enabled them not only to represent their own interests in dealings with London's trade and political communities but also to keep hold of access to Moskitia's mahogany resources by taking up the special relationship with the incumbent Miskitu king.

The leaders of the mahogany elite thus also made up the British Honduras magistracy. This body, comprising seven members elected annually by the public assembly, acted as the executive branch of government. It was responsible for implementing and following up on the decisions taken by the settlement's public meetings, but its primary task was to run the colony. Magistrates had to be white settlers of British descent owning "visible property" worth at least JM£500.[69] In 1820, the year in which George Frederic signed the concession granting Poyais to MacGregor, the magistracy included John W. Wright, George Gibson, Thomas Frain, Thomas Paslow, John Wright R. N., and Charles Craig. Thereafter, at least until 1825, the members were replaced annually based on the principle of rotating elected positions. Their replacements were Charles Evans, James Colquhoun, Manfield W. Brown, Thomas Iles, Edward Meighan, James Hyde, William Gentle, David Betson, Thomas Pickstock, S. August, and William Hall.[70] As major slaveowners, all of these magistrates were involved in trading and exploiting mahogany. According to an 1820 census, some, including James Hyde, William Gentle, and Thomas Paslow, were among the settlement's biggest owners of slave labor, with more than fifty slaves.[71]

One man in particular emerges as a key figure in the colony: Marshall Bennett. Aside from a brief absence between 1821 and 1822, when he was replaced by John W. Wright, he was the only magistrate reelected every year from 1819 to 1825. In addition to being the most consistent member of the Belizean magistracy, Bennett was first and foremost the settlement's wealthiest man. Although it is difficult to put an exact figure on his fortune, an estimate can be made based on the number of his slaves. During population censuses of the colony in 1816, 1820, and 1823, Bennett is consistently shown to be the largest slaveowner, with 211, 250, and 243 individuals respectively, far more than the other magistrates.[72] Over the course of his terms of office, Bennett came to control a large share of the colony's enslaved labor force. Whereas the number of slaves held in British Honduras between 1806 and 1823 decreased by approximately 30 percent from 3,626 to 2,468 individuals, and the number of slaveowners with at least fifty slaves also declined, from seventeen to eight, the number of slaves held by Bennett stayed roughly the same.[73]

Some other major slaveowners, however, were excluded from the coterie of wealthy mahogany loggers. Grace Tucker Anderson, a free person of color, was one of them. After a unique life journey—recounted in a romanticized but historically erudite novel by Zee Edgell titled *Time and the River*[74]—she inherited her late husband's estate in 1820. As a result, she became the owner of 110 slaves, most of them employed in mahogany logging.[75] Under local rules, however, magistrates had to be of pure British descent, which was obviously not the case for a former slave such as Anderson.

In addition to running the settlement, magistrates leveraged their political position to reserve economic privileges for themselves, individually as well as collectively. More than anything, the oligarchy functioned as a way for the members to help one another. When a magistrate, past or present, had to leave the colony, the task of overseeing and operating his personal estate or assets under his responsibility was often delegated to another magistrate.[76] Members of the magistracy were also empowered to handle the liquidation of the estates of settlers or their descendants based in Britain. For example, John Wright was engaged by Louise Hill, who lived in London, to represent her in the sale of the estate of her late father, John Emmons Hill, which she did not wish to keep.[77] Since they were responsible for drawing up the inventories of the estates, magistrates had inside information about estimated asset values, handing them an advantage when it came to a potential acquisition of those properties. In 1822, Bennett, for example, purchased the estate of two Somerset heiresses for £3,000.[78]

The magistracy also headed the colony's judiciary, which in the 1820s was divided into three separate courts: the Grand Court, the Petty Court, and the Slave Court. Sitting in quarterly sessions, the Grand Court was chaired by the magistrates, assisted by a jury of thirteen citizens selected by local residents.[79] Records reveal that the Grand Court primarily heard civil cases, mainly of a commercial nature.[80] Plaintiffs typically brought proceedings on matters involving noncompliance with the contractual clauses of an agreement, official and public recognition of slave emancipation procedures, and, above all, failure to settle debts.[81] The court did also occasionally hear cases involving defamation, blasphemy, and other serious crimes set down in the legal texts compiled by William Burnaby in 1765, which were gradually amended and expanded to create a kind of common law for the settlement known as the Burnaby Code, published for the first time in 1809.[82]

In cases before the Grand Court, the jury and magistrates tended to rule overwhelmingly in favor of the plaintiff. As *Sproat v. France* shows, this approach was intrinsically linked to the colony's judicial system. On October 31, 1822, George Sproat accused Alexander France of selling mahogany logs without his consent. Whereas France had been hired by Sproat to transport three logs from his works on the Manatee River south of Belize to a sorting and measuring center in Belize, the plaintiff accused him of selling the product illegally to Wright & Young, a wholesaler. Expecting to be ruled against, France begged the jurors to set the fees at a sufficiently reasonable amount so that he could recover the expense through the suit that he was planning to bring against Sproat during the court's next session.[83] While the court's rulings could not officially be appealed against, it would seem that, as the French threats show, judgments were challenged through successive trials or out-of-court settlements.

A notable feature of the types of cases brought before British Honduras's highest court is the absence of suits involving violent crimes. While occasional notes offer evidence of terrible violence inflicted on slaves, the magistracy, acting through court decisions or through its own meetings, generally regarded these actions either as unimportant or, alternatively, of sufficient importance, based on medical reports from the settlement's physician, Dr. Young, for the superintendent to be notified.[84] However, on the basis of the cases heard by the court, there appear to have been few instances of violence by settlers toward other settlers.

Before rushing to the conclusion that all the colony's inhabitants lived together in harmony, barring the odd business dispute, one specific case points to a system of social control that was instigated and monopolized by the members of the magistracy. On September 16, 1822, the jury of a court chaired by three magistrates found Frederick Bowen guilty of threatening, and endangering the life of, Marshall Bennett. During the trial, six witnesses, including at least two magistrates, accused the defendant of following Bennett and threatening him in the street, declaring openly and loudly that he would not mind running him through with a blade.[85] Bowen was found guilty and sentenced to three months in prison, given a fine of JM£100, and required to post bail of at least JM£400. Following Bowen's three months' imprisonment, his creditors, including magistrates Bennett and Gibson, agreed to cancel his personal debts and return his bail money on condition that he leave British Honduras for the United States. Bowen reluctantly agreed.[86]

Yet just a few years earlier, Bowen had been on good terms with the magistracy, being employed from time to time as a police officer and enforcer, and even assaulting some settlers who had defied the magistrates' wishes. In 1818, for example, Thomas Osburn accused Bowen of assaulting him and arresting him without a warrant. But Bowen was cleared by a jury after the timely discovery during the trial that the magistrates had actually issued a warrant against Osburn but had seemingly forgotten to mention its existence.[87] In the space of a few years, though, Bowen turned from being a henchman into a foe that Bennett needed to dispose of. As this case illustrates, through their command of the executive and the judiciary, the magistrates controlled a parallel legal system that discouraged most settlers from stepping out of line and breaking the colony's rules and customs, especially where this involved leveling any kind of accusation at magistrates.

Although the private reasons why Bowen came to hate Bennett remain unclear, this case reveals the means that were brought to bear on anyone who stood up to the established order. Specifically, these mechanisms composed the formal legal process of an official judgment, coupled with a more informal dispute settlement system linked essentially to questions of debt and the penalties for which extended to banishment of an undesirable party. This peculiar order, embodied here by Bennett, against whom Bowen turned to his cost, was partly based on the ties of power that bound Belize's inhabitants to the magistrates, who, as we shall see, controlled the financial flows connected with the mahogany trade.

Mahogany logging, so central to the operation of British Honduras and the power of the magistracy, was a seasonal business. The trees were felled between August and March, often in remote areas. The logs were then transported by river during the rainy season in June.[88] As many loggers did not have sufficient capital to keep operating until the results of their labor (and that of their slaves) could be sold to wholesalers, they often relied on short-term loans to finance their businesses and settle current expenses. For this, they turned to the wealthiest men in British Honduras, namely the magistrates. Bennett, Thomas Paslow, James Hyde, and Thomas Iles all extended loans, ranging from tens to thousands of Jamaican pounds, to many local businessmen, providing the liquidity they needed to continue operating.[89] The loans were typically divided into bonds without a specific coupon, while the terms went from a few months to two or three years depending on the amount. Bonds were secured against the borrower's estate or a set number of slaves. If a borrower failed to meet their obligations, their property or labor was seized for the benefit of the lender.

As they stepped up their lending, the magistrates gained control over the colony's cutting practices. Within this system, some magistrates acted as exclusive buyers and exporters of timber to be shipped to Britain. Magistrate John Wright, for example, was head of the firm of Wright & Young, which bought mahogany logs from the settlement's loggers for shipment to Britain.[90] By forcing debt on the loggers, who often had to deliver their product to the same individuals who had extended the loans to them, the Belizean oligarchy was able to steer—or at least heavily influence—the production system used to exploit local mahogany resources. As primary suppliers of the capital required to exploit the colony's natural resources, the magistrates ensured that they had exclusive access to the supply of logs needed for their own affairs to run smoothly.

The ties linking magistrates and lesser loggers were not always just financial. Sometimes, loggers who were in debt to the magistrates hired these rich owners to be their legal representatives. On April 16, 1823, for example, Grace Tucker Anderson appointed Thomas Iles as:

> My true and lawful attorney revocable for me, in my name and to my use to ask, claim, demand, recover, take and receive of, and from all and singular such sum and sums of money whatsoever as never is, or at any times or times hereafter shall be due payable and belonging unto me, And also of all person, or persons whatsoever all and singular such other sum, and sums of money, salary, wages, goods, wares an merchandize, freight, profits, rents, and arrears of rent, debts dues, duties, claims, and demands

whatsoever, which now is, or at any time or times hereafter shall be due, owing, payable and belonging unto me, by any ways or means, right or title whatsoever or giving and hereby granting, unto my said attorney his substitutes and assigns, all my authority and lawful power in the premises for receiving, recovering, compounding and discharging, the same as fully and effectually to all uses, intents and purposes as I might or possibly could do, being personally present, And acquittances, releases or any other discharges in law or equity required in my name to make, sign, seal and deliver and my person in any court or courts where my presence may be requisite and necessary to represent.[91]

Anderson was not alone. Many of the settlement's merchants, loggers, and even ordinary citizens hired magistrates to act as their personal commercial and legal agents. Bound by a contract witnessed by two other magistrates and recorded in a central register, these agents were responsible for performing the tasks involved in recovering personal claims, handling movements of capital and other payments, and representing their clients in court.[92]

Although the contracts do not mention how the new agents were compensated, as their numbers swelled, these agreements represented a powerful financial tool for members of the Belizean executive. Since the agents were likely paid a commission on the amounts managed, the establishment of a network comprising many such contracts held by members of the magistracy (one representative could choose to appoint a substitute to replace him) indirectly created a payment system in the hands of the same men who already issued many of the loans needed for the local economy to run smoothly. Appointing a magistrate as agent was also a means of acquiring legal protection, as illustrated in the case of Anderson. In a settlement devoid of a single professional lawyer, there were certainly benefits to being represented by an individual who was also in charge of dispensing justice in the colony and enforcing its laws with wide latitude for interpretation, even if, in return, the client had to surrender control over the capital movements connected with their business.[93]

By maintaining a grip on the payment system, magistrates exerted economic and political control over the entire colony. With many of the inhabitants bound either financially or contractually to one of the magistrates, it became hard to challenge the magistracy's practices, decisions, legislative proposals, and appointments or reappointments presented at the public meetings. Yet with a political, social, and economic hold over the colony, magistrates were also able to retain exclusive control over an area that was effectively rendered out-of-bounds for the rest of British Honduras's population: external affairs. Through their economic position as the chief mahogany exporters and lenders to small and mid-sized businesses, as well as their political status, magistrates could claim the political power to shape the mahogany trade in Central America and beyond.

One of the ways in which the magistrates controlled the colony's foreign relations, and in particular its mahogany trade, was by appointing one of their own to act as London agent, charged with representing the economic and political interests of the local mahogany business.[94] For example, on March 4, 1822, a public meeting appointed John Young as agent, to be based in London to represent the interests of the colony. Young was who none other than John Wright's partner in the Belizean mahogany trading company Wright & Young. The public meeting agreed to release £300 annually for this purpose.[95] The agent's main job was to ensure that goods shipments arrived safely in London's ports, that the sales were recorded, and that the bills of exchange to pay the British Honduran loggers were duly dispatched.[96] Young was also responsible for coordinating, maintaining, and fostering a network of London merchants with an interest in mahogany shipments from British Honduras. Although the names of these merchants have not been formally identified for the period covered by this book, they appear to have comprised a small group. Following a discussion in the British Parliament in 1826 on possible changes to the preferential duties levied on Belizean mahogany, Young approached Messrs. Forsyth, Angus, Poingdestre, and Cox to send a message in support of the interests of the British Honduras magistracy.[97]

Although appointing an agent in London provided some control over the outflow of the colony's production, the magistrates also ensured that they were able to control the colony's supply of natural resources, particularly outside its territory. The most important of those resources was the Shore's mahogany. British Honduras's financial and trade system was more than merely a means of securing the economic, commercial, political, and social control needed for the oligarchy to perpetuate its own power; it was heavily dependent on steady access to the mahogany in the forests on Miskitu territory. To maintain that access, British Honduran mahogany loggers needed privileged access to the relationships of negotiation and cohabitation established with—and partly by—local Indigenous peoples. Starting in the late eighteenth century, the system of control established by the magistracy allowed the colony's wealthiest loggers to act as the sole and preferred talking partners of the Miskitu king, through whom access to Moskitia's mahogany resources was negotiated. Ostensibly, the magistracy refrained from acting outside British Honduras as delineated in the 1786 Treaty of London, ensuring that, as far as Spain was concerned, its behavior was politically and diplomatically irreproachable, at least formally. Privately and unofficially, though, the oligarchs had managed to secure exclusive access to dealings with the Miskitu king. They did so by training Miskitu kings as cultural intermediaries. In 1805, for example, the magistracy assumed responsibility for educating the young Miskitu prince John (likely the future George Frederic), who was sent to Jamaica "to impress upon his mind the advantage of our alliance."[98] Likewise, the magistracy's coffers funded the purchase of gifts to be distributed by the king among representatives of the Miskitu communities.[99]

However, individuals outside this political regime struggled to exert influence, both internally and externally, because of the magistracy's grip on local and external relations. The case of James and George Hyde is particularly illustrative in this respect. To sell its local mahogany production on the English market, the Belizean magistrates dealt heavily with a London merchant firm called Inglis Ellice & Co., led by two merchant bankers, John Inglis and Edward Ellice.[100] Although chiefly active in the North American fur market, the firm had some dealings in British Honduras. Following the death of John Inglis and the subsequent departure of Edward Ellice for the Hudson's Bay Company, Inglis's son formed a new business, Inglis and Co., with the aim of taking over the old firm's activities to refocus on Central America.[101] To do so, the firm began buying up the debts of some of the magistrates, in hopes of channeling mahogany exports toward itself. Bennett mounted a revolt against these financial maneuvers and sought to challenge Inglis's aspirations through the Belizean court system. Several wealthy local mahogany merchants sued Lewis Evans Williams, Inglis and Co.'s local agent, for failing to pay bills of exchange.[102]

But not everyone backed Bennett. After running short of cash in 1821, the woodcutter James Hyde signed an exclusive contract with Inglis and Co., promising to sell the firm the mahogany from his works. He also handed over his entire property, including his estate and slaves, to the foreign firm.[103] In return he and his brother George became commercial agents of Inglis, with responsibility for exploiting the mahogany resources of an estate that now belonged to the British financier. Named to represent Inglis on Belizean soil, as evidenced by suits brought against them over unpaid bills of exchange, the Hydes abruptly became local outcasts.[104] After previously being elected magistrates periodically before 1821, neither of them would ever hold that office again.[105] The number of slaves that they owned fell by about one-third between 1820 and 1826, perhaps in a sign that the brothers were suffering from business troubles and struggling to maintain their social and economic standing within the colony.[106]

Moskitia in the early nineteenth century was characterized by a peculiar political economy. Established over the course of the eighteenth century, this regime of political and economic cooperation between Indigenous peoples and representatives of British private enterprises operating in the region was fragile and at times unequal. Nonetheless, it was rooted in a cohabitation that was both tolerated and essential to safeguarding and growing the commercial and political benefits of both sets of players. In exchange for goods and firearms that enabled them to assert their military and political hold, Miskitu elites guaranteed access to the natural resources coveted by the British enterprises that set up on the Shore in the eighteenth century. Within this system, Indigenous kings acted as cultural go-betweens appointed by trading partners. Following diplomatic decisions taken in London, the heart of the British regime shifted to British Honduras in the final third of the eighteenth century. There, an oligarchy made up of mahogany loggers and merchants secured exclusive access to the Shore's natural resources by building up social, political, and legal control based primarily on command of the settlement's internal finances.

By unpicking the political and economic dynamics that structured the social, cultural, and colonial interactions connecting British private merchants to local Indigenous peoples, this chapter shines a brighter light on the conditions that set the stage for MacGregor's arrival on the Shore. However, as the next chapter will show, it was not so much the successful preservation and implementation of this system of cohabitation that led King George Frederic to allocate a huge plot of land to the future cacique of Poyais but rather that the system itself was called into question in the first decades of the nineteenth century, both internally and externally.

TWO

A Miskitu Land Grant

ON JANUARY 17, 1820, the Belizean magistracy wrote to the superintendent of British Honduras expressing concern about the depletion of the main official mahogany reserves in the territory named by the London agreement of 1786.[1] The loggers felt squeezed, as the gradual expansion of their activities beyond the territorial limits set by Britain and Spain seems to indicate. In addition to making temporary incursions into Moskitia with the blessing of the Miskitu, in 1814 the Belizean settlers, hoping to set a precedent that would prompt Spain to extend the forestry areas, had announced that mahogany logging had been extended to the banks of the Moho River, well beyond the settlement's southern border.[2]

The loggers' complaints may have been well-founded, justifying their desire to continue exploiting resources beyond the previously defined territorial limits—particularly those on the Shore. However, their claims of distant yet plentiful timber resources, set against tales of depleted reserves at home, may also have been driven by stress within a political ecology that either supplemented or superseded the true state of affairs amid changing times.[3] In fact, rather than reflecting a genuine shortage, the sharp decrease in access to mahogany resources reported by the magistrates in early 1820 was primarily attributable to the emergence of a significant impediment a few years earlier: On October 28, 1817, Colonel George Arthur, His Majesty's Superintendent in British Honduras since 1814 (Fig. 7), forbade the extension of any logging concession without his express consent.[4] The measure, which forced loggers to notify the superintendent when acquiring or operating new concessions, was just one of several attempts by Arthur to counter the local political economy operated and controlled by the mahogany oligarchy to control trade and finance.

As this chapter illustrates, the actions of Superintendent Arthur led to significant disruptions to the political economy of British Honduras by opposing the consolidation of a political and judicial system that favored the settlement's most powerful logging interests and, more widely, to the political and economic cooperation between English settlers and Miskitu elites, which underpinned the extraction of mahogany in Central America. However, these disruptions would also combine with other Atlantic dynamics. These included the spillover into Moskitia of American revolutionary claims, or the development of anti-slavery movements. This peculiar combination of local and Atlantic change would go on to have particular repercussions in Central America, offering King George Frederic the opportunity to reposition himself politically within Moskitia. Like other South American independence or abolitionist projects of the time, he envisioned the establishment of a Moskitia that would be commercially and politically independent. In other words, George Frederic essentially tried to shape Britain's drive to improve trade in the Americas and turn it to his own commercial and political benefit. Against the backdrop of these colonial conflicts and Atlantic disruptions, George Frederic sought to leverage English eagerness to boost British trade—particularly in mahogany—in the Americas and to turn this enthusiasm to his own commercial and political ends. This, as we shall see, included allowing MacGregor to create Poyais.

———

Arthur was appointed Superintendent of British Honduras in 1814.[5] At that time, a British Honduran superintendent held a position specific to the private colony. Rather than act as an official Crown agent sent to enforce a British legal framework, he was primarily tasked with representing His Majesty's interests in an observer's role.[6] As British Honduras was not a colony under a formal British legal regime properly speaking, his presence was possible chiefly because the magistrates tolerated it. In return, they gained a preferred channel of communication with the Jamaican authorities (who were in charge of appointing him) and with His Majesty's Government, to which he regularly reported.

From time to time, however, the British Honduras oligarchs took it upon

Figure 7. George Arthur. Source: Major-General Sir George Arthur, Bart., KCB [Lieutenant Governor of Upper Canada, 1838–41], 1887, 693137, Archives of Ontario.

themselves to remind the superintendent—and hence Britain—about the primacy of their own legal and political regime, as illustrated by the abortive attempt by Lieutenant Colonel Alexander Mark Kerr Hamilton, one of Arthur's predecessors, to impose local law reforms. In 1807, Hamilton attempted to prevent Marshall Bennett from renewing his seat on the magistracy. He accused Bennett of being ineligible, because he had been found guilty in a 1799 case involving a man named John Moss. However, a meeting of the settlers decided to annul the verdict and, at Bennett's request, to expunge the minutes of the ruling from the court register, to ensure that the details of the trial remained secret. In early 1808, under pressure from Superintendent Hamilton, the case was retried, and Bennett was cleared once again. The new court overturned the 1799 ruling outright, deeming it to be invalid as one of the jurors had gone to the restroom when the jury voted. With Bennett cleared again, the British Honduras magistracy declared Hamilton's attempt to oust one of their own—and not the least important—member of the group as a degrading insult to the settlement's legal and political institutions. The superintendent's actions were seen as an attack on their "ancient uses and regulations." In retaliation, the magistrates decided to suspend Hamilton's wage, which was paid by the local treasury.[7]

The magistracy's publication of Burnaby's Code the following year therefore clarified, in writing, these "ancient uses and regulations."[8] These texts set fines for blasphemy and theft, the legislative terms for imposing new taxes, and the rules for setting up local courts of justice. The code comprised twelve articles and a few amendments, often couched in vague terms.[9] Yet its publication sent a signal to Britain, as it was designed not just to formally establish a legal framework exclusive to the colony. It was also meant to curb the powers of the British superintendent posted in Belize, who is mentioned just three times in a few minor appendices.

The function attached to the post of superintendent remained loosely defined.[10] The leader of British forces stationed in Belize, Arthur himself described his job as administering the colony and enforcing compliance with the Burnaby Code. However, he also complained that his task was impossible because "these [laws] have been found in many respects prejudicial; in others impracticable, and in [. . .] all inefficient."[11] Since British Honduras was a private colony, the superintendent was not authorized to interfere in practical ways as he wished in local affairs. In theory, for example, he was charged with ratifying the elections of new magistrates and could even ask the British Secretary to the Colonies to dismiss those found guilty of improper behavior.[12] But Arthur's superior, Under-Secretary of State for the Colonies Robert Wilmot-Horton, actually considered that "the authority of a superintendent [. . .] is of so doubtful a nature in print of law that it may be considered rather conventional than strictly legal."[13]

He nevertheless believed that there was room to maneuver. A superintendent needed, from time to time, to exploit the gray areas within the frameworks that underpinned the magistrates' local legal prerogatives in order to uphold the primacy of English law in specific instances. To ensure that British authority in the region was not rejected, potentially to Spain's benefit, such opportunities needed to be used sparingly, and only when bringing official British influence to bear might serve the magistrates' interest. Although

Arthur complained that the lack of clarity about the functions entrusted to the superintendent might be detrimental to the English Crown's "legitimate" rights in the region, His Majesty's Government could nevertheless benefit, at times, from the continued ambiguity.[14] Acting more like a tolerated guest of the Belizean loggers, the superintendent, posted to a geographical location whose sovereignty was disputed by two imperial powers, offered an official local anchor point, provided that he stayed on the right side of the magistracy. Wilmot-Horton himself thus advised Arthur to avoid getting overly involved in the magistrates' affairs, including in several cases concerning the brutal mistreatment of slaves.[15]

This seems to have been the case, at least initially, as Superintendent Arthur appeared, shortly after his appointment, to foster relatively good relations with the British Honduras oligarchy. A letter from the magistrates to the British government in 1817 mentioned the "great services" rendered by the superintendent.[16] Wilmot-Horton also said that he liked being in Belize. In reports to London in 1816, he compared British Honduras with other colonies in the British West Indies, including Jamaica, and described his settlement as a paradise, especially for its slaves.[17] He likewise appeared to be on good terms with the men that he called "respectable magistrates," including Marshall Bennett.[18]

Over the course of his time there, however, his position toward these men gradually changed. In addition to imposing reporting requirements on the operation of mahogany concessions, Arthur became less willing to lobby the British government in support of the magistrates' complaints and grievances. Following a discussion by the British Parliament in 1820 on rescinding a 1817 law offering preferential duties to British Honduras mahogany, Arthur forwarded a petition to the Colonial Office.[19] Signed by many loggers, the petition requested that the proposed increase in import duties on Belizean mahogany be reconsidered. In a report accompanying the petition sent, out of duty, to Earl Bathurst, Secretary of State for War and the Colonies, Arthur said, however, that he believed the "loggers' fears" to be "wholly unfounded," since British Honduras mahogany was, in his view, of inferior quality and unable to compete with foreign merchants.[20]

This change of feeling toward the biggest loggers in British Honduras was probably due to a gradual firming of Arthur's religious beliefs, particularly regarding the abolition of slavery. As indicated in letters to his wife,

Elizabeth, who had remained in London, Arthur was a devout evangelical and opposed to slavery.[21] On arriving in Jamaica in 1812 as major in the 7th Infantry Regiment, he described himself as "a Perfect Wilberforce as to Slavery," in a reference to William Wilberforce, a British Member of Parliament (MP) leading the movement to abolish slavery.[22] His sudden opposition to the British Honduran magistrates' business activities may also have been exacerbated by events following a slave uprising in 1820. He was especially repelled by the means used to quell the rebellion and wrote to express his utter outrage over "the extreme inhumanity of many of the lower class of Settlers, residing in the town of Belize, towards their Slaves; and, as it appeared to be an evil greatly increasing, [. . .] the total inadequacy of the Courts of this Settlement to check this vicious disposition."[23]

The way that the local authorities deliberately ignored the violence with which some slave owners attempted to prevent any new uprising doubtless further encouraged Arthur in his changed attitude toward the loggers of British Honduras. The case of a slave called Peggy was an especially flagrant example. After she was accused of stealing some handkerchiefs, Mansfield Bowen, her owner, had her flogged and confined for five days in a rat-infested hut. After recovering from her injuries, Peggy lodged a complaint against Bowen, for which she was once again harshly punished. Further, the magistrates found Bowen not guilty, deeming the testimonies provided by three slaves during the trial to be inadmissible, since they were submitted by individuals without rights.[24]

Besides condemning the loggers' mistreatment of their slaves, Arthur also embarked on a crusade to free slaves of Indigenous descent. Many descendants of British settlers that had formerly lived on the Shore owned such slaves, who were probably initially acquired through commercial trade with the Miskitu. Responding to practices that he personally condemned, Arthur decided to enforce in British Honduras a 1775 act issued by William Legge, Earl of Dartmouth and British Secretary of State to the Colonies, which then made it illegal to enslave local Indigenous people in Pitt's Black River settlement on the Shore.[25] Arthur set up a committee to discuss the legality of such practices in British Honduras, while also getting many slaves from Moskitia to safety, under the authority of the provost marshal, the officer in charge of the military police unit attached to the troops under Arthur's command.[26]

Some of Arthur's reports were taken up by William Wilberforce, who in 1823 gave an impassioned reading of one of the superintendent's reports in the House of Commons, stressing the systematic mistreatment of slaves and especially the problem of Indigenous slaves.[27] Wilberforce's speech also propelled to the forefront of the London scene a private and independent British colony that had hitherto received praise for allegedly providing a safe and happy environment for its slaves. A few years earlier, a pamphlet published in 1809 urging the British government to step in to assist a colony that was economically threatened by its inability to expand the geographical reach of its mahogany industry had offered a vivid description of British Honduras's logging activities. Written by George Henderson, a soldier posted in Belize, it proclaimed: "in no part of the world, where slavery prevails, can the condition of beings so circumstanced be found of milder or more indulgent form."[28]

To try to draw a comparative scale of the sufferings endured within the West Indian slavery system would be futile. However, without offering any kind of justification for the practices in Belize, the conditions of slaves working in the mahogany trade do appear to have been qualitatively different than those of other British colonies, especially the sugar-producing centers. This finding was recently illustrated by James Walvin, who records the treatment of slaves laboring in the Belizean mahogany industry.[29] During successive harvesting seasons, owners and slaves would often find themselves isolated and alone in remote forests. With both groups equipped with the tools needed to fell trees but also firearms to defend against the dangers roaming the forests of Central America, owners needed to treat their slaves relatively well to avoid a rebellion using the arms that they themselves had supplied. Before each logging season, a few slaves were also sent out as scouts deep into the forest to find and identify which trees to fell. At that time of the year, mahogany leaves are orange-tinged, making the trees easier to spot. Fears that these scouts might sell their intelligence to other loggers were another incentive for owners to offer their slaves better living conditions.[30] However, as Peggy's case shows, these good conditions were still relative. In addition to the unspeakably cruel and intolerable punishments inflicted on them, slaves were given far and away the hardest and most dangerous jobs. These included the transportation and loading of mahogany logs on merchant ships, during which many accidents occurred.[31]

Responding to the fallout in London following Arthur's stand against their slavery practices, some loggers openly opposed him. A defense published in London and Kingston and drafted by order of the "inhabitants of Honduras" protested that Arthur's accusations about the mistreatment of Belizean slaves were slanderous. The authors argued that the slave owners running the settlement were far more benign than those in other British colonies. That their slaves could supposedly take every Sunday off, or that some had joined the ranks of the Belizean militia during the 1798 Battle of St. George's Caye, purportedly signing up of their own free will alongside their masters to fight the Spanish foe, offered proof that Belize's slavery practices rested on solid foundations.[32] The authors likewise cast the superintendent's accusations as part of a strategy to undermine their business activities to his own benefit, suggesting that his reporting requirements on mahogany loggers to London and Kingston gave him intelligence that he could then use for his own business activities, proven or otherwise. His public accusations of cruel slavery practices, the inhabitants claimed, were therefore chiefly aimed at stirring up bad press in London to sour relations between the main mahogany merchants and their London trading partners.

While Arthur was undoubtedly sincere in his critique of British Honduran slavery, he was actually engaged in parallel activities that potentially hurt the business interests of the Belizean loggers to his own gain. On April 5, 1820, he sent a letter to the Miskitu king, George Frederic, in which he set out a project to build a missionary-led school on the king's land, "in order, if possible, to provide some instruction to the children."[33] Keen to see his plan come to fruition, the superintendent even sent a report to Josiah Pratt the day after contacting George Frederic about the matter. In it, he set out his progress and intentions, detailing what he saw as a well-thought-out collaborative undertaking. At the time, Pratt was the secretary of the deeply evangelical Church Missionary Society in London, and therefore seen by Arthur as ideally placed to supply the best missionaries to execute his plan to teach Moskitia's "poor miserable Indians."[34]

Arthur's plan, which he deemed should be "highly agreeable to the Miskitu people" and a "blessing for the country," looks laudable on the face of it. But a different conclusion may be reached when the plan is held up against the accusations made in defense of the British Honduras loggers, not to mention the broader context in which attempts at evangelization became entangled with colonial momentum in Central America. Pratt also appears to have had close ties to anti-slavery champion William Wilberforce. In addition to being the founders of the Church Missionary Society, the two men kept up a friendly correspondence.[35] Pratt also had links to the Clapham Sect, an evangelical abolitionist group to which Wilberforce belonged, since William Hey, founder of the *Christian Observer*, the sect's official publication, was the uncle of Pratt's wife. In fact, Hey appointed Pratt to be the paper's first editor.[36] At any rate, Pratt seems to have held Wilberforce in high regard, proposing in 1815 to name a ship of the Church Missionary Society intended to carry missionaries to Africa after him.[37] Since Arthur supplied reports to Pratt's society on progress in evangelizing the Miskitu, and Wilberforce obtained the superintendent's reports for his speech before Parliament denouncing Indigenous slavery in British Honduras, it seems reasonable to conjecture that Arthur, Pratt, and Wilberforce shared a similar understanding of the elements linking anti-slavery arguments and the evangelical faith.[38]

These affinities were also reflected in some of the canons of English anti-slavery at the time, in particular in Wilberforce's 1823 *An Appeal to the Religion, Justice, and Humanity of the Inhabitants of the British Empire*. In it, he called for slavery to be totally abolished. As proof, he gave readers many examples of cruelty, including rapes and floggings, inflicted on slaves in the British West Indies. More importantly, he dwelled on the cruel absence of a practice forbidden to slaves but considered fundamental and essential to fulfillment of the human condition, as well as to the productivity of the Caribbean sugar trade. Specifically, Wilberforce believed that abolishing slavery would pave the way for the repeal of laws and regulations in West Indian colonies prohibiting slaves from entering into holy matrimony.[39] In his view, depriving slaves of the opportunity to enter more "Christian" unions was an impediment to moral fulfillment and drove them to engage in "licentious" practices, including having multiple sexual partners. If slavery were to be abolished, former slaves would therefore be automatically allowed to marry. The sanctification of unions within future communities of former slaves would then lead to a "natural" increase in their numbers. Flagged by Wilberforce as a prerequisite for healthy and numerous births, marriage was implicitly identified as an essential alternative to the decrease in the West Indian labor forces following the abolition of the slave trade in 1807.[40]

Wilberforce's argument that marriage was the expression of a higher level of civilization chimed with conservative ideas that emerged in the second half of the eighteenth century, inspired notably by the thinking of Edmund Burke. An Irish-born philosopher, member of the Whig party, and long-serving MP, Burke saw marriage, and especially its indissolubility, as a key factor in the superiority of British civilization.[41] Accordingly, and as a fierce critic of the French Revolution, he identified measures introduced during France's First Republic to facilitate divorce as reflective of severe civilizational decline.[42] However, whereas Burke bemoaned the way in which French revolutionaries reduced marriage to a simple civil contract, Wilberforce implicitly raised it to the status of the quintessential contract. He considered marriage, like any religious rite, to be essentially designed to sanctify a contract.[43] Actively disseminating such values within communities described as being in a precarious moral state would therefore contribute to a "regular improvement in [Christian] religion, morality, and civilization."[44] In turn, this would lay the foundation for a spiritual revelation, understanding, and realization of the importance of the sacred agreement made by the two parties. By extension, the marriage contract was the basic model used to regulate and organize of all forms of interaction, whether social, commercial, or, as in this case, labor-related.

With this in mind, the measures taken by Arthur against the Belizean magistracy can be seen as a strategy to sap the latter's power on the Shore. Arthur's plans to convert the Miskitu to Christianity appeared to form part of a campaign to transform the structure of the interactions linking the colonial and Indigenous polities.[45] Although the colony's prosperity was rooted, by his own admission, in the extraction of valuable timber resources, Arthur nevertheless considered the settlement to be run by a gang of incompetent magistrates.[46] To resolve this situation, he planned to engineer a deep shift in the paradigm underlying relations between British mahogany loggers and the Miskitu. Since interactions between Indigenous and colonial elites dictated the allocation of preferred access to the coveted resources, the teaching of "Christian" values, based on respect for contractual relations by all members of a group, would pave the way for new colonial practices to be adopted.

Arthur's model was thus seen as a potential replacement for the existing form of cohabitation practiced by the settlers and the Miskitu and so critical to the activities of the Belizean oligarchy. Setting up a missionary-run school that would promote religious ceremonies sanctifying the importance of respect for contractual relations seems like a strategy that could ultimately drive a fundamental shift in the cultural practices underpinning the Miskitu's internal power systems. Moreover, while polygamy—practiced by Miskitu elites to consolidate ties of vassalage—underpinned the establishment and mutual recognition of alliances within the Indigenous communities, the introduction of arrangements designed to establish couples based on monogamous Christian marriages would undermine the local political structures.[47]

Crucially, Arthur's plans sought to introduce a system in which Indigenous peoples were encouraged to comply with values essentially based on compliance with contractually established and clearly defined associations, which were given almost sanctified status. Instilling such values in the Miskitu community would offer a way to circumvent one of the prerequisites of the existing political and economic relationship binding British Honduras and Moskitia, namely the arbitration processes through which the Miskitu king mediated relations between representatives of both communities' elites. Arthur's education plan would inculcate Miskitu communities with contractual values. Once local populations were schooled and converted to Christianity, anyone would be able to establish and maintain direct relations with Indigenous persons without having to go through the king. According to Arthur, this would enable the Miskitu and other Indigenous polities of the region to enter a "system of industry."[48] Notably, free and contractually bound Indigenous peoples would provide an adequate labor force to cut and process the region's mahogany resources, which Arthur implies by mentioning that he wants to instruct a few "intelligent boys" from Moskitia in carpentry.[49]

Ultimately, the contractualization of labor relations between those exploiting natural resources and the labor force, against the backdrop of a dialogue infused with Christian values, was a way to compensate settler populations for the likely end of slavery practices following the abolition of the slave trade in 1807. The introduction of a strict and clearly defined framework, underpinned by the sanctification of contractual relations, would support a new approach to replace the flexible negotiating practices stemming from the cooperative process that had hitherto linked British settlers and the Miskitu. Introduced into the heart of the Indigenous polities, these evangelizing practices would eventually obviate the need for authorization from the king or any other member of the Indigenous elite.

A bystander in the confrontation opposing the colonial practices of the local oligarchs with Superintendent Arthur's Wilberforcian approach, King George Frederic hoped to take advantage of the situation to shore up or even improve his specific mode of interaction with the Belizeans, which had hitherto had a decisive effect on his own political and material situation. This, as we shall see, involved granting the Poyais territory to MacGregor in 1820. Yet George Frederic's status and role should not normally have encouraged him to act in this manner. Like the rulers that came before him, George Frederic was essentially raised from his earliest days to play the role of cultural go-between, bridging the gap between the business and political interests of the Miskitu and British. To some extent, in adopting a new stance, against a backdrop of political and economic unrest in Central America, George Frederic far exceeded a king's usual functions. Yet a few biographical details give insights as to why George Frederic distanced himself from the role assigned to generations of previous Miskitu monarchs.[50]

Born in the 1790s, George Frederic Augustus was destined to become another Miskitu leader in the old mold. He and his younger brother, Robert Charles Frederic, were taken to Kingston in June 1805.[51] To safeguard his political legacy, their father, George II, had previously negotiated with Alexander Lindsay, Earl of Balcarres and then governor of Jamaica, to have both sons educated in Kingston.[52] Their great-uncle Isaac went along as chaperone for the two princes, ensuring that their education was suited to their future position. The Jamaican authorities also provided him with £100 a year for his personal needs and those of his entourage.[53]

As a child, George Frederic was regularly presented to some of the island's most important residents. On August 13, 1804, a dinner was organized at the governor's residence, attended by a small group of high-ranking British officers and dignitaries. Although the young prince threw an age-appropriate tantrum that evening—much to the displeasure of the governor's wife, Lady Maria Nugent, who recorded the incident in her journal—the aim of the gathering was clear: to maintain the interest of those present in Moskitia's commercial potential. Throughout the evening, George Frederic's great-uncle was at pains to remind the guests of the "fine and hospitable customs of his country," which would soon be governed by the prince, who, at that exact moment, was receiving a British education in order to maintain the preferred access of British merchants to Moskitia's trade.[54] Accordingly, George Frederic's education not only made him aware of his English talking partners and their customs but also hammered home the message that the legitimacy of his royal position depended on the state of Moskitia's foreign trade.[55]

However, George Frederic was not educated by English tutors only. Many foreign merchants were also involved in training the future royal intermediary. Hoping to ensure that the future king would provide continued access to the resources of the Miskitu Shore, some merchants sought to keep in regular contact with the prince during his time in Jamaica. For example, Peter Shepherd, a British merchant, regularly brought leaders from the Valiente (members of a Rama polity based in the southern part of Moskitia) to Jamaica to visit George Frederic.[56] Allowing the young prince to get used to commanding his future subjects and assert his role as Moskitia's gatekeeper for foreigners, these frequent meetings also enabled Shepherd to foster good contacts with George Frederic, in hopes of maintaining his flourishing business. As a merchant, Shepherd not only dominated the trade between Moskitia, Jamaica, San Andreas, and Old Providence; he also acted as an intermediary for North American merchants trading in Miskitu goods.[57] More importantly, by interacting with British merchants such as Shepherd, George Frederic was able to forge ties to foreign merchants while also learning how to play an active role in facilitating long-distance trade.[58]

While George Frederic continued his cultural and commercial education in Jamaica, Moskitia was governed by his uncle, Stephen.[59] After the death of George Frederic's father in 1800, Stephen, acting as regent, upheld his late brother's policy of trade conciliation with foreigners established in the region, which was essential to safeguard the political regime of the Miskitu. However, Stephen had to fill the trade vacuum created by the forced abandonment of the Black River settlement following the 1786 treaty between Spain and Britain, under which Britain accepted Spain's full sovereignty over Central America and agreed to evacuate Britain's presence from Moskitia. Miskitu interest then shifted swiftly to the British Honduras settlement. After taking in many Black River evacuees, the Belizean magistrates could see significant commercial advantage to maintaining long-term relations with the Miskitu. So they courted them, and in 1802, for example, sent gifts worth a total amount of £40 to the young George Frederic, who was then in Jamaica.[60]

In November 1815, once George Frederic was deemed to be of age, Stephen organized a meeting with thirty or so Indigenous leaders, at which they all agreed to sign a submission "giving [their] assent, consent, choice, and declaration to, for, and of the appointment of the hereditary Prince Frederic [. . .] to his father's Crown, Franc, and Government, as [their] lawful King and Sovereign."[61] Backed by this support, George Frederic was ready to take on his royal role. In January 1816, he wrote to the then superintendent of British Honduras, George Arthur, requesting to be crowned in the settlement's capital, Belize.[62] The superintendent agreed, pleased that the young king might be officially counted on as the new go-between in charge of maintaining a political and trade alliance between British Honduras and the Miskitu.[63] The ceremony took place on January 18, 1816. George Frederic charted a British sloop of war from Jamaica to Belize for the occasion. Flanked by his own chiefs, as well as British merchants and officers from the colony, George Frederic, in the uniform of an English major, rode on horseback to Belize's main church, where he was enthroned as "King and Sovereign of the Miskitu Nation" during a coronation service conducted in English, accompanied by cries of "Long Live the King."[64]

After his coronation, George Frederic took up residence in Cape Gracias a Dios. The farthest point on the headland jutting out into the Caribbean between the Yucatán Peninsula and the South American mainland, the cape was a key crossing point and center of political and trade negotiations. As the seat of the Miskitu kingdom, it was traditionally a place of mediation for representatives of Moskitia's different communities. The cape was also a gathering point for foreign merchants seeking lawful access to Moskitia's resources. Like his forefathers, George Frederic approved the trade rights of merchants who set up from time to time in the region to build up mahogany, sarsaparilla, or turtle shell supplies for their trade. For example, during a trip in the late 1810s and early 1820s, Orlando Roberts, a British merchant on his way to the cape, met French and British traders whose presence on the Shore depended on regularly renewing their allegiance to the Miskitu sovereign.[65] In July 1815, an American merchant named Jacob Dunham, an American trader who had set up a base in Cape Gracias a Dios, also received permission from George Frederic to "touch and trade in all parts of my dominions in any vessel from North America."[66]

Miskitu nobles and British merchants based on the Shore and especially in British Honduras hoped that George Frederic's coronation would preserve a long-standing situation that benefited British West Indian trade, similar to the system followed under his late father George II. When George Frederic asked to be crowned in Belize, Superintendent Arthur said that he would be honored to grant this privilege, provided that the Miskitu king remembered that he was "in a particular manner under the protection of the British Government."[67] In other words, George Frederic was advised not to disrupt the special ties binding the Miskitu and English merchants and nurtured by his forefathers. Some British merchants even agreed among themselves to enforce this exclusive arrangement. Dunham, the American trader then doing business on the Miskitu Shore, found himself forbidden by British merchants from traveling to Jamaica or sending letters aboard their ships, as they feared that he might "become a rival in trade or become the means of introducing others to the trade."[68]

However, the early years of the king's reign were marked by serious tensions, both internal and external to Moskitia, which stymied and disrupted the model of economic and political colonial cohabitation brokered by the Miskitu ruler.[69]

Within Moskitia's internal context, George Frederic's rule got off to a bad start, as he either could not or would not assert his royal authority over the kingdom. Stephen's fifteen-year regency had given General Robinson and Governor Clementi ample time to shore up their political and economic positions. In the north, Robinson had become a wealthy rancher after boldly distancing himself from Miskitu royal authority. His absence from the leaders' meeting organized by Stephen in 1815 (his signature does not appear on the joint declaration) and George Frederic's coronation caused him to be roundly insulted by the young king.[70] In the south, Clementi, another wealthy rancher, pointedly refused all contact with the new king and actually executed one rather disrespectful envoy. George Frederic also managed to alienate one of his closest allies, Admiral Earnee, by sexually assaulting one of his wives.[71]

Changes taking place far beyond Moskitia also had major consequences for George Frederic's reign, by introducing new actors and ideas to the region. British anti-slavery campaigns had repercussions for Moskitia's political and economic stability. As mentioned earlier, Superintendent Arthur, who was an admirer of English anti-slavery MP William Wilberforce, sought to enforce a ban on holding Indigenous slaves from Moskitia. On the eve of the royal coronation, Arthur strongly urged George Frederic to cease these practices and instead to "administer justice in mercy."[72] Yet these efforts to promote the English anti-slavery movement in Central America posed a problem for George Frederic. The sale of slaves anchored the internal Miskitu economy as well as the system of exchange between the British and the Miskitu, safeguarding the latter's political, military, and commercial grip over the region. Abolishing Indigenous slavery would further undermine the king's faltering power.

The French Revolution and subsequent Napoleonic Wars also had major repercussions on the other side of the Atlantic.[73] Former Spanish colonies saw a sudden upsurge in revolutionary defiance as support swelled for independent republican states.[74] The Haiti uprisings also drove the realization of new slavery-free political possibilities in the Caribbean.[75] The Americas and the Caribbean became key centers of protest where new political projects could be imagined and carried out. But Americans of Spanish origin and former Haitian slaves rising up against their old ruler were not the only ones taking part in these political reconfigurations. Large contingents of British mercenaries hired by Spanish revolutionaries also embraced South American revolutionary ideas and projects, which they helped to spread in their fight against Spanish imperial forces.[76]

Some of these battles took place very close to Moskitia. Jean-Louis Aury, a French privateer on the payroll of several new South American republics, attacked the Spanish ports of Omoa and Truxillo between 1819 and April 1820.[77] These settlements in the Bay of Honduras were only a short distance from Moskitia. In preparation for the attack, Aury sent representatives to George Frederic to request military support, or failing that, right of passage. Intrigued by the idea of allying with the South American insurgents, George Frederic allowed Aury's fleet to circulate in the region and even provided livestock to replenish their supplies, to the fury of General Robinson, the head of large Paya and Sumu communities in the north of Moskitia who had commercial dealings with the Spanish.[78]

The potential trade opportunities opened up by the emerging independent American territories also drew new foreign merchants to the Spanish Main. Interested in more direct transatlantic trade, many of them arrived alongside the mercenaries hired to support revolutionary movements around the continent.[79] George Frederic's kingdom was one of their stops. The Shore's precious mahogany resources, depicted so colorfully in the travel writing of the time, had piqued the interest of British merchants besides West Indian traders and Belizean loggers, to the loggers' annoyance.[80] George Frederic was well aware of the trade potential represented by his territory's precious timber resources. For example, he commissioned Roberts to transport two large mahogany dories to British Honduras to convince the region's merchants of Moskitia's high-quality wood.[81] The possibility of building a transoceanic passage was a particular source of interest. In the south of George Frederic's kingdom, some, including Jeremy Bentham, saw potential to connect several rivers by canal to the Pacific via Lake Nicaragua. Roberts's account of his journey along Moskitia describes, for example, his search for the perfect passage to link the two oceans.[82]

With George Arthur and the magistrates at loggerheads, George Frederic held simultaneous talks with both parties, ensuring that he would avoid having to rely entirely on either of the rivals, no matter what the outcome of the colonial confrontation.[83] So while keeping up his ties to the British Honduras oligarchy, George Frederic also sent gifts to Arthur, and in April 1820 the superintendent thanked the king warmly for a gift-laden canoe.[84] The king was likely seeking to measure the kind of response he might receive from the potential winner of the Belizean dispute. Primarily, though, the gifts were a further reminder to his partner of the kinds of wealth he might hope to find on the Shore. Sending a canoe that was surely made of mahogany was a symbol of the future victor's spoils: access to Moskitia's timber.[85]

In response, Arthur, upholding the practices of negotiation—or at least of flattery—still in effect, was at pains to honor George Frederic's gesture. In response to the requests that accompanied the canoe, Arthur sent the monarch a schooner bearing the requisite tribute.[86] However, George Frederic had his doubts over Arthur's ostensible loyalty and obedience. The superintendent seemed set on ending the Miskitu king's role of exclusive cultural intermediary, as he was beginning to maintain direct relations with other representatives of the Indigenous elite, including General Robinson. Following the assassination of George Frederic's father, George II, in 1800, Robinson sought forcefully to ensure that the existing regal line was maintained, by preventing the dead monarch's brother Stephen, who was suspected by some of the murder, from being crowned king.[87] Thus, especially since he was challenging George Frederic's authority, Robinson could have become a disruptive political element had he decided to throw his weight behind a faction opposed to the sovereign. That Arthur had offered to pay for the

London education of Robinson's son and nephew was a threat to the material and symbolic position of the Miskitu king.[88] If political disruption from the Belizean colonial and ideological clash were to spill over to the Shore in earnest, Robinson and his heirs might side with Arthur, infuriating the British Honduras loggers, but more particularly George Frederic.

Caught in the crossfire between the magistrates and Arthur, both of whom he was trying to woo, George Frederic feared for his position and personal privileges. However, the arrival of new foreign merchants and mercenaries in Central America radically changed the lives of Moskitia's inhabitants. As Orlando Roberts writes of the Valiente, the arrival of new strangers in their lands "made a considerable impression on [their] minds."[89] For George Frederic, contact with the new foreigners had other consequences, by allowing him to broaden his own political and commercial prospects during these times of imperial, Miskitu, and Atlantic transformations. As internal political strife on the Shore brought him increasingly into conflict with other Miskitu nobles, and amid mounting foreign criticism of Indigenous slavery, George Frederic now considered becoming something else: an actor of change on the Shore and beyond. As such, he gladly "associated with, and listened to, every visionary scheme submitted to him by the traders."[90]

Taking counsel, as he had often done during his teenage years in Jamaica, from foreign merchants passing through Cape Gracias a Dios, George Frederic decided to seize the opportunity offered by these internal and Atlantic dynamics. Like other Spanish-American and Haitian insurgents and foreign mercenaries such as Aury, he saw the possibility of building his own independent situation, for his own political and economic benefit, imagining himself freed of the rigid system of Miskitu-British cohabitation, which was now coveted by other external actors and within which he merely acted as a go-between. Instead, in a number of fragmented primary sources, he set out a project in which he would play a more active role.[91] George Frederic saw himself as the sole sovereign of a new state, overseeing the exploitation of natural resources, which would both benefit and strengthen his reign. He would gain new prerogatives, including the power to levy taxes (in cash or in kind), dispense justice, and form an army, under the supervision of well-educated commissioners and other "men of wisdom and integrity" appointed by him. All this would be for the betterment of the different peoples living in the region, whom he felt to be suffering under the violent rule of General

Robinson and Governor Clementi. Rather than being reduced to slavery—a practice threatened by George Arthur's ceaseless efforts—these communities would be educated, so that they could help to improve their country. Moskitia's inhabitants would answer to the king, ultimately preferring to be governed by George Frederic rather than the local Miskitu elites.

Just as Aury had asked George Frederic for assistance to carry out his military enterprise, George Frederic now needed help to pursue his own political project. He hired foreign workers to develop his kingdom's agriculture, forestry, and trade. In 1820, he took in Garifuna refugees evacuated from St. Vincent to the island of Roatan, off the coast of Truxillo, after their defeat in the Second Carib War of 1797, to establish settlements between Cape Camarón and the Patook River.[92] This area was on lands that had been under the control of Robinson. But the general had just died on the operating table in Belize in 1820, leaving behind an heir who was too young to govern and a regent who was seen as too cruel for the northern communities.[93]

George Frederic sought to further exploit the vacuum left by General Robinson's death by backing the establishment of new settlements that would improve the region. Instead of slaves, but in addition to the Garifuna settlers, he wanted to bring in foreigners who were interested in unlocking Moskitia's commercial potential, but who also had experience in state-building and finance—namely the foreign mercenaries fighting in the Spanish-American wars. He saw just such an opportunity in the person of Gregor MacGregor, who had arrived on the Shore in April 1820 after suffering several defeats against Spanish positions in Central America in the previous year. As an outsider in the struggle pitting the loggers against Superintendent Arthur to preserve or reshape relations with the Indigenous sovereign, MacGregor was a godsend for George Frederic, who used the disruption of the local political and economic system as an opportunity to better his own political situation.

On April 29, 1820, George Frederic granted MacGregor the territory of Poyais. Already known to certain chroniclers since the eighteenth century, these lands were chiefly inhabited by the Payas, a people under the late Robinson's authority. Given to "His Excellency General Sir Gregor MacGregor and his Heirs for ever," these lands of Poyais spanned just over thirteen thousand square miles, extending from the Caribbean Sea far into the interior of Moskitia. The Miskitu king also precisely indicated in the deed the geographical coordinates of the vast territory, based on a map of the

Bay of Honduras charted several decades earlier by the English geographer Thomas Jefferys.[94] The agreement signed by George Frederic with MacGregor granted the right to take the legal measures and apply the duties needed to ensure the prosperity of Poyais. However, the grant also stipulated that no form of sovereignty was ceded under the agreement. In other words, the deed granted the beneficiary some of the prerogatives of the true head of state, here George Frederic. Yet making such grant exceeded the traditional powers held by George Frederic, who was ultimately supposed to act less like a king and more like a liaison between the Miskitu and foreign settlers, and to approve decisions adopted at the local level. Instead, by making significant land grants to foreigners such as MacGregor, the king sought to style himself as a true sovereign in the eyes of his new interlocutor, who knew nothing about the practices underpinning colonial interactions on the Shore.

In other words, the Poyais grant delegated powers associated with a position that George Frederic hoped to occupy, given the political upheaval taking place at that time: that of a true head of state with full executive powers. Through MacGregor's ingenuity, the Miskitu king took a gamble on his potential political future amid possible changes to the position of British Honduras magistracy and broader European imperial dynamics in the region with the collapse of Spain's empire in the Americas. At best, openly affirming a sovereignty that had seemingly existed before in de facto form might enable George Frederic to potentially claim de jure sovereign rights when the imperial cards might be reshuffled on the Shore. At worst, the grant could always be repealed and transferred to a rival on the grounds that the region had been occupied in a way that contravened the agreement.

This chapter has sought to show that the allocation by Miskitu king George Frederic of a substantial land grant to MacGregor was the consequence of disruptions to the system of economic, social, and cultural negotiation specific to Moskitia. Established over the course of the eighteenth century, this regime of cooperation between Indigenous communities and representatives of British private enterprises operating in the region was rooted in a cohabitation that was both tolerated and essential to safeguarding and growing the commercial and political benefits of both sets of players. But in the early 1820s, George Arthur, the British superintendent posted to British Honduras, sought to upend this system of arrangement and cohabitation by attempting to instill evangelical and anti-slavery values within the Miskitu communities. These values chiefly aimed to challenge the monopoly held by the British and Indigenous elites on negotiations granting access to local mahogany resources.

Seen in this light, George Frederic's decision to grant MacGregor—a foreigner—preferred access to Moskitia's lands was less the act of an incurable alcoholic, as he is often depicted in history, but rather that of a political actor looking to position himself at a time when the region's political and economic practices were being overhauled. In fact, the decision was an active, deliberate, and well-informed strategy for the political reform and economic improvement of Moskitia. Aimed at promoting centralization of George Frederic's power as king, it was based on the commercial improvement and political independence of his subjects and territory, which, given his education, he believed could play an important role in Caribbean and Atlantic trade. British agents hired specifically to mobilize foreign capital and labor were tasked with giving concrete form to George Frederic's political and commercial project.

If we understand the interactions linking and opposing the Miskitu and British colonial enterprises in the region as forming specific political, social, and environmental dynamics, we come to see George Frederic's grant to MacGregor as part of a unique arrangement. By sidelining his usual interlocutors and offering land to MacGregor, George Frederic was anticipating the political changes heralded by the gradual collapse of Spain's empire in the region. To do this, he sought to position himself as a true head of state, rather than a mere cultural intermediary. In other words, rather than being a minor or nonexistent figure in the political and commercial transformation of the Atlantic, George Frederic was the mastermind behind a story of American Indigenous state-making. Rather than duping an alcoholic native chieflet into granting him a huge tract of land in Central America, MacGregor actually became the pawn of a Miskitu king seeking to capitalize on changes in the colonial situation within his own environment. In the next chapter, we will explore the reasons that prompted the Scot to accept the king's offer, and the conditions behind the design of a very particular colonial project in a part of Moskitia henceforth known as Poyais.

THREE

A Protean Plan

BIOGRAPHERS SELDOM DWELL on the period between April 1820, when MacGregor obtained the Poyais concession from George Frederic, King of the Miskitu Nation, and October 1822, when he raised a loan in the City of London for the State of Poyais. Although these events are more than two years apart, they are generally and implicitly understood as the start and finish of a necessary, quasi-natural and obvious gestation period for the Poyais scam.[1]

However, primary sources on Poyais cast doubt on the interpretation whereby, for well over two years, MacGregor decided secretly to foment and arrange an obscure financial deal in London. In the months after he acquired the Miskitu concession, MacGregor gave little thought to conceptualizing or setting up any kind of plan for developing his newly acquired land and turning it into a state. Instead, his activities were heavily focused on his military and political efforts as a mercenary hired under the republican flag. As recounted by Alexander Alexander, a Scottish traveler, former mercenary, and sugar plantation overseer, MacGregor was elected in December 1820—just a few months after obtaining the Poyais concession—to represent Margarita, an island off what is now Venezuela, at the forthcoming Congress of Cúcuta.[2] On behalf of the many Margarita-based mercenaries working for the Latin American cause, he was due to be present for the opening of the first constituent assembly to legitimize the birth of the Republic of Colombia. In the end, however, he did not attend.

Although MacGregor was eventually refused entry to Cúcuta, this chapter will show that his activities after obtaining the Poyais concession did not consist in fomenting some kind of dishonest conspiracy. Accordingly, it is worth asking what might have influenced him during this period to dream up a colonial plan aimed specifically at developing Poyais. It is also relevant to question the reasons that led MacGregor to consider financing his venture on the London capital market. This chapter focuses on MacGregor's career between his final years as a mercenary in the Latin American cause and his arrival in Britain with the Poyais concession in hand. The aim is to better understand how various financiers and businessmen influenced MacGregor's decision to consider Poyais as a commercial and political project, and to choose London as the ideal place to raise the capital needed to carry it out. Analyzing the uncertainties that MacGregor encountered in the two years before leaving for Britain shows that his enterprise evolved and took shape as a result of the interactions and obstacles he faced, mainly in the Caribbean, in the aftermath of successive military failures.

According to this analysis, Poyais was not a scam that sprang up in the mind of a natural-born fraudster. Rather, following George Frederic's bequest, Poyais was originally, and above all, a significant plot of land destined to become an independent military base, thus legitimizing the issuance of letters of marque to privateers hired to attack Spanish possessions. But when MacGregor finally arrived in London two years later, he had a different political and commercial project altogether. It was carefully planned and based mainly on improving the extraction of the Miskitu Shore's natural resources and supporting the consolidation of a Miskitu polity. Choosing the London capital market to finance his Poyais plan was therefore a last resort, on which he relied opportunistically because of the economic and structural difficulties involved in drumming up private investment on either side of the Atlantic.

The actual reasons why MacGregor arrived at George Frederic's court in April 1820 are unclear. They are generally presented as self-evident, part of a fraud devised by a swindler convinced that he could persuade an alcoholic Indigenous ruler—whom he had never met—to grant him land on which to build a nonexistent country. In this reading, the Miskitu king was the chosen victim of a man who had never set foot on the Shore during his career as a mercenary serving the cause of Latin American independence.[3]

An alternative explanation is that Gregor MacGregor stumbled upon

Cape Gracias a Dios by chance. Following his last two military defeats, at Porto Bello and Rio de la Hacha, he may have wanted to get back to his family, who were waiting safely for him in Jamaica. However, the return voyage may have been made difficult by the strong currents flowing from the Isthmus of Panama and present-day Guajira (where Rio de la Hacha is located) to Cape Gracias a Dios, forcing his ship to reroute to George Frederic's home base.[4]

Archives retracing the last months of MacGregor's career as a mercenary suggest another explanation, however. His arrival at the Miskitu ruler's court may have been part of a strategy often favored by foreign mercenaries hired under an American republican banner. Acquiring a major territorial concession on the Shore was actually the culmination of a carefully planned tactic by a handful of British mercenaries, who saw the Indigenous sovereign's desire for political autonomy as a godsent opportunity to consolidate a military and colonial presence that would boost Latin American independence.

The life of a foreign mercenary in the service of the American republican cause generally consisted of engagements under the orders of senior revolutionary officers. Accordingly, MacGregor found himself serving under Antonio Nariño, Manuel Piar, and Juan Bautista Arismendi, successively, during his voluntary service in America in the early 1810s.[5] Sent to fight on several fronts, he gradually adopted a particular military strategy—similar to the one pursued by eighteenth-century privateers and taken up by some of his foreign fellow-mercenaries—that consisted of establishing forward positions on or near disputed Spanish territories. Once captured, these positions were temporarily declared independent, with a view to incorporating them into future new American independent states if all went according to plan. Meanwhile, the territories became quasi-sovereign military bases from which privateers plundered neighboring Spanish possessions. These operations were of military benefit to the Creole revolutionary efforts and advantageous to foreign merchants, who often supported independence uprisings financially and commercially in the hope of expanding their direct transatlantic trade. Retracing MacGregor's military operations in the years before he obtained the Poyais concession illustrates the political, economic, and legal foundations of this strategy.

MacGregor first attempted in 1817 to establish a power base on Amelia Island, which lay off the coast of Florida and was occupied by a small Spanish garrison. Essentially, he took the island, on the advice of the then governor of Margarita, Juan Bautista Arismendi, in order to capture a new fallback base for republican operations in Central America. If MacGregor succeeded, his Latin American career would be significantly advanced, and the captured base could help to create a military center for newly recruited European and American mercenaries.[6] Sailing from Margarita to the north of the American continent with orders to capture the Floridian island, MacGregor disembarked at various ports between New York and Savannah to recruit men and raise funds from commercial agents. In Philadelphia, he received an official commission from agents representing Latin American republican interests, who confirmed that he was to capture Amelia Island on the revolutionary's behalf.[7]

The apparent ease with which MacGregor was able both to recruit volunteers and to raise the capital needed to prepare and carry out the military invasion of Amelia reveals a particular facet of the activities of foreign mercenaries fighting on behalf of American independence—and something at which MacGregor seemed to excel: communicating about or "selling" his military projects and ventures. In MacGregor's case, recruiting soldiers and raising American funds to mount a military operation was the culmination of months, even years, of experience. His success was largely based on the ability to present himself as a serious, capable, and experienced partner who was fully aware of political, military, and economic events in the places he planned to attack and conquer. He put his talents to work as soon as he set foot on the American continent in 1812. As a mercenary freshly recruited by Francisco de Miranda, Generalissimo of the First Republic of Venezuela, MacGregor set about presenting himself as an experienced Scottish soldier. Keen to make an impression, he even made it a point of honor to fight only in full Highland dress, accompanied by a bagpiper. Above all, as someone with front-line experience, MacGregor made a point of keeping his actual or potential interlocutors and partners informed about his actions and, more broadly, about the situation in Latin America. In this way, he actively portrayed himself as a privileged and competent provider of information, ideally placed to handle any undertaking, both military and, later on, commercial. For example, in letters written in the 1810s to the British prime minister, Spencer Perceval, and to Prince Edward Augustus, Duke of Kent and Strathearn and promoter of Britain's expansion on the American continent, Mac-

Gregor was at pains to describe in detail not only his military exploits but also the region's characteristics and commercial and political potential.[8]

On June 29, 1817, MacGregor and a force of around a hundred men took Fernandina, the main town on Amelia Island. The defending Spanish commander panicked and surrendered without a fight. In his place, MacGregor appointed himself brigadier general and declared Amelia to be liberated on behalf of the governments of South America.[9] As with Margarita, MacGregor saw his new territory as a base for privateers and mercenaries recruited on behalf of the republican forces. To this end, he proclaimed the island's independence from its former Spanish occupants, renaming it the Republic of the Floridas. He hoisted a new flag—a green St. George's cross on a white background—and awarded his men the Order of the Green Cross, a military decoration invented on the spot to commemorate the "liberation" of the island.[10]

To ensure a degree of financial and agricultural self-sufficiency for his territory, MacGregor planned initially to recruit American settlers, to whom he had already sold plots of land before launching his military operation. He ordered the opening of a post office and, more importantly, a court of justice; he also set up a printing press to publish a newspaper as well as legislation to govern the island's population, previously under Spanish rule. In reality, these new laws served to discipline the American mercenaries under MacGregor's command, who were reluctant to follow the orders of an officer who was in fact awaiting military reinforcements and cash from the American continent. In the meantime, MacGregor used his press to print banknotes in order to pay his soldiers' wages.[11]

MacGregor's biographers often interpret the issuance of paper money as an early sign of the man's mischievous nature.[12] However, these payment instruments were more like letters of credit than counterfeit currency. Indeed, similar securities had been issued in the British colony of Massachusetts in the seventeenth century. In the immediate absence of cash, which was taking a long time to arrive from the mainland, the colony's administration decided to print promissory notes as a way of calming anxious soldiers still awaiting their pay.[13]

More generally, authors who have dealt with MacGregor's invasion of Amelia consider his declarations about the newly liberated island or the raising of a specially designed flag as a first failed attempt to create a fake country. However, the work of David Head adds some perspective on the underlying reasons for MacGregor's actions in the region.[14] Head's study of the invasion of Amelia Island and the subsequent declaration of independence highlights a rationale—or even a distinctive business model—underlying a plan that is systematically portrayed as the beginnings of a monumental fraud. Above all, Amelia was not an isolated case, as the story of Galveston Island demonstrates.[15]

Located on the Texas Gulf Coast, the island, which had similar geostrategic advantages to Amelia, was captured in August 1816 by Jean-Louis Aury, a former French privateer who had become a commodore under Simón Bolívar. However, owing to a political disagreement with Bolívar, Aury joined the Mexican cause as a mercenary. José Manuel de Herrera, a member of the Mexican Congress, saw the uninhabited Galveston Island as an ideally placed port that would strengthen Mexico's commercial and military independence in what was still Spanish Texas. So he commissioned Aury to capture it and appointed him as governor.

Aury's takeover of Galveston was swift. The island was destined to become Mexican but, in the meanwhile, Aury established it as a temporarily independent zone under his authority. This enabled him to set up courts, which not only rendered justice but, above all, legitimized the capture of Spanish ships by privateers holding letters of marque recognized and issued by him on behalf of the Mexican government. These large, often ornate documents authorized shipowners and their crews to seek out, attack, and seize specific categories of vessels from a designated enemy on behalf of the issuing authority. In this case, the authority was Aury, Galveston's temporary ruler. Once a captured vessel was brought back to the island, the newly established court of justice would legitimize the seizure, ruling that the ship was the property of the issuing authority. As a result, privateers were able to lawfully resell their spoils to foreign merchants who, in turn, recognized the legitimacy of the temporary authority.[16]

Aury's actions in Galveston were not very different from those of MacGregor in establishing an independent government on Amelia Island at the behest of Bolívarian agents based in North America. Uninhabited following a military landing, Amelia became a military fallback zone for new mercenaries. Although ostensibly claiming independence, Amelia was a new kind of "republic" that could eventually be incorporated into the Latin American independence movement.[17] In the meantime, it was governed by a legal and independent entity. Like Galveston, Amelia was an independent territory with its own government. More importantly, it issued letters of marque granted by MacGregor to privateers who were free to set up bases in Amelia, provided they attacked only ships from, and positions in, Spanish Florida. Once they brought their spoils back to the island, a MacGregor-appointed judge granted them ownership of the captured goods so that they could then lawfully sell them on to British and North American merchants, while almost certainly giving priority to those who had advanced the funds to finance the invasion of Amelia in the first place.[18]

However, the success of this military operation, which ultimately was also political and financial, was not due to MacGregor alone; it was above all a collective effort. In addition to the many fighters under his command, MacGregor was accompanied and advised by a number of junior mercenaries who would also play a part in the Poyais story. The newly appointed overlord of Amelia was soon joined by Colonel George Woodbine, a former comrade in arms of Robert Christie Ambrister and Alexander Arbuthnot, both of whom were infamous for having been tried and executed by Andrew Jackson during the first Florida Seminole War in the 1810s. During these North American wars, Woodbine was a British agent responsible for recruiting Seminoles and Creeks to assist British resistance against American expansion into Florida.[19] The contacts he made during his talks and negotiations earned him both a personal grant of Seminole land and a Wanted poster on the orders of Jackson. The future president of the United States would apparently have preferred to see Woodbine dangling at the end of a rope instead of Ambrister and Arbuthnot.[20] Following his involvement in the Seminole Wars, Woodbine may have become a privateer in search of letters of marque. On learning of MacGregor's successful incursion, he set sail for Amelia Island from his base in the Bahamas.[21]

In Amelia, Woodbine convinced the island's new master to roll back other Spanish positions in Florida. The plan was to land MacGregor and a company of mercenaries in Tampa, in southwestern Florida, where more than 1,500 Indigenous soldiers recruited by Woodbine would be waiting for them. From this position, MacGregor would then attack Saint Augustine, a little farther to the south of Amelia.[22] However, the success of this plan depended on whether MacGregor could avoid leaving the island without a military presence. To that end, he had to await the arrival of military reinforcements and cash from the mainland. Since fresh supplies were always painfully slow in arriving, MacGregor was unable to stem a general decline in troop morale. Worse yet, learning of an imminent Spanish attack, he abandoned Amelia less than three months after conquering it. Woodbine agreed to evacuate MacGregor aboard his schooner bound for the Bahamian island of New Providence.[23]

MacGregor did not admit defeat. He still planned to attack Spanish strongholds in Florida, but finding himself short of volunteers, he traveled to London to stock up on men and materiel. While there, he met Thomas Newte, a British merchant and commercial agent for the revolutionary forces in New Grenada. Newte agreed immediately to give MacGregor the lines of credit needed to acquire weapons and military supplies and, above all, to cover more than £5,000 in advances owed to MacGregor's English and Irish volunteer soldiers and officers.[24] MacGregor left England in 1819 with his new recruits. He made an initial stop at Aux Cayes, the main port of Haiti, then the first free Black republic in America after gaining independence in 1804, and home to many South American revolutionaries taken in by the Haitian president, Alexandre Pétion.[25] MacGregor gave his men a single order: to stay put in Aux Cayes and wait for him. Meanwhile, he set off for Jamaica to ensure his family's safekeeping ahead of the fighting to come.[26]

MacGregor's arrival in Kingston coincided with a change of plan. A new attack in Florida no longer seemed a priority, since the territory had been annexed by Andrew Jackson's forces.[27] More importantly, MacGregor was not alone in his analysis. By advancing the funds needed to attract new recruits, Newte encouraged, or may even have recommended, MacGregor to redeploy his forces to New Grenada rather than back to Amelia. In line with Newte's strategic shift, MacGregor's trip to Jamaica served a crucial purpose, allowing him to glean "information among the merchants at Kingston, concerning the most eligible part of the Spanish Main on which to make a descent."[28]

One of the Kingston merchants interested in MacGregor's upcoming campaigns was one Wellwood Hyslop, a partner in the trading company founded with his brother Maxwell, who had arrived in Jamaica in 1792. In the early nineteenth century, it must have been quite difficult for "latecomers" such as the Hyslops to enter the local sugar market, which had been developed since the eighteenth century and was well established. Nonetheless, they tried, albeit unsuccessfully, to develop a shipping business. After some unsuccessful deals in New York, the brothers saw some room for maneuver in the Latin American revolutionary movements. In the 1810s, they seized the opportunity arising from the relinquishment of Spanish rule in some Latin American territories to establish trading links there. To that end, Maxwell remained in Kingston, while Wellwood in 1813 set up a trading branch in Cartagena, which had seceded from Spain in 1810. Unfortunately for their new economic aspirations, the Hyslops were forced to abandon their new activities when Spanish troops under Pablo Morillo laid siege to the city in 1815. Their brief period of contact with independence movements nevertheless brought them closer not only to mercenaries committed to the Latin American cause—including MacGregor, who often visited the city during his republican period—but also to Simón Bolívar himself.[29] Following the siege of Cartagena, Bolívar would go on to receive considerable financial support from Maxwell Hyslop during his exile in Jamaica.[30] Subsequently, the Hyslop brothers introduced themselves as Bolívar's commercial agents for New Granada. Wellwood Hyslop was even appointed minister plenipotentiary for Britain, commissioned by the 1817 Venezuelan Congress of Cariaco to negotiate a trade treaty.[31]

However, following the recapture of Cartagena, the gradual reconquest of New Granada by Morillo's forces compromised the trade links between the Hyslops and the lands liberated by Bolívar. When MacGregor arrived in Kingston in 1819 to drum up support from local merchants for his future military plans, Wellwood Hyslop jumped at the opportunity to open up new commercial gateways to the Spanish Main. He even went so far as to keep MacGregor "almost entirely secluded from society, in the hope of monopolizing the commercial advantages to be derived from the capture of Porto Bello," a Spanish port in the northern part of the Isthmus of Panama.[32]

Convinced by Hyslop, MacGregor set the capture of Porto Bello as the priority for his future military operations. And he assured the Jamaican merchant community that their "property, as far as can be identified as to be bona fide British, shall be respected." Leaving his wife and child in Jamaica, MacGregor returned to his men in Aux Cayes and, as agreed with Hyslop, launched an attack and invasion of Porto Bello on April 1, 1819. News that the Spanish port had been recaptured delighted the Jamaican merchants.[33] But the celebrations were short-lived. Surprised by a counterattack from the

Spanish forces, MacGregor fled Porto Bello—once again—with some of his officers aboard Woodbine's ship, leaving his men with no choice but to surrender.[34]

MacGregor could not disappoint his backers so, on his way to Aux Cayes, he arranged a new military campaign. This time, he planned to attack Rio de la Hacha, a port north of New Grenada used mainly for trading in pernambuco, a dyewood.[35] With reinforcements and equipment sent from Britain and financed by Newte, MacGregor embarked with a battalion of just under two hundred mercenaries for Rio de la Hacha in September 1819. His men quickly captured the stronghold, despite Spanish opposition. Using a now well-known military tactic, MacGregor went so far as to declare the territory independent, while styling himself as His Majesty the Inca of New Granada. However, short of reinforcements and funds, he was unable to cope with insubordination within his ranks. Once again, he abandoned his men, still accompanied by Woodbine. Many of them were eventually executed or captured during a Spanish counterattack.[36] MacGregor reached Aux Cayes with a handful of officers in October 1819. From there, he sheepishly sought refuge in the north, at the court of the Haitian king, Henri Christophe, a major supporter of the Latin American republican cause.[37]

All the authors dealing with Poyais seemed to agree on one point: MacGregor's movements are impossible to retrace from that point onward. However, his decision to appear at the court of the Miskitu king was motivated by the fact that another British mercenary, James David Roy Gordon, introduced him to George Frederic.

While little information remains about Gordon, we know that he was also involved in the capture of Amelia Island. However, rather than landing under MacGregor's orders, he was hired as a colonel by the mercenary Jean-Louis Aury. Aury, who recaptured the island from Spain on behalf of Mexico after MacGregor's hasty departure, was unable to repel an attack launched by the government of the United States to appropriate the territory, on the pretext of combating the illegal slave trade organized by Aury. (The real reason, apparently, was that President James Monroe was concerned about the risk posed by the arrival in America of West Indian slaves who might have been trained in sedition.)[38] After losing the island, Gordon followed Aury in an attempt to invade the Spanish stronghold of Truxillo on the Bay of Honduras in April 1820.[39]

Although the attack on Truxillo proved unsuccessful, it was nevertheless well prepared. Anticipating a military operation to rid the region of Spanish presence, Aury's men presented themselves to George Frederic. As well as acquiring information about the region, their mission was to rally the Miskitu to their cause or, failing that, to ensure that they did not get involved.[40] Gordon was among the officers sent by Aury to Moskitia to secure the cooperation of the Miskitu. He won the favor of King George Frederic, who was doubtless already seeking to diversify the number of interlocutors who might damp down the steadily mounting tensions in British Honduras. Apparently, Gordon and George Frederic became close, so much so that the king appointed in 1819 the mercenary, whom he named his "truly and well-beloved friend," as general of a future Miskitu army and an ambassador "authorized to act for us with foreign Nations in any way or manner he may judge of the greatest utility in our public Service."[41]

Although George Frederic was initially enthusiastic, Gordon was not immediately able to honor his new commitments, at least not prior to the battle of Truxillo, which would be led by Aury. Yet the outcome of that confrontation would ultimately be in favor of Spain. In fact, Aury's failed landing prompted the Miskitu king to officially renounce any form of involvement with the French mercenary, particularly since his Belizean partners had accused him of favoring foreign intervention in the region.[42] At the same time, some of Aury's men, probably disappointed by this latest setback, decided to disown him. Gordon thus left Aury's service and took refuge at George Frederic's court. This time, he was accompanied by some other Scottish mercenaries fighting for American revolutionaries, including Captains Murray and Hosmore, and a North American named Samuel Warren.[43] MacGregor was also there. A week after the failed attack on Truxillo, MacGregor, who had certainly taken part in Aury's assault, was introduced to the Miskitu royal court by Gordon, who already had his entrée.[44] In addition to Gordon's help, Woodbine very likely lent a hand, given his experience with negotiations involving representatives of Indigenous populations.

Wishing perhaps to distance themselves from the battles against Spanish forces, the two men were tempted by the offer that George Frederic had previously made to Gordon, namely to establish themselves as close military allies and diplomatic representatives of the Shore. The Miskitu king subsequently made them a new offer, inviting them to set up a commercial and political operation on the Shore on an enormous tract of land, Poyais, beginning at Black River and extending far into the interior.

———

George Frederic and MacGregor signed an agreement on April 29, 1820, that constituted a territorial concession.[45] It authorized MacGregor to draw up all the measures, notably laws and customs formalities, necessary for the prosperity of Poyais, provided that he did not usurp any form of sovereignty over the territory. The document also named MacGregor and his descendants as the owners of the important concession. This essentially established a form of vassalage vis-à-vis the Miskitu king.

For MacGregor, the Poyais agreement not only gave him an enormous swathe of land. It also gave him an ideal opportunity to establish a potentially lasting military position in a region undergoing a major redrawing of its sovereign map. As he himself would later write, after the failure at Amelia, he originally saw Poyais as a suitable site for a second military recruitment base or a fallback position for foreign mercenaries near Margarita.[46] In other words, the territory obtained from the Indigenous sovereign was seen to be suitable for a private military colony. Like the initial plan for Amelia Island, Poyais would be a temporarily independent base that issued letters of marque to privateers engaged against Spanish forces in the region, while awaiting formal incorporation into one of the new Latin American republics. In the event that the recognition of Spain's formal predominance on the Miskitu Shore were to change in favor of another power, such as a Latin American republic or Britain, an Indigenous concession would also serve as a precedent for recognizing any property rights in the region.[47]

For George Frederic, hiring foreigners was an expedient for improving Moskitia and emerging as the full Miskitu ruler he sought to become by asserting an effective sovereign right over his territory. At the same time, an imperial reshuffle was expected to take place in or near his envisioned kingdom. Gordon and his associates were to bring the necessary skill, labor, and capital needed to fulfil George Frederic's desire for political independence. As mercenaries, they had already made several trips to London to enlist new British volunteers as military labor in the American republican cause. Most importantly, they had experience in raising transatlantic capital. MacGregor had already taken out large loans in London from merchant bankers to acquire military provisions and pay advances that had been promised to volunteers. One thing was to be clear to everyone, however: The Miskitu king would cede no sovereignty whatsoever to these new partners.

It did not take long for George Frederic to impress upon these mercenaries the important commercial and military potential of their new colony, with its agricultural potential and abundance of natural resources, including precious woods. William Boggs, an old Irish merchant living in Cape Gracias a Dios who acted as a counselor to Miskitu kings, must have also considered allowing the British to participate in improving Moskitia, thereby strengthening the commercial power of his counselee and benefiting his own business. His signature can be found, alongside that of George Frederic's, on the concession granted to MacGregor.

George Frederic's first British settlement was to become a prosperous colony. The venture started well. Hiring some of the nearby Garifuna settlers, MacGregor and Gordon, along with Captains Murray and Hosmore and Samuel Warren, established their colony on the banks of Black River—near the point where the former English settlement, evacuated in 1786, had been located. They rapidly cleared a considerable area of land on which they planted significant quantities of corn. Proud of the settlement whose creation he had commissioned, George Frederic showcased it as a model to encourage other foreign merchants to invest in the improvement of Moskitia. When the Miskitu king gave a tour of the Black River colony to Orlando Roberts, an English West Indian merchant who visited the Shore regularly between 1816 and 1822, the latter was impressed with the quality of the first crops harvested and the resources to be obtained from the area.[48]

On the day he was granted his concession, MacGregor set about raising the capital needed to exploit and economically develop his new territory. Setting up a proper agricultural and commercial economy would meet the nutritional and monetary needs of the future troops and other privateers stationed there. From this perspective, MacGregor seems to have been following the practices of British owners of new West Indian lands intended to be a source of natural resources or cash crops. As Thomas Roughley described in a guide written for Jamaican planters, a capital injection was needed to develop any new land deemed suitable for farming. He gave the example of a landowner who saw the economic potential of one of his plots located in a hilly area of Jamaica. Although the initial harvests seemed promising, they could not have been achieved without first obtaining tools and other equipment to clear the land and get the plantation up and running. Since the planters' capital was usually tied up in estates or slaves, Roughley wrote that the funds needed for initial outlays on the heavy goods needed to get started had to be borrowed from merchants, who often delivered those supplies and tools on credit.[49]

However, the relationship described by Roughley chiefly concerned a situation specific to and concentrated in the Jamaican economy, which was already a well-established cash-crop environment comprising British planters and merchants operating in the British West Indies. At first glance, this configuration seems relatively dissimilar to that of the Shore. Indeed, it was difficult for MacGregor to mobilize the capital resources of a region devoid of any lasting British presence since its evacuation in 1787. His transition from a leader who had just suffered military setbacks in Rio de la Hacha, Porto Bello, and Truxillo to a landowner in charge of the economic and military development of a vast estate must have been a major challenge. While similar career changes occurred in nineteenth-century Latin America, MacGregor's venture was unique in that it seemed to rest entirely on his shoulders.[50] Apart from a few noncommissioned officers, notably Woodbine and Gordon, who stayed with him after his escape from Porto Bello and Truxillo, MacGregor was the sole owner of the Poyais concession granted by George Frederic.

However, obtaining a territorial concession was only the beginning of a colonial process requiring not only capital but also the assurance of being able to sell the fruits of economic development—for example, agricultural produce or privateer prizes—and to import the goods needed to build up a military colony. Immediately after he acquired title to the Poyais land, MacGregor wrote to Nathan Mayer Rothschild, the most important merchant banker in the City of London. In this first letter, written at Cape Gracias a Dios, he apparently asked Rothschild to take a stake in the development of the territory.[51] He offered to send, in a subsequent missive, a concession for German "Hebrews," who would be free to settle in Poyais. He described the territory as a potential haven of peace for Jews, who were often victims of pogroms in Europe (including perhaps the 1819 Hep-Hep riots, in which the Rothschild family was among those targeted).[52]

MacGregor's aim was not simply humanitarian: He wanted to charm the financier into joining a colonization project in Central America. Nevertheless, he was following a strategy often used by transatlantic merchants in the latter half of the eighteenth century. As Robert East illustrates, American merchants engaged in transatlantic trade prior to the 1776 Revolution still depended heavily on British export houses to sell their goods into the European continent.[53] While these houses allocated a significant proportion of the credit needed for trade to run smoothly, the British merchant bankers who ran them would assess the creditworthiness of the merchants, whether already established or seeking to become so, on the basis of their actual or potential connections and referrals. As a result, an American merchant establishing a business relationship with an English merchant would benefit from a credit commensurate with the prestige of the London house that agreed to do business with him. This was a major distinguishing factor in the competitive market for transatlantic trade. Although the dynamics highlighted by East concern mainly the period immediately before the Napoleonic Wars, transatlantic trade nonetheless seems to have continued to be organized and structured in the same way, if not more intensely because international business recentralized on London in the aftermath of the Congress of Vienna. By contacting Rothschild as a freshly arrived colonial entrepreneur, MacGregor seems to have been seeking the same kind of recognition and commercial credit. This was probably all the more necessary as he owed his former patrons a debt for his recent military defeats. At worst, MacGregor may have been hoping that if Rothschild was not interested in Poyais, he would at least provide a recommendation to another financier.

If writing to Rothschild on his own initiative was MacGregor's first choice in his search for funding, it also reveals another peculiar feature of transatlantic finance and trade in the early nineteenth century, namely the existence of information transmission channels specific to the financial practices of leading merchant bankers such as Rothschild. Some historical studies attempting to explain Nathan Rothschild's dominant and unrivaled position in British finance in the early nineteenth century generally point to his ability to deploy, organize, and safeguard an extensive network of agents.[54] Obtaining privileged information through such private channels (including his brothers' banking houses) would have enabled Rothschild to survey a variety of markets on the lookout for potential investment opportunities. Above all, it would have allowed him to better evaluate, anticipate, or react to current or future commercial positions.

In the case of Poyais, however, Nathan Rothschild was not the one who initially sought information about MacGregor or his plan. Rather than arriving on the financier's desk through a proprietary information channel or an active search for potential investments in Central America, the information about the Poyais plan came from MacGregor himself. MacGregor "simply" asked the most prestigious banker of the time to provide him with the capital needed to develop his concession. Rothschild's reputation and position as the City's leading merchant banker and a dominant force in financial and commercial markets ensured that information came right to the door of New Court, the headquarters of his banking house.[55] Rothschild could thus boast the privilege of choosing projects in search of British financing.

The stocks and companies of these "happy few" in turn received a special "brand," signaling to the markets that they were an investment of higher apparent quality, since they had been approved by Rothschild himself.[56] A private company boasting the Rothschild "seal of approval" could probably signal an apparent guarantee of quality to other merchants, or even compensate for a previous troubled financial relationship. In MacGregor's case, this would prove extremely useful for the Poyais plan. The recent military failures at Rio de la Hacha and Porto Bello forced him to sever some of the ties he had previously enjoyed with other British merchant bankers. After his various defeats, he was heavily in debt to Thomas Newte, the English merchant who had sponsored and financed his ill-fated military operations in Central America. MacGregor would even go so far as to sue Newte in the Court of Chancery in London in 1823, accusing him of having contracted debts in his name, without his express consent.[57]

While MacGregor was writing to Rothschild in an effort to raise capital, Gordon sailed to British Honduras shortly after founding their Black River colony, and later to Jamaica. In both places, Gordon sought tools, capital, and future outlets from which to sell his new settlement's products. Interestingly, it was understood within British Honduras that he had been hired by and was acting on behalf of George Frederic, who had authorized his new general to act abroad in the name of the Miskitu king. In a letter to the Colonial Office, Superintendent Arthur of British Honduras reported that Gordon had "entered very much into the affairs of the Miskitu King, under what Instructions he was acting [and] appointing him a General in his service."[58] This authority also enabled Gordon to ask the Spanish forces in the region—after assuring them that he was no longer under Aury's orders—to politically tolerate the existence of the settlement and to engage commercially with its improvement.[59]

MacGregor, meanwhile, was still waiting for a reply from Rothschild, whom he wanted to count among his financial and commercial backers. So, a little less than a year after the first contact, he wrote again. Sent from Santa Marta and dated March 16, 1821, the letter was primarily a reminder of the first missive sent the previous April. MacGregor also apologized for not yet having sent Rothschild the concession for the "Hebrews."[60] Above all, he explained his various travels in the West Indies, whence the delay in sending the promised documents. Shortly after obtaining the Poyais concession, MacGregor had traveled to the Windward Islands, before moving on to Santa Marta, a port town in present-day Colombia, under republican control. Because of these comings and goings, MacGregor worried that he might have missed Rothschild's reply or, worse still, that he had not been taken seriously. So he sent a duplicate of his initial contact, as well as a copy of the concession agreement.[61]

And for fear of missing a reply, he begged Rothschild to write to him at "Messrs Thos Higson & Co., merchants at Kingston, Jamaica." By his own account, MacGregor was on his way to the Congress of Cúcuta. The aim of this assembly, initially scheduled for January 1821, was to formalize the creation of the independent republic of Gran Colombia. Ordered by the Venezuelan Congress meeting in Angostura in October 1820 following the Battle of Boyacá, the new republic was to unite Venezuela and New Granada. However, it had to be legitimized by a congress of elected representatives from its constituent regions, thus providing it with a constitution governing and formalizing the political principles laid down at Angostura.[62]

With Gordon still absent from the settlement, Warren (the North American) was to oversee the colony in the absence of MacGregor, along with Murray and Hosmore. But on his way to the Windward Islands, MacGregor stopped off at Margarita Island, one of the first areas captured by Latin American republican forces and incorporated into the free territory of Venezuela in 1814. Margarita was primarily an arrival and rest stop for foreign legions (notably British), and a place of retreat for many soldiers and refugees.[63] As a result, although it was populated by many local farming families, the area revolved mainly around the various legions. Because of its position and early involvement in the Bolívarian cause, Margarita was one of the territories represented at the Congress of Cúcuta. MacGregor may have been on his way to Margarita to inform his superiors that he was now the proud owner of Poyais, where he could finally set up the military base he had been desperately trying to create since the failure at Amelia. But once on the island, MacGregor got caught up in American revolutionary politics. He was elected as one of the few Margarita deputies sent to the constitutional congress in Cúcuta. His election on December 18, 1820, was apparently attributable to his own soldiers and to North American residents of the island.[64]

Poyais was never far from MacGregor's thoughts as he traveled to Cúcuta. He worried that he had still not received a reply to his first letter to Rothschild, so, drawing on his talents as a skilled communicator, he wrote to the British Chancellor of the Exchequer, Nicholas Vansittart.[65] He began by citing the regular correspondence he had maintained with the Duke of Kent and Strathearn, giving details of his activities in Latin American revolutionary movements from his arrival in Latin America in 1812 until the duke's death in 1820. Enthusiastic at the idea of following Francisco de Miranda in his revolutionary aspirations, he had nevertheless offered his services as a privileged informant to the then English prime minister, Spencer Perceval.[66] When Perceval died in 1812, the Duke of Kent may have taken over the correspondence with MacGregor. Thus, in writing to Vansittart, MacGregor clearly considered him a worthy successor to the Duke of Kent as a special correspondent for sending his reports on the state of the Latin American uprisings.

In his letter to Vansittart, MacGregor said that Amelia had been captured primarily to provide a new channel for Britain's emigrant population. He also informed the chancellor of the recent capture of Lima by José de San Martín's revolutionary forces, as well as the appointment of a former North American mercenary based in Margarita named Todd as agent for the United States of America for the whole of the West Indies. Above all, MacGregor's letter indicated that he had obtained a concession in Moskitia, that he intended to set up a state there (while also recalling his previous actions in Amelia, officially constituted as an independent state to allow the allocation of letters of marque) and that he wanted to obtain support from the British government. But as with the Rothschild letters, MacGregor's request for support from Britain went unanswered.

MacGregor never did set foot in Cúcuta. In the short memoirs he wrote in 1839 for the Venezuelan government to seek a pension as a former officer, he said that he was systematically refused access to the town despite being an elected representative.[67] Although the exact reasons are unclear, MacGregor's previous military failures may have prompted Bolívar, who was known for his sudden temper tantrums, to dismiss his officer.[68] In fact, it appears also that Francisco de Paula Santander, then vice president of Gran Colombia, was so enraged by the fiascos of Porto Bello and Rio de la Hacha that he wanted to see MacGregor hanged.[69]

Frustrated by his ejection by Bolívar, MacGregor abandoned all his military commitments to the Latin American cause in order to concentrate on the opportunities of the Poyais concession. But apparently he was not alone in beginning to feel a degree of frustration after years of service to the cause of American independence. As he noted in his report to Vansittart, many of the British mercenaries he met on his way to Cúcuta were tired of the fact that their only payment for the services rendered to the newly emerging Latin American governments consisted of their food rations.[70] Only a handful of those hired under Bolívar's orders could hope to occupy a prominent political position and acquire a genuine sense of belonging to America following the first enduring victories in the Latin American independence projects. As Matthew Brown notes, volunteers could at times find it challenging to integrate into their new societies due to the complex relationships between Hispanic Americans and foreigners, not least because of their inadequate command of Spanish.[71] The case of MacGregor himself is revealing. While still a noncommissioned officer under de Miranda, he apparently wrote all of his Latin American correspondence in English.[72]

The Poyais plan gave many of these expatriates an opportunity to settle down and build a home and shelter of their own. Stripped of its initial military goals, the Poyais concession became an unrivaled opportunity for the handful of foreign mercenaries already based in Black River and, as we shall see, all the others who would join MacGregor later on. Poyais could be crafted into a suitable environment for some of these neglected mercenaries who wanted to quit the military and live in an independent colony that might, as MacGregor outlined in his letter to Vansittart, be recognized and ultimately endorsed by the British government.[73]

Driven back by Bolívarian forces to Rio Seco, a town between Santa

Marta and Cúcuta, MacGregor changed what Poyais was to become. He drew up a proclamation on April 13, 1821, outlining the new direction he intended to take (Fig. 8). He actually planned to implement his agreement with George Frederic by acting as the Miskitu king's agent. MacGregor introduced himself as the "cazique" of a territory allocated by the Indigenous ruler and said he intended to declare Poyais neutral, both in its relations with the new, independent Latin American states and with the Spanish empire. In his proclamation, MacGregor addressed the "Poyers" (Paya) and other "inhabitants of the territory of Poyais," promising to improve their situation "by every means in my power." To this end, he said that he wanted to sail to London to recruit settlers who could serve as "religious and moral instructors," as well as to establish livestock farms and assist "in the cultivation of valuable productions, for which our soils and climate are so well adapted." In his absence, MacGregor appointed George Woodbine as vice-cazique, charging him "to pay the most paternal attention to [the Poyers'] interests," and giving him "positive orders to observe the most strict neutrality with respect to the adjoining provinces."[74]

MacGregor's adoption of the cazique title is often described as yet another dishonest move to seize sovereignty over Poyais.[75] However, his proclamation actually reveals a bond of vassalage linking him to George Frederic. The very use of the term "cazique" shows that MacGregor recognized a hierarchical relationship with the Miskitu king. The title, derived from the Indigenous Taíno language of Santo Domingo, designates a local political leader who sets himself up as an intermediary between the population and some higher sovereign authority.[76] In this way, MacGregor's use of a Spanish American honorific title recalls the political symbolism developed and deployed by some Latin American leaders, a doctrine called "Incaísmo" by writers such as Jesús Díaz Caballero.[77] This symbolic political imagery, developed by Latin American Creole revolutionaries like Francisco de Miranda and Manuel Belgrano, was a line of reasoning that legitimized the replacement of Spanish political institutions. These "liberators" portrayed themselves as patriotic fathers descended directly from pre-Columbian Inca dynasties. The Indigenous peoples of these newly independent territories, seen as essentially inferior, owed their self-fulfillment solely to the political abilities of revolutionaries who occupied a hereditary position within a system founded on a nostalgic and romantic view of the pre-Columbus era.

PROCLAMATION,

To the Inhabitants of the Territory of Poyais.

POYERS!

On the 29th April 1820, the King of the Mosquito Nation, by a deed, executed at Cape Gracias a Dios, granted to me and my heirs for ever, the Territory of Poyais.

The moment that the situation of affairs in Colombia would permit me, I have hastened to assure you of my firm and unalterable determination to come and spend the remainder of my days, I trust, in peace and tranquillity, amongst you.

POYERS! It shall be my constant study to render you happy, and to exert myself in improving your situation, by every means in my power.

The Territory of Poyais shall be an asylum only for the industrious and honest,—none others shall be admitted amongst us; and THOSE, I trust, you will receive with open arms, as brothers and fellow-citizens.

With a view of avoiding a misunderstanding with our Spanish neighbours, which, under *all circumstances*, would be disadvantageous to both parties, I have this day published a MANIFESTO, addressed to the AUTHORITIES and INHABITANTS of the adjoining SPANISH AMERICAN PROVINCES of HONDURAS and NICARAGUA, giving them the most positive assurances, " that I have no other views *here*, than those which my duty as Chief of this Territory inspires."

Animated with the hope of establishing our neutrality upon a safe and solid basis, as well as to enable me to take the most active measures for procuring you religious and moral instructors, the implements of husbandry, and persons to guide and assist you in the cultivation of the valuable productions for which our soil and climate are so well adapted, I have determined upon visiting Europe; and in consequence, have this day appointed the Governor of San Andres, H. E. BRIGADIER GENERAL GEORGE WOODBINE, M. G. C. to act and take upon him the office of my VICE-CAZIQUE during my absence; charging him to pay the most paternal attention to your interests, and with positive orders to observe the most strict neutrality with respect to the adjoining provinces of HONDURAS and NICARAGUA, as the most certain and sure means of encouraging emigrants to come and settle in our country, and of avoiding the expense of maintaining a large military force, at a moment when all our resources are required for carrying into effect the establishments already projected, and in progress; and I confidently trust, that you will shew to the said Vice-Casique that respect and attachment which the citizens of all countries are bound to pay and feel towards those who lawfully command, particularly when they exercise their authority with justice and impartiality.

POYERS! I now bid you farewell for a while, in the full confidence that the measures I have adopted for your security, defence, government, and future prosperity, will be fully realized; and I trust, that through the kindness of Almighty Providence, I shall be again enabled to return amongst you, and that then it will be my pleasing duty to hail you as affectionate friends, and yours to receive me as your faithful Cazique and Father.

By H. H. Command,
G. DRUMMOND,
Secretary.

Given at Head Quarters, in the Camp of Rio Seco, this 13th day of April 1821.

GREGOR, CAZIQUE OF POYAIS.

A TRUE COPY OF THE ORIGINAL.
THOMAS STRANGEWAYS, *Aid-de-camp,*
and Captain 1st Native Poyer Regiment.

Figure 8. Proclamation to the Inhabitants of the Territory of Poyais. Source: Gregor MacGregor, *Proclamation to the Inhabitants of the Territory of Poyais* (Rio Seco, 1821). RB.l.38, National Library of Scotland, Edinburgh.

Yet aside from presenting Poyais as a potential haven for rejected British mercenaries in the service of the Miskitu, MacGregor was still unable to find the funds needed to finance any form of colonial enterprise. Rothschild had not yet answered his letters. When MacGregor was dismissed from Cúcuta, he may have gone to see Thomas Higson, the person responsible for collecting his correspondence in his absence.[78] Higson was a fairly wealthy Jamaican planter and cattle breeder. By 1820, he had four estates in the Jamaican county of Surrey and owned more than 150 slaves.[79] James Hakewill, author of a famous "picturesque" guide to Jamaica in 1825, painted a view of Port Royal seen from Windsor Farm, one of Higson's residences (Fig. 9). The foreground of the painting shows a couple—possibly Higson and his wife—strolling through the grounds of Windsor Farm.[80]

Unfortunately for MacGregor, no letters from Rothschild awaited him

Figure 9. Port Royal, seen from Windsor Farm, one of Thomas Higson's properties. Source: James Hakewill, *A Picturesque Tour of the Island of Jamaica* (London: Hurst and Robinson, 1825). Special Collections, Princeton University Library.

at Higson's home. But at least he could look forward to being reunited with his wife and children, who had been taken in by Higson during the military assaults on Porto Bello and Rio de la Hacha in 1819.[81] Higson also benefited from this reunion with MacGregor, who told him about the Poyais concession. Higson probably saw it as a great opportunity that would enable him to improve his situation as a planter and merchant, provided that it took on a different form and scope. In the first place, he considered Poyais as a business that could be based on mahogany logging. As a planter, Higson was also an amateur botanist, an interest that was more than just a hobby. He saw botany as a form of applied research that would improve crop quality and extend the range of agricultural produce in the Jamaican economy. The 1820s saw certain advances in horticultural science, essentially aimed at identifying and introducing new, more productive crops to offset the predicted post-emancipation decline in the local slave labor force and the resulting drop in productivity.[82] Higson thus sought to identify new varieties, such as different types of cotton or other vegetation that could help the Jamaican economy diversify away from its reliance on cotton. He developed a passion for the flora and topography of Central America, taking advantage of his many business trips to identify new species.[83] He is credited, for example, with contributing to the taxonomic description of Central American sorva (*Couma macrocarpa*, or cow tree), renowned for its edible latex.[84] In recognition of his commitment, Higson was appointed official botanist of Jamaica and curator of the Bath Botanical Garden in 1828.[85]

It is therefore safe to assume that, with his knowledge of Central America botany, Higson certainly saw mahogany as a promising diversification option or alternative to the much maligned and possibly languishing sugar trade. Following the model of the private British colonists who came to the Miskitu Shore during the eighteenth century, drawn by the commercial potential of large endemic mahogany resources, Higson probably encouraged MacGregor to see Poyais as a colonial project focused not only on developing a settlement for retired foreign mercenaries and strengthening Miskitu claims to independence. Poyais could build its prosperity on cutting and selling the wood. MacGregor seems to have found that argument convincing. He would later say that mahogany logging was one of the central pillars of his business. The first Poyais coat of arms, which closely resembled that of the MacGregor clan, is printed both on the certificates of one of the Poyais bonds issued in

London in 1823 and on a Poyais bill of exchange dated the same year and denominated in Poyais dollars. Both bear the emblem of a tree, which has often been described as a "tree of liberty" but may actually be a mahogany, thus depicting the natural resource underpinning MacGregor's plan.[86] Moreover, MacGregor later openly announced that the capital raised from the sale of his sovereign bonds would be used to improve the extraction of the territory's resources. In the text accompanying these ornate bond certificates issued in London in 1823, he declared that the inherent purpose was to promote "the general development of the natural advantages of the country."[87] And in 1822 MacGregor also hired a Scottish migrant called Gatmore to supervise mahogany logging in Poyais.[88]

Higson did not think of Poyais only as a mahogany depot. He also considered using the position of Poyais, with its equivocal sovereign status, to benefit Jamaica's beleaguered sugar trade. In his eyes, Poyais could be a possible location for a neutral port, ideally situated as a welcome midway stopover for trade between the United States and the British West Indies. By then, however, those flows had been curtailed because of diplomatic imperatives, as MacGregor had already indicated in a letter to Chancellor of the Exchequer Vansittart.[89] Following the Napoleonic and Anglo-American Wars (1812–1815), Britain signed an agreement with the United States in an attempt to reorganize its transatlantic trade. Dated July 3, 1815, the act authorized American and British vessels to grant each other reciprocal national treatment in the transatlantic trade between the two states. In the process, the United States tried to add similar treatment for its own commercial vessels in the British West Indies. However, the request was turned down by the British government, which considered its colonial trade to be exclusive. In response, the U.S. Congress, under pressure from American shippers, passed three pieces of legislation in retaliation for the commercial isolation of the British West Indian colonies. First, in 1817, Congress imposed a discriminatory tax of $2 per ton of merchandise on foreign ships entering American ports from foreign ports where American ships were barred. The Navigation Act of April 1818 closed U.S. ports to British vessels from any British colonial port that denied access to American ships. And in May 1820, Congress put a complete stop to trade with any British-owned vessel operating between U.S. ports and the West Indies.[90]

Jamaican planters feared the gradual introduction of that embargo, since their island depended heavily on maintaining direct trading relations with the United States. Should it be cut off from this market, the Jamaican sugar industry would no longer be able to obtain the American timber it needed to make barrels for sugar or rum, or to construct or repair buildings and other infrastructure.[91] The United States was also a potentially attractive outlet for Jamaica's ailing sugar economy. For many planters, the abolition of the slave trade in 1807 had increased the cost of maintaining their workforces. The ban on legally sourcing labor directly from the African continent forced them to rear and educate laborers directly in the Caribbean rather than buying them. Planters argued that caring for children who would become working slaves on their fourteenth birthday was an additional cost burden amounting to at least £120 per person.[92] Added to this was the cost of so-called improvement measures for slaves, which included the recommended introduction of better working conditions to supposedly enable an increase in sugar productivity.[93] Furthermore, the Jamaican sugar trade continued to suffer from the growth of new Caribbean sugar companies. Former colonies of Spain (Trinidad), France (St. Lucia, Tobago) and Holland (Demerara, Berbice, Essequibo) acquired by Britain in 1802 provided stiff competition, since their land had not been eroded to the same extent by generations of exhaustive plantation.[94] However, these new West Indian islands were not alone in competing with Jamaican sugar planters. The British mainland was also supplied with cheaper imports from the British East Indies, colonial Brazil, and Spanish-held Cuba.[95]

Pending the lifting of trade restrictions, Jamaican planters could only legally obtain shipments of American timber and other goods through foreign West Indian ports. Between 1818 and 1820, the trade routes used by merchants carrying American supplies, priced with a markup, to the British West Indies passed through the French, Dutch, and Spanish islands.[96] Smuggling was also organized between the United States and Jamaica.[97] The transaction costs on these operations involved different levels of risk depending on the types of growers. Top-tier Jamaican planters such as the Beckford, Hibbert, and Codrington families, who had several hundred slaves and much larger amounts of capital, certainly found it easier to set up smuggling operations.[98]

However, for a representative of a second-tier planter such as Higson, smuggling certainly posed a considerable risk. Since Poyais was technically a foreign territory with regard to the British West Indies, it was an ideal location for a neutral port. Just like the Danish or Dutch possessions that played a neutral role in West Indian trade during the War of the Spanish Succession, Poyais would allow Jamaican planters to trade freely with the United States, thus easing commercial pressures in the short term.[99] In the long term, wood from the Poyais forests would even be a substitute for American timber. In this way, the Poyais plan could meet the needs of people like Higson, hindered by commercial and diplomatic constraints specific to Jamaica.

After his stay with Higson, MacGregor envisaged several different operational methods for Poyais, including cutting and trading in mahogany and operating as a neutral port. To feed future residents, it was also to become an agricultural colony. This was at least how MacGregor presented the Poyais plan in a final letter to Rothschild on June 20, 1821, whom he still hoped to involve in his project. In it, he reiterated his request for the financier to invest in developing the concession granted by the Miskitu king. However, this presentation of his plan to establish a settlement in Moskitia differed substantially from the one described in MacGregor's earlier letters. Rather than simply setting up a colony to house settlers, he now presented a much more elaborate project. According to MacGregor, twenty or thirty Jewish families would be recruited to exploit the region's vast natural reserves, particularly mahogany. He estimated that developing and exporting resources such as lumber, dyewoods, and sarsaparilla would generate huge profits. He also said that he was determined not to involve Poyais in the conflict between Spain and its colonies. In other words, he emphasized the neutrality of a territory that lay beyond the borders of European empires. Poyais, he said, could become "a free port, which will immediately give it considerable trade, as there is no port to Leeward of Jamaica for reception of American produce."[100]

While the increased complexity of the Poyais plan addressed the business concerns of Jamaican planters such as Higson, it was also a response to Rothschild's lack of reaction to MacGregor's initial letters. However, making the Poyais plan more elaborate in the eyes of Rothschild would also make it riskier, hence seemingly more profitable. Although the new version of the plan would have needed more capital—to build a port, for example—it would certainly have offered higher potential profits.[101] MacGregor emphasized this point, estimating that the quantity of imports required for the colony to operate would cost "a considerable sum." However, he said, the likely proceeds from "the Custom House, sale of lands, and various other sources" could yield "at least one million dollars." Added to this would be the income from natural resource exports, envisaged at "one million five hundred thousand dollars, together with bullion and specie of a value at least equal to that amount."[102]

Another reason for MacGregor to write once again to Rothschild was that he needed capital from outside the British West Indies. While the new version of the Poyais plan addressed Higson's likely commercial concerns and hopes, he would not have been able to raise the substantial funding necessary to bring it to fruition. Most planters had their capital tied up in land and slaves, so the many investments they needed to develop or maintain their plantations were generally secured through credit from the island's merchants, leaving them heavily in debt. This general lack of liquidity caused by the difficulties of the Jamaican sugar trade meant that many West Indian creditors suddenly found themselves—often unwillingly—owning large plantations and inheriting the debts that went with them.[103] This was particularly true in the 1820s. As one anonymous planter put it in an 1826 pamphlet slamming the likely abolition of slavery: "The very large balances due by the Planters of the West Indies to the Merchants of this Country can never be paid!"[104]

But as MacGregor surely knew from having previously borrowed money in London to fund his military campaigns, many metropolitan investors seemed to be more financially inclined to take such a risk. And this might include Rothschild. The British economy had seen a significant easing of liquidity since the end of the Napoleonic Wars in 1815, the return to the gold standard in 1821, and the conversion from 5 percent to 4 percent interest on millions of pounds' worth of consols by the British government. In that climate, many investors were willing to put some of their money into relatively risky companies and political projects, including American ones, with potentially high returns.[105]

Unfortunately for Gregor MacGregor, he chose the wrong investor. Rothschild did not respond to this last letter. The financier's silence was probably attributable to fears arising from the political and military climate in Latin America, which was still broadly unstable. Another factor may also have been Britain's wavering policy on the recognition of the new Latin American states.[106] It is also conceivable that the first version of the Poyais plan—a settlement intended simply as a military base to support the independence movement—was not a worthy investment for a financier who had greater affinity with monarchical political aspirations, as evidenced by his family's close ties to Austria.[107] More importantly, Rothschild was known for his tendency to choose only those investments he considered safe.[108] For example, he was late in entering the Latin American sovereign debt market. In 1825 he took part in the issuance of a second loan on behalf of the Empire of Brazil, shortly after the British government told Spain that it intended to open formal negotiations with some Latin American states on diplomatic recognition.[109] In other words, Rothschild appears to have refused to take part in the Poyais adventure not only because he was wary of the unsettled political, diplomatic, commercial, and military situation in Central America but perhaps also because he found the Poyais plan too hazy, since it changed radically with every letter from MacGregor.

Although he certainly expected yet another refusal from Rothschild, MacGregor still saw London as the best financial center to raise the funding for his new project. For that reason, he was already on his way to Britain when he wrote his last letter to Rothschild on June 20, 1821, which he sent from Donaghadee, a small port in northeast Ireland. His plans were to travel to London, with an initial stopover in Scotland, so he asked the merchant banker to send all future correspondence to Callander, a small town in Perthshire, where one of MacGregor's sisters, Jane, apparently lived.[110]

The main reason for his Scottish sojourn was not so much to get back to his roots and family as to contact a merchant recommended by James David Roy Gordon, a former comrade in arms of Commodore Aury, who had introduced MacGregor to the Miskitu ruler. It appears that Gordon helped, if not urged, MacGregor to travel to Scotland to meet a person who could help him find the funds necessary for their Poyais plan.

This chapter has illustrated how MacGregor's reasons for considering the creation of a colony on the Miskitu Shore were initially consistent with his activities as a mercenary under the republican banner. Because the country was located in an area under approximate Spanish imperial control, its sovereignty could be instrumentalized to temporarily establish a territory that could issue letters of marque, a military and political strategy that MacGregor had already followed on previous occasions. Yet his unfortunate dismissal by the Colombian army, coupled with his inability to raise funds from prestigious British merchant bankers, forced him to turn instead to Jamaican-

British merchants and planters. Seeing how Poyais could benefit their own businesses, they urged MacGregor to reconsider his original allocation of territory. Accordingly, Poyais turned into a project based on exploiting extensive mahogany resources and establishing a neutral port to allow the West Indian sugar trade to bypass the tariff barriers imposed by the United States. However, MacGregor's inability to raise the large amounts of capital needed for the new version of the Poyais colonial project either in the West Indies or from leading English merchant bankers forced him to go to London in the hope of tapping the City's more liquid pool of local capital.

By retracing the birth and evolution of the colonial plan for Poyais, it is possible to qualify its founding myth. Rather than being entirely rooted in London finance and the speculative Latin American securities bubble of the 1820s, MacGregor's plan originated chiefly in the economic and political upheavals that followed the Napoleonic Wars and the abolition of the slave trade. The economic difficulties encountered by midrange Jamaican planters seems to have contributed greatly to the conceptualization of Poyais as a political and commercial project.[111] Adapting to the needs of planters such as Thomas Higson, who saw the Poyais concession as an opportunity to escape an effective and expected decline of Jamaican commercial and agricultural productivity, MacGregor's plan thus appears to be intrinsically defined by the economic and political dynamics specific to the British West Indies. The idea of establishing a colony on the Shore offered a timely solution to the need to find outlets for a Jamaican market increasingly cut off from its sources of timber supply, as well as new territories in which to diversify agriculture and exploit natural resources.

FOUR

A Foreign Loan

AFTER AN EVENTFUL ATLANTIC CROSSING, MacGregor and his family arrived in the Irish port of Donaghadee on June 4, 1821.[1] From there, they traveled to Scotland to join MacGregor's sister Jane, who lived in the village of Callander. While his family relaxed in the area, MacGregor worked to defend his name, which had been sullied by a pamphlet published in London and detailing the military fiascos of Porto Bello and Rio de la Hacha. Written by Michael Rafter, one of his former officers, the document paints an unflattering, even slanderous, picture of MacGregor, describing him as an alcoholic, bereft of morals, devoid of compassion, and driven primarily by concern for his own public prestige.[2]

Rafter was a British soldier who served under MacGregor during the Rio de la Hacha campaign. He had enlisted not out of sympathy for the Latin American cause but in hopes of tracking down his brother, about whom he had had no news. He later learned that his brother had been a colonel in a battalion led by MacGregor but had been reported lost following battles near Panama. In 1820, Rafter published a pamphlet that was essentially a tirade directed against his former commanding officer. Determined to preserve his image—so crucial to his military career and his recent endeavors as a colonial promoter—MacGregor in turn wrote several letters for publication in British newspapers, offering his own version of the heavy defeats sustained following the republican attacks.[3] He may have also exercised oversight in the publication of a book authored by a former medical officer who had served in his military campaign. This text sought to rehabilitate MacGregor's tarnished reputation through a more favorable portrayal of his ill-fated engagements in Central America—albeit with varying degrees of success.[4]

The period that MacGregor spent with his sister also gave him the opportunity to head to Edinburgh, where an acquaintance of James David Roy Gordon, with whom he had sowed the seeds of Poyais, awaited him. Gordon, who was still in the British West Indies at the time, had persuaded George Ogilvie to take part in the Poyais project. Not much is known about Ogilvie besides the fact that when Gordon later became military secretary of Poyais and colonel of the 4th Poyaisian Regiment, George Ogilvie was given command of a company within that regiment.[5] It is probably through Ogilvie that Gordon told MacGregor to get in touch with James Ogilvie, one of George's Scottish relatives, when he was in Scotland.

James Ogilvie was a Scottish shipper, a commission agent on behalf of individual creditors and a gunpowder works, and a director on the boards of several fire insurers.[6] He was also a former merchant banker. Toward the end of the eighteenth century, he took over the London trading house of Jean-Jacques Ogilvie and founded James Ogilvie & Cie, a Paris-based bank. Although he wound up the London firm in 1802, he kept his Paris business activities, specializing in providing credit to British merchants trading in France. With the outbreak of the Napoleonic Wars, however, he was forced to liquidate the company and transfer its operations to one Mr. Martin.[7]

Accompanied by Ogilvie, now named the first British agent for the Poyais project, MacGregor headed to London sometime between late 1821 and early 1822.[8] Although a skilled communicator, MacGregor needed the help of a seasoned merchant banker to raise the funds needed to put his Poyais plans into motion. Moreover, he had to rely on the talents of new agents, in view of the difficulties experienced with a previous intermediary, Thomas Newte, who had been responsible for raising funds to finance his previous military ventures and to whom he was now heavily indebted. Thus hiring Ogilvie certainly came in handy, since MacGregor probably had less of a foothold in the City's trade and financial networks. His past as a soldier and mercenary had not allowed him to master all the (in)formal codes and dynamics of British international finance. Reflecting this, MacGregor's correspondence contains no technical financial details about the London fund-raising campaign, barring occasional references to seeking the money needed to execute his project.

Ogilvie's help was especially valuable because the City in the early nineteenth century offered a wide range of potential fund-raising options for MacGregor. If we treat Poyais as a trade venture designed to harness Moskitia's abundant mahogany resources and build a neutral port to support British trade in the Caribbean, it is useful to identify some of the sources of financing available at that time. In this particular case, we can imagine at least two scenarios that would have enabled MacGregor and his agents to raise the funds needed to carry out the Poyais venture, for example establishing a partnership not requiring official incorporation, or founding a joint-stock company.

By establishing a private company or a partnership not requiring official recognition, such as a sole proprietorship, closed family firm, or general partnership, for example, a transatlantic trading firm could finance itself by means of bills of exchange. Such credit tools were often a preferred means of payment and financing for transatlantic trade activities.[9] In this case, however, there appears to have been one big obstacle. Since the Poyais project was not backed by any previous trading deals, as none had taken place yet, funds probably needed to be secured for a longer period than the few months for which bills of exchange were usually valid, in order to pay to purchase equipment and send the required labor.

Technically, founding a joint-stock company could have been another option for MacGregor. It could have helped him deal with two key problems: He could have secured long-term funds while spreading the financial risk more effectively among his investors, since stockholders in a joint-stock company are considered to bear liability in proportion to their holding. However, under the 1720 Bubble Act, which was still in effect at that time, a royal or parliamentary charter was needed to form such a business. Setting up a joint-stock company was therefore a way to implicitly crowd out potential rivals, both symbolically and in fact.[10]

However, setting up a joint-stock company was also, and above all, a popular solution at the time for many ventures looking to expand into the Americas. Although they were still governed by the Bubble Act, the ranks of joint-stock companies swelled steadily in the early decades of the nineteenth century.[11] Establishing these chartered ventures was seemingly more straightforward, since the approval process likely acted as a means for lawmakers to extract rents and obtain directorships.[12] Yet the creation of a joint-stock company was still a relatively risky proposition for its backers. This was especially true if the legalities required to form such firms were not observed, as illustrated by the case of the Equitable Loan Bank Company. Founded in

April 1824 and operating as a pawnbroker based on the French mont-de-piété model, the Equitable Loan Bank Company had capital of £2 million, divided into forty thousand shares worth £50 each. As a means to attract investors, shares could be acquired by paying £1, with the remainder to be settled in successive installments determined by the company's directors. The Equitable Loan Bank Company presented itself as an institution that "will afford Capitalists a secure and beneficent employment of their wealth. [. . .] the object is the accommodation of all classes of persons suffering under occasional distress."[13] Sure of their success, the company's directors began selling negotiable stocks early on, while the application for a royal charter was still underway. But although the House of Commons approved the company's incorporation, the House of Lords refused to follow suit, deeming that the firm had acted illegally by selling negotiable securities without a charter.[14]

Although officially due to the fact that the company had issued and distributed negotiable shares in a manner that was not in accordance with the British legal framework governing the creation of joint-stock companies, the failure of the Equitable Loan Bank Company sheds an interesting light on some of the political dynamics and risks involved in setting up a joint-stock company. In fact, it seems that the fiasco was not entirely attributable to fraudulent practices or mismanagement by the directors. The Lords' refusal to grant a charter was also the result of internal dynamics within Parliament, which actually posed a much bigger threat to efforts to set up such firms. Parliamentarians themselves were the main barrier, as Ron Harris shows.[15] After reviewing the arguments put forward by a group of rival pawnbrokers fearful that the incorporation of a competitor capable of offering far cheaper loans would crowd them out of their own sector, several members of the House of Lords (who were apparently also involved in financial activities) concluded that granting a charter would be at odds with the principle of free trade. Deeming that the Equitable Loan Bank Company might be able, by issuing cheap loans given legitimacy by the institution's philanthropic and moralizing stance, to monopolize a significant share of financial flows from the City's financiers, this group of Lords allegedly blocked the company's incorporation on legal grounds to preserve the interests of their advocacy groups.[16]

Although the Equitable Loan Bank Company is just one example, it is quite possible that, when the threat of criminal charges in the event of bankruptcy was factored in as well, forming a joint-stock company might have seemed like a risky proposition.[17] At least, this may have been the case for Poyais. Since MacGregor's project was based essentially on the need to circumvent the obstacles blocking the sugar trade between Jamaica and the United States, incorporation would surely have upset the faction within Parliament that was aiming to bring down the slave-based Caribbean economy. Including as it did William Wilberforce, a fierce opponent of West Indian slavery practices, this group would perhaps have blocked any application for a charter and, consequently, delayed the possibility of raising the necessary funds—at least without too much political risk—for an indefinite period.

But in 1822, a trade project such as MacGregor's had another funding option: a sovereign debt issue. Technically, this was an interest-bearing financial instrument that served as an IOU for a government. A loan of this kind would offer a way to obtain a long-term financing solution, spread the risk among investors in proportion to their outlay, and avoid the difficulty of seeking a royal charter. Critically, in London at that time, changes and improvements to payment and trading technologies had made it easier to issue and trade financial securities. The City had, for example, already introduced a number of major financial and informational innovations over the eighteenth century to support international trade through bills of exchange.[18] A few years before the Poyais loan, these financial dynamics had been amplified in particular by the recent development of the sovereign debt market, with two particular loan issues. In 1817, France, which had to pay substantial amounts of war compensation, took out an initial loan. Banker Alexander Baring, who was in charge of the deal, working with his Dutch partner, Hope & Co., decided to place the bonds on several European exchanges. Although the loan was denominated in francs, with interest payable in Paris, the deal put London, and especially Baring, at the heart of the European and international financial landscape. The following year, another innovative move affirmed the supremacy of the English foreign loans market. Managed by Nathan Rothschild, the Prussian loan of 1818 was issued in pounds sterling, rather than thalers, with interest paid in London instead of Berlin.[19]

MacGregor and Ogilvie's fund-raising efforts in London also took place at a pivotal moment for the creation and trading of bonds issued by new sovereign entities. The two men arrived in the English capital shortly after the issuance on the London Stock Exchange of foreign bonds by other politically disputed Latin American territories. Indeed, in 1822, Colombia, Peru, and Chile all issued bonds on the exchange worth a total £4.2 million and carrying a 6 percent coupon. With interest already kindled by the low returns on English domestic debt, the appeal of the Latin American debt market was further fueled by public support for Latin American independence movements, which held the promise of increased and more direct transatlantic trade with the continent, a region viewed by many as a source of limitless natural resources following the 1811 publication of Alexander von Humboldt's *Political Essay on the Kingdom of New Spain*.[20]

The relatively higher coupons paid on Latin American loans compared with other foreign bonds issued in the same years—Denmark and Russia both issued bonds at 5 percent, for example—and traded on the London Stock Exchange generally reflected the financial risks associated with these investments. These stemmed from the ambiguous political status of the new borrowers, which were viewed as commercially promising but about which information often arrived with some delay, as it had to cross the Atlantic by sailing ship.[21] Yet strategies were deployed in the City to offset the risky features of these securities and make them more attractive to potential investors. For example, while the interest on these securities was paid at face value, the bonds were often sold at a discount and settled in installments, drastically increasing the effective rate of return as long as the securities had not been fully paid for. These loans technically enabled the borrowers, that is, Latin American revolutionaries, to obtain fresh capital (less discounts and commissions paid to intermediaries) to fund their wars of independence and, even more importantly, to pay back earlier private loans granted to them by British merchant bankers to carry out their military operations.

And yet, in the early 1820s, acknowledging the existence of this kind of polity was not necessarily a forgone conclusion, particularly in the case of the new states spawned by Latin American revolutions. To avoid upsetting diplomatic relations with Spain, many European governments refused to officially and formally recognize these new governments.[22] Although it acknowledged the existence of the newly independent territories, the British government, for example, did not rush to recognize them formally. During a debate in the House of Lords in June 1822 on an amendment to Britain's Navigation Laws, Prime Minister Robert Banks Jenkinson, Earl of Liverpool, gave an address on the need to build trade relations between British colonies and the United States, in which he spoke of opening "a commercial intercourse [. . .] with the independent parts of South America."[23] In this way, Liverpool openly recognized the existence of the new Latin American states without specifically naming any of them. It was not until Great Britain and Colombia signed a trade treaty in 1826 that a South American government was officially acknowledged for the first time by London.[24] Yet it would be wrong to say that Britain's leaders did not take a stance on Latin America's independence movements. Thoroughly lax enforcement of a ban preventing British mercenaries from enlisting in Latin American revolutionary armies points to an implied but fairly clear position by His Majesty's Government on the outcome of the political unrest on the other side of the Atlantic.[25] Still, the four-year window between when the first Latin American loans were issued in 1822 and formal recognition of the first new states in 1826 was thus essentially characterized by the absence of a formal decision by the British government on acknowledging specific independent governments in Latin America. As long as Britain refused to grant formal recognition, these loans were essentially confined to future political (and trade) projects.

During the same period, however, the London Stock Exchange was much less preoccupied by this question. Specific requirements governed access to the foreign loans market but were less concerned with the features of securities actually exchanged on the trading floor. In fact, in 1822, there were no rules covering the introduction and acceptance of new securities by the exchange. The official rulebook of the London Stock Exchange, adopted in 1812, stipulated that securities should be exchanged between co-opted members or their recognized clerks. Members needed to be British nationals and could not have been involved in bankruptcies in the past, unless cleared of these by the Committee for General Purposes. Although off-exchange trading of securities was banned, no rules regulated the features required for new shares or bonds to be introduced or accepted.[26] A business relationship between two members of the London Stock Exchange appeared to be all that was needed to introduce a new security on the foreign loans market.

The daily trading prices of securities seen as worthy of interest were then gathered and published by an individual authorized to do so by the Committee for General Purposes, in this instance James Wetenhall. Since 1786, Wetenhall had been the editor of the *Course of the Exchange*, which was first created in 1718 by James Castaign and had been the official list of the London

Stock Exchange since 1803.[27] As such, he was permitted to include the prices of new securities in his publication, provided that they were deemed to be "bona fide" in the market, giving him some latitude in his selection.[28] The inclusion of the trading prices of these bonds in Wetenhall's official list amounted to a kind of indirect political recognition for the Latin American securities, by placing them, in a sense, on an equal footing with loans issued by European powers. The loans issued by Colombia and Peru were listed alongside those of Russia and Austria, not only for the audience made up of investors following Wetenhall's publication but also for a broader readership, since the daily trading prices of these bonds also appeared regularly in widely circulated newspapers.[29]

However, to access the capital markets, a would-be sovereign debt issuer had to be established as an independent political entity. In other words, only a sovereign state could, one may think, issue sovereign debt. But as the rules of the London Stock Exchange were less concerned with the defining characteristics of the traded securities than with those of its own members, the central element qualifying a borrower as a sovereign—namely the existence of a sovereign political entity—could be created by an agreement between investors, borrowers, and agents. In this setting, the contracting of a foreign loan was the result of an arrangement between the borrower (or the borrower's representative) and its financial intermediaries. The Colombia loan of 1822 is instructive in this regard. Authorization to contract a loan was signed by Antonio Francisco Zea, the minister plenipotentiary of the Republic of Colombia in London, who was acting without the express agreement of his government. In point of fact, Herring, Graham, and Powles, the bank in charge of setting up the loan, provided much of the impetus for the decision.[30]

The creation of such "fictions" by financial or trade partners—in this case formally establishing the existence of a country to enable a foreign loan to be contracted—was not a reprehensible or unusual criminal act, at least in the eyes of the English legal system. As Daniel Klerman shows, the creation of scenarios that seemingly distorted reality was a specific legal strategy sometimes employed in English courts. By building a consensus around a nonexistent situation, several parties could come to a joint agreement about the possibilities emerging from a newly created universe. For instance, some English civil cases include in their opening statements the transcription of an agreement between defendant and plaintiff doing business in France stating openly that Paris is in the kingdom of England. The creation of such a "legal fiction" in private commercial or financial relations allowed the parties, who were aware that they had distorted reality, to temporarily modify the configuration of their own world of possibilities, allowing them, in this instance, to settle their dispute within the English legal system.[31] Operating within a similar framework, Ogilvie essentially planned for a sovereign debt issue by creating a Poyais legal fiction, as an alternative to other forms of financing. To do this, he would simply copy the transactions already conducted by the likes of Colombia, Peru, and Chile.

As MacGregor's official London agent, Ogilvie thus became open to proposals from potential contractors, that is, merchant bankers or investors given the task of setting the loan issuance terms.[32] Interestingly, Ogilvie was approached by a number of financial players who were active in the capital market and keen to earn fees from setting up a major deal. Commissions for such services could indeed be extremely lucrative, rising as high as 8 percent for the Mexican loan of 1824.[33] During the contractual stage of setting up a loan, it was common for financial intermediaries to respond, either unprompted or by invitation, to calls for bids by potential borrowers. Decisions were made through a sealed auction or via a system of open negotiations with bids and counterbids.[34] Different merchant bankers could thus make proposals to a potential borrower to set up a loan for a specific amount, at a given interest rate (on the face value) for a pre-agreed term. But financial agents could also suggest measures to sweeten a loan for potential investors. For example, in the case of foreign loans, bonds were often sold initially at a deep discount to their face value. Sometimes, bonds could also be purchased through a pre-agreed payment plan, which allowed investors to put up the necessary funds in instalments. For instance, the bonds from the 1824 Buenos Aires loan were initially sold at £85, but the securities were nominally worth £100. Although the purchase price of these securities could be paid in six installments spread over six months, interest calculated on the face value of each bond was guaranteed.[35]

Daniel Mocatta was the first to make a proposal to Ogilvie. Mocatta was a merchant banker and the son of Abraham Mocatta, who together with Asher Goldsmid cofounded Mocatta and Goldsmid, gold bullion brokers for the Bank of England.[36] As such, he made a proposal to Ogilvie for a £200,000 loan divided into two thousand bonds worth £100 each. Mocatta additionally suggested that the bonds should be sold initially at a price of £67, that is, a 33 percent difference between the face value and selling price of the future securities.[37] Interestingly, it appears that Mocatta's proposal was not prompted merely by a need or keenness to enter the Latin American sovereign debt market. It is true that he had hitherto been absent from this particular market, although it may be that he was looking to retain a clientele of investors that had pulled out of trading in European bonds, which had become less attractive since the end of the war.[38] In fact, his interest in setting up a partnership with MacGregor's financial representative in Britain may have been underpinned by other, broader commercial motivations. These seem to have rested primarily on the economic potential that Central America seemed to offer at the time. In the first place indeed, many British travel accounts published between the second half of the eighteenth century and the early years of the nineteenth century not only painted the Shore as a reserve of boundless natural resources, including mahogany. They also praised its strategic geocommercial location as a trading post ideally placed between the Spanish Main and the Caribbean colonies.[39] As such, the land and advantages of the territory earmarked for the Poyais project were likely well known to people such as Mocatta, certainly alert to trade opportunities in a region that was free of any formal imperial involvement.

Second, Mocatta potentially had a far more direct interest in a project that might contribute to the growth of the West Indian sugar trade, especially in Jamaica, as revealed by research to identify his direct business partners. These, interestingly, included the Belisarios. Like the Mocattas, the Belisarios were descended from Portuguese Sephardic Jews, but part of the family had been based in Jamaica since the seventeenth century. As merchants, they were involved in the slave trade as well as the sugar trade, for which they were attempting to introduce improvement strategies to address the troubles affecting the sector in the early nineteenth century.[40] Although based in the Caribbean, the Jamaican branch of the Belisario family maintained close ties with London, even sending some of its members to the City to apprentice. In the early decades of the nineteenth century, this included successively Jacob and Isaac Mendes Belisario. Isaac generally tends to be better known for his artistic output, as he was the first noted painter of works showing cultural figures from the Jamaican slave community (Fig. 10).[41] Yet he spent several years in London as clerk and broker for his uncle Jacob Be-

Figure 10. *Jonkonnu*, by Isaac Mendes Belisario, 1837. Source: Isaac Mendes Belisario, *Sketches of Character, in Illustration of the Habits, Occupation, and Costume of the Negro Population in the Island of Jamaica* (Kingston: published by the artist, 1837). Folio A 2011 24, Paul Mellon Collection, Rare Books and Manuscripts, Yale Center for British Art.

lisario, an art dealer and stockbroker at the head of a company founded with Aaron Mocatta, Daniel's brother.[42] Although that company was dissolved in 1819 and ceased to trade, business dealings between the Mocatta and Belisario families continued. As proof of this, Daniel Mocatta and Jacob Belisario handled, for example, trading in the Poyaisian bonds issued in 1827 for MacGregor but rejected the Scotsman's entreaties to pay his bail after he was imprisoned for challenging Francis Mellite Spong, a wealthy soldier who had openly and publicly insulted him, to a duel. This had nothing to do with Poyais, incidentally: While her husband was away, Spong's wife had run off to join MacGregor, with whom she had been acquainted prior to her marriage a few years earlier.[43]

Mocatta's involvement in Poyais thus seems to have been spurred not only by the profits that could potentially be opened up by the proposed loan, such as contractor fees, for example. He was certainly also motivated by the interest that he and Jacob Belisario, as occasional partners, shared in growing the Jamaican sugar industry they were involved in, at least through family ties. Like many others, Mocatta was on the lookout for opportunities that would allow him to act as agent or financial liaison in projects backing commercial interests that might benefit his own trading activities.[44]

Although he initially accepted Mocatta's offer of financial services, Ogilvie suddenly broke off their partnership agreement. A counterbid had in fact been put forward by John Lowe, a broker operating in the City of London, whose background and interests seemed to be aligned with those of Ogilvie.

Shortly after Austria's brutal repression of the Neapolitan uprising of 1820, Lowe was in Genoa on behalf of Nathan Rothschild. Carl Rothschild, Nathan's brother and the head of the future Naples branch of the family banking house, was responsible for raising a loan for the Sardinian government at the demand of Austria, which insisted on being reimbursed for the costs incurred during its military intervention against the insurgents led by Guglielmo Pepe.[45] At the time, Lowe was therefore tasked not only with recovering the unpaid claims of some of Nathan Rothschild's customers but also with passing on information about the Sardinian military situation to London.[46] In one report, he expressed his disdain for the Austrian forces stationed in Genoa, writing: "I have a great dislike to Bayonets & muskets in the hands of fellows with greasy moustachios," in a derogatory description of the Austrian army dragoons patrolling the streets.[47]

On his return from Sardinia, Lowe began to view Latin America's revolutionary movements as a commercial windfall. In a letter dated July 4, 1822, to Robert Stewart, Lord Castlereagh, Marquess of Londonderry and the Foreign Secretary of the day, he indeed urged His Majesty's Government to cultivate good diplomatic relations with Colombia and other territories freed from the failing Spanish yoke. Lowe argued that these new relations would pave the way for direct and openly recognized trade lines with a Latin American continent that had hitherto been accessible largely indirectly via the British West Indies. While acknowledging that this would be detrimental to Britain's colonial interests in the Caribbean, he suggested that direct access to these lands, guaranteed by political agreements, would nevertheless open up new markets to British industry. As Lowe saw it, this would mitigate the risks associated with organizing trade crossings, thereby also drastically lowering the maritime insurance premiums typically paid by shippers conveying goods to republican movements.[48]

Doubtless intrigued by the Poyais project, John Lowe approached Ogilvie, claiming to be able to propose a loan on more attractive terms. He also suggested a loan with a face value of £200,000 divided into two thousand bonds, each with a face value of £100. However, his proposed issue price was £75. Although the term of the loan was not specified (as with Mocatta's proposal), Lowe's proposal set a coupon of 6 percent. Accordingly, under his proposal, more funds would be available to carry out the Poyais project than under the bid by Mocatta, whose proposed issue price of £67 would result in a difference of £16,000 after payment in full of the installments. In addition, involving a former Rothschild agent in the project might also lead to a connection to the famed financier.[49]

Dismissing Mocatta's bid, Ogilvie signed and accepted Lowe's offer on October 22, 1822.[50] The next day, Lowe engaged Perring, Shaw, Barber & Co., a banking house led by John Perring, baronet, MP, and a former mayor of London, and Nathan Shaw, a member of the committee of marine insurer Lloyd's of London, to take care of interest payments.[51] A loan was then contracted for the "Service of the State of Poyais." Worth a nominal £200,000, the debt was secured by all future revenue raised on the territory of Poyais. Promising a coupon of 6 percent, the loan was divided into two thousand bearer bonds, sold at an initial price of £80, a 20 percent discount to their nominal value. Interested investors could acquire these securities through a specific financing plan. While £15 needed to be paid on the delivery of each bond, the remaining amount was to be settled in two installments of £35 and £30, due on January 17 and February 14, 1823, respectively. If all the installments were not paid in full, the bond was canceled.

In his apparent haste to issue the loan, Lowe did not have enough time to print bond certificates, instead distributing scrips.[52] These temporary certificates (Fig. 11) had a face value of £100, £200, or £500, and entitled the bearer to an equivalent number of future permanent certificates, conditional on payment in full of the requisite installments. For their services, Ogilvie paid Lowe a commission of approximately 8 percent on the nominal value of bonds sold, plus another 5 percent or so to Perring, Shaw, Barber & Co.[53]

After the loan was issued, the securities were traded on the London Stock Exchange. They were probably introduced to the trading floor by Lowe, who may have been a member of the exchange. Wetenhall quickly added the Poyais bonds to his *Course of the Exchange*, perhaps because he anticipated a surge in trading in the securities after their introduction. This was quickly confirmed. Initially sold at £80, they traded at over £82 on October 26, 1822, three days after the loan was put in place (see Chart 1 in Chapter 5 to view the evolution of Poyais bond prices). On October 29, they broke £86 after being mentioned in a short newspaper article.[54] As rumors spread in November 1822 about the possibility of a new war in Europe, the price of Poyais bonds, like those of other Latin American securities, stayed relatively high (£79). According to an article published in the *Dublin Evening Post*, reporting on news from London, this was because "this Security is little offered on the Market, and [would appear] to be in few but very respectable hands."[55]

Since there are no archives that exactly retrace the activities of Perring, Shaw, Barber & Co., as the records were probably destroyed after the 1825 crisis that caused the firm to go bust, it is hard to know who these "very respectable hands," which held a majority of MacGregor's securities, actually were.[56] Poyais scrips were bearer securities that were not assigned to any specific person and thus belonged to whoever held them. However, insights into how the Poyais capital was allocated may offer some clues. And indeed, some of the funds borrowed were allocated to building and improving the Poyais territory. In fact, accompanying the issuance of the Poyais loan in 1822, several announcements were published in British newspapers, which reported on the imminent departure of the *Honduras Packet* for Poyais. The ship was

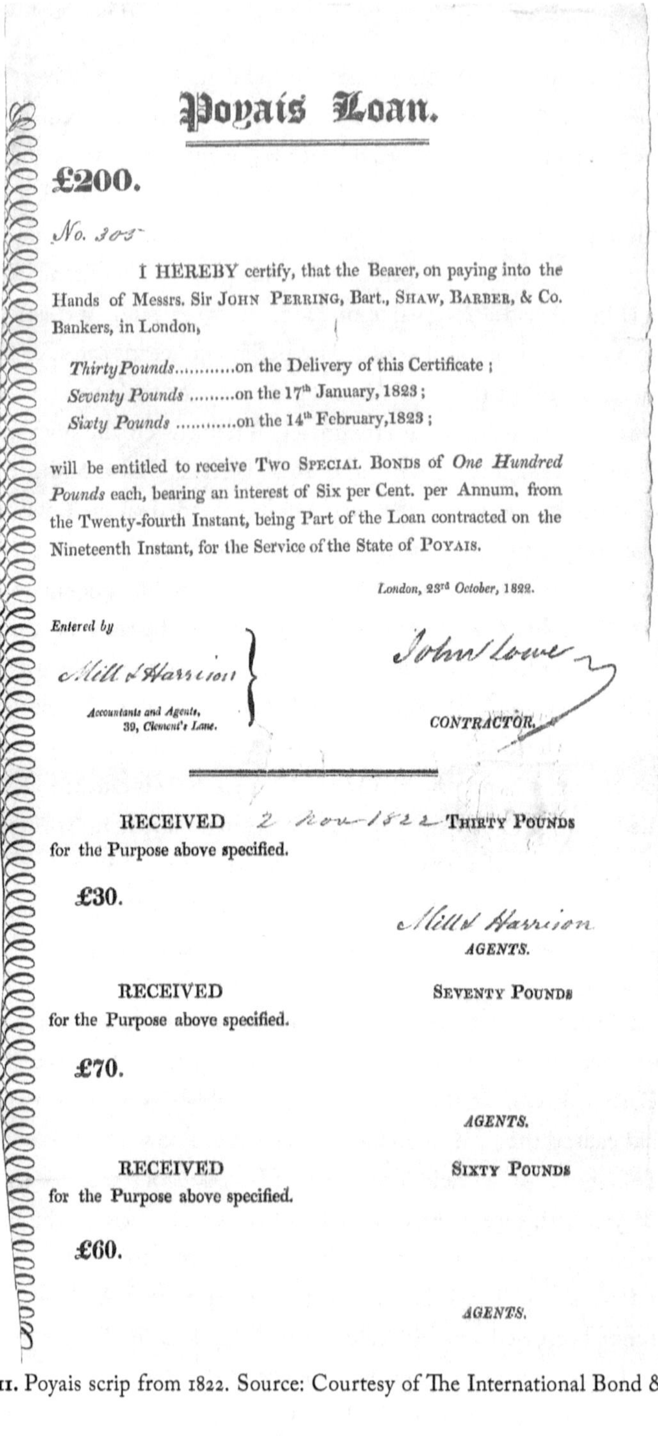

Poyais Loan.

£200.

No. 305

I HEREBY certify, that the Bearer, on paying into the Hands of Messrs. Sir JOHN PERRING, Bart., SHAW, BARBER, & Co. Bankers, in London,

Thirty Pounds............on the Delivery of this Certificate;
Seventy Pounds ....on the 17th January, 1823;
Sixty Pounds ....on the 14th February, 1823;

will be entitled to receive TWO SPECIAL BONDS of *One Hundred Pounds* each, bearing an interest of Six per Cent. per Annum, from the Twenty-fourth Instant, being Part of the Loan contracted on the Nineteenth Instant, for the Service of the State of POYAIS.

London, 23rd October, 1822.

Entered by
Mills & Harrison
Accountants and Agents,
39, Clement's Lane.

John Lowe
CONTRACTOR.

RECEIVED 2 Nov 1822 THIRTY POUNDS
for the Purpose above specified.

£30.

Mills Harrison
AGENTS.

RECEIVED   SEVENTY POUNDS
for the Purpose above specified.

£70.

AGENTS.

RECEIVED   SIXTY POUNDS
for the Purpose above specified.

£60.

AGENTS.

Figure 11. Poyais scrip from 1822. Source: Courtesy of The International Bond & Share Society.

scheduled to transport just under one hundred passengers along with sufficient provisions to build the initial encampments and sawmills needed to start developing MacGregor's territory. Under the command of Captain Thomas Hedgcock, the *Honduras Packet* set sail from the port of Gravesend on the banks of the Thames on November 22, 1822, followed two months later by another ship, the *Kennersley Castle*.[57]

The combined value of the shipments sent to Poyais on board the two vessels can be estimated at £16,000: £6,000 for the *Honduras Packet* and £10,000 for the *Kennersley Castle*.[58] As well as being the total value of the cargo on board the two ships, £16,000 was also two-thirds of the expected amount from the sale of the scrips issued by Lowe based on payment of the first instalment (£15 per bond) less commissions for Ogilvie, Lowe, and Perring, Shaw, and Barber. In addition to acting as MacGregor's London agent, Ogilvie was also a shipper. In this capacity, he instructed Alexander Arnott, thought to be the father of the future first Baronet Sir John Alexander Arnott, to charter the *Honduras Packet* and the *Kennersley Castle* for Poyais "on account and risk of General McGregor, as Cazique of Poyais."[59] The funds needed to dispatch the ships may have come simply from the sale of the Poyais scrips. But it could also be that Ogilvie saw MacGregor's project as an opportunity to extend his business activities beyond the Atlantic and therefore acquired two-thirds of the scrips in return for fronting the value of the provisions sent to Poyais, with the promise of paying the subsequent instalments at the agreed dates. This would in turn explain why some sources indicate that MacGregor had sold his rights to "some merchants in London" for £16,000.[60]

While Ogilvie had two-thirds of the Poyais scrips, the remainder was initially held by Lowe.[61] Having guaranteed that the borrower would receive the amount arising from the sale of the securities in his possession, Lowe worked to offload his scrips on the London Stock Exchange, hoping to boost the price above the initial level, as any difference would represent a personal profit for the contractor. By establishing a market in Poyais bonds on the London Stock Exchange and selling them to buyers who were likely aware that the securities were in short supply, since Ogilvie held a majority share, Lowe was able to get the price to quickly and easily exceed the initial level of £80 just days after the securities made their debut on the exchange.

To promote the existence of Poyais as a borrower and as a sovereign, Lowe published an open letter to George Canning[62]—who had just become Foreign Secretary after Castlereagh's suicide. Written in the final weeks of 1822, the letter reiterates the positions already presented to Canning's predecessor, stressing the importance of recognizing the independent republican nations of South America as way to open up the new markets needed by British industry, which had been weakened by the Napoleonic Wars. Although the political structures of the new territories were not yet fully consolidated, Lowe said that Britain should nevertheless seize the opportunity created by the presence of so many mercenaries fighting alongside republican armies, which he identified as a possible means to gain a strong commercial foothold in these regions. He suggested that Canning might consider the potential of Poyais in this respect. As a fertile land granted by an Indigenous ruler to a British subject, Poyais could be considered in a prime commercial location between wealthy Colombia and the colonies of the British West Indies. Through development of the territory, there was also the possibility of constructing a transoceanic canal via neighboring Lake Nicaragua in the hopefully not-too-distant future.[63]

Yet the promotion of Poyais was not based solely on a message aimed at English politicians. It was also aimed at investors and, more importantly, future residents. Indeed, another publication praising the idea of a colony on the Shore was—at least partly—written by one Thomas Strangeways.[64] Released by Scottish publisher William Blackwood, the book is presented as a guide to prospective settlers. Although often thought to have been a pen name used by MacGregor himself, Strangeways was actually the name of a former officer of the British 65th Regiment.[65] Before taking retirement in 1820, Strangeways had been posted to the British West Indies. On his return to London, he was commissioned by Poyaisian agents to write the promotional guide. Borrowing heavily from previous books describing Moskitia, Strangeways depicted a country with vast reserves of precious timber, including mahogany, which he describes in glowing terms: "the whole appearance of this tree is the most beautiful that can be imagined." To back up his words, his book contained a detailed map of Moskitia, with a representation of what the Poyais coast must have looked like (Fig. 12). The book also offered tips on forging friendly relations with the Indigenous peoples of the region to gain

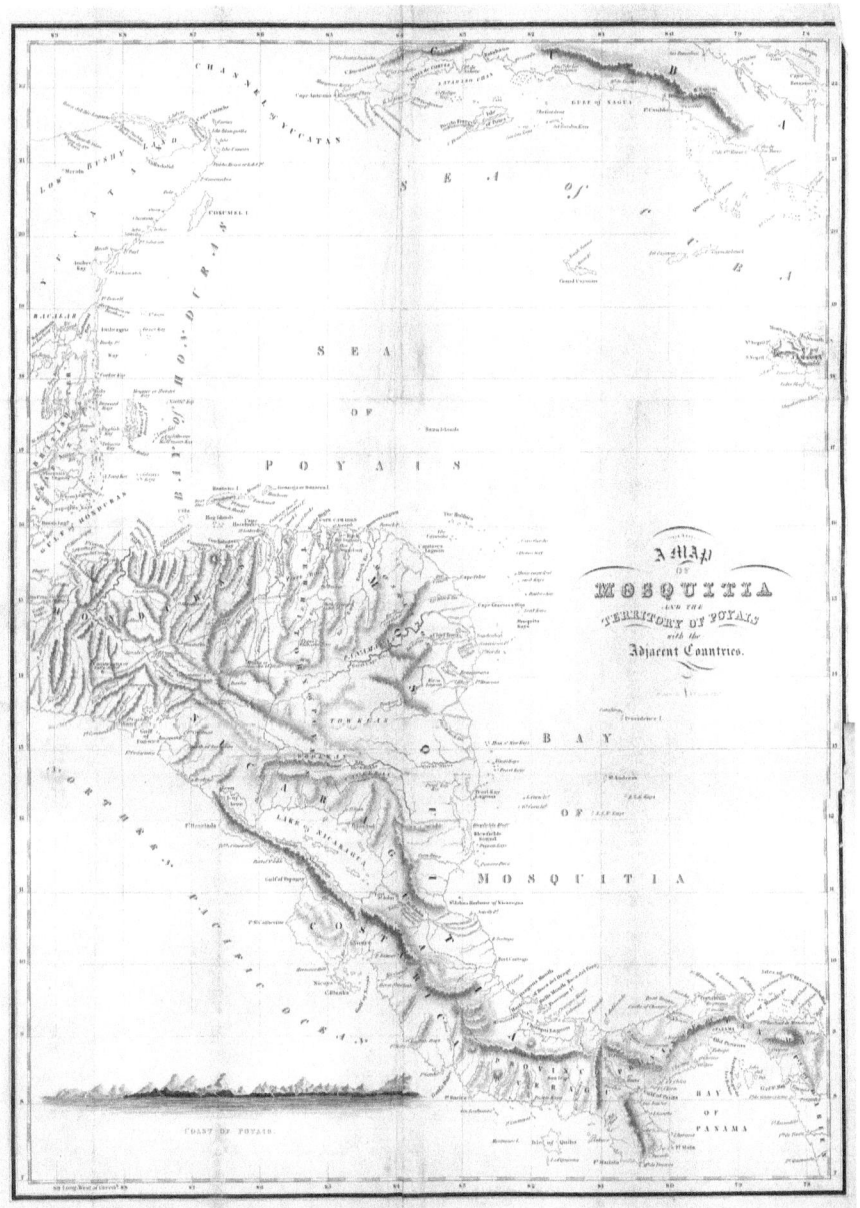

Figure 12. A map of Moskitia and the territory of Poyais. Source: Thomas Strangeways, *Sketch of the Mosquito Shore, Including the Territory of Poyais* (Edinburgh: W. Blackwood, 1822). Courtesy of the John Carter Brown Library.

access to local natural resources. Like others, Strangeways stressed that trade in Poyais would benefit in time from the construction of a transoceanic canal via Lake Nicaragua.⁶⁶

Strangeways' book was not only a puff piece for a country but also a visual advertisement for its promoter. It opens with a full-page portrait of MacGregor (Fig. 13), decorated with Poyaisian medals and wearing the military regalia of an officer. He poses against the backdrop of a battlefield above which

Figure 13. Gregor MacGregor, Cacique of Poyais. Source: Thomas Strangeways, *Sketch of the Mosquito Shore, Including the Territory of Poyais* (Edinburgh: W. Blackwood, 1822). Courtesy of the John Carter Brown Library.

flies the Poyais flag, a green St. George's Cross against a white background, similar to that created in Amelia a few years earlier. The painting also boasts the new Poyais coat of arms, featuring the emblem of a tree (mahogany, perhaps?) topped with the MacGregor clan motto in Scottish Gaelic, *S Rioghail Mo Dhream*, "My Blood Is Royal." Commissioned between 1820 and 1822, the original painting was by Simon Jacques Rochard, a London-based French artist who was well known for his portraits of the British nobility. The painting was subsequently engraved by Scottish artist William Home Lizars.[67]

Continuing to promote MacGregor, Strangeways lavishes praise in the preface on "His Highness the Cacique." MacGregor is described as the noble son of a line of Scottish chieftains descended from the royal house of Alpin and the folk hero Rob Roy MacGregor, further underlining his indisputable rights to the Poyaisian territory. These allusions would certainly have resonated with the renewed interest and recognition that Clan MacGregor was enjoying in the 1820s, after being out of favor for many years. Clan members were even sworn to protect the Scottish crown jewels and to act as royal bodyguard during the Edinburgh visit of George IV in 1822.[68] The same year, a play about the legend of Rob Roy MacGregor was put on at the Theatre Royal in London's Covent Garden.[69]

So MacGregor was all but pushed, albeit willingly, into playing the role of the flamboyant cacique. Portraying him as the personification of Poyais certainly helped to promote the project but, arguably, it also served a financial function by enabling the deal's intermediaries to insulate themselves against some of the risks associated with London's financial markets in the early decades of the nineteenth century. Setting up a loan of this nature came with numerous risks because of how long it took for information to cross the Atlantic. Despite employing multiple strategies to mitigate risk by making their ventures more attractive to potential investors, including a high interest rate, a discount on the initial selling price, and payment in installments, merchant bankers could still be hurt if a project fell through. And the price of failure could be high. An analysis of the rules and regulations of the London Stock Exchange reveals that the fabric of London's financial world was at least partially based on discretionary rules. While any member who was bankrupt or who defaulted on payments would be expelled automatically from the market, so would "every member who may be guilty of dishonorable or disgraceful conduct."[70] He could then be readmitted by the Committee for General Purposes only if he submitted his accounts for review or had his name listed on the exchange's Black Board.[71] For players operating in a competitive financial space characterized by significant default probabilities, financial failure might mean not only financial loss but also reputational damage that could jeopardize involvement in parallel or future business. Yet promoting MacGregor personally as the embodiment of Poyais's enterprise potentially protected his financial intermediaries from the risk of failure. If some factor threatened the viability of the Poyais project—a takeover of the region by Spanish forces, say—responsibility for paying interest or repaying invested capital would fall to MacGregor as the loan's political representative. In other words, in their capacity as financial intermediaries, Ogilvie and Lowe could be sure that MacGregor, Poyais's public figurehead, would bear any reputational costs in the event of failure.[72]

Strangeways' guide was handed out to anyone interested in enlisting in MacGregor's venture. As its name indicates ("Chiefly Intended for the Use of Settlers"), it was primarily offered to settler families expressing interest in emigrating to Poyais. It was probably also circulated to promote the Poyais securities still being traded in London. Yet Strangeways' guide was fiercely criticized by an article in the October 1822 issue of the *Quarterly Review*, a periodical published by John Murray. The article's anonymous author called the Poyais project a fantasy and said it was unachievable for two reasons. First, Spain still had legal sovereignty over the Shore, at least until it formally relinquished its American territories altogether. Hence, the loan's underlying political project had no legitimacy. Second, in the writer's view, it was unthinkable that the territory's sovereign ruler, Miskitu king George Frederic, would have willingly made such a significant grant of land to a man like MacGregor. The author dismissed the coronation of George Frederic as a "foolish" ceremony and compared the ruler's power to that of West African "King Toms and King Jacks," concluding that "the 'lands' and the 'loan' [. . .] are non-entities, and the whole affair merely, what is vulgarly called, a hoax."[73]

However, the critique laid out in the article had less do with the non-existence of an actual Poyaisian state than with the author's conviction that establishing a settlement on the Shore would surely come into competition with the settlers of British Honduras and their long-standing resource extraction activities. Yet discrediting a financial project led by a mercenary cast out by South America's revolutionary movements was also a roundabout way to throw more favorable light on loans issued by other nascent republics backed by Murray, who had released several memoirs by English mercenaries fighting for Latin American causes.[74] The successful publisher of works by Thomas Malthus, Lord Byron, and Sir Walter Scott, Murray was indeed also involved in promoting the Colombian financial and mining interests of John Diston Powles, one of the contractors to the Colombian loan of 1822. As part of this, Murray commissioned articles lauding the rich prospects opened up by the Latin American capital market, even at one point hiring a young Benjamin Disraeli, future British prime minister, as a ghostwriter. Disraeli described Colombia in extremely fanciful terms despite never actually setting foot in South America.[75] Calling Poyais out as a fraud, Strangeways' critic offered to help his readers spot "fraudulent" securities out of the many on offer, while presenting the loan issued by the Republic of Colombia as thoroughly legitimate, not least because its investors included Powles, Disraeli, and (probably) Murray.[76]

The critique of Strangeways' book, particularly regarding the implausibility of successfully raising capital in London for a project of Central American state-making, sparked wider discussion in English newspapers. In the same month as the *Quarterly Review* article's publication, the *London Courier* released a short piece titled "More Loans!!!" Its anonymous author mockingly welcomed the arrival of imaginary agents in London, "each charged with authority to negotiate a Loan [. . .] for the improvement and advantage of the Tribes of Indians which inhabit the Coasts of the Mississippi."[77] While it certainly implicitly mocked the Miskitu king's attempts to secure funding through MacGregor, the piece extended this ridicule to all Indigenous peoples of the Americas. The following day, the *London Courier* published another article, further ridiculing the fictitious arrival of agents supposedly raising funds for American Indigenous peoples.[78]

A letter to the editor responding to the *Quarterly Review* article was published at the start of 1823.[79] Written by one Verax, it praised the Poyais venture as an unrivaled opportunity to support Jamaican trade, which was then hamstrung by difficult diplomatic relations between Britain and the United States. The author also described MacGregor's project as having been formally accepted and recognized by Miskitu king George Frederic. The Verax riposte was a neat attempt to keep the Poyaisian legal fiction alive in the face of numerous attacks by presenting it as a politically legitimate endeavor. It reported that while George Frederic, Moskitia's de facto sovereign, had granted the concession, MacGregor had also secured authorization from the Spanish crown, which at the time still had de jure sovereignty over the territory. However, Verax's assurances that contact had been made with the Spanish government constituted a statement of intent, rather than actual fact. It was to be several months before a diplomatic envoy was sent to Madrid to request Spain's recognition of Poyais.[80]

Ultimately, Verax's letter sought to scotch the growing rumors that the recently issued loan was at risk of defaulting on payment of the promised interest to investors. And it is interesting to note that some of the rumors about Poyais being unable to deliver on the promises made to investors may well have been true. In fact, MacGregor's enterprise was running very low on cash. Indeed, a few days prior to payment of the second installment scheduled for January 17, 1823, Lowe, the contractor for the Poyais loan, fled to Paris, leaving with just over one-third of the £30,000 paid out under the first installment.[81] He justified this by saying that the amount—more than £12,000—was an advance on the total fees owing to him. In other words, Lowe pocketed the money that he was due to receive once all the Poyaisian bonds had been distributed and all the installments duly paid. By going to the London Stock Exchange to trade the securities that he held, which amounted to approximately one-third of all the scrips, with the remaining two-thirds probably in Ogilvie's hands, Lowe managed to obtain advance payment of his full fees while also earning a juicy profit by offloading the securities for more than their initial selling price.

Perhaps Lowe's decision was hasty. It may even have been fraudulent. Yet this sudden exit also reflected Lowe's decision to distance himself from Poyais and eventually refocus in particular on supporting the Colombian independence movement, a project that was dear to his heart. Alongside his Poyais venture, Lowe also paid out more than £13,000 to send provisions and reinforcements on four ships to mercenaries battling royalist forces in Maracaibo (Venezuela).[82] The basically anti-Colombian portrait of Poyais painted by the *Quarterly Review* may have prompted Lowe to pull out of a project that he ultimately thought might damage his other interests, although he made sure to earn a healthy profit on his way out.

MacGregor was less than impressed by his contractor's actions and abrupt flight to Paris. A portion of the money had been earmarked for the first interest payment, to reassure scrip holders that their investments were in sound health.[83] Although roundly condemned by MacGregor in a letter sent to an acquaintance, Lowe never really paid for his actions. After his former contractor returned to London, MacGregor brought a suit against him before the Court of King's Bench (the highest court of common law) in April 1824—the trial referenced at the opening of this book—publicly accusing him of misappropriating some of the project's funds. To prove the significance of the amounts in question, a list of Poyais bondholders was supplied. But the suit slammed to a halt when the presiding judge said that he wanted to see concrete evidence proving the formal existence of the State of Poyais. Although a representative for the Poyais project argued that the fact that settlers were sent to a territory that belonged legally to MacGregor was sufficient to prove that Poyais existed, the judge dismissed the plaintiff's claims as inadequate, and the charges against Lowe were dropped outright, leaving the borrower to take responsibility for the poor performance of the securities and bear the creditors' complaints.[84] His name cleared, Lowe continued doing business and would once again be hired as an agent by Nathan Rothschild, who had seemingly paid little heed to the former's Poyais dealings.[85]

Publication of the criticism of Strangeways' guide in the *Quarterly Review* and Lowe's abrupt departure caused the financial performance of Poyais securities to deteriorate. After trading at over £89 toward the end of October 1822, Poyais bonds lost almost 25 percent as they hit £67 in January 1823. To reassure the investors recruited by Lowe, who were shortly due to pay the second installment on their bonds, an announcement was made in several British newspapers (*Public Ledger and Daily Advertiser*, *The Scotsman*). Signed by John Lowe, even though he was supposedly in Paris, the announcement stated that payment of the second installment of £35, scheduled for January 17, was postponed to February 10 and reduced to £10. Meanwhile, the payment date for the final installment, scheduled for February 14, was pushed back to an unspecified time.[86] As the first deadline approached, a further public notice was issued announcing that payment of the second installment would be postponed to March 17 and reduced to £5.[87]

To shore up the public credibility of a project whose viability was being openly challenged, the departure of a second ship for Poyais, the *Kennersley Castle*, was announced.[88] The vessel set sail from the port of Leith near Edinburgh on January 22, 1823, with more than one hundred passengers aboard, a few months after the *Honduras Packet*. Her departure was announced by the sound of cannons and was formally hailed by MacGregor.[89] However, not everyone was reassured by these announcements. Ogilvie, who was also the shipper of the *Honduras Packet*, was either unable or unwilling to make the required installment payments. Instead, he, along with Alexander Arnott, attempted to partially offset the losses incurred in sending the two ships by appropriating the revenue from the sale of ownership deeds to Scottish and English candidates to emigrate to Poyais.[90] Ogilvie was also extremely keen to sell the bonds in his possession and by offloading his holdings further fueled the collapse in the price of Poyais securities. Yet with sales seemingly taking place off the official exchange, prices were not reported in the *Course of the Exchange*, which explains why the price of the bonds was not recorded after February 1823. However, MacGregor complained bitterly about the actions of Lowe and Ogilvie, saying, "The conduct of the contractor and Mr. Ogilvie have knocked the Loan upon the head."[91]

As Ogilvie and Lowe abandoned MacGregor, just under two hundred future settlers were en route for Poyais. As soon as the Poyais loan was contracted, two recruitment offices opened their doors to these would-be emigrants. The first was at No. 1 Dowgate Hill, in London; the second at No. 63 North Bridge in Edinburgh.[92] Describing Poyais as a country of bountiful natural resources, the agents running these "Poyais Land Offices" handed out copies of Strangeways' guide to future emigrants and urged them to buy farming concessions, which were being sold at an initial price of three shillings an acre. The acquisition price could even be paid in installments. Besides an annual tenure license fee (feu-duty), which cost about half a penny per acre and was waived for the first five years, settlers were not required to pay any other taxes.[93]

As mentioned, two ships making for Black River were chartered using funds put up by Ogilvie and laden with provisions and volunteers. The first wave left aboard the *Honduras Packet* from the port of Gravesend near London on November 22, 1822. On board was Hector Hall, a former lieutenant colonel of the 22nd Regiment of Foot recently returned from a posting in the East Indies and Mauritius.[94] MacGregor tasked him with ensuring that the first group of settlers was properly established. As lieutenant governor, he was given a set of twenty-six instructions detailing the measures that he should take, such as creating a militia to defend the settlement and building good relations with the Indigenous communities. Hall's orders also included erecting the town of St. Joseph's on the site of the ruins of the old English town at Black River (point 5); ensuring that each settler belonged to either the yeomanry or the militia (point 11); sending a messenger to Miskitu king George Frederic at Cape Gracias a Dios to announce the settlers' arrival (point 14); and preventing settlers from buying land belonging to other Indigenous peoples of the Shore (point 17). While acknowledging that it was impossible to foresee every situation, MacGregor also told Hall: "You are hereby authorized, in all such cases, to act according to the best of your judgment, and as may appear to you most advisable for his [Miskitu] Highness's honour and interests, as well as beneficial or necessary to any other party or parties concerned" (point 26).[95] Hall was accompanied by forty-two other passengers, many of whom were traveling alone.[96] These emigrants were to establish an administrative and labor base that would enable them to quickly and effectively build their embryonic settlement. Accordingly, just under half of them were to hold positions in administration and overall supervision of the onsite works, while the rest were divided into laborers, famers, and skilled workers.

For all its promise, the Poyais emigration project got off to a rocky start. Testimony from the settlement's doctor, James Douglas, reveals that misfortune struck the first wave of Poyais settlers.[97] After a crossing that included stopovers on St. Thomas (now part of the U.S. Virgin Islands) and at Port Royal in Jamaica, the *Honduras Packet* arrived off Black River in February 1823. Initially delayed by a hurricane, the passengers eventually set to unloading the provisions and other cargo from the ship's hold, and quickly put up tents and huts. They received essential assistance from the local native communities, trading medical treatments provided by Douglas or gunpowder in exchange for food and help in setting up their accommodations. Five days after their arrival, however, Douglas was astonished to see the *Honduras Packet* departing. As an excuse, the captain told the settlers that he was worried about another hurricane and was heading to Cape Gracias a Dios to unload the rest of his cargo.

Overall, however, the first few weeks went relatively well for the new

Poyais settlement. But the help from the locals suddenly dried up in March 1823. Douglas could not find any explanation for the abrupt change. It appears that local peoples were dissatisfied with the salary paid by the settlers, which was less than what Gordon and MacGregor had initially promised when obtaining the grant of land from George Frederic. Sources indicate that local laborers had anticipated a daily wage of half a dollar, supplemented with rations.[98] Previous dealings had provided a vital source of food and logistical assistance that had helped the settlers to find their feet and survive. Without it, their situation, which was already fairly precarious, soon worsened. The dwindling food supplies and meager reserves may have accounted for the change in the behavior by their Indigenous counterparts, since it became difficult to keep up the gift exchanges that had cemented their good relations until that point. Without the diversified diet made possible by exchanges with the local population, the relatively positive mood within the Poyais settlement quickly soured. In charge of the settlement's well-being, Hall decided to mount an expedition to Cape Gracias a Dios to recover the remaining provisions that had been in the hold of the *Honduras Packet* and that were needed for the settlement's survival. In fact, an envoy from the Miskitu king had arrived a few days earlier to inform him that the ship was currently docked and waiting to be unloaded.

In the meantime, a second ship was on its way to Poyais. Under the command of Captain Henry Crouch, the *Kennersley Castle*, the second vessel chartered by Ogilvie, left Leith on January 22, 1823. To the roar of a cannon salute, the *Kennersley Castle* and its passengers bid farewell to MacGregor, who had come expressly to tell them that he would bear the full costs of the crossing. Among the 150 or so Scottish settlers on board, constituting ninety-three households, was James Hastie, a woodcutter on his way to Poyais with a work contract stipulating that he would provide a minimum of two years' service to MacGregor.[99] Of the Scots recruited by the Edinburgh land office, around seventeen volunteer households were on their way to support the administrators and supervisors supposedly already on site in Poyais, while twenty-four households were engaged as laborers. Some forty-nine households were planning to work in the secondary sector and formed a pool of skilled labor destined to drive the settlement's forestry and furniture-building production chain. With its budding luxury timber industry, which included cutters but also carpenters and cabinetmakers, Poyais was earmarked as a future export hub for mahogany logs and finished products. This burgeoning venture was to be supported by local agricultural production and managed by administrators and workers. Sailors, customs officers, coopers, and bankers on board the ship would oversee efforts to set up a commercial harbor, while masons, smiths, weavers, and others would take care of constructing and maintaining the requisite infrastructure.[100]

Following a voyage lasting fifty-seven days, the *Kennersley Castle* arrived off Poyais three days after Hall's sudden, desperate departure for Cape Gracias a Dios. On viewing the coast, Hastie was initially disappointed by what he saw. Instead of admiring the panorama shown by the engraving on the cover of Strangeways' guide, which depicted the former harbor of Black River as an inhabited and soon-to-be wealthy inhabited trading post (Fig. 14), he saw only empty beaches, devoid of human activity. On coming ashore, he found a settlement in desperate straits, living in the bush and running down its last reserves. Yet the *Kennersley Castle* could not provide any great logistical assistance. Besides some food, the ship did not carry enough additional provisions or materials.[101]

Figure 14. View of the port of Black River in the territory of Poyais. Source: Thomas Strangeways, *Sketch of the Mosquito Shore, Including the Territory of Poyais* (Edinburgh: W. Blackwood, 1822). Courtesy of the John Carter Brown Library.

After overcoming their initial disappointment, Hastie and his freshly arrived travel companions got to work. Helping the first round of settlers who had arrived a few months earlier, they built a few rudimentary dwelling places, a cellar and a storehouse for provisions and other materials.[102] However, at this point, not only had the local Indigenous peoples already stopped providing assistance, but medical supplies began to run out. This caused an outbreak of "fever" (most likely dysentery or malaria), which gradually infected all the settlers. Dr. Douglas's bleeding treatments failed to contain the spread, and on April 25, he reported that 111 people were sick.[103] In the meantime, the unfortunate Poyaisians continued to await the return of Hall's expedition.

Meanwhile, Hall reached George Frederic's court in late March. Tasked with bringing the *Honduras Packet*'s cargo back to Black River, he met with a flat refusal from the ship's commander, Captain Hedgcock, on the grounds that he (Hedgcock) had not been fully paid for his crossing. While he allowed Hall to unload the medical supplies, Hedgcock kept the rest of the ship's cargo, intending to sell it to the highest bidder.[104] Appealing to George Frederic for assistance, Hall was unsuccessful in his search for help. As the officer in charge of settling the first Poyais emigrants, he learned why the king had abruptly ordered his subjects to stop providing help.

For his part, George Frederic, who had probably been delegitimized in the eyes of any merchants wishing to conduct Caribbean or Atlantic trade with him because of the unfolding sanitary disaster in his Black River settlement, actually decided to distance himself from MacGregor. Without divulging the source of his information, he said that he had felt betrayed by the Scotsman, who had contracted a sovereign loan without royal authorization and claimed for himself the title of cacique of the independent state of Poyais. Believing that MacGregor had failed to meet his obligations and overstepped his rights, George Frederic declared on March 23, 1823, that he was rescinding the concession granting Poyais to MacGregor. However, in a show of magnanimity, he said that if the Poyaisian emigrants already in place pledged allegiance to him, they could stay and keep the lands given to them by MacGregor. The king's decision was intended essentially to clarify the full strength of his political authority in the land to which these foreign laborers would belong and to establish the legal framework with which they had to comply. George Frederic also sought to raise more funds locally. Although no taxes would be collected for the first year, settlers would need to purchase, within five years, the appropriated plots of land at the price of twenty-five cents per acre paid "in money, goods, or service."[105]

Back in Black River, the lack of provisions needed for the settlement to survive and thrive spelled a premature end for the colonial venture. With Hall still en route, the colony's sanitary conditions grew steadily worse. A widespread sense of defeat sapped the settlers' morale, and some even took their own lives. Others attempted to flee on a makeshift raft, including five exhausted men who landed in a woeful state in British Honduras in early April 1823. Yet by that time, British Honduras had seen significant political change in the intervening period since April 1820, when George Frederic had first allocated the Poyais concession against the backdrop of the conflict between the Belizean magistrature and Superintendent George Arthur. Outraged by the attacks against him, Arthur had resigned his superintendency. Abandoning his quest to reform the practices linking the Shore's Indigenous and settler populations, he was transferred to Van Diemen's Land (present-day Tasmania), officially because of poor health, leaving the cutters of British Honduras to celebrate victory in their feud.[106] This would eventually have important repercussions for the fate of Poyais.

Edward Codd was appointed in January 1823 as superintendent to replace Arthur (and Allen Hampden Pye, the interim replacement). A former major general from the 60th Foot Regiment, Codd was named superintendent of the settlement without any knowledge of how it actually functioned internally.[107] For example, when George Frederic's successor, Robert Charles Frederic, would officially be crowned in Belize in March 1824, Codd expressed concern about the existence of such practices, not understanding how regional politics operated.[108] According to some sources, he even displayed visible signs of dementia or psychological distress and, as such, posed much less of threat to the magistrates.[109]

But despite Codd's appointment, the magistrates did not emerge unscathed from their battle with Superintendent Arthur. Massive efforts were required to counter the bad press generated by the publication in London of the former superintendent's reports. To recap, Superintendent Arthur was an evangelist with ties to William Wilberforce, a recognized and respected anti-slavery champion who was widely admired by London public opinion. To the dismay of the Belizean magistrates, Wilberforce had taken up some of Arthur's reports criticizing the slavery practices of the mahogany cutters of British Honduras in his speeches before Parliament. This was a potential source of damage to the image of an economy that put itself forward as a model in the treatment of its enslaved labor force.

And although Arthur had left his post, he was still a potential threat. As he passed through London before being redeployed as governor of Van Diemen's Land, he personally vouched before the British government for the claims made in his official correspondence. William Bullock, secretary to the governor of Jamaica, even counseled the magistrates of British Honduras to keep a low profile over the unresolved question of Indigenous slaves.[110] Arthur's return to London gave him direct access to Henry Bathurst, Earl Bathurst and Secretary of State for War and the Colonies at the head of the Colonial Office. Bullock in turn advised the magistrates to avoid attracting too much attention, encouraging them to let the courts tackle the issue and recommending measures to ensure that Indigenous slaves were provided with adequate legal resources to request their freedom.[111] Worse still, while not only undermining the magistrates' cherished legal and judicial independence, Arthur, with his anti-slavery ideas, had also sparked an increase in slave escapes in the area.[112] As we will see, however, the woes of MacGregor's settlers provided a gilt-edged political and economic opportunity for the mahogany cutters of British Honduras.

In early April 1823, desperate and exhausted after a grueling journey, the five settlers who had fled Poyais aboard a makeshift raft that landed in Belize were brought by the local magistrates before the new superintendent of British Honduras. Unaware of the situation, Codd was greatly moved by the pitiful state of the men, whose names are never revealed in the sources documenting the event. He therefore instructed the settlement's main magistrate, Marshall Bennett, accompanied by magistrate George Westby, to go immediately to Moskitia to determine the condition of the other emigrants and provide any assistance needed.[113]

A newcomer to the region, Superintendent Codd was certainly unaware of the wider issues. The same was not true of the colony's resident magistrates. Although they claimed to have learned about MacGregor's venture from the five Black River refugees who had recently arrived in Belize, the magistrates of British Honduras had in fact been aware of the Poyais project for two years. On January 15, 1821, then-superintendent George Arthur told

Earl Bathurst that he had learned from James David Roy Gordon, a former British mercenary who had fought under Jean-Louis Aury and who had introduced MacGregor to George Frederic, that MacGregor was the owner of a large land concession granted by the Miskitu king.[114] Having informed Arthur about the nascent Poyaisian venture, Gordon may well have passed on the information to the Belizean magistrates as well. At the time, George Frederic's decision to grant a concession to MacGregor was not in and of itself a problem for the Belizean cutters, who saw the move as an empty promise by a frustrated ruler. Moreover, they hoped that Arthur's eventual redeployment would open the way for things to get back to normal, as his departure from Belize in April 1822 left the magistrature free to rebuild its preferred relationship with the Miskitu king. However, the magistrature was caught off-guard by the establishment of a more concrete colonial venture in Poyais, which formed a genuine obstacle to their logging business.

On April 26, 1823, Bennett landed in Black River aboard a schooner, the *Mexican Eagle*. Before going ashore, however, he sent a letter to George Frederic informing him of his arrival at the settlement. Bennett also told the king in his letter that he was bringing gifts specifically for him. He said that he planned to stay for six days and would await the arrival of the king in hopes of having a discussion with him, begging him "to be assured of my unalterable good wishes and desire to promote the peace and prosperity of your country."[115] While it is not sure that an interview took place on Bennett's schooner, the letter speaks of a desire to clarify or resume the relations threatened by the land grant to MacGregor. However, once on shore, both Bennett and Westby were taken aback by the dramatic situation that MacGregor's settlers found themselves in. Bennett cut short his stay in Poyais and took the sickest individuals aboard his ship to bring them to safety in Belize.[116] Since he could not take all the settlers with him, Bennett promised to come back.

The healthiest settlers who stayed behind witnessed the arrival of Hall on May 1, 1823, just a few days after Bennett's departure. Yet the leader of the Poyais settlement came back from Cape Gracias a Dios empty-handed, besides a few medical supplies. Desperate, and with support from Dr. Douglas, the settlement's physician, who confirmed the medical distress of the settlers, Hall gave the order for the settlement to be dismantled.[117] Through Bennett, who returned just a few days later, he begged Superintendent Codd to help him to evacuate the settlers and their provisions.[118]

For some settlers, Bennett came too late. One of them, dismayed by the failure to establish a settlement on the Shore, was Hugh Frazer. A Scottish cabinetmaker who arrived on the *Kennersley Castle*, he did not want to wait for the *Mexican Eagle* to return; instead, he fled Poyais by paying some locals to take him and two countrymen, George Davison and William Law, who were likewise disheartened by the conditions in Poyais, away by boat. Just a few days before the *Mexican Eagle* arrived, they set out with their native guides for British Honduras. After a few days at sea, however, the crew, who were presumably unhappy at the paltry pay they had received, threw Frazer and his companions overboard. Frazer was luckier than his companions and managed to swim ashore at Truxillo, where a family of Spanish settlers living on an isolated part of the coast took him in. He gradually recovered from his ordeal before reaching British Honduras a few weeks after the first set of Bennett's evacuees.[119]

Arrested by the Belizean authorities on his arrival, Frazer was questioned by the magistrates, who were keener to learn about the nature of the boat's cargo than about the activities of the emigrants dispatched by MacGregor to Moskitia. Nevertheless, their aim was to show that they could deliver justice. On the same day that he gave witness, the magistrates brought before Frazer sixteen Indigenous men suspected of having taken part in his attempted murder.[120] Frazer did not recognize any of them. The magistrates did not stop there, however. Two days later, magistrate Thomas Pickstock summoned Frazer again and brought before him an Indigenous man called Gibson, whom Frazer instantly recognized as the captain of the boat in which he had fled Poyais.[121] Following a series of interrogations, the identity of the crew of the boat that had transported Frazer was gradually pieced together, and six Indigenous men were arrested for the murder of Frazer's unfortunate companions.[122] They were also accused of belonging (at least according to the magistrates, as no Indigenous testimony was recorded) to the retinue of the recently deceased General Robinson. The sudden discovery of a formal link between those accused of attempting to murder Frazer and one of the main Indigenous allies of former superintendent George Arthur (who had offered to pay to educate Robinson's children) offered further grounds to support the Poyaisian emigrants. The fact that the Poyais settlers, already disregarded due to MacGregor's apparent neglect, had been attacked and killed by some followers of Robinson, a man viewed as a potential enemy of the Belizean magistrature's interests because of his former alignment with Arthur, represented an opportunity for the magistrates to support and justify dismantling the Poyais venture. The Belizean magistrates once again appeared as the saviors of the Poyais settlers who had already been repatriated to British Honduras and whose grateful testimonies were carefully recorded.[123]

While Bennett's mission was certainly humanitarian, it was also deliberately and publicly presented as such. On June 9, 1823, the London *Times* and the *Morning Post* published extracts from a letter sent to Lloyd's by its agent in British Honduras, Thomas Paslow, a former magistrate who had been appointed as one of the settlement's London agents in 1822.[124] The dispatch, dated April 13 of the same year, just a few days after the arrival of the first Poyais escapees in Belize and before Belizean magistrates dismantled the settlement, describes MacGregor's venture as a pitiful failure. Recounted in graphic detail, the living conditions of the Poyais settlers are depicted as inhuman and awful: "Out of the 55 who arrived at one time at the shore, nine remain, some put out to sea to reach Belize, others up the river, and have never been heard of, and others died miserably near to where they were landed, which was absolutely among mangrove trees, which they had to cut down."[125]

Based on Douglas's and Hastie's descriptions, the settlers sent by MacGregor endured a torrid time in Poyais. In addition to having to cope with a harsh climate, most fell ill for want of logistical, food, and medical supplies. Yet the letter to Lloyd's did much more than simply describe the woes of MacGregor's colony. The unsigned dispatch described MacGregor as an opportunist who had little regard for the true needs of these "poor souls" and who was incapable of planning a colonial venture. Depicted as a self-centered and vain despot, MacGregor was held up by the letter as solely responsible for the venture's failure and the shocking situation of a group of people left inadequately prepared to fend for themselves in a dangerous environment.

This chapter reveals how, in 1822, issuing a foreign loan was an alternative to the credit instruments typically used to fund British trade ventures. Recent innovations in European sovereign debt issues, combined with the lack of clear and formal rules at the government level or within capital markets, opened the way for financial intermediaries tasked with raising the funds for the Poyais project to circumvent the legal approaches typically used in Britain for this purpose, such as setting up a joint-stock company, for example. But to create such a loan, those in charge of setting it up had to agree on the potential existence of a future sovereign political entity. However, this innovative use of a particular kind of credit instrument—namely the issuance of a sovereign debt founded on a legal fiction—left the borrower at a disadvantage. Issuance of the debt benefited, and even protected, the speculative transactions of the financial intermediaries hired to set up the loan, to the detriment of MacGregor as borrower.

While eschewing the interpretations commonly put forward by historians characterizing Poyais as a fraud, this chapter highlights the micromechanisms underpinning foreign loan issues and underlines the importance of the roles played by financial intermediaries in the capital markets of the early nineteenth century. Small bit-part players such as John Lowe had a thorough understanding of the legal complexities and technicalities of the financial markets, giving them significant leverage to profit personally while being shielded from reputational concerns, at the expense of their borrowers. Rather than being the only way for a sovereign political entity to fund its economic expansion, the issuance of a loan in London is revealed, through the Poyais prism, to be the result of Atlantic historical constraints and the specific features of the City's legal and political frameworks. Yet, as MacGregor and many Poyais bondholders would discover, the success and survival over time of a foreign loan such as that raised by Poyais depended on political, economic, and legal matters extending far beyond the scope of the City alone.

FIVE

Saving Poyais

NO MATTER THAT THE FIRST two convoys of Poyais emigrants had to flee the awful conditions that met them as they attempted to establish their colony, MacGregor remained convinced of his venture's merits. On July 4, 1823, he wrote to Hector Hall, the commander sent aboard the *Honduras Packet* to develop the settlement, expressing delight that his colony would soon be flourishing and even speaking of recruiting new settlers and British mercenaries in the near future. He said that the new arrivals could be confident of finding in Poyais a sanctuary maintained by a self-sufficient local system of agricultural production. From there, foreign armed forces could deploy garrisons at military outposts. MacGregor was even planning to expand his territory by occupying Spark's island (perhaps Utila island) in the Bay of Honduras at the mouth of the Roman River (perhaps Río Aguán). The site had strategic value as a defense against the feeble Spanish presence that persisted in a number of smaller, remote settlements, such as Truxillo.[1]

Although brimming with confidence, MacGregor nevertheless felt that the success of his project was reliant on fresh intelligence about the State of Poyais reaching London. It is certainly true that news dissemination played a vital role in the viability of his undertaking. As mentioned earlier, the initial architects and several other key participants in the scheme and in the Poyais loan of 1822 pulled out after the dissemination of information openly questioning the very existence of Poyais, in particular a scathing piece in the *Quarterly Review*. When the Poyais plans were portrayed as detrimental to Colombia's republican aspirations, Lowe and Ogilvie severed their ties, even if that meant enduring significant monetary losses.

Coincidentally, MacGregor also lost his initial business supporters—

those Jamaican British merchants who saw a settlement in Poyais as a golden opportunity to grow their own affairs in the sugar trade. Several men who had played a central role in designing the project presented in London withdrew, including Thomas Higson and the Hyslop brothers, who had been named agents for Poyais in the West Indies.[2] Higson had been a vital pillar in MacGregor's relations with the British West Indies, but now his name drops out of the story, perhaps as diplomatic and trade tensions between Britain's West Indian colonies and the United States eased over the course of June 1822.[3] This caused MacGregor to claim that he had been the victim of "foul play" in Jamaica.[4] MacGregor's two principal colonial partners also vanished from the scene. Rather than wait for the convoys of settlers and provisions to arrive in Poyais from London, James David Roy Gordon and George Woodbine, the two fellow mercenaries who had introduced MacGregor to the Miskitu ruler, chose instead to cultivate closer, more personal ties in George Frederic's court at Cape Gracias a Dios.[5]

These defections left MacGregor alone and short of money. Without aid, he was not in a position to pursue a project that had already sent many emigrants to Black River. Worse still, following through on his initial plans to keep up a sustained flow of settlers to Poyais, MacGregor found himself even deeper in debt after chartering a third ship, the *Skeene*.[6] Desperate, he resolved to raise additional funds by turning to the holders of the remaining Poyais securities, who he hoped might be interested in ensuring that their initial investments did not go up in smoke. However, MacGregor was unable to provide them with assurances that they would be paid the promised interest via Perring, Shaw, Barber & Co. He therefore returned to the London capital market in an effort to fund the continued development of his project.

On April 7, 1823, MacGregor appointed William John Richardson as chargé d'affaires and new London agent for Poyais, replacing Ogilvie.[7] Although we do not have a great deal of information about Richardson, we know that he was one of the initial buyers of the Poyaisian scrips issued by Lowe in 1822. He was also a man of means and the owner of Oak Hall, a manor house in the London suburb of Wanstead.[8] Fearing that he might forfeit not only his initial outlay but also the promised interest payments if the project were to fail, Richardson resolved to get MacGregor's loan back on track.

The day after his appointment by MacGregor, Richardson called a meeting of Poyais scripholders. Since the securities issued by John Lowe were no longer valid because the installments had not been paid, Richardson proposed a plan to set up a new loan divided into tradable bonds, which he presented in a prospectus circulated among the investors at the meeting. Deeming Richardson's proposal to be the "fairest and most liberal," since it guaranteed the deferred payment of an initial dividend, the meeting approved the suggestion and appointed him as contractor to set up the loan.[9]

On May 1, 1823, a new Poyais loan was officially contracted.[10] With a face value of £200,000, it was to be split into two thousand bearer bonds earning annual interest of 5 percent payable semiannually by Perring, Shaw, Barber & Co. for a period of thirty years. To woo fresh investors, the issue price was set at £50. As with the first loan, the bonds could be purchased in installments. Investors needed to pay £5 to purchase a scrip, which allowed them to acquire a true certificate later. The balance could then be paid in three installments of £15, to be settled on dates that would be determined later.

Richardson not only took charge of raising new funds to bring Poyais to fruition; he was also determined to make sure that the new loan had public credibility, given that criticism of the project had sowed doubts about whether the State of Poyais even existed. To that end, he encouraged MacGregor to strut about town, embracing his role as a true sovereign monarch. Sumptuous receptions were held at Oak Hall, during which MacGregor was introduced as the sole political representative of the new State of Poyais. According to the account of a guest at one of the Oak Hall soirées, those present were treated to various proofs establishing MacGregor's credibility, such as the concession from George Frederic, MacGregor's own family genealogy from an important Scottish clan, and his Bolívar family connection.[11] Josepha, MacGregor's wife, was regularly presented to support her spouse's political credentials. Marrying MacGregor when he was still just a mercenary on the payroll of South American revolutionary movements, Josepha Antonia Andrea Aristeguieta y Lovera was a cousin of Simón Bolívar, who gave their union his blessing.[12]

Despite the doubts surrounding the very idea of Poyais, it was presented as already functioning as an independent state. MacGregor and the hosts of these gatherings enthusiastically shared printed lists naming those appointed to key positions in the Poyais government-to-be.[13] As head of the Principality of Poyais, the cazique was presented as entitled to bestow noble titles. Taking his role as leader of the colony and communicator-in-chief to heart,

MacGregor had already named several passengers from the initial Black River convoys to be members of his new Poyais aristocracy. Among those granted Spanish- or British-sounding titles, such as Baron Valoria and Baron Witton, Hector Hall, who led the first convoy of settlers, was named Baron Tinto.[14] Thomas Westcott, who arrived in Black River aboard the *Honduras Packet*, was appointed to be Under Secretary of State in the Home Office. While the letters informing the selected Black River migrants of their ennoblement were being drawn up in readiness to be dispatched on a future ship, the composition of the first Government of Poyais-Council of State was published in the London *Morning Chronicle* of April 1, 1823.[15]

Moving to Black River was one way of acquiring Poyaisian nobility. Acquiring Poyais securities was another. At least, that was what MacGregor and especially Richardson appeared to be promising. Some of the new Poyaisian peers were actually the very men in charge of managing MacGregor's loan. They included one Count Braena and three barons: Arenas, Orellana, and Estrada.[16] As revealed by the cover of a Poyaisian seal box in his possession, Richardson himself was bestowed the title of Count de la Cruz.[17] However, allocating titles of nobility was not just a matter of decorum. As noted by William Rubinstein, acquiring noble rank was often hard for the then-rising financial bourgeoisie.[18] Being granted a title, even in a foreign principality rather than in Britain, where such a thing might be very difficult or impossible to secure, was thus a potential reward for investing in MacGregor's project. Meanwhile, for MacGregor himself, naming a Poyais aristocracy further burnished and formalized his role as head of state. By acquiring noble title and being bound by formal and explicit ties of vassalage, the project's investors also enhanced their protection in the event of failure.

Richardson blamed James Ogilvie, the agent of the first Poyais loan in 1822, for all of Poyais's financial woes, caused by breaking the agreement initially established with Daniel Mocatta "who is worth half a million" in favor of John Lowe "who is not worth 500 pounds."[19] Trying to make up for these past mistakes, Richardson asked Mocatta to handle the exclusive sale of four hundred securities from the new loan, equivalent to £40,000 in face-value terms. In return, he offered a 5 percent commission on the face value of the securities sold.[20] The bonds were then floated on July 7, 1823, with Wetenhall's *Course of the Exchange* listing them at £5, or the price of the first installment required to purchase one security.[21] Working with his son-in-law Horatio

Montefiore, Mocatta did his best to boost the price of the bonds. Using his connections at the London Stock Exchange, he got the price to climb briefly past £20 on July 28 and again on August 8, 1823, which generated gains for investors aiming to profit by trading securities on which the second installment had not been paid.[22]

At the time, however, these new Poyais bonds had to be sold on the Foreign Stock Market. A new venue set up specifically for trading in foreign securities, the Foreign Stock Market was the result of a split between two groups of London Stock Exchange members. Amid the widespread excitement sparked by the introduction of the first Latin American loans, a contingent primarily made up of young brokers (who often did not have much equity) called for trading in these foreign securities to be facilitated. Led by Jacob Ricardo, the brother of famed economist David Ricardo, this faction suggested erecting a new building devoted entirely to trading in foreign securities. However, the proposal came up against staunch opposition from an opposing group mainly made up of well-established and well-funded "jobbers," or market makers, many of whom did business on their own account. This faction, which was led by Abraham Montefiore, the brother-in-law of Nathan Rothschild, argued that foreign securities should not be traded on the London Stock Exchange. Pointing out that the exchange's original Deed of Settlement, drawn up in 1802, authorized only trading in British securities, they claimed that transactions involving foreign instruments were illegal.[23]

Keen to avoid internal strife, the owners of the London Stock Exchange gave the go-ahead to split the capital market.[24] A new building devoted to trading in foreign securities was acquired in late 1822, and it was there that the inauguration of the Foreign Stock Market was celebrated on New Year's Day 1823.[25] The new market, which had its own operating rules, accepted all trades in foreign securities, including bonds from Latin American loans already in circulation, such as those of Colombia, Chile, Peru, and Poyais. Although a specialized and separate entity, the Foreign Stock Market followed operational rules that seemed similar to those of the London Stock Exchange, particularly insofar as they were less concerned with the characteristics of the securities traded on the market (besides the fact that they were foreign) than with those of the exchange's members. Closing prices at the end of each session were also collected and published by James Wetenhall, whose sole criterion for including securities in his list was that they be considered bona fide on the exchange.²⁶

As contractor, Richardson reserved the right to keep the remaining 1,600 Poyais bonds that Mocatta had not introduced onto the new Foreign Stock Market.²⁷ He privately persuaded a small group of investors to acquire four hundred of his securities. Probably holders of the 1822 Poyais scrips, the group included G. Nicholson, P. Johnson, and George Alexander—all three of whom are difficult to identify—along with James Thick and James William Sowerby.²⁸ Thick was a member of the London Stock Exchange, while Sowerby was a London merchant who financed and traded in steam engines.²⁹

Richardson, Nicholson, Johnson, Alexander, Thick, and especially Sowerby certainly saw the acquisition of Poyais securities as a way of investing their own funds. Yet they also all appear to have viewed it as an opportunity to expand their own business and financial activities. By investing with Richardson, for example, Sowerby may have spied a chance that his services might be called on, fueling the growth of his own steamship business. The other five investors may have been contemplating the possibility of expanding their trading activities by joining forces with the Poyais endeavor, which they were essentially financing. If MacGregor's venture was to materialize, this group—which resembled an investor club as identified by Naomi Lamoreaux—could then have benefited from its proximity to Richardson, MacGregor's agent, and gained privileged access to the promising Atlantic and Caribbean trade that Poyais was promising. In other words, purchasing Poyais securities was a targeted investment for placing funds in a specific polity and for gaining an indirect but preferred stake in future entrepreneurial activities.³⁰

On June 9, 1823, the London *Times* and the *Morning Post* published excerpts of a letter sent by one of the British Honduras magistrates to marine insurer Lloyd's of London. As mentioned earlier, the dispatch, dated April 13 of the same year, described the abject failure of MacGregor's venture.³¹ The first two convoys of emigrants sent to Poyais on the *Honduras Packet* and the *Kennersley Castle* had been unable to cope with the conditions on the Shore and had been urgently evacuated by the magistrates of British Honduras.

Richardson was forced to delay the sale of his bonds on the Foreign Stock Market to prevent their trading price from collapsing after news broke in London of the misfortunes suffered by the Poyais settlers. Yet he was not ready for MacGregor's project to be shut down. Responding to the allegations published by the British Honduras magistrates, he organized a media campaign in support of establishing a colony on the Shore. On the day following the release of the Lloyd's dispatch, the *Times* published a letter by Poyais's London agent. In it, Richardson openly accused the magistrates of deliberately sabotaging the venture led by MacGregor and unfairly charging him with incompetence and fraud. He claimed that the Belizean loggers had done everything in their power to confound the establishment of a European settlement on the Shore and stifle any potential competition that might interfere with their own business activities. According to Richardson, the difficulties preventing the initial round of emigrants from establishing a permanent base were simply due to a few recruitment issues, and he took pains to stress that these problems were being ironed out.[32]

News that the situation had improved came quickly. A few days after publication of the Lloyd's dispatch, some English newspapers announced that another ship was already bound for Poyais.[33] Setting out from Leith on June 4, 1823, just days before the Lloyd's dispatch came out, the *Skeene* carried one hundred or so emigrants, provisions and materials to build the new colony, and letters of nobility for the new Poyaisian peers.[34] Richardson's sale of Poyais bonds to his small investor group provided the bulk of the funds needed to send the *Skeene*. More than £2,000 was raised in all, making it possible to pay off the debt incurred by MacGregor to charter the vessel.

After a trouble-free crossing, the *Skeene* arrived off the coast of Black River sometime in August 1823. Scanning the coastline, those onboard saw no signs of human activity, as the settlers sent ahead on the *Honduras Packet* and the *Kennersley Castle* had already been evacuated by a magistrate, Marshall Bennett. The *Skeene*'s panicked passengers quickly despaired of being able to set up a settlement at that location, and the *Skeene* soon made for British Honduras, arriving on August 13.[35] Surprised by the ship's arrival, the settlement's magistrates were caught off-guard by a letter signed by the passengers appealing to be taken in by the local authorities.[36] The magistrates issued emergency authorization for the *Skeene* to unload at the port of Belize but were leery of adopting the emigrants as new citizens of British Honduras.

Having already paid out considerable sums to look after the first Poyaisians evacuated from Black River a few months earlier, the magistrates did not relish the idea of welcoming yet another batch of strays.[37]

After giving the matter some thought, however, the magistrates changed tack as they realized that the *Skeene*'s arrival might prove a boon in more ways than one. Their first move was to seize all correspondence on board in order to gain intelligence about the current state of the Poyais scheme.[38] With the arrival of the new emigrants, the magistrates also saw an opportunity for their own settlement to flourish. Many of the newcomers were skilled workers who could be taken in by local workshops. Anyone selected and sponsored by three magistrates could be accepted into unpaid indentured service for one year, except for smiths, carpenters, and sailors, who were paid between JM£20 and JM£50 annually. Those unable to find a placement with a Belizean employer could set up their own settlement on Honduran soil under the de facto authority of the magistracy. And so, under the command of one John Campbell, a passenger on the *Skeene*, a group of emigrants traveled to Stan Creek, an area in southern British Honduras boasting extensive natural resources that the local loggers had not yet exploited because of a lack of labor. However, the magistrates were finicky. A handful of passengers deemed to be of "unsuitable character" were sent back to Britain.[39]

To cover the remaining costs of evacuating Black River, as well as establishing a permanent Belizean presence in Stan Creek and sending any undesirables back to Britain, the magistracy confiscated the *Skeene*'s cargo and sold it to a few wealthy merchants and other residents of British Honduras. This tribute was taken in addition to the provisions and other cargo transported by the *Honduras Packet* and seized by Bennett after Poyais was evacuated.[40]

Following this latest setback, some of Poyais's London agents tried to reassure the ill-fated emigrants and persuade them to return to Poyais. Edward Irving, who became involved in the project in 1823 as secretary to Richardson, wrote a letter on December 8 of that year to John Campbell, the man tasked with leading the *Skeene*'s passengers to their new abode.[41] Assuring him that he understood the discontent felt by the passengers on discovering no colonial activity in Poyais, Irving nevertheless urged Campbell to stick to his initial mission of helping to develop MacGregor's colony in Poyais. He warned Campbell to beware of the claims made by the Belizean magistrates, who might be tempted to exaggerate the misfortunes of the *Honduras Packet* and the *Kennersley Castle*. To reassure him, Irving told Campbell that another ship was on the way, loaded with the provisions and equipment needed to rescue MacGregor's colony, along with funds to pay the emigrants recruited to build the settlement. At the same time, Irving apologized for not providing more details, as he was afraid that his letter might fall into the wrong hands.[42]

A fourth ship, the *Albion*, was indeed bound for Poyais at the order of Richardson and his partners, who hired Herman Hendriks to charter the vessel. A former resident of Jamaica, Hendriks owned sugar plantations and descended, like Jacob Belisario, from a Jewish family of Portuguese origin that had left the Netherlands in the seventeenth century.[43] A member of the Foreign Stock Market, Hendriks met MacGregor and Richardson at Oak Hall in the month of August 1823. Over the course of various dinners and conversations, MacGregor and Richardson made several presentations to Hendriks. Recounting the financial failure of the previous year's loan, they nevertheless pitched Poyais as a sound venture. Designed as a settlement that could ultimately be a linchpin in the Jamaican sugar trade, MacGregor's scheme was described as deriving its original legitimacy from the land grant by Miskitu king George Frederic.

Having lived for some years in Jamaica, Hendriks was well aware of what opening up Moskitia might mean for the sugar trade. He was delighted by the idea of being part of a project led by a man related by marriage to Bolívar and a partner of the Hyslop brothers, the Jamaican merchants who were (probably inaccurately) presented as Poyais's agents on the island.[44] More generally, Hendriks was also keenly interested in the plans being set up in London to fund the new American republics. A few months earlier, he had offered his services to Jean-Pierre Boyer, president of the Republic of Haiti, to issue a £500,000 loan at 6 percent.[45] Confident that MacGregor's venture was on a solid footing and offered genuine trade and financial potential, Hendriks was taken on to supply the equipment, goods, and provisions to be shipped on the *Albion*. By way of payment, Richardson offered him Poyais scrips with a face value of over £9,000.[46]

Leveraging the positive prospects opened up by the *Albion*'s forthcoming journey, the agreement signed with Hendriks in August 1823 also included plans to issue a new loan for which Hendriks would be the contractor. Worth a nominal £300,000, this new loan would be divided into three thousand bearer bonds earning annual interest of 5 percent, payable semiannually for a period of thirty years by, once again, Perring, Shaw, Barber & Co.[47] The banking house's recurring involvement in the business of Poyais probably reflected a determination to stay engaged in the booming sovereign debt market. Since the first Poyais bonds were issued in 1822, the sovereign debt market had expanded, as several Latin American states, along with Spain, Russia, and Naples, issued loans.[48] Accordingly, Perring, Shaw, Barber & Co. was careful to keep a hand in the Poyais project, even if the venture was under pressure. Withdrawal by the issuing bank might not only have hurt the already struggling image of the Poyais bonds. Amid a boom in trading, the bank's own reputation would have probably been damaged as well.

Leaving London around September 17, 1823, the *Albion* transported fifty passengers along with cargo worth just under £10,000. In addition to the food and drink needed for the crossing, the shipment also included all the provisions, materials, and equipment required to build a permanent fortified encampment (Fig. 15). Among other things, the *Albion* carried hundreds of firearms and cavalry sabers, several thousand bricks, casks of nails, military uniforms, medicines, sheets, and other household linens.[49]

John Wright, a former British naval officer (not to be confused with the prominent Belizean magistrate of the same name), was tasked with accompanying this latest batch of Poyais settlers to Moskitia. As commander of His Majesty's Navy in Central America around 1805, he had acquired a knowledge of the area and viewed the Shore as a region that could, if properly settled, allow Britain to fortify its presence on the continent following the failed British invasion of Buenos Aires in 1806. In 1808, he had published a book describing the resources, including mahogany, that could be extracted from the territory.[50] For Wright, joining MacGregor's venture was an opportunity to play his part in realizing a plan for colonization, trade, and imperial expansion that he had only dreamed of when he wrote his book. For MacGregor, Richardson, and the other Poyais agents, enlisting the services of Wright, whose book was cited multiple times in Strangeways' promotional guide, was a way to give a boost and public credibility to a struggling colonial project.

After a lengthy crossing, the *Albion* eventually arrived off the coast of Poyais in November 1823. Like their predecessors, the ship's passengers found

Contents of the Albion's Cargo.

2000 dollars in money
120 tierces of beef
80 pork
20 firkins butter
20 puncheons rum
20 cases sugar
5 bags coffee
200 bags bread
100 large casks flour
25 ditto pease
20 boxes soap
20 candles
30 casks porter
54 coils cables, and ropes
10 bales canvass and twines
1 ditto hides
1 ditto match-rope
Rope-making machines
Pig lead—Sheet ditto
100 casks nails
Surveyor's tools
Sail-maker's ditto
Cases medicines
100 military caps
Cases harness
Bales stationary
Crates and casks of earthen-ware and glass-ware, for use and for trade
Ditto of tin-ware for use soldiers' use and for trade
Household furniture of every description, with linen, beds, plate, &c. intended for the Admiral's residence
100 muskets

100 pair pistols
200 cavalry sabres
50 barrels gunpowder
6 cases accoutrements.
6 18-pound guns, mounted complete
6 12 ditto, ditto
6 6 ditto ditto
200 round of shot for each gun
8 iron cables, with anchors, &c.
80 bundles, iron and steel
200 bars iron
9 jack-screws
10 grindstones
20,000 bricks
35 hogsheads coals
Blacksmith's tools, complete
Carpenter's ditto ditto
Mason's and shipwright's ditto
Bales of military clothing for Lancers, Artillery, and Guards, both for dress and undress, with boots, spurs, &c.
Blocks, and various other articles for the building and equipment of 8-gun vessels
Paints, oil, tar, &c.]
Bales of blankets
serges
bedding
slops
Water casks, and provisions for fifty passengers, and various other articles both for use and trade.

Figure 15. Contents of the *Albion*'s cargo, according to Herman Hendriks. Source: Herman Hendriks, *A Plain Narrative of Facts* (London: Stephen Couchman, 1824). The Hume Tracts Collection, UCL Library Services, Special Collections.

a place devoid of human activity, besides the scattered remains of a hastily abandoned encampment. Although a landing was tried, the quest to revive the settlement in Poyais ended in failure. The initial attempt was complicated by challenging tides and sandbanks and was instantly struck by tragedy as several passengers drowned. Plagued by clouds of mosquitoes and sandflies, the crew of the *Albion* quickly decided to abandon Poyais.[51]

The ship cruised for some time around the Bay of Honduras. It was initially refused entry to Belize by the local authorities, as it carried military equipment that could potentially be used against "friendly neighboring states," namely the Miskitu, new republican outposts, and the few remaining Spanish colonies around the Bay, with which the magistrates of British Honduras had dealings from time to time.[52] Toward the end of February 1824, more than five months after leaving London, Wright wrote to the Miskitu king, George Frederic, asking for assistance. Concerned by the ship's arrival, the king advised Wright to head for Belize and wrote to the superintendent of British Honduras to inform him of his wish.[53] As with the *Skeene*, the *Albion*'s passengers were eventually taken in by the magistracy and sent to join their fellows in Stan Creek, while the ship's valuable cargo was confiscated and sold.

Back in Britain, things were not going any better for Poyais. With preparations underway to issue a new loan and the *Albion* sailing for Poyais, the publication of yet another dispatch from Central America struck a fresh blow. In early September 1823, several British papers published the proclamation given on March 23 of the same year by George Frederic to Hector Hall, the officer in charge of settling the first Poyais emigrants. The announcement stated publicly that the Miskitu king had rescinded the concession granted several years previously to MacGregor, because the latter had "failed to fulfil his contract with me in accordance with his instructions."[54]

MacGregor left London shortly after the king's proclamation was published. Officially, he said that he wanted to go to the north of Italy to seek treatment for his ailing wife, who struggled with English winters. In fact, he headed for Paris, perhaps on the trail of John Lowe, who had made off with a portion of the funds from the first loan. MacGregor took up residence at "Maison Villette" on the Champs Élysées.[55] He may have thought that reclaiming some of the funds appropriated by his former contractor would alleviate some of his woes. According to some of his agents, he also went there in search of powerful allies who might back his project.[56] MacGregor was accompanied by Thomas Irving, brother of Edward, and later by Gustavus Hippisley, a British mercenary who had formerly fought for the Bolívarian cause.[57]

MacGregor's Paris trip, it turned out, was also aimed at forging new alliances that might support the development of a settlement on the Shore. Ever the opportunist, MacGregor now posed as an ardent supporter of the powers that had emerged from the French Restoration and wrote two letters on November 25, 1823, one to the French Foreign Minister, François René de Chateaubriand, and the other to Spanish secretary of state Víctor Damián Sáez, asking them to formally recognize the Principality of Poyais.[58] In return, he offered to provide them with information about the best options for reasserting their influence in South America. MacGregor painted Poyais as the prime location for a military base from which to launch a series of Spanish-led offensives against the newly established Central American Federation. As with his state-building plans following the capture of Amelia Island, MacGregor saw a possibility to establish a temporarily independent state that could play a strategically vital role through the assignment of letters of marque, in this instance to defend Spanish interests.

By aligning himself with the French and Spanish regimes, and looking ahead to a possible joint intervention in South and Central America, MacGregor was able to gain access to Parisian money men with ties to absolutist interests.[59] In the French capital, MacGregor quickly made contact with Gabriel-Julien Ouvrard, financier of Ferdinand VII and supplier to the French army during the Spanish campaign of 1823. Presenting himself as a fervent absolutist, MacGregor begged Ouvrard to intercede for him at the Spanish court so that he might be recognized as the lawful owner of Poyais. But Ouvrard ignored the Scotsman's entreaties, considering MacGregor to be in the same mold as Theodore von Neuhoff, who enjoyed a short-lived reign as Theodore I, king of Corsica.[60]

MacGregor also reached out to Henri Dard, a lawyer known for defending the property of French émigrés. Specifically, Dard represented royalists who had fled to safety outside France during the revolutionary unrest and whose assets had been confiscated by the nation to pay down its debt and punish the enemies of the French Revolution. Arguing for Spain to reassert its authority in its American territories and for France to defend its West Indian colonial economy against English commercial interests, Dard was surely interested in the scheme proposed by MacGregor, who now presented himself as upholding Spanish imperial interests in Central America.[61]

Dard agreed to introduce MacGregor to Joseph Mérilhou.[62] A lawyer in the Périgord region of France, Mérilhou was legal counsel to Compagnie de la Nouvelle-Neustrie, a private colonization company led by Jean-François Lehuby. Following a failed initial attempt to establish a colony in the United States, Lehuby was given the opportunity by MacGregor on June 4, 1825, via Mérilhou and Dard, to set up his colonial project in Poyais. Concessions were also offered to Mérilhou and a number of new French allies at the same time.[63] Full of enthusiasm, Lehuby quickly drew up a colonization plan, which included sending several hundred settlers to Poyais aboard a ship chartered for the purpose at Le Havre. But the Paris police soon put an end to the project. As reports of events in Poyais arrived from Britain, they arrested Lehuby, MacGregor, and several members of his entourage in September 1825 on suspicion of fraud. After spending several months in La Force and Bicêtre prisons, MacGregor and his supporters (although not Lehuby) were eventually found not guilty during a high-profile trial in 1826.[64]

As Matthew Brown explains, disenchantment with the republican cause may have been behind MacGregor's abrupt identity U-turn, as he went from being a mercenary fighting for the Bolívarian revolution to a pro-Spanish absolutist.[65] In this light, MacGregor certainly reassessed his stance on South America's republicans after Bolívar, enraged by the losses at Rio de la Hacha and Porto Bello, expelled him from his revolutionary army. Yet MacGregor's about-face was not solely due to newfound feelings for absolutist institutions better able to serve his own interests. After being kicked out of France following his attention-grabbing trial, MacGregor was also keen to get back into Bolívar's good books. In a letter dated December 24, 1826, MacGregor begged Bolívar to lift "this odious decree [and] that you would honor my pleasure for the cause of humanity, taking under your immediate protection the said territory of Poyais."[66]

But when he left abruptly for Paris after the Poyais scandal broke in London, MacGregor's conversion into a European pro-absolutist appears to have been a strategy to allow him to raise funds somewhere other than

London, where his efforts to borrow the capital needed to develop Poyais were now stymied by a major obstacle, as support firmed in the world of finance and trade for the political and military activities of other Latin America's revolutionary movements. The publication a few months earlier in the *Quarterly Review* of a scathing critique of the Poyais project, which accused MacGregor of seeking to build a rival territory that would compete with the Bolívarian campaign for independence, was certainly behind some of his difficulties in raising the funds needed for Poyais (such as the departure of John Lowe). Since Poyais could no longer be presented as yet another South American revolutionary project, its access to financial backing from the City of London seems to have been closed off. Worse still, being labelled as anti-Colombian would have been a serious handicap for anyone seeking to raise money in London at that time among merchant bankers involved in one way or another in providing financial support for other Latin American independence projects. Amid increased trading in Latin American securities on the Foreign Stock Market, many of the City's merchant bankers openly backed republican projects. A large reception was even organized in November 1822 at a London tavern in honor of Antonio Francisco Zea, Colombia's diplomatic representative.[67] A petition signed by many merchant bankers, calling on the government to formally recognize the newly independent states of South America, including Colombia, was also presented to the House of Commons in June 1824.[68]

With his hasty departure from London in 1823, MacGregor distanced himself from Poyais, at least in London. From that point on, Richardson acted as the figurehead for the project in the City, and MacGregor's name appears only sporadically in documents. However, MacGregor's withdrawal from his own venture was not a major stumbling block for Richardson and his partners.

With MacGregor gone, Richardson pressed on with the plan to issue bond certificates from the new loan discussed with Hendriks in August 1823, which was intended to pay for sending the *Albion* to Poyais. To do this, he had new securities printed. Dated October 6, 1823, each certificate bore the handwritten signatures of a witness (J. Schmied), a notary (H. Durien), and Richardson himself, who was described as having received full authority from MacGregor to issue the securities.[69] Printed by James Whiting, a well-known printer of English lottery tickets, the new certificates were magnificently decorated (Fig. 16).[70] Their intricate designs were intended to prevent forgeries. Yet like the certificates issued by other Latin American states such as Colombia for its loan of 1824, they may also have been a way of sending a strong message of official and sovereign legitimacy, highlighting a borrower's ability to implement these security features in its own bonds.[71]

The new Poyais certificates had sixty detachable coupons that gave the right, when torn off and presented, to payment by Perring, Shaw, Barber & Co. of a semiannual dividend at an annual interest rate of 5 percent. As stated on the coupons attached to the certificate, the dividends were to be paid over a period of thirty years, after which the loan would be redeemed in full. The certificates bore a declaration signed "Gregor MacGregor, P." (with "P." possibly standing for "Prince"), and the loan was described as secured by "all the Revenues of the said STATE OF POYAIS" and by a duty of 2.5 percent laid on all merchandise imported into the territory. The funds raised were to be used not only for the general development of Poyais but also to establish a sinking fund financed by future revenues from the territory, which would be used over time to pay off the debt. MacGregor's declaration, dated September 15, 1823, as he was journeying to France, was signed before a witness, George Clarke, and a notary from Boulogne-sur-Mer, Achille Dutertre.[72]

The amount of the loan printed on the certificates was £200,000, divided according to the printed information into two thousand securities, each with a face value of £100. But the loan was supposed to be for £300,000. At least, this is what seems to have been initially intended as per the original agreement with MacGregor and according to a draft manuscript of the certificate that MacGregor had with him on his journey to France and also to information found in Joseph Mérilhou's papers.[73] This is further confirmed by Richard Gregg, who undertook the arduous task of recompiling the serial numbers of these securities and found that three thousand one-hundred-pound certificates were indeed printed.[74] Their combined face value was thus £300,000, as agreed by Richardson and Hendriks. The exact reason for the discrepancy, which was seemingly decided in MacGregor's absence, is somewhat vague. It may have been that deliberately underestimating the number of bonds in circulation was seen as a way to dupe potential buyers and potentially boost the price of the bonds, at least when they were issued.

Figure 16. Poyais bond certificate, October 1823. Source: "Poyais Share Certificate A501," 1823, British Museum London, Coins & Medals CIB.14660 © The Trustees of the British Museum.

As contractor for the new loan, Hendriks found himself in possession of three thousand share certificates. The issue price of the certificates was £10—a full £90 less than the printed face value of £100—and could be paid in two £5 installments.[75] Hendriks thus undertook to provide £30,000 to Richardson.[76] Obviously, Hendriks stood to make a sizable personal profit if he managed to offload the securities for more than their issue price. Through trading on the Foreign Stock Market throughout October 1823, Hendriks managed to keep the price of the Poyais securities above £10, thanks notably to advertisements in the press highlighting the new loan's attractive terms.[77] According to the *Course of the Exchange*, Poyais bonds in turn traded at between £10 and £17 during that period.[78]

However, the furor accompanying the return of the *Honduras Packet* and *Kennersley Castle* escapees spelled yet more trouble for Poyais. It should be remembered that after their rescue from Black River, the emigrants were taken to Belize. After receiving treatment, some were offered a free crossing back to Britain on a ship chartered by the Belizean magistracy. James Hastie and his family were among the evacuees. After arriving in London on October 13, 1823, they were quickly brought before the Lord Mayor by one Mr. Prince, who was a member of the Court of Common Council, the City of London's primary decision-making body. Prince called for justice to be done and for financial assistance to be provided to the Poyais emigrants and especially to any orphaned children. He begged the Lord Mayor to provide assistance to the returning settlers, whom he presented as the victims of a diabolical fraud.

Hastie and the other emigrants were questioned about the events that led to their evacuation from Moskitia at a public hearing with the Lord Mayor. According to a transcription of the hearing published on October 21 in the *Times* and the *Morning Chronicle*, the witnesses claimed to have been recruited by MacGregor on the basis of scurrilous lies.[79] Hastie reportedly said that his dealings with the local Indigenous people, who were outraged by the settlers' presence there, had shown him that no sovereign Poyais state truly existed. Instead of a developed colony complete with a theater, as promised by the lively descriptions provided by the Poyais agents, Hastie had found nothing but an empty beach. In his absence, MacGregor was constantly presented as the cause of all the ills of the refugees. The mere mention of his name led to calls of "Yaw! Yaw!" and widespread condemnation by those present at the hearing conducted by the Lord Mayor.

The Lord Mayor, who approved payment of assistance to help the Scottish settlers to return to Edinburgh, left the hearing convinced that he had never before heard of such a deception. Prince also offered to set up a charitable fund to support Poyais orphans. He said that he, together with his brother and Messrs. Fry and Chapman, had deposited a sum of money in an account with a bank run by Fry and Chapman. Interestingly, the banking house happened to be the same institution that was in charge of paying the interest on the Peru loan of 1822.[80] Joseph Fry's wife even volunteered to help the young girls rescued from the Poyais misadventure.

The next day, however, on reading reports of his and his comrades' testimonies in the London papers, Hastie was taken aback and claimed that they in no way matched what had been said the previous day. He added that his hearing before the Lord Mayor, to whom he expressed immense gratitude for providing financial assistance, had been primarily orchestrated by Prince, who seemingly had business ties to Belizean magistrate Marshall Bennett and wanted to discredit MacGregor's project even further.[81]

In an affidavit dated October 22, 1823, submitted to the Lord Mayor, signed by himself and five other returnees from Black River—and further backed up a few months later by the publication of the tale of his own journey to Poyais—Hastie claimed that the published report of the hearing before the Lord Mayor conveyed a false image of MacGregor. Hastie described MacGregor as an honest man, not the evil liar and crook portrayed by the *Times* article of the previous day. MacGregor had not only footed the bill for their passage to Poyais but had never made any claim that Poyais was a wealthy and well-governed state. In fact, the discontent of many of the settlers on arriving at the Shore was fueled by the ravings of a few passengers on the *Kennersley Castle* who were delighted at leaving Britain behind and had possibly overromanticized their new settlement. According to the signatories of the affidavit, the failure of Poyais could not be attributed to MacGregor alone. It was, in fact, due mainly to poor recruitment, with a surfeit of soldiers and other people in command positions who were unsuitable for building a new colony from scratch.[82]

Three days after these rectifications were issued, an anonymous statement published in the *Times* accused Richardson of forcing Hastie and his fellow evacuees to write the affidavit exonerating MacGregor and his agents.[83] Outraged, Richardson dispatched a tough-looking former soldier to carry a message directly to Prince. Accusing him of being behind the claims against him, Richardson challenged Prince to a duel. The affair was eventually brought before the Lord Mayor, who arrested Richardson for disturbing the peace and refused to release him unless bail was paid. Challenging Prince to a duel, in the knowledge that this would likely end in jail rather than an actual confrontation, was surely a tactic used by Richardson to clear his name after it had been sullied by the previous day's accusations.[84] His arrest was short-lived: James William Sowerby, the London steam engine merchant and holder of Poyais scrips purchased from Richardson, and Herman Hendriks stood as guarantors and paid the money to secure his release.[85]

Successive reports of these events further eroded the financial foundations of a project already rocked by the earlier desertions of James Ogilvie and John Lowe. Poyais was henceforth painted as a dubious sovereign project led by an incompetent adventurer who could not even prove his legal ownership of the territory he hoped to develop.[86] These problems were exacerbated by a letter published in the *Times* by Marshall Bennett and George Westby, which, in addition to an account of the humanitarian evacuation of Poyais, included a statement by George Frederic rescinding MacGregor's concession. The two Belizean magistrates said:

> There is no Poyais sea or city of Poyais in existence, nor any appearance in that part of the country to warrant such an assertion; and indeed, to sum up the whole, we cannot better exemplify it than by declaring that the whole scheme of the establishment has been built upon the baseless fabric of a vision.[87]

With MacGregor in Paris, and Poyais now being touted as a monumental fraud, Richardson and some of his followers may have begun to envision an ending that was a little less glorious than initially expected. Plagued by accusations of being a fraudulent venture, MacGregor's commercial plans and, above all, his financial project suddenly seemed harder to realize. Those problems were evidenced by the judicial scandals facing Richardson and other agents of the Poyais scheme, combined with the repudiation of the concession granted by King George Frederic, on which the entire MacGregor project ultimately rested. Richardson and other Poyais bondholders nevertheless made a last attempt: they tried to recover some of the nonperishable goods confiscated by the magistracy. These were valuable assets, as the three ships chartered and dispatched to Poyais, the *Honduras Packet*, the *Kennersley Castle*, and the *Skeene*, had transported provisions and construction materials worth around £22,000.[88] As investors, they wanted to make sure that the money invested in the shipments of materials and provisions sent to set up the settlement was not confiscated by the Belizean magistracy without compensation.

George Augustus Low was dispatched to Poyais to retrieve what he could.[89] Like MacGregor, Low was a former British officer who had fought in the Bolívarian armies. He enlisted with James Towers English, an Irish mercenary in command of a British legion assembled in 1818, but then fought with republican forces until sometime in 1823. After the disappointment of his annulled marriage to Mary English, the widow of James Towers English (who had died in 1819) and a merchant woman active in Britain's Central American trade, Low was expelled from the revolutionary army for misconduct and decided to throw in his lot with MacGregor, his former brother in arms.[90] Since some of his friends had "large properties at stake in this colony [Poyais]," Low volunteered to travel to assess the situation on the Shore in the wake of the dispatches recounting the disasters that had befallen the *Honduras Packet* and the *Kennersley Castle*. While en route for Poyais, he stopped off in the Bahamas and Colombia to settle some personal business and eventually made it to Black River on August 24, 1823.

After being shown around by Indigenous guides for a few days, Low saw that neither the settlers nor the materials that were supposed to have been unloaded a few weeks earlier were there. His guides told him that the British Honduran magistrate Marshall Bennett had evacuated the entire settlement to British Honduras, including the settlers and, above all, their equipment.[91] Low then sailed for British Honduras. On arriving in Belize, on September 5 and 9, 1823, Low filed a formal complaint with the magistracy. Referring to himself as a colonel in the service of Colombia, he requested to right to lodge a complaint naming Marshall Bennett, the owner of the *Mexican Eagle*, along with magistrate Thomas Pickstock, Bennett's secretary William Walsh, John W. Wright, and George Westby.[92] He also wanted to name Colonel Hall, the man initially tasked with leading the settlement project and who had authorized the Black River evacuation.

According to standard practice followed by the colony in the absence of a notary, William Gentle, in his capacity as magistrate, was appointed to hear the complaint. Acting in his own name and that of General Sir Gregor MacGregor, Major William John Richardson, and—importantly—"other merchants of Great Britain," Low formally accused Bennett and his men of appropriating and making off with the property and cargo of the plaintiffs carried aboard the *Honduras Packet* and the *Kennersley Castle*.[93] However, after Low refused to provide supporting documents to the magistrate hearing the complaint, the case was dismissed. Low justified his refusal to present the ownership deeds for the cargo contained in the ships sent to Poyais on the grounds that he did not consider that the dispute could be settled under the law applied by the magistrates of British Honduras. He argued instead that English law should be followed. Indeed, did he not consider that all the protagonists involved in the theft of the Poyais goods cited in his complaint were "from Great Britain"?

Instead, Low returned to London, where he published a pamphlet titled *The Belise Merchants Unmasked* in 1824, which basically conveyed his deep disagreement with the settlement's legal practices. In it, he was scathingly critical of what he described as the magistrates' total complicity in the downfall of the Poyais project. Low openly accused the magistracy, led by Bennett, of conspiring to bring down a venture that might have threatened the magistrates' business activities. Low's pamphlet described British Honduras as a territory in the grip of an oligarchy that manipulated the settlement's legal foundations to its own ends. In his view, the utter absence of any lawyers or any other man of law in the settlement perfectly illustrated the magistrates' control and unfettered power.[94]

Low's complaint ultimately sounds like an admission of failure to recover the goods from the Poyais project, after they had been seized by a legal authority that he did not recognize but against which he and the Poyais bondholders were totally powerless. The loss of the goods was a major setback for the architects of the Poyais scheme, as the magistrates' seizure of the shipments of tools and foodstuffs—paid for at great expense by the promoters of MacGregor's project—was upheld by a legal system over which they had little power. Belizean "habits and customs," in other words the sole authority of the magistracy, prevailed.

Powerless to recover their cargo from the first two ships sailing for Poyais, Richardson and other investors sought to enlist the help of the British government. On learning that their third ship, the *Albion*, and its cargo had been seized by the magistracy some weeks earlier, Richardson and the other main Poyais backers (Sowerby, Nicholson, Johnson, Thick, and Alexander) wrote a joint letter in early March 1824 to Earl Bathurst, Secretary of State for the Colonies. Stating that they were acting on behalf of the cazique of Poyais, they protested the theft by the magistrates of British Honduras of equipment worth some £30,000 that had been sent to Moskitia. Richardson and the letter's other authors called for ministerial intervention or assistance, claiming that the magistrates had not only refused to return the confiscated goods, on the grounds that the matter was not subject to British law, but had also forced the dismantlement of the colonization project currently underway in Poyais.[95] As a response from Bathurst was not immediately forthcoming, a few weeks later Richardson wrote to Under-Secretary of State for the Colonies Robert Wilmot-Horton, reminding him of their request.[96]

Meanwhile, Richardson and the other Poyais investors made another attempt to recover their property. Low was again dispatched to British Honduras. Traveling aboard the schooner *Mary*, on May 24, 1824, he announced to Superintendent Codd his arrival at the port of Belize, once again with the goal of recovering the property seized by the local magistracy.[97] This time, though, he was prepared to do whatever necessary to try to recover even a fraction of the Poyaisian investment, even if that meant doing battle with the British Honduran legal system. The magistrates, however, had no intention of settling any questions concerning appropriation of the *Albion*'s cargo. Rather, Low's return handed them an unexpected opportunity to respond to his attacks on them in *The Belise Merchants Unmasked*. They sued him for slandering the three British Honduran men principally named in the pamphlet, namely magistrates Bennett, Wright, and Pickstock.

The King v. Low George Augustine was brought before the Grand Court of Belize on June 29, 1824, almost one month after the arrival of Low, who had spent the intervening time behind bars in Belize. Chaired by an assembly of magistrates, the court was challenged by Low as soon as its composition was announced. But his objections were denied and the procedure continued, with statements from the defense. The arguments put forward by the magistrates named in the pamphlet followed a two-pronged strategy. The first objective was to demonstrate that most of the British Honduran magistrates accused by Low of causing Poyais's downfall were not present during the Belizean intervention on the Shore. Second, citing excerpts from Low's pamphlet, they argued that it was unthinkable that the magistrates could be described in such derogatory terms by an individual who was completely unknown to them. At the same time, the defense attempted to prove that Low was indeed the pamphlet's author, for although the document was signed with his surname and initials (G. A. Low), Low always denied being the writer.[98]

Of course, the magistrates' case against Low was based first and foremost on charges of libel and publication of defamatory statements. But the proceedings were about more than just that. Above all, they were a challenge to judicial legitimacy. As in his first confrontation with the British Honduran legal system, Low made a point of challenging the very legitimacy of the Belizean court. Any case involving British merchants had to be settled in an English court. Yet in contrast to Low's assertions, the magistrates hearing the case made sure to systematically quash these claims. They presented themselves as the proper representatives of British royal judicial authority. The case's title alone seemed to confer legitimacy upon them. Supposedly acting in the name of the crown, the magistracy was portrayed as an extension of British royal authority. More precisely, it argued that the British Honduran legal system was an extension of that headed by the king of England, with appropriate adjustments to meet the settlement's particular needs through the creation of a specific legal regime based on local "habits and customs."[99]

In his defense, Low presented himself as physically infirm and weak, apparently because of an attack of gout, but he said that his conscience was clear and he considered his imprisonment and trial to be illegal.[100] In addition to challenging the assertion that he was the author of the pamphlet named in the case, he insisted that the Belizean court was not competent to judge the suit. Low, who based his arguments on the writings of a well-known judge, William Blackstone, said that for his crime (insofar as his actions could be considered as such) to be prosecuted locally, the incriminating text also had to have been produced locally. As he saw it, only a London court was competent. Low therefore challenged the authority and right claimed by the local magistracy to hear cases that, by its own interpretation, were deemed to affect the interests of British Honduras.

In his closing statement, Magistrate Wright urged the jurors to impose the harshest possible sentence on the defendant for smearing the business and political reputation of the magistrates with his pamphlet. As proof that the legal proceedings went beyond a simple case of defamation, he also sought to justify not only the seizure by Belizean magistrates of the provisions and other property brought to Black River aboard the Poyais ships, but also their subsequent sale to meet the escalating costs of rescuing the Poyais settlers. Above all, Wright described Low's pamphlet as an attack on the settlement's judicial and political system. Justifying his arguments, but also the entire trial, as representative of and based on an extension of English common law, the magistrate denounced Low's actions as an attack not only on the legal system embodied by the Belizean magistracy but also therefore on that of Great Britain as a whole.

Confident of winning the case, the presiding magistrates and those called on to testify against Low were nevertheless surprised by the time taken by the jury to reach a decision. The following evening, to speed up the jury's deliberations, the magistracy ordered the police officer responsible for supervising the jurors and protecting them from outside influence to stop providing the jury with any more food, drink, or lighting without the express authorization of the court, that is, the magistrates themselves.[101] Duly prodded, the jury presented itself before the court the next morning. To widespread surprise, the jurors found Low not guilty, for want of sufficient proof.[102] A furious Bennett accused one of the jurors of harboring grievances against him, notably over a property-line dispute. Wright and Pickstock also suspected that a third party, one Captain Willer, who was opposed to the magistracy's policies, had swayed the jury's decision.

The same day, Superintendent Codd received a letter signed by Bennett, Wright, and Pickstock informing him of their resignation with immediate effect. The magistrates said that they felt unable to remain in their position unless the affront to their political and business reputation was cleared.[103] More than a mere exoneration, the jury's decision was a clear attack or at least a fierce critique aimed at the oligarchy's regime. This may have had something to do with the makeup of these juries. Jurors had to be officially recognized inhabitants of the settlements, namely people of British descent who had been resident for a number of years. Most of these were small and medium-sized mahogany business owners, who were typically financially dependent on the wealthy natural-resource exporters who also controlled the settlement's executive and judicial branches of power.[104]

Witnessing a shift that could potentially threaten Belize's social and political stability, Superintendent Codd sought to intervene. Up until that point, the magistrates had seemingly played on his complete ignorance of Poyais to get around some of the obstacles put up by his predecessor, Superintendent George Arthur, to block the slavery practices employed by the settlement's main mahogany cutters. Appalled by the misfortunes of the Poyaisians who had sought refuge in Belize in April 1823, Codd had no hesitation in giving his strong backing to the "humanitarian" mission led by Bennett.[105] In a report to his London superiors about the situation in Poyais following the Black River evacuation, he even described the magistrates in glowing terms. As he said in the introduction to his report, which was subsequently published in London in 1824, his primary goal in writing the document was to restore the reputation of the magistrates. Their honor had been besmirched by the slanderous accusations made against them, particularly in Low's pamphlet, which accused the British Honduras cutters of causing Poyais's downfall. In response, Codd asserted that it fell to him to elucidate the "true situation of the imaginary state of Poyais."[106]

Convinced that the three resigning magistrates were justified in their actions, and that the author of *The Belise Merchants Unmasked* had acted in bad faith, Codd called for a retrial. Responding to the superintendent's request, two jurors from the initial trial came before the court. While claiming not to challenge the previous day's ruling exonerating Low, they nevertheless acknowledged that a formal judicial ruling was needed on the matter of the slanderous nature of the pamphlet purportedly written by the accused.[107] The sudden challenge handed the magistracy legal grounds to bring a new suit against Low. Of course, he protested fiercely against the naming of a new jury, insisting that under English law, the procedure could be repeated only for the benefit of the defendant, and not for that of his accusers. Low's arguments were once again dismissed, and a new trial was organized. The three presiding magistrates conducted an examination that was virtually the same as the first, right down to the questions and answers, with the sole exception that a new jury was appointed.

After a brief deliberation, the jury in the second trial once again found Low not guilty due to insufficient evidence. However, in a statement sent to Superintendent Codd, the jurors said that their verdict in no way implied any loss of stature or prestige for the three magistrates named in the pamphlet, and that their resignation therefore was unfounded. In fact, the jurors begged Bennett, Pickstock, and Wright to resume their duties, which they subsequently did as if nothing had happened.[108]

The magistrates then published their own book. Titled *Falsehood Detected*, it told potential readers beyond the colony that their reputation had been formally restored and their name cleared, after being sullied by the accusations of William Wilberforce regarding their involvement in Indigenous slavery and the claims of Poyais agents. Published in Jamaica and circulated in London, the document was written by Hector Hall, the officer in charge of settling the first Poyais emigrants.[109] Who better than a former Poyais official to challenge his former bosses and restore the credit of the Belizean magistrates who had rescued him from a failing settlement? The book essentially retold the tragedy of the Poyais settlers from the perspective of the man who was in charge—and who was so grateful to his Belizean saviors. Hall's diagnosis was clear: Poyais failed because those in charge ignored the need for proper recruitment for the sake of economic gain. Crafted as a response to Low's document, *Falsehood Detected* accused the pamphlet of being nothing but a pack of lies and libelous remarks about the magistrates, who had acted entirely selflessly during the Poyais affair to rescue the victims of a scheme designed to trick them into believing in the existence of an imaginary country.

Although the Low trial gave the magistrates an opportunity to put themselves forward once again as the saviors of the hapless emigrants, it was nevertheless a serious test of the exceptionalism of the legal regime controlled by the Belizean mahogany oligarchy. At a local level, the legal attack mounted by Low enabled the settlement's small and medium-sized natural-resource companies to send a clear signal to an oligarchy that took its economic, political, and social position for granted. More broadly, the failed attempt by the Poyais backers to recoup their investments underlined the continued exceptionalism of a legal regime that safeguarded the legal and political independence of British enterprises based in British Honduras.

Low's trial allowed the magistracy to avoid having to rule on the question of ownership rights to the confiscated Poyais shipments. Although Low was ultimately found not guilty, the rehabilitation of the resigning magistrates lent legitimacy to their seizure. Richardson and the other Poyais bondholders had to content themselves with not losing any more money to the project.

Surely grateful that they had not yet paid the additional installments that would normally have been due on their bonds, many Poyais financial backers moved on. Writing to MacGregor, Hendriks himself said:

> Your cause has been injured by the selection of men not fit to be entrusted with the management of the settlement, they have thwarted your views, and the property sent out by the *Honduras Packet* and *Kennersley Castle* has been sacrificed; some lives have also been lost from the endurance of toil, fatigue, and want; and that same public blame you for it [. . .] all this is lost, and I repeat, all your future hopes of title, possession, or any thing else, are also lost.[110]

Despite these British Honduran attacks challenging the legitimacy of Poyais as a political entity and questioning the credibility of the whole colonial venture, Poyais bonds continued to trade on the Foreign Stock Market. On the day following publication of the letter by the magistracy stating that Poyais did not exist, Poyais securities traded in a range of around £10 to £15. Even after suits were brought against MacGregor for endangering the *Kennersley Castle* refugees, the bonds continued to trade at similar prices. Speculation probably fueled some of the trading in Poyais securities on the Foreign Stock Market, as investors hoped that the value of their bonds would rise on news of an improvement in the colony's fortunes.

But continued trading in Poyais bonds, as recorded in the exchange's official list, may also have reflected the need to keep these transactions within the Foreign Stock Market. For, in addition to making it easier to sell securities and facilitate access to the City's capital, trading on the Foreign Stock Market also established the legal framework applicable to disputes between investors and holders of securities. As Marc Flandreau shows, the London Stock Exchange and the Foreign Stock Market acted independently as legal bodies with full authority over transactions in all of the securities recognized and traded within each market.[111] Briefly, these markets enjoyed a kind of extraterritoriality within the British legal system, which prohibited certain types of contracts and trades as defined by the Barnard Act of 1734.[112]

The executive committees of the London Stock Exchange and the Foreign Stock Market were in charge of settling disputes between creditors about on-exchange trades, often through arbitration. These committees were known to impose significant settlement terms in their arbitration rulings.[113] However, there were advantages to settling disputes within these markets, not least the fact that cases involving financial transactions could be settled much faster by one of the committees compared with the standard process offered through the British legal system. The committee of the Foreign Stock Market needed sometimes just a few days to rule, whereas the Court of Chancery might have taken several months.[114] In fact, the Court of Chancery was widely criticized in this regard: Charles Dickens's novel *Bleak House*, published a few years later, served up a biting criticism of that court and the glacial pace of its dispute settlement regime.[115]

Public exposure was also relatively restricted. The press loved stories about British court cases, especially ones involving some kind of conflict or fraud.[116] But reports on the disputes settled by these markets were essentially confined to meeting minutes. Although information was sometimes circulated through the *Times*, publications dealing with cases brought before the committees usually came about as a result of internal consultations, with details about disputes between market members sometimes made public through pamphlets and letters—some highly poetic—to newspaper editors.[117] Therefore, the decision to publish such information was often made by the very participants in the dispute.

As a rule, these markets formed a legal environment that was reserved essentially for their respective members. The press typically had access only by proxy. Bringing a dispute for arbitration before the committee of one of these exchanges could thus be a way to ensure that the matter was settled in an independent, closed environment made up of known and recognized peers.[118] Some Poyais bondholders understood this very well. In August 1825, for example, the Foreign Stock Market Committee was convened to settle a disagreement over Poyais bonds between two market members: Herman Hendriks and one Edward Josephs. The quarrel emerged over the calculations used to convert the Poyais scrips of 1822 and 1823.[119]

But this system did not suit everyone. It might be imposed on borrowers or clash with a different legal regime, notably in instances where the debt was contracted without the borrower's full and informed consent. In this regard, the performance and fate of the Poyais loans appear to have been affected by the experiences of other foreign political and trade initiatives. In particular, this was the case for those of Colombia and Greece, which had to settle financial disputes with investors after engaging, voluntarily or otherwise, in contracts involving large quantities of capital in London during the 1820s. Highlighting the specific features of these cases helps to more accurately describe the environment in which Poyais investors and securities were operating and reveals developments in dispute settlement practices in the London capital markets of the day. The cases of Colombia and Greece offer particularly instructive insights into how the executive committees of the City stock markets were influenced in their decisions regarding the securities traded on those markets, including, ultimately, the Poyais bonds.

The Colombia loan of 1822 is a prime example. Antonio Francisco Zea had been granted a power of attorney in December 1819 by his friend Simón Bolívar, the president of the Republic of Colombia as envoy extraordinary and minister plenipotentiary to establish diplomatic, commercial, and financial relations with European powers and mercantile communities. On March 13, 1822, Zea signed an agreement with three London merchant bankers—Charles Herring, William Graham, and John Diston Powles—for a 6 percent loan of £2 million. The loan was divided into twenty thousand bearer bonds with a nominal value of £100. Briefly, the purpose of the loan was to redeem outstanding debentures contracted since the 1810s to finance the recruitment of British mercenaries committed to the American republican cause and the purchase of military equipment.

Quickly oversubscribed and actively traded in London, the new 1822 loan was a great success in the eyes of English financiers, but not so much in those of the Colombian Congress, which openly disapproved of Zea's loan. In June 1822, the Congress argued that Zea—who in the meantime had died—had exceeded a mandate that was no longer valid. Indeed, he had been appointed before the signing of the constitution of the Republic of Colombia at the 1821 Congress of Cúcuta, which terminated all the "faculties of all its former functionaries and public agents." Put another way, Colombia considered its own loan illegitimate.[120] However, deeming that the mistake might in the end provide a significant windfall of funds, Colombia's lawmakers decided to recognize and honor the debt. But in a letter to the committee of the Foreign Stock Market delivered through a Mr. Jones (an agent of Herring, Graham, and Powles), they stipulated that they wanted to name the judges responsible for hearing any potential future disputes with the country's creditors.[121]

In other words, the Republic of Colombia refused to recognize the Foreign Stock Market Committee as the default court of arbitration.

Colombia's stance caused consternation in the City, as it had the potential to set a precedent for other borrowers thinking about challenging the institution's authority in the event of future disputes. John William Richardson (not to be confused with the William John Richardson on MacGregor's payroll), a holder of Colombian securities, wrote to the Foreign Stock Market Committee. Based on information supposedly obtained directly from the vice president of Colombia, Francisco de Paula Santander, he suggested that Jones had merely mistranslated the message from the Colombian government, which had already ratified the loan's principal clauses and had sent a senator to London to sort out the problems caused by Zea in his haste to contract the debt.[122]

Although seemingly settled, Colombia's challenge to the position of the committee of the Foreign Stock Market as the de facto court of arbitration for disputes involving its bondholders nevertheless meant that the committee needed to act to head off new potential challenges. Consequently, committee member Joseph Cohen proposed at a meeting of the Foreign Stock Market Committee in November 1823 to amend the market's internal rules. Cohen, who was a business partner and brother-in-law of Nathan Rothschild, recommended that only new foreign securities given express approval by the committee should be authorized to be introduced to the exchange.[123] Considered by an ad hoc subcommittee, Cohen's question eventually led to the adoption of a resolution on November 19, 1823, following extensive discussions that are only partly recorded in the institution's minutes. The resolution states: "The Person authorised by the Committee to publish the Prices of Foreign Stocks, shall in future only Publish such as may be laid before the Committee for their Sanction."[124] Put another way, rather than regulating assessments of the quality of new bonds traded on the exchange, as Cohen had requested, the committee decided to restrict the official publication of prices to those of securities that had received express authorization from the Foreign Stock Market to be traded. Until then, this role had been played by Wetenhall, publisher of the *Course of the Exchange*.

Yet the next day, the committee clarified its decision. It stated that it would recognize as bona fide any security issued in connection with a new sovereign loan traded on the market, provided that the loan was duly contracted by a diplomatic representative or another person with the authority to wield effective sovereign power.[125] With this move, the Foreign Stock Market Committee empowered itself to rule on the quality of foreign loans to be traded on the City exchanges in the future. Market access would be granted only to political entities that the committee itself decided to recognize. Likewise, the committee itself would decide who the proper representatives of those entities were.

Cohen wanted to go further. In addition to making the introduction of new foreign securities subject to a review by the Foreign Stock Market Committee, he wanted to strip Wetenhall of his de facto monopoly on publishing the market prices of foreign funds in his *Course of the Exchange*, as he felt that the prices were not published "correctly."[126] Unfortunately for Cohen, the committee itself took a more benevolent attitude toward Wetenhall. Preferring to make the role played by the *Course of the Exchange* official, it elected merely to require Wetenhall, who seemed contrite when summoned before the committee, to publish the prices of preapproved securities only.[127]

In this way, the Foreign Stock Market Committee set itself up as the only body that could rule on the market introduction of new sovereign bonds. It also became the sole authority with the power to recognize borrower countries as truly existing. Persuading a member of the exchange to introduce securities to the trading floor, in hopes that sufficient transactions would prompt Wetenhall to list the price in his *Course of the Exchange*—as was the case when MacGregor's initial loans were introduced to the London Stock Exchange and the Foreign Stock Market in 1822 and 1823 respectively—would no longer suffice. From this point onward, the committee of the Foreign Stock Market reviewed each new sovereign loan put forward for trading. It did so for the loans of Austria (December 1823), Mexico (January 1824) and Guatemala (April 1824).[128]

The loan contracted by Greece in 1824 is particularly illustrative of the new financial and political dynamics governing the introduction of new bonds on the City's stock markets. Like Colombia's challenge to the Foreign Stock Market's dispute resolution system, the Greek loan of 1824 is not directly related to the story of Poyais. But it had a specific bearing on how the London capital markets worked and thus shaped the fate of MacGregor's financial dealings and political and business ventures.

On January 21, 1824, the Foreign Stock Market Committee received a letter from John Bowring, a British merchant formerly involved in raising funds for Spanish liberals, who went on to represent the interests of the London Philhellenic Committee set up in 1822 to support Greek independence. Boasting high-profile members such as Jeremy Bentham, Joseph Hume, and Lord Byron, the Philhellenic Committee was raising funds to provide material assistance to the Greek independence movement, at the behest of Jean Orlandos and Andreas Louriottes, merchants and representatives in the National Assembly at Epidaurus.[129] At the time, Bowring was representing the financial interests of the Greek independence movement and preparing its first loan issue in the City of London. Yet in his letter to the Foreign Stock Market Committee, Bowring denounced another proposal for a Greek loan, this one led by Count General de Wintz. Bowring described de Wintz as lacking lawful authority assigned by the independent Greek government, whose own legitimacy was openly disputed, including by the Chancellor and Foreign Minister of the Austrian Empire, Klemenz Wenzel von Metternich.[130] In Bowring's view, there could only be one Greek loan: his own. So he asked the committee to consider it as the sole true Greek loan, since it had been authorized by two lawful representatives empowered by the future borrower's Parliament. He added that Orlandos and Louriottes were already en route for London to formalize the financial mission entrusted to the Philhellenic Committee.

The following day, de Wintz defended his own financial enterprise before the Foreign Stock Market Committee.[131] De Wintz was a Montenegrin officer, who had been made a general by Louis XVI and a Knight of the Order of Saint Stanislaus by the king of Poland. He was proposing to raise money to help Greece repel Ottoman forces by capturing Cyprus for the Knights of Malta.[132] De Wintz asked to be formally recognized as Greece's diplomatic representative based on the authority assigned by his unnamed contractors. Moreover, he requested formal recognition of his titles of nobility under the aristocratic orders of the Ancien Régime, which, he argued, were widely recognized by Austria, Prussia, and Russia. In other words, he asked to be treated on the same footing as Bowring.[133]

In view of these two requests, the committee had to decide which of the Greek bonds would be eligible for issue on the Foreign Stock Market. And in line with its own recent decisions, it had to take a position on recognizing the diplomatic representative of the sovereign borrower in question. After remaining silent on the issue for several days, on February 23, 1824, the Foreign Stock Market Committee abruptly ordered Wetenhall to list Bowring's Greek loan.[134] In so doing, it took a clear stance in favor of the independence movement backed by the London Philhellenic Committee. This decision coincided with the publication a few days earlier by Daniel Mocatta, Bowring's contractor, of a prospectus presenting a loan of £800,000, "to assist in bringing the pending contest to a just and happy conclusion," in anticipation of the "speedy recognition [of the Greek Nation] by the different Powers of Europe."[135]

Keen to offer formal and lawful recognition to Bowring's Greek project, the committee of the Foreign Stock Market needed to be able to base its decision on more solid-seeming evidence. Thus, in early March 1824, Orlandos and Louriottes wrote directly to the committee. Highlighting their position as the diplomatic representatives of the Greek National Assembly, they insisted that they did not want to dispute Ottoman sovereignty over Cyprus and implicitly denounced Wintz's loan.[136] William Evans, an eminent member of the Philhellenic Committee and a British MP, also wrote urging the Foreign Stock Market Committee to fully recognize Bowring's loan.[137] Backed by these new elements, the committee determined Bowring's Greek loan—and by extension the underlying political structure of the new state—to be bona fide, authorizing its inclusion in Wetenhall's list.

As the Colombian loan of 1823 and the Greek loan of 1824 show, from November 1823 onward, the Foreign Stock Market Committee took it upon itself to recognize the legitimacy of the underlying political entities responsible for issuing foreign loans. This would have significant ramifications for MacGregor and Poyais. At the time when the internal rules were changed, the *Course of the Exchange* was still recording the odd trade in Poyais bonds, which were listed at £5 when the Foreign Stock Market closed on November 28, 1823. Thereafter, however, trades dried up, and the Poyais price remained essentially empty for the following weeks. The return to London a few days earlier of MacGregor's first settlers, following their failed attempts to set up a base in Poyais and subsequent evacuation from the Shore by the magistrates of British Honduras, may have caused business in Poyais bonds to come to a standstill. Certainly no member of the Foreign Stock Market wanted to trade in the Poyais securities, preferring either to sell them off-exchange in trades that were not recorded by Wetenhall's list or to hold on to them in hopes that the Poyais situation might improve and so push the price up. Amid the prolonged absence of trading in Poyais bonds, Wetenhall withdrew the securities from the *Course of the Exchange* on January 23, 1824, pending a pickup in volumes. Unfortunately for MacGregor and his backers, the financial destiny of Poyais did not improve sufficiently following the bonds' removal from the official list.

On November 9, 1824, Edward Josephs, a holder of Poyais certificates, brought a case before the Foreign Stock Market Committee. Josephs said that a few weeks previously he had obtained 550 Poyais bonds for just over £4 each from one Mr. Symons. When Josephs attempted to sell his securities to a Mr. Zwinger a few days later, Zwinger had refused to go through with the deal on the grounds that the securities were "spurious & not marketable." Accusing Symons of pressuring him to buy the securities, Josephs asked the committee of the Foreign Stock Market to rule on the validity of the transactions made by the three parties and to convince Zwinger to acquire the Poyais bonds that he (Josephs) held.[138]

The securities involved in the dispute between Josephs, Symons, and Zwinger were not part of the 1823 Poyais loan. They actually belonged to a brand-new series issued in connection with MacGregor's latest financial scheme. Whether stubborn or merely opportunistic, some of MacGregor's agents tried in 1824 to bankroll yet another rescue of Poyais by once again raising capital in the City. With MacGregor seemingly still in Paris, his representatives proposed to issue a new loan on the Foreign Stock Market. This latest loan was to be worth £725,000, considerably larger than the previous fund-raising efforts. It was to be issued partly to repay the earlier loans and was to be divided into magnificent certificates with a face value of £250 or £500. Titled "Poyaisian Redemption Loan," the bonds were to be sold initially at 40 percent of their face value, with annual interest of 2 percent based on their face value payable for twenty years (Fig. 17).[139]

Josephs and Symons were at odds over these new Poyais bonds. But when Josephs asked Symons to explain the nature of the securities, the Foreign Stock Market Committee gave a definitive ruling, stating: "The Committee decide that the Poyais Bonds not being considered as Secu-

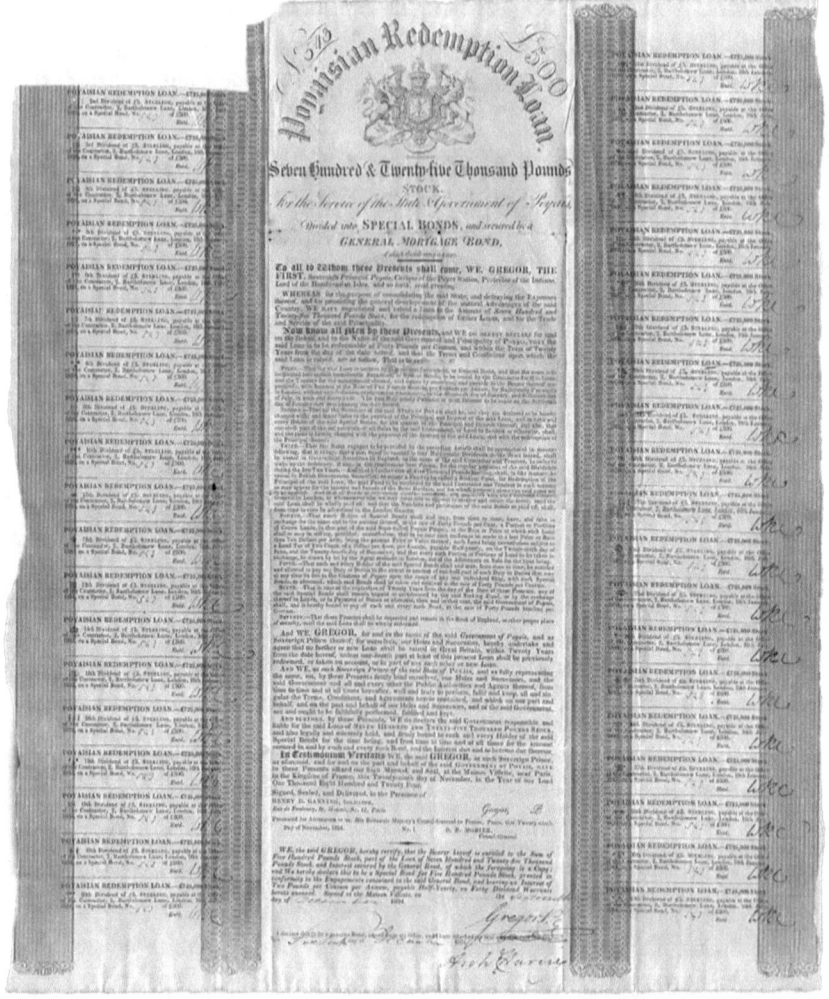

Figure 17. Poyais Redemption Loan bond certificate, 1824. Source: Courtesy of Scripoworld.

rities cognizable by the Committee they cannot interfere in this transaction."[140] Poyais's fate was sealed. While not saying it in so many words, the committee seemingly used the arbitration request from Josephs as an opportunity to decide not to get involved in matters related to a transaction involving securities it did not recognize. This was because the new Poyais securities had not gone through an authorization process similar to that undergone by other recent borrowers such as Greece. The Foreign Stock Market Committee also took the arbitration request as an opportunity to pronounce on the quality of the disputed bonds from the new Poyais loan of 1824. Consistent with decisions on the Colombia and Greece loans a few months earlier, the committee expressed a negative opinion on Poyais's political legitimacy as a borrower. Although the exact reasons why the committee reached this decision are not recorded in the minutes, it is possible that the bad reputation of MacGregor's venture and the lack of trading in Poyais bonds over several months played a part in stripping the project of its bona fide status. By this time, Poyais's notoriety had grown to such an extent that it was being compared to the infamous Darien scheme of the late 1690s. Highlighting this parallel, an author writing about Poyais in a Canadian journal just weeks earlier had remarked that "there perhaps never was a scheme, entered into with so great and general an avidity since the celebrated Darien settlement."[141]

By no longer recognizing the Poyais bonds, the Foreign Stock Market Committee sounded the death knell for any Poyais project, current or, especially, future. Thus, while the bonds of other not-yet-diplomatically-recognized Latin American states continued to be included in the official list, the legal fiction of Poyais was no longer maintained, at least on the Foreign Stock Market. So in addition to being portrayed as a massive fraud and having its bonds removed from Wetenhall's *Course of the Exchange*, MacGregor's project also now saw its bonds excluded from the Foreign Stock Market. No trade would ever be listed on it nor would any dispute over Poyais bonds be arbitrated by its committee. Even so, the bonds did not vanish from the City altogether. Now, though, they traded hands for pennies outside the Foreign Stock Market, exchanged by investors and speculators with limited interest in MacGregor's affairs or in Poyais.[142]

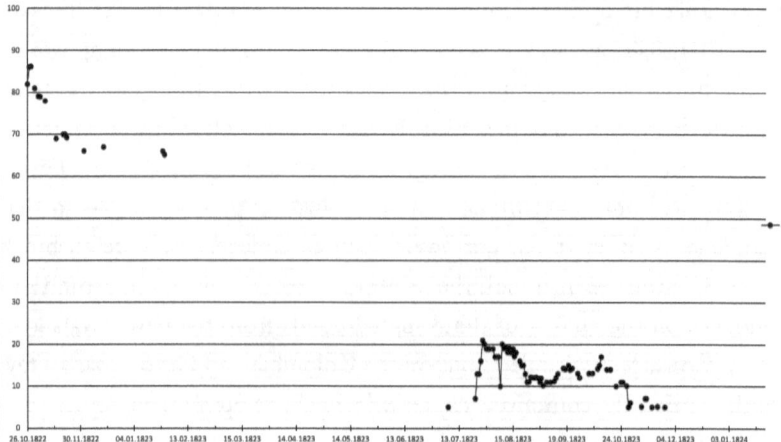

Chart 1. Price of Poyais Bonds Traded on the London Stock Exchange and Foreign Stock Market, 1822–1824. Source: Prices compiled by the author based on Wetenhall's *Course of the Exchange*, 1822–1824. Only daily closing prices were considered and were decimalized.

Undeterred by news of the fiasco surrounding the landings of the *Honduras Packet* and the *Kennersley Castle*, a number of major Poyais bondholders pressed on with the campaign to establish a British settlement on the Miskitu Shore. Led by William John Richardson, the project's backers dispatched two more ships, the *Skeene* and the *Albion*, loaded with settlers and provisions for Poyais, and met the chartering costs by issuing fresh loans in London. Although they set off full of hope, the subsequent arrivals likewise saw their efforts end in failure, and the ships' cargo was confiscated by the oligarchy controlled by the mahogany cutters of British Honduras. Keenly aware of the consequences attached to his position as formal political representative and figurehead for the Poyais sovereign loans after these fresh setbacks, MacGregor fled London. He headed for Paris, where he hoped to kick-start a new colonial venture without the baggage of his British misfortunes. MacGregor's abandonment did not dim the colonial enthusiasm of the investors recruited by Richardson. Seeing in Poyais an investment opportunity and potential returns, they made plans to organize new loans and dispatch more ships to Black River.

Two events dealt a deadly blow to any hopes of one day building a private British colony on the Shore, or at least of recovering some of the capital invested. First, English law did not apply to the dispute between the Poyais investors and the Belizean cutters who had confiscated the shipments sent to the settlement. Only the private colony of British Honduras, which was independent of Great Britain and controlled by the local oligarchy, had jurisdiction over the case. Second, amendments to the internal rules of the Foreign Stock Market compromised the present and future legitimacy of the Poyais legal fiction. Following disputes that brought it into conflict with Colombia and Greece, the Foreign Stock Market Committee decided to take responsibility for vetting the quality of new securities issued on the market, notably by ruling on the legitimacy of political projects underpinning new foreign loan issues.

SIX

Shadow Government

FRANZ KAFKA'S NOVEL *The Castle* narrates the misfortunes of K, a land surveyor apparently hired by the administrator of the titular castle. K tries desperately yet unsuccessfully to learn more about his mysterious assignment. His repeated setbacks stem mainly from the inaction of Klamm, a senior civil servant. Although Klamm never actually appears in the novel, he is arguably the real protagonist. Conspicuous by his absence, he nonetheless embodies a central figure whose reluctance to act is the root of K's misfortunes.[1]

Like the elusive bureaucrat who plays such a prominent role in *The Castle*, a shadowy institution lurks in the background of the Poyais affair, namely the Colonial Office, a government department overseen by the British Secretary of State for War and the Colonies and responsible for the affairs of the British colonies. In general, it was careful not to openly express an opinion on MacGregor's colonial plans. Yet it followed his every move from the outset. Several examples illustrate the extent to which the Colonial Office was kept well-informed of MacGregor's activities. As mentioned earlier, he wrote in March 1821 to the Chancellor of the Exchequer, Nicholas Vansittart, to announce that he had acquired the Poyais concession a few months prior. He said that he planned to turn his new territory into a colony that could ultimately benefit English trade as well as the new independence movements in Latin America. He also asked Vansittart for material and financial assistance to set up a campaign to promote British emigration to Poyais.[2]

Although Vansittart seems not to have answered, other members of the British government were mindful of MacGregor's plans for the Miskitu Shore. The Colonial Office, then headed by Earl Henry Bathurst, monitored the project, getting regular reports on the political and commercial situation of British Honduras by corresponding with local superintendents, first George Arthur, then Edward Codd.[3] In this way, information about Poyais reached London directly on several occasions. On June 20, 1823, shortly after British Honduran magistrates had evacuated Poyais, Codd sent Bathurst a report detailing the misfortunes of the Scottish settlers recruited by Mac-Gregor and taken to Belize.[4] On January 15, 1821, more than a year and a half before the Poyais loan was offered for sale, Superintendent Arthur wrote to Bathurst to tell him about a major concession that the king of the Miskitu had granted MacGregor.[5]

Although Bathurst usually received this kind of communication directly, he apparently paid scant attention to what was happening in Central America. As Douglas Murray-Young explains, the Colonial Office in the first part of the nineteenth century was still organized and governed on the basis of the dynamics that had emerged since its founding in 1794. The work of the secretariat was mainly handled by the Secretary of State, assisted by several clerks.[6] Often unable to deal with correspondence and other duties on his own, Bathurst was free to delegate tasks to his under-secretary or a clerk. Since he was closely involved in the affairs of the Cabinet, Bathurst seems to have scaled back his executive duties in the Colonial Office, concentrating instead on issues relating to Gibraltar, Malta, the Ionian Islands, and Saint Helena. Thus, neglected by Bathurst, West Indian and Central American affairs were handled by the Under-Secretary of State, Robert Wilmot-Horton.[7]

And indeed, the vast majority of Colonial Office correspondence with the British Honduran superintendents was signed by the under-secretary.[8] In fact, Wilmot-Horton's position was privileged. It enabled him to observe and assess Central America's economic and political potential through MacGregor's journeys. At first, Wilmot-Horton's interest in Poyais was largely tied to his professional responsibilities as under-secretary in charge of Central American and Caribbean affairs. Receiving dispatches on Poyais was contingent on obtaining broader information on the political and economic state of Central America, particularly in relation to slavery in the Caribbean general and British Honduras in particular. But receiving information about Poyais also served his own personal political interests and desires for advancement, so much so that he expressly asked to be kept informed of the developments in MacGregor's enterprise. He saw the Poyais colony as a prototypical model which, if successful, could serve as a blueprint for mass emigration campaigns, which Wilmot-Horton saw as the solution to Britain's economic and political problems.

———

Before taking up the position of under-secretary of the Colonial Office in 1821, Wilmot-Horton (Fig. 18), the Third Baronet of Osmaston in Derbyshire, sat in the House of Commons. Elected in 1818 to the borough of Newcastle-under-Lyme, he was close to the Conservative-Liberal interests of George Canning, who served two terms as Foreign Secretary, from 1807 to 1809, and then from 1822 to 1827. He was soon spotted by Henry Bathurst because of his affinity with Canning and was offered the post of Under-Secretary of State for War and the Colonies in 1821. In that role, Wilmot-Horton concentrated mainly on arranging migration programs, particularly to Upper Canada, and overhauling the Colonial Office by delegating more tasks to secretaries and clerks. He resigned dramatically in 1828, upset that some of his political projects, notably organized emigration, were being held up in Parliament. He was appointed governor of Ceylon in 1831. (Wilmot-Horton was also the cousin of George Gordon Byron, the poet famous for his involvement in the Greek independence movement in the 1820s. On Byron's death, Wilmot-Horton was tasked with destroying the poet's personal diary.)[9]

Arriving at the Colonial Office in 1821, Wilmot-Horton was put in charge of Caribbean affairs. In that capacity he had to tackle the problems arising from the sugar trade in the British West Indies, which had been compromised by the abolition of the slave trade in 1807. Although Wilmot-Horton was not opposed to complete abolition, his administrative position nevertheless required him to consider a political solution that would allow the lucrative trade in sugar to continue. With regard to planters, he adopted the same broadly conciliatory stance as his superior, Earl Bathurst.[10] Responding to William Wilberforce's 1823 pamphlet *An Appeal to the Religion, Justice, and Humanity of the Inhabitants of the British Empire*, which called for total and immediate abolition of slavery in the Caribbean, Wilmot-Horton instead recommended a gradual process based principally on consultation with slave owners.[11] However, Britain's West Indian colonies had been rocked by a series of slave uprisings, fueled as much by the 1791 Haitian revolt as by the emancipation policies adopted by some newly formed Latin American republics. As a consequence, Wilmot-Horton had to guarantee that so-called ameliora-

Figure 18. Robert Wilmot-Horton. Source: Richard James Lane, *Sir Robert John Wilmot-Horton*, 182?, National Library of Australia, PIC Drawer 7741 #U6819 NK3493.

tive measures, such as curtailing punitive torture, would also be introduced. Pending full emancipation, these measures were supposed to maintain the productivity of local slaves while not harming the interests of planters.[12]

But Wilmot-Horton's inability to compel slave owners to treat their slaves more humanely exposed him to grave political risk. The example of British Honduras is revealing in this respect. Wilmot-Horton's supervisory activities were marred—as revealed in reports from Superintendent George Arthur—by issues arising from the torture of slaves by influential Belizean cutters and by the enslavement of Indigenous peoples from Moskitia, in defiance of legislation passed by the English courts in 1775. Arthur's reports formed the basis of heated accusations against Wilmot-Horton. Abolitionist parliamentarians, led by Wilberforce, accused him of failing to prevent the mistreatment of slaves who were supposed to benefit from programs to improve their condition, or who, in the case of the descendants of the Indigenous peoples of Moskitia, were not to be coerced into forced labor.[13] Above all, as an independent colony, British Honduras was suspected of being a hub for the illegal Caribbean slave trade. In a letter to George Arthur, Wilmot-Horton pointed out that although Belize was an independent colony, magistrates could not allow slaves to transit through it on the way to a British colony or elsewhere.[14]

The special status of British Honduras was a thorn in Wilmot-Horton's side. The treatment inflicted on the colony's slave population, upheld and legitimized by the local independent authority of the Belizean magistracy, exposed the under-secretary to broadsides from abolitionists in Parliament. However, because British Honduras was a formally independent colony, Wilmot-Horton was unable to intervene and properly enforce local measures to improve slaves' conditions. Responding to Superintendent Arthur, who was concerned about cruel treatment by two magistrates in particular, he said:

> It would be quite impossible for the Crown to interfere to prevent [these gentlemen] from holding slave property either personally or by representation, but at the same time it is equally impossible to express too strong indignation at [this] gross brutality.[15]

The legal independence of British Honduras was also a hurdle to strengthening Britain's commercial and political footprint in the Caribbean. As Superintendent Arthur wrote in a confidential letter to an unknown officer in July 1819, imposing an English-style legal structure on British Honduras would make it possible to standardize procedures for settling trade disputes between English merchant bankers and Belizean cutters.[16]

At the time of the Poyais affair, however, most trade disputes involving British Honduras were settled in accordance with the particular legal regime used in Belize, which was commanded and controlled by the colony's magistrates. The bulk of these rulings favored the interests of the Belizean mahogany trade. It should be remembered that between 1823 and 1824, William John Richardson and other Poyais bondholders attempted, through the agency of George Augustus Low, to recover goods that had been sent to Poyais but were later confiscated by British Honduran magistrates following the evacuation of Poyais settlers from Moskitia. However, the Poyais investors' attempts floundered, mainly because the parties were unable to agree on which of the two legal systems—English or Belizean—ought to apply. Consequently, Superintendent Arthur saw only one way for Britain to control the actions of the Belizean judiciary, which were legally unassailable but detrimental to a concerted abolitionist or meliorist effort, and to install a political counterweight in a region progressively dominated by multiple foreign interests, notably Spain, the United States, and newly independent Latin American states. In Arthur's view, the status of British Honduras should be formalized as an official British colony governed by a legal regime dependent on London.

Robert Wilmot-Horton had joined the Colonial Office at a time of widespread social and political unrest, particularly in England. The aftermath of the Napoleonic Wars had exposed deep-seated social ills in British society. In 1816, the so-called Year Without a Summer, crops failed on a massive scale because of the previous year's eruption of Mount Tambora, a volcano in the Dutch East Indies (now Indonesia). Those misfortunes were compounded in 1819 by the Peterloo Massacre, the disastrous culmination of growing labor unrest caused, among other things, by a textile crisis due to the postwar economic slump.[17]

For some, salvation came in the form of increasing participatory access to political institutions. The risks of actual or potential unrest prompted some British parliamentarians, including the Radical journalist William Cobbett, to predict as early as 1819 that "all the Evils of our Population would cease" if parliamentary reforms such as universal male suffrage were introduced.[18] Yet Wilmot-Horton, who was still a Member of Parliament in 1819, rejected Cobbett's proposal, partly for fear that popular revolt would translate into mass support for Parliament's Radical fringe. Rather than introducing more democracy, his solution lay outside Great Britain. In a letter to Thomas Robert Malthus written some years later, he said that instead of parliamentary reform, he had favored an overhaul of the Poor Laws, a set of statutes that provided financial support for the needy. The overhaul would be accompanied by a large-scale "System of Emigration [. . .] to our own Colonies."[19]

Faced with the risks posed by a nonproductive indigent population, with the potential for widespread social destabilization, Wilmot-Horton believed that emigration programs would ease the burden on cities and foster the development of British colonies in general. Above all, he believed that government-run migration programs would compensate for or replace the Poor Laws, which had been sharply criticized since the late eighteenth century.[20] Throughout his career at the Colonial Office, Wilmot-Horton believed that Britan's demographic problems could be solved through emigration. That belief was to have huge repercussions for MacGregor's Poyais project.

However, Wilmot-Horton was not alone in thinking that the expansion of Britain's population would create major problems. In his 1798 *Essay on the Principle of Population*, Robert Malthus posited a correlation between population growth and famine. To mitigate the inevitable emergence of a food crisis and the attendant risks, he recommended applying "preventive brakes," such as celibacy or delayed marriage, to the exponential demographic growth of contemporary societies. Those curbs would be aimed principally at the poorest segments of the population. Some of Wilmot-Horton's contemporaries were critical of Malthus for not considering emigration as a remedy against a demographic time bomb.[21] Yet Malthus initially saw emigration plans as "a very weak palliative."[22] In his opinion, it would merely create a demographic vacuum that would quickly be filled by a hypothetical increase in the birth rate, encouraged by a relative abundance of resources. Moreover, Scotland loomed large in Malthus's pessimistic vision of Britain's economic development. As Fredrik Albritton Jonsson shows, critics worried about the risk of overpopulation focused primarily on northern Britain. Scotland had been seen in the latter half of the eighteenth century as a frontier land with huge potential that demanded large-scale and optimistic development plans. But the economic bottlenecks that were hampering Britain, caused by both the loss of its North American colonies and the Napoleonic Wars, led to the view that Scotland was gradually becoming a statistically proven demographic burden rather than a potential reservoir of agricultural land.[23]

Despite Malthus's reservations, the government was considering colonial initiatives as a way of ridding Great Britain—Scotland in particular—of some of its inhabitants. And this was before Wilmot-Horton arrived at the Colonial Office. In July 1819, Chancellor Vansittart submitted an experimental plan to Parliament that consisted in relocating indigent workers to the Cape of Good Hope. In an ironic response, the Radical MP Joseph Hume regretted that the plan did not go further by offering the possibility of forcibly removing reluctant candidates for emigration.[24] (Vansittart's plan also helps to explain why MacGregor wrote to him in 1821 to inform him of the Poyais concession, which he saw as a potential new destination for British emigration.[25])

The government's Cape of Good Hope plan ended in a resounding financial and human failure, thereby dampening parliamentary support for this type of solution.[26] As soon as he was appointed, Wilmot-Horton nevertheless intended to take advantage of his appointment as under-secretary to apply his own migration solution to what he saw as an underlying problem of overpopulation. In his view, moving inactive sections of the population receiving assistance under the Poor Laws would ultimately cost less than keeping them in Britain and putting a strain on parish finances. He argued that emigration could not only help develop Britain's undervalued colonies in North America but would also be a saving grace for people mired in poverty because of a lack of sufficiently paid work. As Wilmot-Horton wrote, Britain's imperial expansion should go hand in hand with emigration programs designed to move indigent English people, and above all Scots, to specific locations. Described as "the most desirable thing in a country," emigration could provide the labor needed for colonial land use and natural resource extraction. But it would only be successful if organized and channeled by the government, thereby facilitating the movement of underemployed, hence indigent, British workers. Such movements would rapidly expand the population needed to optimize the development of environments where the Indigenous workforce or slave labor was considered lacking or insufficiently skilled.[27]

In early 1823, Robert Wilmot-Horton published his *Outline of a Plan of Emigration to Upper Canada*.[28] Under the plan, British parishes would be responsible for selecting candidates for emigration. Using loans from the British government, they could provide funds to pay both for publicly organized transatlantic crossings and for the costs of settling in Upper Canada. Although they would eventually have to repay the loan at 4 percent interest, the parishes would avoid both potential overpopulation by indigents and excessive initial outlays. Wilmot-Horton was convinced that his program was sound and decided to apply it on a wider scale. He was involved in a number of government bodies dealing with emigration programs. These included the Select Committee on the Employment of the Poor in Ireland, in 1823, and the Select Committee on Emigration, set up in 1826, which he chaired.[29]

Initially, however, Wilmot-Horton's colonial plan, centered solely on the situation in Upper Canada in 1823 or thereabouts, marked the culmination of a personal period of training and experimentation. Some biographers have noted that his view of emigration as a sufficient or necessary solution to the risks posed by gradual population growth, as highlighted by Malthus, took some time to take root. For example, Eric Richards points out that although Wilmot-Horton first mentioned his interest in emigration issues in or around 1819, he did not talk specifically or publicly about a practical migration project until his Upper Canada plan was published.[30] In other words, his conception of a specific migration policy was the culmination of an acknowledged experimental process, to which MacGregor's Poyais project would contribute.

This process of experimentation was prompted by the need to link his obligations as under-secretary to certain English slaveholding interests in the Caribbean, and by his personal aspirations to see the government set up emigration campaigns. However, Wilmot-Horton's actions attracted considerable political criticism. By advocating a personal vision of emigration-based colonial expansionism while endorsing effective measures to improve the living conditions of slaves, Wilmot-Horton became an ideal scapegoat for Radical parliamentarians opposed to the export of British labor. Joseph Hume, for example, agreed with Malthus that only a cap on the number of births would have a decisive effect on the perceived increase in the number of impoverished people. In 1825, Hume described the government's request to Parliament to extend funding for ongoing emigration projects as "a most outrageous extravagance."[31] William Cobbett, the same Radical MP with whom Wilmot-Horton had clashed in 1819 over parliamentary reforms, accused the under-secretary—and indeed the entire government machinery in charge of migratory projects—of duping the Irish and Scots by involving them in risky experiments at their own expense. He described the scheme as a "thing" that echoed a murky "old Roman plan" for large-scale colonization.[32]

The Radicals' criticisms of Wilmot-Horton, while excessive, did seem partially justified. His plans were prepared for Upper Canada but they also envisioned a system that could eventually ship migrants to parts of the British Empire, the development of which would not only relieve England of a population burden but also contribute to its overall prosperity.[33] Moreover, as Wilmot-Horton admitted to the Select Committee on Emigration, the plans organized as early as 1819 and financed by the government were actually experimental. In his view, they were needed to conduct a vital assessment of the possible effects of earmarking a large portion of the national budget for expanding the government's emigration programs.[34]

As Wilmot-Horton pointed out, his position as Under-Secretary of State for the Colonies allowed him to assess the results of colonial projects launched by the Colonial Office prior to his appointment, both in North America and in the new colony of the Cape. He saw these projects as ongoing migration experiments that would form the basis for his own colonial plans in Upper Canada from 1823 onward.[35] However, since there were no official "experimental" emigration projects in the southern United States, Wilmot-Horton was unable to gauge the potential of moving British emigrants to these areas. Since it was already hard to secure parliamentary funding to push ahead with ongoing North American migration experiments, which were fiercely criticized by the Radical opposition, no new government initiatives were likely to materialize.

Luckily, thanks to his position in the Colonial Office, Wilmot-Horton was able to witness another "experiment"—the inception and collapse of Poyais—that was unexpected yet highly enlightening. As MacGregor himself pointed out, Poyais was an ideal place for Scottish migrants to settle. It was far more than a trading colony intended to support the Caribbean maritime economy. In MacGregor's eyes, Poyais was also a potential bulwark against possible expansion by the United States. It would open up a "new channel for the emigrant population of Britain," acting as an effective counterweight and supporting a British presence in the north of the continent against the expansion of the "invading power" of his country's former "sister," the new United States of America.[36]

As a project based on population transfers, and in comparison with the so-called colonization "experiments" conducted by the British government during the same period, Poyais constituted, for Wilmot-Horton, a unique and specific case that made it possible to identify factors that would determine the outcome of colonization projects in Central America. The arrival after 1815 of a handful of Scottish plowmen, hired by West Indian plantations to train their slaves, allowed an initial analysis of the potential effects of migratory movements from Britain.[37] Ultimately, however, only a few of these migrants went to the British West Indies; most headed directly for the United States, at least from the second half of the eighteenth century onward.[38]

For Wilmot-Horton, Poyais was thus a welcome "experiment." Owing to the organizational structure of the Colonial Office, the Under-Secretary of State for the Colonies was responsible for monitoring the progress of MacGregor's project. Although Wilmot-Horton gave no instructions to the British Honduran superintendents regarding King George Frederic's grant of a major land concession to the Scottish mercenary, he was nonetheless anxious to monitor the progress of the Poyais venture. He took advantage of his position to gather information about the activities of MacGregor and his associates through reports drafted by the superintendents posted to Belize. For example, on March 7, 1823, he asked the incumbent superintendent to pass along any news about Poyais merely "as a subject of general interest."[39]

However, Wilmot-Horton remained constantly in MacGregor's shadow. Although he received news about Poyais fairly regularly, in public he expressed no interest in following or intervening in the mercenary's affairs. He even seems to have ignored letters that Richardson and other Poyais investors sent in March 1823, first to Secretary of State Bathurst and then directly to the under-secretary, asking the Colonial Office to intervene in their favor in disputes with British Honduran magistrates over confiscated Poyais property.[40]

By following the progress of the Poyais project from afar, however, Wilmot-Horton was able to identify and confirm why British projects on the Gulf of Honduras were so hard to carry out. The excessive political and, above all, legal independence enjoyed by British Honduras, which enabled local oligarchs to claim that they were acting legitimately in the name of the British crown, was a serious hindrance to any migration program or slavery reforms in the region. As the Poyais situation revealed, the existence of an independent legal system governing British citizens outside a framework compatible with that of their compatriots was one of the factors that led to MacGregor's downfall. This was later confirmed when British Honduran magistrates took legal action against the agent representing Poyais, George Augustus Low. The fact that Poyais investors were unable to lawfully recover cargoes sent at great expense to the Shore was a major stumbling block for any future attempt to set up a colony in Central America. In other words, it was impossible to extend a migration program to Central America as long as British Honduran magistrates enjoyed their own legal and political regime.

However, on July 3, 1823, shortly after the magistrates had evacuated Poyais, Wilmot-Horton informed Superintendent Codd that the Secretary of State for the Colonies intended to introduce a bill to Parliament that would regulate British Honduras's legal framework by imposing a civil court under British jurisdiction. Without offering further details or explanations, other than asking to be kept personally informed about the situation in Poyais, he asked Codd to tell him what the inhabitants of British Honduras thought of the draft legislation. The purpose of the bill was to change the way that local civil law cases, such as debt proceedings and trade disputes, were handled by scrapping the requirement to conduct them in court with a jury and a presiding magistrate. Instead, cases would be settled by a Supreme Court of Civil Justice in and for the colony of Honduras, made up of judges appointed by a commission under British royal authority. In addition to appointing the judges, the commission would have the power to renew or dismiss the court's members at any time. Cases would be heard and decided "according to the rules and practices of the law of that part of the United Kingdom called England." In addition, the court's decisions could be submitted for appeal to a legal body in London, provided that they were duly referred to the superintendent within fourteen days, accompanied by a deposit, and that the amount in question was greater than £300 or unquantifiable in monetary terms.[41]

Far from being insignificant, Wilmot-Horton's bill was a direct attack by the British government on British Honduras's independent legal system. It sought to take away the Belizean magistrates' power to handle commercial cases, which had previously been settled mainly by the Grand Court of British Honduras. As a result, any dispute under civil jurisdiction would be governed by a regime similar to England's. More importantly, the introduction of a hitherto nonexistent right of appeal would relegate British Honduras to the lowest rung of the British civil courts. In his letter, Wilmot-Horton referred to British Honduras as "a settlement" rather than "a colony," since he did not consider it to be officially under British sovereignty. However, his reform would incorporate it indirectly and partially into a formal legal framework governed directly by the British Parliament. In this way, British Honduras would be tacitly recognized as a territory subject to English commercial law.

Wilmot-Horton's consultation request was sent to Superintendent Codd several days after a dispatch from representatives of the British Honduran oligarchy to Lloyd's was published in London, reporting on the failure of Poyais's first settlement attempt.[42] The under-secretary's letter did not go down well with the Belizean magistrates. At a public meeting on November 3, 1823, a group of British Honduran residents instructed the magistrates to persuade Codd to use his influence in order to maintain the status quo.[43] Convinced that the magistrates had acted properly in the evacuation of the Poyais settlement, the superintendent adopted a simple strategy. On December 12, he wrote briefly to the Colonial Office, forwarding a copy of the minutes of the residents' meeting. However, apart from a short paragraph about the inhabitants not wanting to change their legal status, the document contained a full transcript of a letter that Codd had sent to the magistrates, congratulating them and praising their role in the evacuation of the Poyaisian colony. He also commended them for warmly welcoming the unfortunate passengers of the *Skeene*, who had arrived a few months earlier.[44]

Along with praise for the magistrates, and a line describing MacGregor as a rogue, the minutes also recorded another discussion between British Hondurans. Magistrate John Wright discussed the accusations against the magistracy that had been made by the settlement's former superintendent, George Arthur, in various reports and repeated—notably by abolitionist MP Thomas Fowell Buxton—in a parliamentary debate on the abolition of slavery.[45] The British Hondurans considered that Arthur's description of the treatment they meted out to their slaves was untrue and defamatory. So, likely convinced or urged on by the magistrates, they decided to respond to their former superintendent's claims. To that end, a magistrates' commission, which included Marshall Bennett, was appointed "to draw up a defense of the colony."[46] This led to the publication in 1824 of a book commissioned by the "inhabitants of Honduras," in which they claimed that all the accusations against them were slanderous insofar as their author, Arthur, was a devious hypocrite. Regarding the mistreatment of slaves, the book questioned the legitimacy of the previous superintendent's allegations leveled against the magistrates, allowing them to call into question the accusations made by abolitionists in the British Parliament. Above all, they described the slaves held in British Honduras as being among the happiest in the world.[47]

Despite their official statement that the existing legal situation should be maintained, the magistrates openly told Bathurst and Wilmot-Horton that they strongly disagreed with the Colonial Office's bill. The fact of disclosing the meeting minutes was a clear indication of the retaliatory powers of the Belizean magistracy, supported by Codd, who probably placed too much faith in its sincerity.[48] In the case of Poyais, Codd's support for the magistrates caused even greater embarrassment for Wilmot-Horton. Were he to question the superintendent's advocacy, he would be considered incapable of managing an expatriate agent who backed the "humanitarian" dismantling of an independent colonial project. Above all, to disavow Codd, and thus the Belizeans' actions toward the Poyais settlers, would be an admission of indirect support for an emigration project that had been publicly described as a resounding fiasco.

Following Codd's reply, Wilmot-Horton suddenly expressed strong encouragement for the magistrates and the superintendent. He sent them his congratulations, along with those of the king, on their participation in the relief effort for unfortunate Poyaisians. Above all, he thanked Codd for being able to work independently with the magistrates, unlike some of his predecessors.[49]

―

The Colonial Office, which had been aware of the Poyais project almost from the outset, was careful not to divulge any information about it in its rare public statements about MacGregor's downfall. Poyais was mentioned occasionally and anecdotally during parliamentary sessions, and the issue was raised very few times in a serious fashion in the House of Commons.[50] During the sitting on March 4, 1824, the Radical MP for Aberdeen, Joseph Hume, noted the supposed existence of a new office responsible for managing Poyais's interests, which had been collecting subscriptions to organize migrant voyages to New Zealand.[51] Speaking directly to the Under-Secretary of State for the Colonial Office just over a year after the Poyais scandal broke, Hume wondered whether His Majesty's Government could provide him with proof of any such a project. Above all, he demanded to know whether the government intended to support MacGregor's new project, if indeed there was one. Replying to Hume (who was the trustee of the sinking fund for the 1824 Greek loan[52]), Wilmot-Horton said that the government certainly did not recognize the project. In addition, he urged greater caution with regard to promises from mercenaries such as MacGregor about the fortunes to be made in the colonies.[53]

On the face of it, Wilmot-Horton's response seemed to chime with a benevolent government stance, consistent with the official policy that had thus far applied to American independence movements. It was benevolent insofar as the government's representative felt it necessary to prevent a repetition of what was commonly regarded as a fraud. Consequently, MacGregor's project was designated in the public, financial, and political arenas as the sad, anecdotal embodiment of a private scam that had impinged on many unfortunate migrants.[54] As the publicly recognized architect of the Poyais project, MacGregor was already being portrayed as a ludicrous or even grotesque figure. Hume himself described the project as the source of "the evils which had resulted from the emigration to Poyais [and which] were well known to the House."[55]

Wilmot-Horton's statement was consistent with the official policy on American independence movements, since it avoided anything that might relate to recognizing the independence of new Latin American countries. Thus, his response seemed to have been sufficient both for Hume and for Parliament as a whole, which continued to regard Poyais as an emblematic fraud.[56] But it was probably also a rhetorical diversion, enabling Wilmot-Horton to avoid delving too deeply into the issue when answering an MP well-known for his Radical affinities. He thus seems to have deflected Parliament's interest in highlighting the Colonial Office's involvement, however passive, in the MacGregor affair. As a personal memo from Wilmot-Horton suggests, he did indeed seem to take personal satisfaction in the fact that the Poyais scandal did not arouse more intense and widespread indignation among the parliamentary opposition. In a summary of the affair written in December 1824, Wilmot-Horton mentioned his fear that some Poyais investors, including Richardson and his associates, might have raised questions in Parliament if the property seized by the British Honduran magistrates were not handed back to them.[57] He feared that the publicity surrounding the Poyais scandal would affect his position as Under-Secretary of State and might hinder his political ambitions. If Wilmot-Horton's extensive and detailed knowledge of Poyais were to be brought to Parliament's attention, the government's failure to deal with what was acknowledged as a disastrous colonial and migratory undertaking might serve as ammunition for opposition

MPs, including Hume, who were less than enthusiastic about the activities of the War and Colonies Office.[58]

Indeed, Wilmot-Horton's false claim that the Colonial Office was completely unaware of MacGregor's activities on the Shore seems to have been part of an effort to shield the government from criticism from the Radicals. But it also enabled the under-secretary to hold on to his position and forge ahead with his political advancement. As H.J.M. Johnston shows, the administrative structure of the Colonial Office in the early part of the nineteenth century was limited, so its activities were delegated and shared between the secretary and his under-secretary, with the latter having discretionary power over regulation and some of the government's business. But this arrangement could also lead to a situation in which the needs of a region were intertwined with the personal interests of the senior civil servant tasked with overseeing that region.[59]

In consequence, Wilmot-Horton's political calculation does not seem unusual. As this short chapter has sought to illustrate, the British government's refusal to intervene in the Poyais affair was prompted less by empire-building imperatives than by a national, or even personal, political calculation. The turmoil from the Poyais scandal posed a major threat to the political career of a senior British civil servant who had to deal with British West Indian issues and was planning major government emigration programs.

Conclusion

A FEW DAYS AFTER THE Foreign Stock Market Committee decided not to consider Poyais bonds as "cognizable" securities, the *Times* reported a peculiar incident. One of the agents involved in the distribution and resale of the bonds hastily exchanged a significant quantity of them for a bill of exchange worth £50. Despite not knowing the origin of the bill, the agent quickly concluded the deal, offloading a nominal £2,500 worth of Poyais bonds. It turned out that the bill in question had been stolen a few days earlier. Nevertheless, the agent preferred to deal in a security of dubious origin, even if it meant having to defend himself before a debt recovery court, rather than being stuck with his Poyais bonds, which had become quasi worthless.[1]

Excluded as a recognized borrower from the London Foreign Stock Market, MacGregor's political project was eventually also rejected as a colonial project of potential interest to British expansion overseas. As recalled in this book, senior officials of the Colonial Office had understood, in the wake of MacGregor's troubles, how difficult it would be to support a formal colonization project and state-sponsored immigration plan in the Bay of Honduras. Instead, they preferred to publicly dismiss it as a joke, rather than acknowledge having taken the enterprise seriously during the early years of its development. As a result, Poyais would be remembered as nothing more than a monumental fraud. The scandal was never again discussed by Foreign Stock Market officials, except to stress that it was why the committee had to scrutinize proposed transactions in foreign loans.[2] The committee's decision simply not to recognize MacGregor's transactions and exchanges of securities on the market floor eventually reinforced—and possibly actualized—the accusations that had remained mere mockery for several months.

Some of MacGregor's agents sought to recoup their losses. They notably aimed to restore public confidence in the bonds by demonstrating the borrower's financial capacity. On December 3, 1824, advertisements appeared in newspapers, announcing that a "half-yearly dividend of one per cent" would be paid to bondholders. These transactions were unsuccessful, however, with MacGregor's old partners accusing one another of fraud by announcing that the payment would be made by competing banking houses.[3] Meanwhile, some of MacGregor's former partners announced that they were collecting complaints from dissatisfied bondholders, stalling while promising to deliver justice "on the transmission of the proper documents."[4] However, the attempt to group the complaints, likely to resolve them quietly, would also eventually prove futile. Any semblance of seriousness in MacGregor's project was swept away with a stock market crisis that soon saw a collapse in value of the vast majority of Latin American securities traded in London.[5] From then on, Poyais would never again appear as a serious project. Allegations of misconduct against MacGregor's financial enterprise had erased from the memories of his contemporaries (and subsequently historians) the project on which it was based: Instead of having sought to contribute to the political and commercial improvement of a new country in Moskitia, Poyais was now remembered as a gigantic fraud.

As we now know, Poyais survived MacGregor. Yet it was the accusations leveled against his financial project that took on a life of their own. More than the history of Poyais itself, these accusations quickly formed the foundation on which subsequent recollections of MacGregor's story endured for over two centuries, taking on the contours of a recurring myth and reappearing here and there in similar guises. In 1839, while Alexandre Dumas reimagined the Poyais myth through the character of Captain Pamphile, the London playwright Douglas William Jerrold satirized MacGregor by creating the fictional Captain Barabbas Whitefeather, dubbed the "principal inventor of Poyais stock" in a mock "Handbook of Swindling."[6] By this point, merely invoking the name of the tract of Moskitia land was sufficient to conjure up images of fraud and folly. This cultural shorthand has since endured. Fast-forward to the 2008 crisis, when MacGregor's animus reappeared multiple times, sometimes as the mad inventor of a nonexistent country, sometimes as a brilliant con artist swindling overly credulous investors. In this way, he became something of a godfather to the fraudsters thought to be at the origin of one of the most significant financial crises of the early twenty-first century. In our own time, these ghosts of Poyais seem to walk again in the form of cryptocurrency debacles and Silicon Valley hubris.[7]

Historical perception might have been shaped by the hostility of those who opposed MacGregor's project as the embodiment of a Miskitu path to state-making and sovereign financing in Central America rather than by an understanding of its true historical foundations. Since that time, MacGregor's colorful legacy has served a paradoxical purpose in contemporary narratives. On the one hand, MacGregor became a comforting reference point, suggesting that while modern investors may have foolishly poured money into dubious financial products, at least they had not fallen for something as outlandish as a nonexistent country. On the other hand, he symbolized the inherent and enduring corruption within financial systems. The commonly told story of MacGregor as a grotesque or brilliant con artist has since become a self-sufficient myth, a self-evident truth whose original context is no longer necessary to convey a commonly accepted meaning. Simply invoking MacGregor, whether directly or indirectly, often serves to either underscore the gravity of a current financial crisis or to put its impact into perspective through historical comparison. Consequently, the Poyais myth functions more as a financial barometer, a story that we are told is necessarily fraudulent. In sum, MacGregor's adventure is hardly considered more than a tragicomic anecdote, a historical accident caused by perhaps the most audacious Scottish fraudster. While economists and historians have mentioned the episode in passing, often producing high-quality work in economic or imperial history, the vast majority remain prisoners of the myth of a financial scandal born straight from MacGregor's unhealthy mind.

This book has taken a different approach. Fraud is seen not as the starting point of the Poyais story but as its conclusion. We first endeavor to consider MacGregor's actions seriously. At the very least, it was necessary to lift the veil of preconceptions that too often hangs over MacGregor's actions and the documents he produced, and that has hitherto prevented us from understanding what Poyais really was. By breaking with tradition, we can present a markedly different narrative. In this story, MacGregor's Caribbean, transatlantic, and British ventures appear more akin to an extended military career dedicated to establishing new trade routes for British merchants in the politically unstable environment of Spanish America and the Atlantic world, both of which were changing radically, politically as well as economically.

From the birth of the Poyais project in 1820 following a territorial grant from the Miskitu king, George Frederic, to its death four years later with formal nonrecognition of its securities by the Foreign Stock Market Committee, the story is often misread. Our change of approach allows for a new biography of MacGregor and his involvement in the Poyais affair. In this light, the man becomes a financial intermediary, an instrument in a larger, eventually failed enterprise, rather than the mastermind behind an elaborate fraud. Our new story recounts a seemingly complicated, labyrinthine, at times laborious undertaking to organize and finance a British colony dedicated to the commercial development of a region with hazily defined sovereignty. That aim was achieved first by widening a frontier that might be useful for newly independent Latin American countries and, eventually, by consolidating Moskitia as a country.

This reexamination eventually reveals a more coherent but nonetheless more complex trajectory in MacGregor's endeavors, which can be summarized as follows: The last years of his mercenary career, which began in 1812 under the South American republican banner, were focused mainly on annexing new territories whose sovereign legitimacy could be instrumentalized—a strategy considered both fair and essential to the Bolívarian cause. Seen as militarily, territorially, and politically beneficial to these newly independent countries, the attempts to settle Amelia Island (1817), Porto Bello, and Rio de la Hacha (1819), though ill-fated, were also a potentially profitable strategy for British merchants who backed republican efforts, both financially and commercially. MacGregor's almost obsessive dream of establishing temporarily independent territories with their own political and legal institutions allowed him to contribute to the republican effort by assigning letters of marque and lawfully commandeering the spoils of war. Against the backdrop of major political upheavals following the gradual collapse of the Spanish-American empire, these ventures were optimistic long-term bets on a promising future. By that reasoning, the captured lands would be incorporated into new, independent states that would benefit British West Indian merchants, most of whom had provided the funding for the initial republican military operations.

For Gregor MacGregor, receiving the Poyais concession from Miskitu king George Frederic in 1820 was an unhoped-for opportunity after a series of dismal military failures. Poyais would give him the long-awaited military and colonial base to provide immediate support to revolutionary efforts in Central America, and would eventually become part of a future American republic. However, MacGregor seemed not to understand or care that he acquired the concession because of major changes in the trading and cohabitation arrangements existing since the eighteenth century between the Miskitu and the British mahogany traders who had settled first in the Shore, then in British Honduras. Those changes were essentially the result of disruptions to the complex political ecology and economy particular to Central America, featuring a mahogany trade monopolized by a foreign oligarchy, and an Indigenous Miskitu king determined to break free of his appointed role as a cultural intermediary. Nevertheless, the origins of that turbulence lay far beyond Moskitia. The scale of British anti-slavery campaigns had a major impact on George Frederic's reign. British Honduran Superintendent George Arthur, who admired the anti-slavery MP William Wilberforce, sought to enforce a ban on owning American Indigenous slaves from the Shore, much to the dismay of the colony's leading mahogany merchants and magistrates. For George Frederic, however, these efforts to promote the English antislavery movement in Central America were problematic. The sale of slaves was one of the cornerstones not only of the Shore's domestic economy but also of the middle ground between foreign merchants and the Miskitu, which guaranteed the latter's political, military, and commercial dominance over the region's other Indigenous peoples. By giving away huge swathes of territory to an adventurer such as MacGregor, who was not involved in any of the conflicts linked to the attempted abolition of Indigenous slavery in Moskitia, George Frederic was able to strengthen his shaky political power base amid the widespread economic and political reconfigurations taking place in Central America. Anticipating the imperial reshuffles promised after the collapse of the Spanish empire, the Miskitu king calculated that developing his territory would allow him to position himself as a true head of state.

As the new owner of Poyais, MacGregor needed vast amounts of capital to finance the long-term occupation of his new possession. With his solid military experience, he could see the legal and political potential of a territory with unclear sovereignty at a time of imperial reconfiguration.

He was also well aware of the need to use transatlantic finance and trade to underpin the success of military and colonial campaigns in America. A skilled communicator, MacGregor had been able to finance his earlier military campaigns through English merchant bankers, easily convinced by the commercial potential of countries that would soon be freed from Spanish rule. As in his previous military operations, MacGregor enlisted the services of new fellow travelers, whom he persuaded to support him in expanding his businesses in Poyais. Some were British merchants, who took advantage of the opportunity to reshape MacGregor's military project as a colonial venture aligned more closely with their West Indian trade, which was struggling. In addition to being a military fallback area, Poyais was seen as a future free port in Central America that could earn handsome profits from the region's mahogany resources. However, the handful of British West Indian merchants and planters who urged MacGregor to reshape Poyais in their own interests could not risk using their own funds for a colonial project that grew and became more complex as time went by. Repeated attempts to persuade Nathan Rothschild, England's wealthiest and most powerful merchant banker, to consider contributing financially to the creation of a new Central American colony also proved fruitless.

Some of MacGregor's associates recommended contacting James Ogilvie, a Scottish financial agent and former merchant banker. Together with Ogilvie, he made his way to the City of London, which had been awash with money in search of higher returns since the end of the Napoleonic Wars. Given the legal and political uncertainties involved in recognizing the independence of an American country freshly liberated from Spanish rule, Ogilvie and the other financial agents recruited by MacGregor considered that the best and most efficient fund-raising solution for the Poyais project would be sovereign debt. Indeed, the absence of a legal framework governing the existence or recognition of foreign sovereign political entities made it easy to float foreign loans in the City. This type of fund-raising, particularly by new, developing American republics such as Colombia, Chile, and Peru, whose bonds were already freely traded, was possible because the London Stock Exchange had specific requirements for the foreign loan market. It regulated the quality of its floor members rather than that of the securities traded there.

However, issuing a bond on the London capital market still required public acknowledgment that Poyais actually existed as a state. It was easy to persuade MacGregor, who was used to publicizing his campaigns, to introduce himself as the wealthy, spendthrift political leader of a sovereign state recognized only by himself and his new associates. His strategy—nothing extravagant, simply an embellishment of his initial project—was similar to the tactics used by some other Latin American borrowers to make their own stock more attractive. If organizing lavish banquets and being the talk of London were sufficient to secure the funding for his colonial project, MacGregor's involvement was certainly worthwhile: An initial issue on the London Stock Exchange in October 1822 raised enough capital to send two ships to Poyais, carrying provisions, building materials, and eager colonists.

Nevertheless, Poyais was serially accused of being an anti-revolutionary enterprise hostile to American republican aspirations. In fact, the only accusation that could be fairly leveled against MacGregor was that he had recently been forsworn by Simón Bolívar after a string of military defeats. Nevertheless, as a result of those accusations, Ogilvie and other financial agents pulled out of the project, pocketing substantial sums of money along the way, thus revealing certain financial weaknesses in the Poyais plan. Fortunately, fresh capital was provided by a select group of new investors and the issuance of a new bond in 1823, which was quickly traded on the new Foreign Stock Market. Those inflows also made it possible to send two new ships carrying settlers to Poyais. With the colonization operation back on track, MacGregor could rest easy.

His respite was short-lived, however. In the first four months of 1823, dispatches from Central America written by British Honduran merchants and published in the London press described the first Poyais settlement as a complete fiasco. Alone, underequipped, and ill-prepared, the settlers who were supposed to build a new land had no choice but to leave the Shore aboard a ship owned by wealthy British Honduran magistrates. His nascent colony in ruins, MacGregor was accused in the same dispatches of having pulled off a massive scam by creating a state out of thin air in order to plunder investors gullible enough to have believed in his enterprise. Yet the funds were indeed earmarked for the development of MacGregor's territory. At worst, he was guilty only of being the name and face behind the financing and colonization venture taken over by the London bondholders and merchant bankers who were funding it. Nevertheless, he was accused of being responsible for the appalling conditions endured by the new inhabitants of Poyais. Worse still, as the political figurehead for the sovereign bond traded in the City, MacGregor had to prove the territory's legitimate existence. Although he considered Poyais to be independent of Europe's possessions in Central America, he found it hard to actually prove its sovereign legitimacy in the absence of any other political authority that might attest to it. One of the main investors, William John Richardson, was nevertheless determined to carry out the plan of founding a free colony on the Shore. Richardson even offered to burnish MacGregor's image by organizing lavish parties in his personal manor house and handing out official Poyaisian titles.

However, George Frederic canceled the concession, preferring to realign himself with the British Honduran mahogany merchants—his former trading partners—after the fiasco of the first settler landings at Poyais. When MacGregor found out, he decided to throw in the towel. He fled to Paris in late 1823, hoping to get help in setting up a new Poyais enterprise. This was yet another gamble on the spread of revolutionary uprisings and the impact of changing imperial military alliances on events in America. MacGregor was hoping to win the support of merchants and financiers who espoused French and Spanish aspirations to keep South America within their sphere of influence. All in all, MacGregor seems to have acquired a taste for the pageantry and honors that accompanied his public performance as a head of state. Above all, pursuing his colonization plan was the only honorable way out for a career British army officer and mercenary, with no other prospects than joining in the wars triggered by the French Revolution. However, MacGregor fared no better in Paris. By hiring a small colonial company to organize the transportation of farmers to Poyais, he attracted the attention of the French authorities. He was arrested on suspicion of fraud and languished for several months in Paris jails.

Revisiting the history of MacGregor's ultimately ill-fated endeavors, this book does more than reexamine a misunderstood narrative: it reintegrates the story into a broader framework from which it had been systematically excluded. This crucial context, encompassing early nineteenth-century international finance, Latin American state formation, and ultimately British imperialism, has long been omitted from the traditional account, effectively divorcing MacGregor's actions from their essential historical milieu. By assuming that Poyais was a serious undertaking, we were invited to reject it as a historical accident, while placing the project within a radically changing Atlantic world. Yet the narrative break proposed in this book no longer places MacGregor's figure at its center, but almost in the background of a much larger history. In fact, the story of Poyais told here is no longer just that of MacGregor. It primarily becomes the story of multiple actors hitherto unsuspected or forgotten, but nonetheless all centrally and fundamentally involved in this revisited narrative. Poyais was meant to serve the military and political interests of Latin American revolutionaries and the commercial aspirations of Jamaican planters; to be a testing ground for the imperial aspirations of a senior official of the British Colonial Office; and to embody a commercial competitor that had to be eliminated at all costs by British Honduran slavers. Most importantly, this history is that of the Miskitu king, George Frederic, who emerges as the mastermind of a story of American Indigenous state-making and sovereign financing. In this story, the Poyais loan was the culmination of a political independence enterprise led by this Central American Indigenous leader. Granting the land of Poyais to a foreign mercenary like MacGregor, and then hiring him, proved to be an active, deliberate, and well-informed strategy for political reform and economic improvement of Moskitia.

The Poyais story told in this book in turn extends far beyond a simple English tale of fraud confined to London's Square Mile. Its origins actually lie in Central America, where it began as an ambitious state-building project. As the narrative unfolds, it develops diverse ramifications, with MacGregor's strand tracing a transformative journey toward the City of London. As events unfolded, the project's focus gradually shifted, becoming increasingly dictated by the needs of capital and the prospects of fund-raising. The reconstituted context thus primarily becomes that of Spanish America's decolonization processes. By illustrating how the Poyais project was, above all and originally, that of King George Frederic, this new narrative reveals yet another form of state-making imagined in the wake of transformations shaking the political landscape of a changing American continent. In this version, Poyais is primarily the project of an institutionalized cultural intermediary seeking to assert himself as a true monarch of a new country. George Frederic saw the establishment of a private colony on the Shore as an individual act of resistance to overcome an unsuitable regional political configuration.

By granting a territorial concession to MacGregor, he could cheaply delegate the economic development of a region over which he intended, in time, to present himself as the worthy monarch and political sovereign.

However, by engaging MacGregor as a colonial and financial intermediary to raise the necessary funds for his political independence project, the Miskitu king's grant of Poyais to MacGregor had repercussions in the Caribbean and beyond, even in the City of London. The context thus becomes that of British commercial and financial penetration in the wake of the Spanish empire's economic and political collapse. Elucidating the murkier details of the Poyais story shows that a failed loan had, in fact, existed on the international financial markets in the early nineteenth century. By including that failure in a work of financial history, we uncover some of the factors driving the transformation of institutional frameworks governing the financing of new sovereigns on international financial markets during this period of intense and contested state-making. Although the Poyais story has specific historical features, it emerges as an initially serious financial project typical of its time. Backed by English merchant bankers hoping to expand or consolidate their activities across the Atlantic, it imitated the financial technicalities and issuing processes of other contemporaneous foreign loans, which had an equally uncertain political and commercial future. In this regard, Poyais was born out of legal and political uncertainties concerning recognition of new territories in the Americas, both in the British government and, more importantly, in the financial markets.

By rewriting the Poyais story, we have also highlighted the multiple "worlds" within which it unfolds, which were in a sense all brought together simultaneously and chronologically by the not-always-successful actions of MacGregor. Those worlds include those of West Indian merchants, a Miskitu king, an English abolitionist, British Honduran slavers and mahogany merchants, and London merchant bankers. Essentially, the Poyais enterprise seems to have been shaped financially, commercially, and politically by the various protagonists with whom MacGregor interacted. One after the other, they took part in an effort, led first from the British West Indies and then from London, that aimed to grab a share of the newly opened Latin American market, whatever the cost.

In particular, our revisited narrative has highlighted the sometimes unsuspected links between these spaces and actors. The story of the Poyais loan does not stop at the boundaries of the successive and separate "worlds" revealed by MacGregor's travels, be they the City of London, Moskitia, or the office of a senior Colonial Office official. This story is one of encounters between, and superimpositions of, these different "worlds," each affected in its own way by the global political and economic transformations that occurred in the early decades of the nineteenth century and revealed here in the light of the neglected and forgotten details of MacGregor's ultimately unsuccessful attempts at transatlantic mediation and intermediation.

In a way, the Poyais story offers a sideways glance at the various players involved as much in a British colonization project in Central America as in an attempt at state-making and financing in Moskitia. It reveals some of the unknowns in the still-debated equation underpinning the foundations of a form of British imperial expansion. It also demonstrates that one form of colonial expansion in the Americas, including Central America, was very much on the mind of at least one senior civil servant at the Colonial Office, namely Robert Wilmot-Horton. Yet the Poyais story also shows how other people in MacGregor's different worlds were all trying to benefit—in their own way, on their own terms, and according to their local imperatives—from the transatlantic expansion of British commercial interests that was initiated and tragically coordinated by the Scottish mercenary. Thus, Poyais becomes the story of players such as George Frederic, who operated far away from the City. The positions he adopted amid the commercial and financial expansion at that time were bets on the future improvement of his material, political, legal, and social conditions, in apparent opposition to certain metropolitan interests. Acknowledging this, the book puts the formation of viable financial, commercial, and political entities into context by exploring the potential trajectories of a Central American Indigenous sovereign and financial project that failed to materialize. It highlights the efforts of the Miskitu leader to secure international recognition and financial autonomy amid challenges posed by Latin American revolutions and shifting European foreign loan markets. And ultimately, the book uncovers an alternative path to state-making that ultimately was not taken, despite the best efforts of its financial and political architects.

In a way, Poyais shares many of the same features as other commercial and financial ventures in the early nineteenth century. What sets it apart, however, is that its architects planned to set up for business in a region that was already home to private British settlers. Without fully grasping the implications, MacGregor failed to encroach on the territory of competitors who were familiar with and able to influence the political environment of Central America, which was defined by the ability to interact effectively with Indigenous peoples. MacGregor's many competitors, who included the British Honduran magistracy and English merchant bankers sympathetic to new American republics, also had a better grasp of the tools and mechanisms behind the transmission of legitimate transatlantic information. In the end, MacGregor's trust in the financial agents responsible for raising the funds needed to build Poyais led to the downfall of his colonial endeavors on the Shore.

The aim of this book has been to elucidate the background to the Poyais affair in order to better understand the commercial and financial contours of Britain's infatuation with the American continent in the wake of the collapse of the Spanish empire. For that reason, it seemed only natural to focus on documents linked directly or indirectly to the MacGregor affair. But although this choice provides unprecedented insight into the contours and dynamics of a particular financial and colonial project, it is not without its limitations. Although the book is based on a substantial corpus of often unpublished primary sources, it mainly uses archives and publications that are always linked to the Poyais case in one way or another. Attention has been paid only to those that have survived the passage of time and the conservation policies of the institutions responsible for keeping them. As a result, the financial and commercial environment of the early nineteenth century can be seen only through the prism of the Poyais project's setbacks. The historical dynamics are confined to those occurring within the four-year time span considered here. By restricting ourselves to such a limited research topic and a short period, we cannot consider events or mechanisms beyond those of Poyais.

Although this book is mainly confined to the sources associated with Poyais, it nevertheless sets out to identify some general characteristics in the particularities of MacGregor's project. Its supposed eccentricities and exceptions suddenly become part of the European, Caribbean, and transatlantic dynamics of the fast-changing world in the early nineteenth century. Yet since our study concentrates on Poyais, it does not allow for sufficient contemplation of the issues involved in similar cases such as Colombia or Greece. Accordingly, it is difficult to provide insights that would offer theoretical generalizations to phenomena other than those revealed by an in-depth study of such a specific topic as Poyais. However, as Giovanni Levi explains, "microscopic observation [can] reveal factors previously unobserved." Thus, our research has sought to pinpoint a series of particular historical occurrences and to incorporate them into an intelligible environment and social structures. In this way, an analysis based essentially on the actions and strategies of seemingly statistically "aberrant" actors reveals not only the contradictions of normative systems in which these ultimately "exceptionally normal" objects of study are embedded, but also the "contradictions and plurality of viewpoints which make all systems fluid and open."[8]

MacGregor hastily departed from London in 1823 following the proclamation by King George Frederic that canceled the Poyais concession granted some years earlier. Although MacGregor tried to find other ways to finance a colonial project in Paris, he had no success. Accused of fraud and subsequently imprisoned, he was proved innocent in 1826 on the condition that he leave France. Still convinced that he had a valid and legitimate right to establish a colonial operation in Poyais, he persisted in trying to raise the capital. Between 1827 and 1831, he attempted to issue new foreign loans in London.[9] However, MacGregor's word and, above all, his legitimacy had been tarnished by rumors circulating between Paris and London to the effect that he was nothing but a pathetic swindler. His discredited reputation certainly made it extremely challenging to issue new bonds on English capital markets. The situation was further complicated by a recent requirement for all new issues to receive explicit approval from the Foreign Stock Market Committee. Given MacGregor's new reputation, such approval was highly improbable. To regain his prestige, he sought to make amends with Bolívar. As early as 1825, he had even sought to portray Poyais as a constitutional republic, in the hope of appealing to English investors potentially more interested in backing a republican-based political project than a vague caziquate.[10] Incidentally, MacGregor's efforts to restore his public image also gave a degree of legitimacy to the handful of new Poyais bonds issued after 1824, all of which were trading over the counter rather than on the Foreign Loan Market. But these efforts were to no avail. As the architect of Poyais, Gregor MacGregor became known and recognized as a comic figure who had invented a nonexistent country. In a satirical work published in 1828, he was portrayed as a contemptible wretch, scrambling down the stairs of a London brothel, naked apart from a blanket after being robbed of his clothes by two women whose services he had hired.[11] His Poyais plan was no better regarded. An 1825 satirical engraving by Thomas Howell Jones shows a flight of speculative bubbles heading skyward; the largest of these, marked "Poyais," has burst (Fig. 19).

Nevertheless, Poyais bonds resurfaced after they had been barred by the Foreign Stock Market Committee. Indeed, there were reports of persistent trading. Some of the bonds were exchanged in Amsterdam in 1834. By this time, the Poyais scandal was already well known to the local press.[12] Even so, some British investors went ahead and sold a few of the securities on the Dutch market, probably to arbitrage price differences with the English market.[13] More than ten years after they had been formally barred in London, Poyais bonds were still trading for a few pennies on an obscure unofficial London market specializing in junk bonds. By 1835, MacGregor's project was already considered synonymous with deceit and the absurdity of certain financial practices, so much so that this unofficial junk bond market became known as the "Poyais market."[14]

However, some Poyais investors seem to have had different objectives. Like Émile Zola's Madame Méchain, they bought bonds ridiculously cheaply

Figure 19. "The Reign of Humbug!!" Source: Thomas Howell Jones, 1825, paper, 236 × 388 mm, British Museum, London, 1868,0808.8655 © The Trustees of the British Museum.

then waited patiently for the price to rise before selling them.[15] In 1837, a few such investors even tried to tempt fate. They formed a private colonial venture, the British Central American Land Company, and attempted to revive an agricultural project at Black River. Thomas Hedgcock, the *Honduras Packet* captain who had brought MacGregor's first settlers to Poyais in 1822, was hired to seek confirmation from the then Miskitu king, Robert Charles Frederic, for the concession originally granted to MacGregor in 1820 by his predecessor George Frederic. In fact, the company was founded basically on speculative ambitions for the old Poyais bonds. Instead of reviving transatlantic trade on the Shore, their aim was to briefly rekindle public interest in MacGregor's old project, thus raising its value, in order to be able to sell the old bonds at a profit.[16]

For MacGregor, the Poyais venture came to an end in 1838 with the death of his wife, Josepha. Tired of being ridiculed, he gave up hope of ever seeing a colony flourish in Moskitia. He begged the Venezuelan government to recognize him as a veteran, which it did by allotting him a pension that allowed him to live out his last days peacefully.[17] Gregor MacGregor died of natural causes in Caracas in 1845, and his body apparently rests in the National Pantheon of Venezuela, although, ironically, there appears to be no plaque to confirm his final resting place.[18]

However, to fully appreciate the impact and legacy of this story, we can also consider its aftermath—not just for MacGregor, but for all the key players whose lives were shaped by their involvement in the Poyais venture. By following some of these individual threads to their conclusion, we can better understand if and how the Poyais affair reverberated through time, eventually influencing personal fortunes. In fact, the fates that befell MacGregor's former associates and financial intermediaries, responsible for bringing Poyais to life, were far less dramatic than MacGregor's. Daniel Mocatta, the London financial agent considered for the first Poyais loan issue, continued to operate on the London Foreign Stock Market, apparently without too much difficulty. Indeed, he signed the prospectus for the 1824 Greek loan issued on behalf of representatives of the National Assembly at Epidaurus and the London Philhellenic Committee.[19] In 1834 he was appointed director of the Eastern Coast of Central America Commercial and Agricultural Company, an English firm acquired shortly beforehand in a corporate raid by the directors of the British Central American Land Company, who commissioned it to carry out a vague project to establish a commercial and agricultural colony in the vicinity of Poyais.[20]

Herman Hendriks, owner of the *Albion*, reappeared shortly after his involvement in the 1823 Poyais loan project. He was hired by Count de Wintz as a financial intermediary to organize the issue of his Greek loan, in competition with the London Philhellenic Committee.[21] Hendriks then remained an intermediary of choice for new states that were issuing loans. When Haiti negotiated the recognition of its independence by France in 1825 in return for a substantial indemnity, Hendriks suggested that President Jean-Pierre Boyer put him in charge of the loan issue. He probably took advantage of his close relationship with the Haitian government, having already offered his services to the president of the young republic in June 1822. Thinking that this would guarantee him privileged access to the territory, Hendriks even considered setting up a mining company to exploit the new borrower's natural resources.[22]

The former London agent for Poyais, William John Richardson, was disappointed by his financial adventure and apparently wanted to go back to a life of ease. He did, however, try to invest part of his fortune in British companies, which were perhaps seen to be less risky than commercial and sovereign projects in Latin American. In 1843 he was one of six plaintiffs in a Court of Chancery case against the directors of the British Iron Company, accused of making fraudulent capital calls.[23] Richardson's past as MacGregor's business manager never caught up with him. However, the Poyais venture appears to have brought him true love. In 1834, he married Jane-Augusta Hippisley, sister of Gustavus Hippisley, a former British mercenary who had followed MacGregor to Paris.[24]

And to end this story at its beginning, revisiting the Poyais enterprise reveals that MacGregor's plan was the extension of a political and economic project initiated by George Frederic. By closely following the development of the Poyais venture, our study shows that the Miskitu king, who is often overlooked from a historiographical perspective, wanted to stand out as a true head of state amid the fast-changing political environment in Central America in the early nineteenth century. He tried to present himself as the only protagonist able to grant and authorize territorial concessions for resource development. In doing so, he planned to profit from additional concessions granted under the terms and conditions that he himself had set. MacGregor's territories would, in fact, be joined by others, since the Miskitu king could choose whether to allow other companies to access his territory. But not all the requests he received were granted. In March 1824, George Frederic refused to grant a concession to John Wright, captain of the *Albion*, which set sail for Poyais toward the end of 1823, on the grounds that he had played a part in the Poyais affair. In 1823, he apparently refused to allocate another large plot of land to Pierre Lelacheur, a merchant and former privateer captain from Guernsey.[25] In both these cases, and others, George Frederic paid great attention to his role as ruler of a geographically defined territory. On March 8, 1824, he wrote to Superintendent Codd to say that he would not incorporate his territory into the newly formed Federal Republic of Central America, which declared independence in July 1823. Instead, he said that he wanted to establish "[his] Kingdom" as an independent nation, formally allied to Britain. He even included a sketch of his plan for a national flag: six alternating blue and white stripes, with a Union flag in the upper left-hand corner.[26]

Two days after the letter to Codd, George Frederic's body was found on a beach in Cape Gracias a Dios. The reasons for his death remained obscure for some time. An investigation by some Cape-based foreign merchants confirmed that the young king had drowned because he was drunk.[27] He was succeeded by his brother, Robert Charles Frederic, who adopted a more conciliatory stance toward British Honduras and played his role as a cultural intermediary more dutifully. However, an investigation conducted much later revealed that Pierre Lelacheur had arranged George Frederic's assassination because the king, who had learned the lessons of his failed collaboration with MacGregor, had refused to grant Lelacheur a major territorial concession.[28]

Notes

Preface

1. Hobsbawm, *Age of Revolution*.
2. Ginzburg, *Cheese and the Worms*.

Introduction

1. "Multum in Parvo," *Newcastle Courant*, May 1, 1824.
2. Committee of the Foreign Stock Market, "Minute Book" (1823–1828), 185–86, MS14617/001, GL.
3. "Cazique" (or cacique) refers originally to an Indigenous (Tainos) leader in Latin America and the Caribbean. It was adopted by Spanish colonizers to refer to Indigenous leaders and notables across their American territories and later used by some European adventurers to claim authority in the region. See Pro Ruiz, "Figure du cacique," 30–32.
4. In early nineteenth-century Britain, there were tensions between narrow legal definitions and broader public understandings of fraudulent behavior. However, fraud is here understood as a deliberate deception to secure unfair or unlawful gain. As is often alleged in the case of Poyais, fraud frequently involved false representation or concealment of material facts in commercial or financial transactions. See Taylor, *Boardroom Scandal*, 22.
5. Although the anachronistic term "Latin America" originates from the geopolitical symbolism initially put forward by Michel Chevalier in the 1830s, thus considering the continent as culturally close to France, it will nevertheless sometimes be used throughout this book to describe a territory that encompasses both South America and continental Central America. On the history of the term "Latin America," see Mignolo, *Idea of Latin America*, 77.
6. Neal, "Financial Crisis of 1825," sec. Latin American Securities.
7. "The Poyais Imposture," *The Times*, October 14, 1824.
8. "Take Care of Your Pockets. Another Poyais Humbug" (July 1827), General Reference Collection 1881.c.16.(7.), BL.
9. Among the other bubbles, one finds that of the Colombian Pearl Fishery Association, a joint-stock company with nominal capital of £625,000, set up in 1823 by London merchants for a Colombian concession allowing them to harvest pearls in that

country. Close by is the burst bubble of the Pawnbroking Company, surely a reference to the Equitable Loan Bank Company, a joint-stock pawnbroking company with nominal capital of £2 million that was founded in 1824 but declared illegal in the same year by the House of Lords for failing to comply with laws on the early sale of securities. On the Colombian Pearl Fishery Association, see An Officer Late in the Colombian Service, *Present State of Colombia*, 322–25. On the Equitable Loan Company, see Taylor, *Boardroom Scandal*, 20.

10. Dumas, *Le capitaine Pamphile*, 1839. On the 1837 crises, see Lepler, *Many Panics of 1837*.

11. Dumas, *Le capitaine Pamphile*, 1877. On Bertall, see Beraldi, *Les graveurs du XIXe siècle*, 45–49. On the crisis of 1873, see Marichal, "Historical Reflections on the Causes of Financial Crises," 82–84.

12. Patalano, "Poyais"; Gehrenbeck, *Gregor MacGregor*; Hayes, *Elmyr de Hory*; Bergamin, *Gregor Macgregor*.

13. For a list of the bonds issued on the London Stock Exchange in the 1820s, see Flandreau and Flores, "Bonds and Brands," 665–66.

14. "Who's at Fault?," *The Economist*, September 22, 2008; Julia Finch, Andrew Clark, and David Teather, "Twenty-Five People at the Heart of the Meltdown . . . ," *The Guardian*, January 26, 2009; Sewell Chan, "Financial Crisis Was Avoidable, Inquiry Concludes," *The New York Times*, January 25, 2011; Larry Elliott, "Who to Blame for the Great Recession? So Many Big Names Are in the Frame," *The Guardian*, February 3, 2012; Robert Lenzner, "The 2008 Meltdown and Where the Blame Falls," *Forbes* (blog), June 2, 2012; "25 People to Blame for the Financial Crisis," *Time*, 2009; David Fiderer, "Time Rewrote History With '25 People to Blame for the Financial Crisis,'" *Huffington Post* (blog), May 19, 2009.

15. Olivia Détroyat, "La fraude d'un trader coûtera 2 milliards de dollars à UBS," *Le Figaro*, September 15, 2011; Florentin Collomb, "Le «Kerviel» d'UBS Condamné à Sept Ans de Prison," *Le Figaro*, November 20, 2012; "Fraude à la Société générale : les premiers éléments sur l'identité du responsable," *Le Monde.fr*, January 24, 2008.

16. "Con of the Century," *The Economist*, December 18, 2008.

17. Frankel, *Ponzi Scheme Puzzle*.

18. For example, see Sarna, *History of Greed*; Klose, "Sind wir noch zu retten?"; Robb, "Before Madoff and Ponzi."

19. Returning to the Poyais case, Brian Taylor sees it, for example, as a warning for contemporary investors to beware of "every 'hot' opportunity that comes [his] way": Brian Taylor, "The Fraud of the Prince of Poyais on the London Stock Exchange," Global Financial Data, accessed April 10, 2013, http://www.globalfinancialdata.com/News/Articles/Poyais_article_v2.pdf.

20. Hamel, "Les uchronies fantômes," 436–37; Klaus, *Forging Capitalism*.

21. Nars, *Swindling Billions*; Khatri, "Gregor MacGregor"; Cook and Tate, "Gregor MacGregor."

22. "The King of Con-Men," *The Economist*, December 22, 2012.

23. Sinclair, *Land That Never Was*.

24. Hasbrouck, "Gregor McGregor"; Allan, "Prince of Poyais."

25. Barthes, *Mythologies*.

26. Brown, "Inca, Sailor, Soldier, King"; Brown, "Gregor MacGregor"; Rodríguez, "Gregor MacGregor."

27. Robert Naylor, for example, briefly describes MacGregor's project as an attempt to establish a trading colony in Moskitia, which was nevertheless doomed from the outset to resounding failure because of poor preparation and inadequate recruitment of migrants. Karen Sorsby, while considering MacGregor's plan to be fundamentally a fraud, nevertheless manages to reinscribe the establishment of this project within the geopolitical considerations of British mercenaries in Central America and indigenous political representatives in Moskitia. See Naylor, *Penny Ante Imperialism*, 79–83; Sorsby, "Mosquito Indian King George III."

28. See, for example, Flandreau and Flores, "Bonds and Brands," 354; Marichal, *Century of Debt Crises*, 36–42; Cassis, *Capitals of Capital*, 23.

29. See, for example, Reinhart and Rogoff, *This Time Is Different*, 93–94; Stone, "British Long-Term Investment in Latin America, 1865–1913," n. 3.

30. For a similar approach, see Orain, *La politique du merveilleux*.

31. On the use of clues in scientific and, more specifically, historical inquiry, see Ginzburg, "Morelli, Freud and Sherlock Holmes"; Locard, "Analysis of Dust Traces."

32. The reflection on the absence of Poyais's "national" archives stems from the work of Jean-Philippe Challandes. As Challandes points out, publicly accessible materials held by national archives essentially belong to the nations concerned. Investigating the failed Brazilian liberal uprising of 1842, Challandes pinpoints an apparent lack of primary sources relating to it. From this observation, he suggests that testimonies from dissident realities that do not necessarily contribute to a certain form of national construction could be eliminated, owing to the use of selection procedures that directly or indirectly safeguard documents which build a nation's memory or history. See Challandes, "Les vaincus des archives."

33. Access to ever-greater numbers and types of printed documents, including monographs, pamphlets, and newspapers, has recently increased exponentially, notably thanks to new directories and search engines for digitized archival documents such as Google Books Library Project, Internet Archive, and the British Newspaper Archive. Although historians who have previously dealt with Poyais failed to identify some of this evidence, they should certainly not be blamed, since research undertaken without such computerized tools is long and laborious. Bingham, "Digitization of Newspaper Archives," 226. For a social critique on the unequal access to and accessibility of online archival databases, see Nicholson, "Digital Turn"; Smits, "Problems and Possibilities of Digital Newspaper and Periodical Archives."

34. For a similar approach to the study of financial scandals, see Goldgar, *Tulipmania*, 6.

35. Ginzburg, *Ecstasies*. Recent historiography has witnessed a proliferation of studies analyzing highly specific, localized case studies as a means to illuminate broader global phenomena. This approach contends that by meticulously examining microlevel instances, we can reveal the intricate workings of larger economic and political systems. Such "global microhistories" offer a nuanced lens through which scholars can observe how macrostructures manifest in and are shaped by local contexts. Interesting examples include Jasanoff, *Dawn Watch*; Iglesias-Rogers, "Hispanic-Anglosphere"; Flandreau, "Pricing Moses

Montefiore"; Zaugg, "Le crachoir chinois du roi"; Berg, "Sea Otters and Iron." Significant methodological debates have been taking place regarding the potential of adopting microhistorical analyses in economic and/or global historical studies. On this subject, see Trivellato, "Is There a Future for Italian Microhistory?"; Ginzburg, "Microhistory and World History"; Levi, "Frail Frontiers?"; Lamoreaux, "Rethinking Microhistory"; Bertrand and Calafat, "La microhistoire globale"; Ghobrial, "Secret Life of Elias of Babylon"; Ghobrial, "Introduction: Seeing the World like a Microhistorian"; Magnússon, "Far-Reaching Microhistory"; Rothschild, "Economic History and Nationalism."

36. Hamilton, "Report Relative to a Provision." On Hamilton's First Report on Public Credit, see Holloway, "Establishing the Public Faith"; Hewitt, *Speculative Fictions.*

37. On the silencing or forgetting of history, see Trouillot, *Silencing the Past.*

38. While spelling variations are often found, including Miskito and Mosquito, the terms Miskitu and Moskitia (or simply the Shore) are used throughout the book to refer to members of the Central American ethnic group and the region respectively.

39. For classical accounts in English, see, for example, Bethell, *Cambridge History of Latin America*; Graham, *Independence in Latin America.* For discussions on the historiography of Latin American independence, see Adelman, "Independence in Latin America"; Uribe, "Enigma of Latin American Independence."

40. Belaubre, Dym, and Savage, *Napoleon's Atlantic*; O'Rourke, "Worldwide Economic Impact."

41. Adelman, *Sovereignty and Revolution*, 1.

42. Blaufarb, "Western Question," 743.

43. Brown, *Adventuring Through Spanish Colonies*; Hasbrouck, *Foreign Legionaries*; Rodríguez, *Freedom's Mercenaries: Northern South America*, Vol. 1; Rodríguez, *Freedom's Mercenaries: Southern South America*, Vol. 2; Vale, *Independence or Death!*; Read, "'Independence or Death.'"

44. Pérez Morales, *No Limits to Their Sway*; Jansen, "Aliens in a Revolutionary World"; Millett, *Maroons of Prospect Bluff.*

45. Bassi, *Aqueous Territory*; Colley, *Gun, the Ship, and the Pen*; Sabato, *Republics of the New World*; Cot, "Jeremy Bentham's Spanish American Utopia."

46. See, for example, Tomz, *Reputation and International Cooperation*; Cox, *Marketing Sovereign Promises*; Eichengreen et al., *In Defense of Public Debt.*

47. Bulmer-Thomas, *Economic History of Latin America*; Rippy, *British Investments in Latin America*; Rippy, "Latin America and the British Investment 'Boom'"; Costeloe, *Bubbles and Bonanzas*; Summerhill, *Inglorious Revolution.* For a broader historiographical survey of the argument, see Brown and Paquette, "Between the Age of Atlantic Revolutions and the Age of Empire."

48. Besseghini, "Weapons of Revolution"; Besseghini and Permanyer-Ugartemendia, "Hispanic World at War"; Humphreys, "British Merchants and South American Independence."

49. Dawson, *First Latin American Debt Crisis.*

50. On the formation of transatlantic credit relations, see, for example, Marichal, *Century of Debt Crises*, chaps. 1–2; Rippy, *British Investments in Latin America.* On the microstructures of the burgeoning international finance market, see Flandreau and Flores,

"Bonds and Brands"; Costeloe, *Bonds and Bondholders*; Fodor, "Boom That Never Was?"; Neal, "Financial Crisis of 1825"; Platt, "British Bondholders"; Mathew, "First Anglo-Peruvian Debt and Its Settlement."

51. For studies looking at the individual histories of successful Latin American political projects, see, for example, Halperin Donghi, *Revolución y guerra*; Costeloe, *Primera República Federal de México*; Bethell, "Independence of Brazil."

52. Other examples potentially include Marengo, Jala-Jala, and Nuka-Hiva. On this topic, see Fuligni, *Royaumes d'aventure*.

53. Llorca-Jaña, "British Merchants in New Markets"; Naylor, "British Commercial Relations with Central America."

54. Platt, "Introduction," 8–9. See, for example, the case of Frederick Huth, the merchant banker at the head of one of the first English houses to penetrate the South American market in 1822, who would end up developing what was virtually a global network, and his firm, Huth & Co., played a key role in connecting trade. Llorca-Jaña, "Economic Activities of a Global Merchant-Banker in Chile."

55. Gallagher and Robinson, "Imperialism of Free Trade." For a critique of Gallagher and Robinson's argument, see Platt, "Imperialism of Free Trade"; Platt, "Further Objections to an 'Imperialism of Free Trade'"; Platt, *Business Imperialism*; Jones, "'Business Imperialism' and Argentina"; Hopkins, "Informal Empire in Argentina." For a summary of the debate, see Brown, *Informal Empire in Latin America*.

56. Brown, "British Informal Empire and the Origins of Association Football in South America," 170. For recent examples, see Cohen, "Love and Money in the Informal Empire"; Baeza, *Contacts, Collisions and Relationships*.

57. See, for example, Flandreau, *Anthropologists in the Stock Exchange*; Press, *Rogue Empires*; Lambert and Lester, *Colonial Lives Across the British Empire*.

58. On the little consideration of Central America in the studies of British imperialism in Latin American, see Brown, *Informal Empire in Latin America*, 14. On Moskitia being considered under British influence, see Naylor, *Penny Ante Imperialism*; Potthast, *Mosquitoküste*.

59. On the methodological benefits of studying failures, see Sandage, *Born Losers*; White, *Railroaded*.

60. This reinterpretation of the story of Poyais, presented through the various "worlds" of inquiry unveiled by MacGregor, initially appeared in Clavel, "What's in a Fraud?" On the role played by transatlantic intermediaries as key agents in colonial processes, see Metcalf, *Go-Betweens and the Colonization of Brazil*; Safier, "Global Knowledge on the Move."

Chapter 1

1. "Grant of Land by George Frederic, King of the Mosquito Nation, Caribbean, to Sir Gregor MacGregor" (April 29, 1820), NRAS945/20/19/72, LBGA.

2. See, for example, Dawson, *First Latin American Debt Crisis*, 41.

3. Floyd, *Anglo-Spanish Struggle*; Sorsby, "Spanish Colonization of the Mosquito Coast"; Hagen, "Mosquito Coast."

4. Bard, *Waikna*, 245.

5. Squier and Davis, *Ancient Monuments of the Mississippi Valley*.
6. Stansifer, "Central American Career of E. George Squier"; Olien, "E. G. Squier."
7. For Squier's review of his own book, see Squier, "Something About the Mosquitos." For other works by Squier, see Squier, "Nicaragua"; Squier, *Nicaragua*.
8. A few years after the publication of Squier's book, a new "anthropological" study, by Bedford Pim, a British soldier, painted the Miskitu in a far kinder light: Pim and Seemann, *Dottings on the Roadside*. For a fuller description of the issues involved in using anthropology in colonial and financial enterprises, particularly on the Miskitu Shore, see Flandreau, *Anthropologists in the Stock Exchange*. Squier's other writings on Central America also appear to exhibit the collusion between anthropological and financial interests described by Flandreau. On this topic, see Squier, *Honduras Interoceanic Railway*; Squier, *Information on the Coal Mines*; Squier, *Tropical Fibres*.
9. *Waikna* is cited as a primary source by William Sorsby and Troy Floyd, as well as in the reading suggestions offered by Courtenay de Kalb to researchers looking to find out more about the Miskitu Shore. Kalb, "Bibliography of the Mosquito Coast of Nicaragua."
10. Huntington, *Civilization and Climate*. For a discussion on the environment-eurocentrism nexus, see Blaut, "Environmentalism and Eurocentrism."
11. Moore, "Miskitu National Question in Nicaragua"; Hartzell, "Nation-State Crises in the Absence and Presence of Segment States."
12. This included, for example, Subaltern Studies or the British New Left History. On this topic, see Merle, "Les Subaltern Studies"; Pouchepadass, "Les Subaltern Studies"; Davis, "Marxism of the British New Left"; Sharpe, "History from Below."
13. See, for example, Olien, "Miskito Kings"; Dennis and Olien, "Kingship Among the Miskito"; Olien, "Micro/Macro-Level Linkages"; Olien, "General, Governor, and Admiral."
14. Helms, "Of Kings and Contexts"; Helms, "Miskito Slaving and Culture Contact"; Newson, *Cost of Conquest*, 276–284; Noveck, "Class, Culture, and the Miskito Indians." These critiques have been exemplified by Werner Herzog's poignant film depicting Miskitu child soldiers enlisted in the resistance against Sandinistan forces, *Ballade vom kleinen Soldaten*. For a more recent study developing a similar line of reasoning, see Gabbert, "'God Save the King of the Mosquito Nation!'"
15. Potthast, *Mosquitoküste*, 165.
16. Naylor, *Penny Ante Imperialism*.
17. Naylor, *Penny Ante Imperialism*, 210, 218.
18. White, *Middle Ground*.
19. This line of reasoning follows a similar argument to that proposed by some research in the field of political ecology. See Hecht, *Scramble for the Amazon*; Robbins, *Political Ecology*, 1–100, 231–44; Warsh, "Political Ecology in the Early Spanish Caribbean"; Dempsey, "Tracking Grizzly Bears in British Columbia's Environmental Politics."
20. Naylor, *Penny Ante Imperialism*, 19–22.
21. "Zambo" refers to persons who are of mixed African and Indigenous ancestry.
22. Offen, "Sambo and Tawira Miskitu"; Conzemius, *Ethnographical Survey*; Conzemius, "Tribus indiennes."
23. Irving, *Christopher Columbus*, 461–68.

24. Kupperman, *Providence Island*.

25. Dawson, "William Pitt's Settlement"; Bennett Murray, *They Came to Belize*, 10.

26. According to Craig Revels, who charts the development of Black River exports based on pamphlets written by Miskitu Shore settlers during the second half of the eighteenth century, in 1786 the colony exported approximately one million feet of mahogany, worth a total £15,000. See Revels, "Timber, Trade, and Transformation," 100.

27. Anderson, "Nature's Currency."

28. Chippendale, *Gentleman and Cabinet-Maker's Director*; Shimbo, *Furniture-Makers and Consumers*, 31–39.

29. Waddell, *British Honduras*, 7–27.

30. Offen, "British Logwood Extraction."

31. Naylor, *Penny Ante Imperialism*, 211–12; Chamberlain, *Pax Britannica?*, 13–14.

32. White, *Middle Ground*. For a study giving similar consideration to Moskitia in an earlier period, see García, "Ambivalencia de las representaciones coloniales."

33. See the descriptions by Bryan Edwards from his eighteenth-century travels: Edwards, *Poyais*, 10.

34. Livi-Bacci, "Depopulation of Hispanic America After the Conquest," 208–13; Newson, *Cost of Conquest*.

35. Robert Hodgson, "Memorandum of Presents Delivered to George King of Mosquito Shore Indians" (Sandy Bay, December 9, 1774), 1, SCRO. For travel journals, see Edwards, *Poyais*, 6–7; Henderson, *Account of the British Settlement of Honduras*, 144.

36. Hosler, "Ancient West Mexican Metallurgy"; Wertime, "Beginnings of Metallurgy," 880.

37. Potthast, *Mosquitoküste*, 165.

38. Dziennik, "Miskitu, Military Labour, and the San Juan Expedition."

39. Revels, "Timber, Trade, and Transformation," 32–50; Chaloner and Fleming, *Mahogany Tree*, 40–44.

40. Offen, "Creating Mosquitia," 268–69.

41. Anderson, *Mahogany*, 5.

42. Wang and Scatena, "Regeneration After Hurricane Disturbance." It took until the early twentieth century for scientific understanding of the tree's ecology to advance to the point where the first mahogany plantations could be established. For bibliographic information on this topic, see Anderson, "Nature's Currency," n. 27.

43. On links between local environmental knowledge and Indigenous peoples, see Ellen and Harris, "Introduction." On accounts written by contemporary explorers, see Wright, *Memoir of the Mosquito Territory*, 25, 29–30.

44. McSweeney, "Dugout Canoe Trade in Central America's Mosquitia," 642.

45. Helms, "Cultural Ecology"; Helms, "Of Kings and Contexts"; Helms, "Miskito Slaving and Culture Contact"; Newson, *Cost of Conquest*, 276–84.

46. Olien, "General, Governor, and Admiral."

47. Noveck, "Class, Culture, and the Miskito Indians."

48. Olien, "Miskito Kings."

49. Springer, "American Indians and the Law of Real Property," 31.

50. Metcalf, *Go-Betweens and the Colonization of Brazil*, 3–4. These figures are often

mythologized, as in the following contemporary cultural products: *Pocahontas*; Chicago, *Dinner Party*; Young and Crazy Horse, *Cortez the Killer*.

51. Naylor, *Penny Ante Imperialism*, 69, 75, 78, 133, 135, 141.

52. Bennett Murray, *They Came to Belize*, 362.

53. On this topic, see Gabbert, "'God Save the King,'" 85; Helms, "Of Kings and Contexts."

54. *Collection of All the Treaties*, 375–82.

55. Dawson, "Evacuation of the Mosquito Shore," 67.

56. Parry, "Convention Between Great Britain and Spain."

57. Dawson, "Evacuation of the Mosquito Shore," 68; Bennett Murray, *They Came to Belize*, 105–7, 118–24. A hundred or so British settlers were allowed to stay on the Shore.

58. This estimate is based on a comparison of the number of refugees who landed in Belize in 1787 with a summary census conducted in 1790. These precious data were gathered by Sonia Bennett Murray. See Bennett Murray, *They Came to Belize*, 266–71.

59. Naylor, *Penny Ante Imperialism*, 67–69; Bennett Murray, *They Came to Belize*, 155–56.

60. Humphreys, *Diplomatic History of British Honduras*, 14–15.

61. Humphreys, *Diplomatic History of British Honduras*, 17–18.

62. Sorsby, "Spanish Colonization of the Mosquito Coast."

63. Exploring population and economic patterns in the Brazilian state of São Paulo during the interwar period, Preston James uses the term "hollow frontier" to describe how predatory agricultural activities expanded around the city of São Paulo, whereas permanent settlements were not established. James, "Changing Patterns of Population."

64. Naylor, *Penny Ante Imperialism*, 77–78.

65. Nigel Bolland offers a nice summary of the political, social, and economic history of British Honduras. See Bolland, *Formation of a Colonial Society*.

66. Bolland, *Formation of a Colonial Society*; Naylor, "British Commercial Relations with Central America," 92. An oligarchy is a political system controlled by an elite that uses the wealth concentrated in its hands to gain preferred access to positions of political power, while also acquiring the resources to safeguard and advance its own interests. Winters, *Oligarchy*, xiii.

67. Bolland, *Formation of a Colonial Society*, 43–44. On the potential impact caused by the development of international trade on local political institutions, and particularly on the formation and consolidation of economic and political oligarchies, see Puga and Trefler, "International Trade and Institutional Change."

68. Bolland, "Systems of Domination After Slavery."

69. Burdon, *Archives of British Honduras*, Vol. 2, 127. According to *Le cambiste universel* by Patrick Kelly, and as evidenced by a letter of credit from a Belizean archive, £100 was equivalent to JM£140. See Hyde, James, Recorded by desire of Lewis Evans Williams attorney to Inglis Ellice & Co., Belize, 7/4/1821, Private Records 1822–1823, BSRAS; Kelly, *Le cambiste universel*, 246.

70. *Honduras Almanack*, 126–31.

71. See the transcription of the 1820 census in Bennett Murray, *First Parish Register*, 87–112.

72. For example, in 1816, the next largest slaveowner, with about 120 slaves, was James Hyde. For transcriptions of the 1816, 1820, and 1823 censuses, see Bennett Murray, *First Parish Register*.

73. "Census 1806," 1806, Censuses, BSRAS; Bennett Murray, *First Parish Register*, 184.

74. Edgell, *Time and the River*.

75. King, *Slavery in Belize*, 3–4, 8–9.

76. Mansfield Bowen, "Proceed by Desire of William Walsh, Clarissa Paslow and Manfield W Bowen" (Belize, April 25, 1822), Private Records 1822–1823, BSRAS; Charles Evans, "Recorded by Desire of Marshall Bennett" (Honduras, January 17, 1823), Private Records 1822–1823, BSRAS; Mansfield Bowen, "Recorded by Desire of John W Wright, William Walsh, Francis H Meighan, Clarissa Paslow and Mansfield Bowen as Exec to Estate" (Belize, April 25, 1822), Private Records 1822–1823, BSRAS.

77. Louise Hill, "Recorder by Desire of John Wright" (London, July 5, 1822), Private Records 1822–1823, BSRAS.

78. Luisa Hamilton Bourke and Emma Mary Clifford Bourke, "Recorder by Desire of Marshall Bennett" (London, October 1, 1822), Private Records 1822–1823, BSRAS.

79. Burnaby, *Regulations for the Better Government*, 12–13.

80. For example, of the 101 cases brought before the session of October 1822, the Grand Court heard 96 (95 percent) that were directly linked to trade-related questions (essentially settlement of debts), four (3.9 percent) indirectly linked to trade-related questions (freeing of slaves, violent treatment of slaves, defamation), and one criminal case (0.99 percent) (attack on another settler): "Grand Court Oct 1822–Jun 1823" (Belize, October 1822), BSRAS.

81. In an economy based essentially on slave labor, slave emancipation cases also fall within the category of trade-related questions.

82. Burnaby, *Regulations for the Better Government*; Naylor, *Penny Ante Imperialism*, 56; Burdon, *Archives of British Honduras*, Vol. 2, ix. The Burnaby Code was published in 1809 after William Hunt, one of the colony's legal secretaries, was tasked by the magistracy with putting order into a legal system founded on numerous poorly organized texts and suffering from gaps due to loss of documents.

83. "Sproat George Versus France Alexander" (Belize, October 31, 1822), Grand Court Oct 1822–Jun 1823, BSRAS.

84. William Gentle, Thomas Iles, and Thomas Wright, "Meeting of Magistrates" (Belize, January 30, 1822), Meeting of Magistrates 1822–1823, BSRAS.

85. "Special Court: The King Versus Frederick Bowen" (Belize, September 16, 1822), Summary Court 1821–1828, BSRAS.

86. Young & Wright et al. to Frederick Bowen, "Recorded by Desire of Frederick Bowen," November 1822, Private Records 1822–1823, BSRAS.

87. "The King on Complaint of Thomas Osburn" (Belize, September 1818), Summary Court, BSRAS.

88. Naylor, "Mahogany Trade as a Factor," 44.

89. For example, see Catherine Griszel and James Hyde, "Recorded by Desire of Catherine Griszel" (Belize, April 11, 1818), Private Records 1819–1820, BSRAS; Thomas Isles and Martha Slusher, "Mortgage" (Belize, June 26, 1819), Private Records 1819–1820,

BSRAS; Thomas Paslow and Catherine Griszel, "Mortgage" (Belize, July 3, 1821), Private Records 1821–1822, BSRAS; Thomas Barnes Brick and Marshall Bennett, "This Indenture" (Belize, October 4, 1821), Private Records 1821–1822, BSRAS. Many documents of this type were found in the Belize state archives. A better detailed and systematic analysis of these claims would help to draw a more accurate picture of the historical landscape.

90. "Sproat George Versus France Alexander" (Belize, October 31, 1822), Grand Court Oct 1822–Jun 1823, BSRAS; *Honduras Almanack*, 188–89.

91. Grace Tucker Anderson, "Recorded by Desire of Thomas Iles" (Honduras, April 16, 1823), Private Records 1822–1823, BSRAS.

92. See, for example, Amelia Arthurs, "Recorded by Desire of John W Wright" (Honduras, October 1, 1823), Private Records 1822–1823, BSRAS; Archibald Colquhoun, "Recorded by Desire of John Wright and William Usher" (London, July 5, 1822), Private Records 1822–1823, BSRAS; Catherine Fanel, "Recorded by Desire of Marshall Bennett and William Walsh" (Honduras, October 9, 1822), Private Records 1822–1823, BSRAS; Edward Meighan, "Recorded by Desire of J.S. August" (Honduras, October 31, 1822), Private Records 1822–1823, BSRAS. Once again, a more systematic examination of these documents would help to gain a better insight into their quantitative importance.

93. For a critique about the lack of lawyers in Belize, see Low, *Belise Merchants Unmasked*, 58. This system based on the sale of legal protection echoes in a way the activities of the Sicilian mafia, whose main business was not extortion but private protection. See Gambetta, *Sicilian Mafia*.

94. Finamore, "'Pirate Water,'" 32.

95. "Public Meeting" (Belize, March 4, 1822), Meeting of Magistrates 1822–1823, BSRAS.

96. See, for example, the accounts recording the sale of a cargo of mahogany drawn up in 1821 on behalf of Thomas Pickstock: Thomas Pickstock, "Recorded by Desire of Thomas Pickstock" (Belize, December 18, 1821), Private Records 1822–1823, BSRAS.

97. "Belize," *Honduras Gazette and Commercial Advertiser*, August 19, 1826.

98. Burdon, *Archives of British Honduras*, Vol. 2, 79.

99. Burdon, *Archives of British Honduras*, Vol. 2, 57, 84, 178.

100. "Bennett Marshall Versus Hyde James and George" (Belize, October 30, 1822), Grand Court Oct 1822–Jun 1823, BSRAS.

101. Ellice spearheaded the talks that led to the merger of the Hudson's Bay Company with the North West Company. See Colthart, "Ellice, Edward."

102. "Bennett Marshall Versus Inglis Ellice & Co Late Concern Of" (Belize, June 25, 1823), Grand Court Oct 1822 -Jun 1823, BSRAS.

103. James Hyde, "Recorded by Desire of Lewis Evans Williams Attorney to Inglis Ellice & Co" (Belize, January 18, 1819), Private Records 1822–1823, BSRAS; James Hyde, "Recorded by Desire of Lewis Evans Williams Attorney to Inglis Ellice & Co" (Belize, July 4, 1821), Private Records 1822–1823, BSRAS.

104. "Anderson Grace Tucker Versus Hyde James & George" (Belize, October 1822), Grand Court Oct 1822–Jun 1823, BSRAS; "Bennett Marshall Versus Hyde James and George" (Belize, October 30, 1822), Grand Court Oct 1822–Jun 1823, BSRAS.

105. *Honduras Almanack*, 122–32.

106. Bennett Murray, *First Parish Register*.

Chapter 2

1. Burdon, *Archives of British Honduras*, Vol. 2, 224.

2. Burdon, *Archives of British Honduras*, Vol. 2, 57, 84, 178; Humphreys, *Diplomatic History of British Honduras*, 15–16.

3. The work of Keith Pluymers is nicely illustrative of this process. Studying the expansion of colonial ironworking by the Virginia Company of London toward the close of the sixteenth century, Pluymers describes statements by the company's backers about the plentiful wood resources of the New World, set against tales of depleted reserves at home, as a means for the British forestry trade to set itself apart in the competitive Atlantic market. Pluymers, "Atlantic Iron."

4. Burdon, *Archives of British Honduras*, Vol. 2, 202.

5. William Duke of Manchester (Saint Jago de la Vega, July 7, 1814), GBR/0115/RCMS 270/25, RCSL.

6. Naylor, *Penny Ante Imperialism*, 77.

7. Bennett Murray, *They Came to Belize*, 421–25; Burdon, *Archives of British Honduras*, Vol. 1, 274; Burdon, *Archives of British Honduras*, Vol. 2, 103–4, 110–16.

8. These texts were first compiled in 1806 by William Hunt and eventually selected by a committee of magistrates entrusted with "inspecting and approving the presented laws and regulations of the colony." Burnaby, *Regulations for the Better Government*, 96.

9. For example, "Tenth: All crimes and misdemeanors commited by the inhabitants of the Bay, which are not mentioned in these Regulations, and for which by these articles of agreement no punishment is provided, shall be punished according to the custom of the Bay in like cases." See Burnaby, *Regulations for the Better Government*, 15.

10. Robert Naylor describes the position as ambiguous, occupied essentially by a military officer playing the role of observer rather than administrator. For Nigel Bolland, the superintendent's role was to avoid conflict not so much with the Spanish as with the magistrates. See Naylor, *Penny Ante Imperialism*, 77; Bolland, *Formation of a Colonial Society*, 167–68.

11. Burdon, *Archives of British Honduras*, Vol. 2, 256.

12. Burdon, *Archives of British Honduras*, Vol. 2, 256–61.

13. Robert Wilmot-Horton to George Arthur, March 16, 1822, R3_39, BSRAS.

14. Burdon, *Archives of British Honduras*, Vol. 2, 257.

15. Robert Wilmot-Horton to George Arthur, March 16, 1822, R3_39, BSRAS.

16. Marshall Bennett, James Hyde, and Thomas Paxlou to George Arthur, "Testifying to 'Great Services' Rendered by Col. Arthur to the Community," March 13, 1817, GBR/0115/RCMS 270/14, RCSL.

17. *Substance of the Debate in the House of Commons*, 75–76.

18. Shaw, *Sir George Arthur*, 24.

19. "Cases in Which Alterations Have Been Made in Customs and Excise Duties," 9.

20. George Arthur to Earl Bathurst, September 12, 1820, GBR/0115/RCMS 270/46_34, RCSL.

21. George Arthur to Elizabeth Arthur, 1819, GBR/0115/RCMS 270/41, RCSL. On evangelicalism as a strand of Protestantism that emerged and took hold in the second half of the eighteenth century, see Bebbington, *Evangelicalism in Modern Britain*.

22. Shaw, *Sir George Arthur*, 17. See below for more on William Wilberforce.

23. Burdon, *Archives of British Honduras*, Vol. 2, 235; *Substance of the Debate in the House of Commons*, 206; Inhabitants of Honduras, *Defence of the Settlers of Honduras*, 2. On the slave uprising, see Campbell, *Becoming Belize*, 293–95; King, *Slavery in Belize*, 8–9.

24. Ferguson, Pelayo, and Encalada, *A History of Slavery & Emancipation in Belize*, 10. Emory King sees the verdict as particularly lenient on Bowen, as the jury knew that the mistreatment of Peggy had been inflicted by the defendant's mistress, who was jealous of Bowen's apparent attraction to his slave. Although interesting, King's version, which tends to be indulgent and praises the treatment inflicted on slaves by the inhabitants of British Honduras, is regrettably insufficiently documented. See King, *Slavery in Belize*, 8–12.

25. J. Henry and Thomas Conlys to Bathurst, "Report of His Majesty's Commissioners of Legal Enquiry for the West Indies on the Case of Certain Persons at Honduras Who Claim to Be Entitled to Their Freedom on the Ground of Indian Descent," report, February 20, 1827, CO 318/67, TNA.

26. Burdon, *Archives of British Honduras*, Vol. 2, 247. On this topic, see Millett, "Law, Lineage, Gender."

27. "Slaves at Honduras," *Aberdeen Journal*, July 23, 1823. For biographies describing Wilberforce as the driving force in the movement to abolish the slave trade and slavery, see Belmonte, *William Wilberforce*; Tomkins, *Clapham Sect*; *Amazing Grace*.

28. Henderson, *Account of the British Settlement of Honduras*, 59.

29. Walvin, *Slavery in Small Things*, 82–103.

30. Henderson, *Account of the British Settlement of Honduras*, 48–49.

31. Walvin, *Slavery in Small Things*, 97.

32. Inhabitants of Honduras, *Defence of the Settlers of Honduras*, pt. 1. According to Mavis Campbell, the pride expressed by the British Honduras loggers following the Battle of St. George's Caye, when master and slave fought allegedly hand in hand against the Spanish invader, was a decisive moment in the formation of a national identity. Belizeans saw themselves as good slavers, in contrast with those in the other British West Indian colonies. Arthur's accusations and the publication of his reports by Wilberforce greatly diminished this image of themselves—or at the very least undermined the identity that they were trying to project. See Campbell, *Becoming Belize*, 283–88.

33. George Arthur to George Frederic, April 5, 1820, GBR/0115/RCMS 270/47_88, RCSL.

34. George Arthur to Josiah Pratt, April 6, 1820, GBR/0115/RCMS 270/47_92, RCSL. On Pratt, see Overton and Machin, "Pratt, Josiah (1768–1844)."

35. See, for example, William Wilberforce to Josiah Pratt, August 19, 1819, MS. 498/81, MOA. On the founding of the Church Missionary Society, see Stock, *History of the Church Missionary Society*, 69.

36. Tomkins, *Clapham Sect*, 183.

37. Pratt and Pratt, *Memoir of the Rev. Josiah Pratt, B.D.*, 128–29.

38. For an example of a report written by Arthur, see Church Missionary Society, "Recent Miscellaneous Intelligence," *Missionary Register*, July 1822.

39. Wilberforce, *Appeal to the Religion, Justice, and Humanity*, 16–17.

40. Wilberforce, *Appeal to the Religion, Justice, and Humanity*, 18.
41. Burke, "Speech on Divorce Bill (29 April 1771)," 357–59.
42. Burke, *Thoughts on the Prospect of a Regicide Peace*, 39–42.
43. Wilberforce, *Appeal to the Religion, Justice, and Humanity*, 19.
44. This rhetoric, based on the sanctity of these contracts in God's eyes, can also be found in documents edited by Pratt. See Pratt, *Works of Ezekiel Hopkins*, 116, 117, 121, 137.
45. This process resembles the impact that the evangelical proselytizing of missionary societies had on the expansion of the East India Company in the first half of the nineteenth century. On this topic, see Copland, "Christianity as an Arm of Empire."
46. George Arthur, "Private," July 17, 1819, GBR/0115/RCMS 270/41, RCSL; George Arthur to Earl Bathurst, July 31, 1819, GBR/0115/RCMS 270/46_17, RCSL.
47. On Miskitu polygamy, see Gabbert, "'God Save the King,'" 85.
48. George Arthur to George Frederic, February 14, 1821, GBR/0115/RCMS 270/47_213, RCSL.
49. George Arthur to George Frederic, June 6, 1820, GBR/0115/RCMS 270/47_114, RCSL.
50. This biography of the Miskitu king George Frederic first appeared in Clavel, "Rise and Fall of George Frederic."
51. Burdon, *Archives of British Honduras*, Vol. 2, 79.
52. Fairlieb Mistie to Balcarres, April 20, 1798, CO 137/99, TNA; Balcarres to Portland, April 30, 1798, CO 137/99, TNA.
53. Portland to Balcarres, July 11, 1798, CO 137/99, TNA.
54. Nugent, *Journal of Her Residence in Jamaica*, 211–12.
55. On the appropriation by Miskitu kings of British regalia, see Dennis and Olien, "Kingship Among the Miskito."
56. Foreign Office, *British and Foreign State Papers*, 689.
57. On Shepherd, see Naylor, *Penny Ante Imperialism*, 96–102.
58. Dennis and Olien, "Kingship Among the Miskito," 733–34.
59. Olien, "Miskito Kings," 214–15.
60. Foreign Office, *British and Foreign State Papers*, 674; Bennett Murray, *They Came to Belize*, 118–37; Burdon, *Archives of British Honduras*, Vol. 2, 57.
61. House of Commons, *Correspondence Respecting the Mosquito Territory*, 46–47.
62. George Frederic to George Arthur, January 13, 1816, CO 123/25, TNA.
63. George Arthur to George Frederic, January 14, 1816, CO 123/25, TNA. At this time, Arthur was apparently still on good terms with the magistrates of British Honduras.
64. Stout, *Nicaragua*, 169; Dunham, *Journal of Voyages*, 96.
65. Roberts, *Narratives of Voyages*, 107–108, 130.
66. Dunham, *Journal of Voyages*, 96.
67. Foreign Office, *British and Foreign State Papers*, 680.
68. Dunham, *Journal of Voyages*, 107.
69. These tensions have been identified in Olien, "Miskito Kings," 215–18.
70. House of Commons, *Correspondence Respecting the Mosquito Territory*, 46–47; Strangeways, *Sketch of the Mosquito Shore*, 144; Roberts, *Narratives of Voyages*, 148.

71. Roberts, *Narratives of Voyages*, 137–39.
72. George Arthur to George Frederic, January 14, 1816, CO 123/25, TNA.
73. Belaubre, Dym, and Savage, *Napoleon's Atlantic*.
74. Adelman, *Sovereignty and Revolution*; Cot, "Spanish American Utopia."
75. Geggus, *Impact of the Haitian Revolution*.
76. Brown, *Adventuring Through Spanish Colonies*.
77. On Aury, see Head, *Privateers of the Americas*.
78. George Arthur to Bathurst, May 13, 1819, CO 123/28, TNA; George Arthur to Bathurst, May 29, 1819, CO 123/28, TNA; José María Palomar, "Noticia de La Invasion de Truxillo" (1820), Guatemala Collection_B820|b.P181n, JCBL; José María Palomar to George Arthur, January 13, 1821, CO 123/30, TNA; Roberts, *Narratives of Voyages*, 131.
79. Llorca-Jaña, "British Merchants in New Markets"; Humphreys, "British Merchants and South American Independence."
80. Naylor, "British Commercial Relations with Central America," 14–15. On the depictions of the Shore's natural resources, see Roberts, *Narratives of Voyages*, 120; Hodgson, *Some Account of the Mosquito Territory*, 18.
81. Roberts, *Narratives of Voyages*, 266.
82. Roberts, *Narratives of Voyages*, 64–65, 104, 248–256. On Bentham's interest in Central America, see Bentham, "Proposals for the Junction of the Two Seas."
83. This approach resembles the at-times conflictual interactions maintained by the Narragansett (southern New England) between English and Dutch settlers during the seventeenth century. On this topic, see Richter, "To 'Clear the King's and Indians' Title,'" 59.
84. George Arthur to George Frederic, April 5, 1820, GBR/0115/RCMS 270/47_88, RCSL.
85. On Miskitu mahogany canoes, see McSweeney, "Dugout Canoe Trade in Central America's Mosquitia," 642.
86. George Arthur to George Frederic, April 5, 1820, GBR/0115/RCMS 270/47_88, RCSL.
87. Olien, "General, Governor, and Admiral," 291–93.
88. George Arthur to General Robinson, January 6, 1821, GBR/0115/RCMS 270/47_200, RCSL.
89. Roberts, *Narratives of Voyages*, 68.
90. Roberts, *Narratives of Voyages*, 131, 148.
91. Parts of George Frederic's political and economic project are described in a letter written in 1823. George Frederic to Alexander Murray, March 28, 1823, CO 123/34, TNA.
92. Roberts, *Narratives of Voyages*, 271–74. On the Carib Wars, see Taylor, *Black Carib Wars*.
93. Roberts, *Narratives of Voyages*, 166, 268; Olien, "General, Governor, and Admiral," 291–93.
94. "Grant of Land by George Frederic, King of the Mosquito Nation, Caribbean, to Sir Gregor MacGregor" (April 29, 1820), NRAS945/20/19/72, LBGA. According to the deed, the coordinates of Poyais are the following: "North: All the Sea Coast comprehended between the 84°25′ to the 85°8′ degree of Longitude West from the Meridian of

London. South: by a straight line drawn due West from Longitude 84°42′ to Longitude 85°42′ West, along the 13 Degree of North Latitude. East: From the Longitude of 84°25′ West, by a line drawn due North & South untill it touches the Western bank of Plantain River, in a Latitude 15°37′ North, and then following the Western bank of that river to Latitude 15° N & Longitude 84°42′W and from thence in a straight line drawn due South untill it touches the 13° of N Latitude. West: From the mouth of Zacarylyon River in Longitude 85°8′ W and following the Eastern bank of the said river South, to Latitude 15°28′ N and then by a line drawn due West untill it touches the Rio Grande or Romaine River in Latitude 15°28′N and Longitude 85°42′ West and then by a straight line drawn due South untill it intersects the 13° Degree of North Latitude and in Longitude 85°42′ West from the Meridian of London." A note from George Frederic accompanying the deed indicates that the latitudes and longitudes mentioned in the grant are taken from the work of the English geographer Thomas Jefferys, who already identified the territory as Poyais. Jefferys, *A Complete Pilot for the West-Indies*, fig. 18.

Chapter 3

1. While MacGregor's previous military campaigns are often described in scrupulous detail, authors are generally reluctant to highlight his movements during this particular period. See, for example, Sinclair, *Land That Never Was*.

2. Alexander, *Life of Alexander Alexander*, Vol. 2, 162. On Alexander Alexander, see Brown, "Life of Alexander Alexander."

3. Dawson, *First Latin American Debt Crisis*, 41.

4. On sea conditions and currents in Central America, see Herman Moll, *A Map of the West-Indies Etc with the Adjacent Countries—Also Ye Trade Winds, and Ye Several Tracts Made by Ye Galeons and Flota from Place to Place*, 1727, 1727, Lionel Pincus and Princess Firyal Map Division, TNYPL; Cameron Beccario, "Earth," 2018, http://earth.nullschool.net.

5. On MacGregor's military career, see, for example, Rafter, *Memoirs of Gregor McGregor*; Brown, "Inca, Sailor, Soldier, King."

6. Sinclair, *Land That Never Was*, 175.

7. Lowe, "American Seizure of Amelia Island," 18–19.

8. Gregor MacGregor to Spencer Perceval, January 18, 1812, FO 72/171/1, TNA. Although no letters from MacGregor to the Duke of Kent and Strathearn have been found, MacGregor does mention some correspondence with the man who in 1819 became the father of Queen Victoria; see Gregor MacGregor to Nicholas Vansittart, March 13, 1821, CO 137/152, TNA.

9. "Extract from a Proclamation of Gregor MacGregor."

10. A picture of the medal can be seen in World Coin News Staff, "DNW Sells Historic Amalia Island Medal," *Numismatic News*, March 19, 2019, https://www.numismaticnews.net/world-coins/dnw-sells-historic-amalia-island-medal.

11. Davis, "MacGregor's Invasion of Florida," 25.

12. See, for example, Sinclair, *Land That Never Was*, 175–88.

13. McKay, *Early American Currency*, 13–15; Mather, *Some Considerations on the Bills of Credit*.

14. Head, *Privateers of the Americas*, 102–5, 111, 140–46.

15. Head, *Privateers of the Americas*, 94–99.

16. Head, *Privateers of the Americas*, 95.

17. "Extract from a Proclamation of Gregor MacGregor."

18. Davis, "MacGregor's Invasion of Florida," 22; Head, *Privateers of the Americas*, 102–5. On military enterprises as a form of economic activity, see the work of Louis Bergeron. He describes the central role played by private banks in financing the French state and the conquests of Napoleon Bonaparte in order to benefit from imperial institutions and conquests, which ensured regular flows of funds for the state and thus the repayment of its loans. Bergeron, *Banquiers, négociants et manufacturiers*, chap. 6; Bergeron, *Les révolutions européennes et le partage du monde*, 230–31.

19. Millett, *Maroons of Prospect Bluff*, 40–42; Wright, "Note on the First Seminole War," 572–73; Mahon, "British Strategy and Southern Indians."

20. Owsley, "Ambrister and Arbuthnot," 297.

21. Parton, *Life of Andrew Jackson*, 423.

22. Davis, "MacGregor's Invasion of Florida," 66–67.

23. Head, *Privateers of the Americas*, 102–5, 111, 140–46.

24. On Newte, see Rodríguez, *Freedom's Mercenaries: Northern South America*, Vol. 1, 105–6; Vittorino, *Relaciones colombo-británicas*, 59–61. On the agreement made between MacGregor and Newte, see Court of chancery, "MacGregor v Newte, Bill Only" (London, 1823), C 13/2787/9, TNA.

25. Rodríguez, "Gregor MacGregor," 90.

26. Rafter, *Memoirs of Gregor McGregor*, 142, 167, 383.

27. Bennett, *General MacGregor*, 202.

28. "Letters from Kingston, Jamaica, of the 24th of March," *Kentish Weekly Post or Canterbury Journal*, May 18, 1819; "Letters from Kingston, Jamaica, of the 24th of March," *Public Ledger and Daily Advertiser*, May 17, 1819.

29. Rafter, *Memoirs of Gregor McGregor*, 170.

30. Ian Anderson, "Hyslops," Hyslop-Maxwell, accessed September 29, 2015, http://hyslopmaxwell.com/hyslops; Humphreys, "British Merchants and South American Independence," 117–21. Ian Anderson suggests that Bolívar's famous 1815 Letter from Jamaica, in which he sets out the justifications for Hispanic Americans' republican claims to independence, was intended for Maxwell Hyslop. See Bolivar, "Reply of a South American."

31. Marichal, *Century of Debt Crises*, 19.

32. Rafter, *Memoirs of Gregor McGregor*, 170.

33. Rafter, *Memoirs of Gregor McGregor*, 171, 211.

34. Morillo, *Mémoires du général Morillo*, 219–20.

35. Vittorino, *Relaciones colombo-británicas*, 93.

36. Rodríguez, "Gregor MacGregor," 113–29; Friede, "La expedición de Mac-Gregor a Ríohacha."

37. Rodríguez, "Gregor MacGregor," 128.

38. Head, *Privateers of the Americas*, 108–11.

39. José María Palomar, "Noticia de la invasion de Truxillo" (1820), Guatemala Collection_B820|b.P181n, JCBL.

40. As Matthew Dziennik shows, the Miskitu were often seen as formidable warriors by European colonial and military representatives. More importantly, that assessment also stemmed from a major campaign by the Miskitu themselves to demonstrate their warfighting abilities to British colonials in the region. Dziennik, "Miskitu, Military Labour, and the San Juan Expedition."

41. Hendriks, *A Plain Narrative of Facts*, 21.

42. George Arthur to Carlos Urrutia, June 9, 1820, GBR/0115/RCMS 270/47_120, RCSL.

43. Roberts, *Narratives of Voyages*, 163.

44. George Arthur to Bathurst, January 15, 1821, GBR/0115/RCMS 270/46_41, RCSL.

45. "Grant of Land by George Frederic, King of the Mosquito Nation, Caribbean, to Sir Gregor MacGregor" (April 29, 1820), NRAS945/20/19/72, LBGA.

46. Gregor MacGregor to Brigadier General Baron Tinto, April 7, 1823, CO 123/34, TNA.

47. On similar dynamics, see also Richter, "To 'Clear the King's and Indians' Title,'" 59.

48. Roberts, *Narratives of Voyages*, 154–64.

49. Roughley, *Jamaica Planter's Guide*, 16. See also Ragatz, *Fall of the Planter Class*, 10, 99–102.

50. On such career changes, see, for example, Alessandro Bonvini's work on Argentina's Legión Agrícola-Militar, established in the second half of the nineteenth century by Mazzinian exiles. Bonvini, "«L'aratro e la spada»."

51. It is not possible to confirm the existence of this letter, since the original has not been found. However, in a letter to Rothschild just under a year later, MacGregor mentions an initial contact made on April 29, 1820, and summarizes some of the issues raised in the original letter. See Gregor MacGregor to Nathan M. Rothschild, March 16, 1821, Sundry Letters, 'M' 1821, RAL XI/112/54, RA.

52. Wasserman, "Hep! Hep!," 811–12; Wasserman, Schwarzfuchs, and Lipman, "Rothschild," 489.

53. East, "Business Entrepreneur in a Changing Colonial Economy," 20.

54. Liedtke, "Modern Communication"; Ferguson, "Rise of the Rothschilds"; López-Morell and O'Kean, "Stable Network."

55. Acquisition of privileged information for financiers on the basis of their market share was a feature of European financial systems in the first half of the nineteenth century. In a recent study, Stefano Ugolini notes a similar phenomenon in Geneva's financial system at the time. In view of their considerable market power, local players such as Alexandre Lombard, Charles Odier, and Louis Pictet were able to allow second-tier players, like Jacques Mirabaud, to give them exclusive access to privileged financial information. Ugolini, "Origins of Swiss Wealth Management?"

56. Flandreau and Flores, "Bonds and Brands."

57. Court of Chancery, "MacGregor v Newte, Bill Only" (London, 1823), C 13/2787/9, TNA.

58. George Arthur to Bathurst, January 15, 1821, CO 123/30, TNA.

59. Carlos Urrutia to Gordon, July 18, 1820, CO 123/30, TNA.

60. Gregor MacGregor to Nathan M. Rothschild, March 16, 1821, Sundry Letters, 'M' 1821, RAL XI/112/54, RA.

61. Since neither the first letter of 1820 nor the copy have been found in the Rothschild Archive in London, it is difficult to know whether MacGregor is referring to a duplicate of the concession granted by the Miskitu king or to the one he himself wanted to grant to the "Hebrews."

62. Bushnell, *Santander Regime in Gran Colombia*, 10–22.

63. Alexander, *Life of Alexander Alexander*, Vol. 2, 147–61.

64. MacGregor, *Exposición documentada*, 4; Alexander, *Life of Alexander Alexander*, Vol. 1, 162. The Congress started several months late, in August 1821. See Bushnell, *Santander Regime in Gran Colombia*, 14.

65. Gregor MacGregor to Nicholas Vansittart, March 13, 1821, CO 137/152, TNA.

66. Gregor MacGregor to Spencer Perceval, January 18, 1812, FO 72/171/1, TNA.

67. MacGregor, *Exposición documentada*, 4–5.

68. Jean-Louis Aury, too, apparently bore the consequences of a disagreement with Bolívar. See Head, *Privateers of the Americas*, 94.

69. Rodríguez, "Gregor MacGregor," 129.

70. Gregor MacGregor to Nicholas Vansittart, March 13, 1821, CO 137/152, TNA.

71. On the sometimes challenging participation of foreigners in the formation of national identities of new Latin American independent nations, please see Brown, "Inca, Sailor, Soldier, King," 47–49; Brown, "Uncertain Collective Identities."

72. See the military correspondence between MacGregor and Miranda: Gregor MacGregor to Francisco Miranda, May 16, 1812, Documentos 1811–1816 (Marqués de Rojas)/Documento 281, AGFM.

73. Gregor MacGregor to Nicholas Vansittart, March 13, 1821, CO 137/152, TNA.

74. Gregor MacGregor, "Proclamation of Gregor, Cazique of Poyais, Addressed to the Inhabitants of the Territory of Poyais, Whom He Addresses as 'Poyers,'" April 13, 1821, GD112/74/897/2, NRS.

75. Hasbrouck, "Gregor McGregor," 442.

76. Pro Ruiz, "Figure du cacique," 30–32.

77. Caballero, "Incaísmo as the First Guiding Fiction"; Brown, "Inca, Sailor, Soldier, King," 49; Pagden, *Spanish Imperialism and the Political Imagination*, 138.

78. Gregor MacGregor to Nathan M. Rothschild, March 16, 1821, Sundry Letters, 'M' 1821, RAL XI/112/54, RA; Gregor MacGregor to Nicholas Vansittart, March 13, 1821, CO 137/152, TNA.

79. "1821 Jamaica Almanac Returns of Givings-in for the March Quarter, 1820 County of Surrey Parishes of Port Royal and Andrew," JFSGRL, 2013, http://www.jamaicanfamilysearch.com/Members/al1821_06.htm; "1821 Jamaica Almanac Returns of Givings-in for the March Quarter, 1820 County of Surrey Parishes of Portland and George," JFSGRL, 2013, http://www.jamaicanfamilysearch.com/Members/al1821_08.htm; "Monumental Inscriptions Kingston Parish Church Yard (Contd)," JFSGRL, 2013, http://www.jamaicanfamilysearch.com/Members/Barcheo8.htm. Higson's success as a planter is reflected in the fact that he was able to build a jetty in Port Royal harbor, damaged by a hurricane in 1817. See "Dreadful Hurricane," *Caledonian Mercury*, October 4, 1813. See also "Thomas Higson," LBSD, accessed September 5, 2024, https://www.ucl.ac.uk/lbs/person/view/2146639423.

80. Hakewill, *A Picturesque Tour of the Island of Jamaica*, chap. Kingston and Port Royal from Windsor Farm.

81. Rafter mentions that MacGregor's wife, who was pregnant and accompanied by her first child, had to seek shelter in the hut of a Jamaican slave after running out of money to pay the rent on the room where her husband had housed her. She was eventually "rescued" by Higson, who agreed to take her in until MacGregor returned. While Rafter's account certainly contains some interesting facts about MacGregor's Latin American military career, the passage describing the family's travails seems to be part of a campaign to slander the man he held, as we shall see below, responsible for his brother's death. See Rafter, *Memoirs of Gregor McGregor*, 383.

82. Ragatz, *Fall of the Planter Class*, 68.

83. Hooker, *Journal of Botany*, 138; Madden, *A Twelvemonth's Residence in the West Indies*, 59.

84. "Cow-Tree of America," *Penny Magazine of the Society for the Diffusion of Useful Knowledge*, April 30, 1836.

85. Fawcett, "Public Gardens and Plantations of Jamaica," 348; Cundall, *Historic Jamaica*, 175–76.

86. "Poyais Share Certificate A501," 1823, Coins & Medals CIB.14660, BM; "Bill of Exchange for One Poyaisian Dollar," J 284/ SD 261, ADD; Villiers, "Une vente de terrain," 198.

87. "Poyais Share Certificate 1295," 1823, Coins & Medals CIB.14659, BM.

88. James Colson to Hector MacDonald, "Correspondence: James Colson, Glasgow, to Hector Macdonald Buchanan, WS, Referring to Sir Gregor MacGregor's Estates in Honduras," Correspondence, April 17, 1822, GD47/635, NRS.

89. Gregor MacGregor to Nicholas Vansittart, March 13, 1821, CO 137/152, TNA.

90. Ragatz, *Fall of the Planter Class*, 338–39; Culbertson, *International Economic Policies*, 435–37, 503–4.

91. Ragatz, *Fall of the Planter Class*, 342; Walker, Lea, and Nunn, *Parliamentary Register*, 337; Roughley, *Jamaica Planter's Guide*, 36.

92. Ragatz, *Fall of the Planter Class*, 337.

93. Ward, *British West Indian Slavery*.

94. Draper, "Rise of a New Planter Class?"; Ragatz, *Fall of the Planter Class*, 332–33.

95. Ragatz, *Fall of the Planter Class*, 332–38; Ward, *British West Indian Slavery*, 49.

96. Ragatz, *Fall of the Planter Class*, 342.

97. Ward, *British West Indian Slavery*, 49.

98. Williams, *Capitalism & Slavery*, 87–91; Harper Fender, "Smuggling," 20. Another example may illustrate the kind of risks involved. Pilar Nogues-Marco's study of the eighteenth-century Castilian black market in silver ingots shows that smuggling was controlled mainly by groups of merchants—chiefly French—with greater capital resources. Often benefiting from diplomatic immunity, these merchants used their considerable economic clout to build up international distribution networks. Nogues-Marco, "Microeconomics of Bullionism."

99. On the role of neutral ports in the War of Spanish Succession, see Schnakenbourg, "Neutres et neutralité."

100. Gregor MacGregor to Nathan M. Rothschild, June 20, 1821, Sundry Letters, 'M' 1821, RAL XI/112/54, RA.

101. On the profits promised by English colonial promoters vaunting the merits of American business projects, see also Spence, *British Investments and the American Mining Frontier*, 58–59.

102. Gregor MacGregor to Nathan M. Rothschild, June 20, 1821, Sundry Letters, 'M' 1821, RAL XI/112/54, RA.

103. Ragatz, *Fall of the Planter Class*, 10, 99–102.

104. A West Indian, *No Colonies No Funds!!!*, 18.

105. Jackson, *Impunity and Capitalism*, chap. 6.

106. Dawson, *First Latin American Debt Crisis*, 77.

107. Gille, *Histoire de la maison Rothschild*.

108. Flandreau and Flores, "Bonds and Brands," 664–67.

109. Dawson, *First Latin American Debt Crisis*, 92–94.

110. Bob Lundin, "The Lundin, Scott, & MacGregor Story: Our Family History—Chapter 11," The Clan Gregor Society, 2004, http://www.clangregor.com/lundin-scott-macgregor-story/.

111. This so-called decline of the Jamaican planter class was first identified by Lowell Ragatz in 1828, and then detailed by authors such as Christer Petley and David Ryden. See Ragatz, *Fall of the Planter Class*; Petley, "Rethinking the Fall of the Planter Class"; Ryden, "Does Decline Make Sense?"

Chapter 4

1. "Sir Gregor MacGregor," *Caledonian Mercury*, August 4, 1821.

2. Rafter, *Memoirs of Gregor McGregor*.

3. "General MacGregor," *Morning Post*, October 2, 1821; "General MacGregor," *Caledonian Mercury*, October 20, 1821.

4. Weatherhead, *Account of the Late Expedition Against the Isthmus of Darien*.

5. Hendriks, *Plain Narrative of Facts*, 22–23; Codd, *Proceedings of an Inquiry*, 109.

6. "The Marfield Gunpowder Works," *Caledonian Mercury*, August 24, 1820; "Notice to the Creditors of William Temple," *Caledonian Mercury*, October 26, 1820; "North British Fire Insurance Company," *Aberdeen Press and Journal*, February 2, 1820.

7. "Inventory of the Personal Estate of James Ogilvie" (December 30, 1835), Wills and testaments Reference SC70/1/53 Edinburgh Sheriff Court Inventories, NRS; Ledru-Rollin et al., "Messal C. Sturt," 721.

8. William John Richardson, "To the Editor of the Public Ledger," *Public Ledger and Daily Advertiser*, January 26, 1824.

9. On partnerships not requiring official recognition, see Harris, *Industrializing English Law*, 27–29. On bills of exchange, see Neal, *Rise of Financial Capitalism*.

10. The 1720 Bubble Act made it illegal for any company to take funds or offer stocks like a joint-stock company without first obtaining a royal charter. It was repealed in 1825. On this topic, see Harris, "Bubble Act"; Harris, "Political Economy." As Jean-Philippe Rochat shows in a study on French sociétés anonymes, obtaining a charter gives a company a special "privilege" that functions as an economic policy tool for the issuing au-

thority. On this topic, see Rochat, "La société anonyme en France," 99–100, 252–54. The French société anonyme in the early nineteenth century is considered here to be virtually equivalent to an English joint-stock company: It was also divided into stocks and required political approval to be formed. However, authorization in this instance was granted by the French government. See also "Code de commerce (1807)," 358.

11. Fenn, "British Investment in South America," 129–46; Costeloe, *Bubbles and Bonanzas*, 28–29.

12. Fenn, "British Investment in South America," 135.

13. Equitable Loan Bank Company, *Plan of the Bank*.

14. "On the Transfer of Shares in Joint-Stock Companies," *Legal Observer*, July 27, 1839; Connery, *Essay on Charitable Economy*, 13; Harris, "Political Economy," 679–80.

15. Harris, *Industrializing English Law*, 134–36.

16. A Retired Pawnbroker, *Examination of the Present Modes of Granting Temporary Loans*; Court of Common Council, *Report of the Proceedings in the Court of Common Council Relative to the Equitable Loan Bank Company*; *Defence of the Principles of the Equitable Loan Bank*; *Pawnbrokers' Reply to the Pretended Fair and Candid Statement*.

17. On criminal charges in cases of bankruptcy, see *New Bankrupt Act*; Lester, *Victorian Insolvency*.

18. Neal, *Rise of Financial Capitalism*.

19. Cassis, *Capitals of Capital*, 21–23.

20. Humboldt, *Political Essay on the Kingdom of New Spain*. On the appeal of the Latin American debt market in London, see Neal, "Financial Crisis of 1825."

21. On the speed of transatlantic communication, see Kaukiainen, "Shrinking the World."

22. Paquette, "Intellectual Context of British Diplomatic Recognition."

23. House of Lords, "Navigation Laws" (House of Lords, June 17, 1822), HL Deb 17 June 1822 vol 7 cc1119–22, Hansard.

24. House of Commons, "Treaty of Amity, Commerce, and Navigation with the State of Colombia" (House of Commons, February 6, 1826), HC Deb 06 February 1826 vol 14 cc111–7, Hansard.

25. Rodríguez, *Freedom's Mercenaries: Northern South America*, Vol. 1, 675–77; Waddell, "British Neutrality."

26. Committee for General Purposes of the London Stock Exchange, "Minute Book" (London, 1819–1823), 321–25, MS14600/009, GL; Committee for General Purposes of the London Stock Exchange, *Rules and Regulations*.

27. Cope, "Stock Exchange Revisited," 18.

28. Committee for General Purposes of the London Stock Exchange, *Rules and Regulations*, 41. For an interesting discussion on the use of the *bona fide* label as a means of social control in London's financial markets, see Flandreau, *Anthropologists in the Stock Exchange*, 126–143.

29. See, for example, "Foreign Funds," *The Times*, March 10, 1823; "Foreign Funds," *Observer*, September 1, 1823.

30. Dawson, *First Latin American Debt Crisis*, 22–28. See the following discussion for more information on the Colombian loan of 1822.

31. Klerman, "Legal Fictions as Strategic Instruments," 14–15. I am grateful to Jean-Laurent Rosenthal for suggesting this reference.

32. Costeloe, *Bonds and Bondholders*, 3–4.

33. Fodor, "Boom That Never Was?," 10.

34. Flandreau and Flores, "Bonds and Brands," 652.

35. Costeloe, *Bonds and Bondholders*, 6–7; Fodor, "Boom That Never Was?," 6.

36. MAN Group, "Descendants of Jacob Lumbrozzo de Mattos," accessed August 11, 2013, http://www.manfamily.org/PDFs/Lousada%20Family%20Genealogy%202007.pdf; Cope, "Goldsmids and the Development of the London Money Market," 182; Flandreau, "Pricing Moses Montefiore," 185.

37. Unfortunately, the specific coupon, term, and fee demanded by Mocatta are not given in the sources that mention this loan proposal. William John Richardson, "To the Editor of the Public Ledger," *Public Ledger and Daily Advertiser*, January 26, 1824; Hendriks, *Plain Narrative of Facts*, 6.

38. Neal, "Financial Crisis of 1825," sec. Latin American Securities.

39. See, for example, Hodgson, *Account of the Mosquito Territory*; Henderson, *Account of the British Settlement of Honduras*; Edwards, *Poyais*.

40. Schorsch, "Sephardic Business," 491. On the Mocattas, see Rubinstein, Jolles, and Rubinstein, *Palgrave Dictionary of Anglo-Jewish History*, 680.

41. Richter, *Belisario of Jamaica*; Smalligan, "Effigy for the Enslaved."

42. Ranston, "Belisario." On the relationship between Belisario and Mocatta, see Jacob Mendes Belisario and Aaron Mocatta, "This Is to Give Notice . . . ," *London Gazette*, December 7, 1819.

43. "Police Intelligence: Bow-Street," *Morning Post*, August 27, 1827.

44. On the diversification of the financial and commercial activities of Europe's banking houses in the early nineteenth century, see Gille, *Histoire de la maison Rothschild*, 75; Chapman, *Rise of Merchant Banking*; Llorca-Jaña, "Shaping Globalization," 474.

45. Gille, *Histoire de la maison Rothschild*, 88–95; Pepe, *Relation des événements politiques et militaires*.

46. Lowe seemingly managed to recover claims from one Mr. Thomas of Genoa and his partner Josiah Reis of London; a Mr. Dragan and Giuseppe Serra of Genoa; and a Mr. Schneidler of Hamburg. See John Lowe to Nathan M. Rothschild, April 21, 1821, XI/112/53/2–3, RA.

47. John Lowe to Nathan M. Rothschild, April 21, 1821, XI/112/53/2, RA.

48. Lowe, "Mr. John Lowe to the Marquess of Londonderry."

49. It may be that Rothschild, whose Parisian brother was the inspiration for French novelist Émile Zola, recommended Lowe's services after turning down the Poyais project. In this he acted like Zola's fictitious banker Gundermann, receiving and redirecting a steady flow of people with proposals toward agents who might consider business that he himself did not wish to accept. Zola, *L'argent*. On the Rothschild brothers, their largesse, and the freedom to pick and choose which borrowers they wanted to work with due to their dominant financial position, see Gille, *Histoire de la maison Rothschild*, 69–70.

50. William John Richardson, "To the Editor of the Public Ledger," *Public Ledger and Daily Advertiser*, January 26, 1824.

51. On Perring, see "Sir John Perring, Bart.," *Gentleman's Magazine and Historical Chronicle*, March 1, 1831, sec. Obituary. On Shaw, see "SHAW, Benjamin (?1770–1843), of 29 Lower Brook Street, Mdx. | History of Parliament Online," accessed July 2, 2015, http://www.historyofparliamentonline.org/volume/1790-1820/member/shaw-benjamin-1770-1843.

52. Gregg, *Gregor MacGregor*, 12.

53. William John Richardson, "To the Editor of the Public Ledger," *Public Ledger and Daily Advertiser*, January 26, 1824; Hendriks, *Plain Narrative of Facts*, 6. Although the selling price settled on by Ogilvie and Lowe was higher than that initially agreed on, it was in line with those of other Latin American bonds issued in the same year.

54. "A New Species of Security . . . ," *Morning Post*, October 28, 1822.

55. "Fall of the Funds—Rumours of War," *Dublin Evening Post*, November 12, 1822.

56. On the bankruptcy of the banking house, see "Sir John Perring and Co," *Observer*, April 2, 1826; "Perring, Shaw and Barber (Banking Partnership)," 1829, ACC/2121, LMA.

57. Douglas, *Journals and Reminiscences*, 106.

58. Low, *Belise Merchants Unmasked*, 2–3.

59. The shippers in these bills were Alexander Arnott and James Ogilvie, and it was specially mentioned in the bills that the property was shipped by them on account and risk of General McGregor, as cazique of Poyais. Codd, *Proceedings of an Inquiry*, 125. On Arnott, see Henderson, *History of the Society of Advocates in Aberdeen*, 388; *Dod's Peerage, Baronetage and Knightage*, 59.

60. Douglas, *Journals and Reminiscences*, 106.

61. As Michael Costeloe shows in his book on sovereign debt issuance mechanisms in the early nineteenth century, it was not unusual for a contractor to acquire some or all of the bonds put up for sale. See Costeloe, *Bonds and Bondholders*, 4.

62. "Commercial Relations," *Public Ledger and Daily Advertiser*, December 21, 1822. A full version of the letter was published in 1823 in *The Pamphleteer*. See Lowe, "Letter to the Rt. Hon. George Canning."

63. On the Nicaragua transoceanic canal, see Folkman, *Nicaragua Route*.

64. Strangeways, *Sketch of the Mosquito Shore*.

65. On Strangeways as a pseudonym, see Nicholls, "'All Abbotsford to an Acre of Poyais,'" 738. On Strangeways' military service see War Office, "Returns of Officer's Service: Thomas Strangeways" (London, 1820), WO 25/775/8, TNA. For a history of his regiment, see Broughton, *Memoirs of the 65th Regiment*.

66. Strangeways, *Sketch of the Mosquito Shore*, 34, 84.

67. Samuel William Reynolds and Simon Jacques Rochard, *Sir Gregor Macgregor*, 1822, D10559, NPG. On Simon Rochard, see Remington, "Rochard, Simon Jacques." On William Lizars, see Melville, "Lizars, William Home."

68. Prebble, *King's Jaunt*, 130, 165.

69. "Theatre Royal, Covent Garden," *Morning Post*, October 14, 1822.

70. Committee for General Purposes of the London Stock Exchange, *Rules and Regulations*, 18–19.

71. Committee for General Purposes of the London Stock Exchange, *Rules and Regulations*, 36–37.

232   Notes to Chapter 4

72. In a way, these financial agents played the role of impresarios, much like Thomas Wade West, a theater promoter in the South of the United States toward the end of the eighteenth century, managing their "actors," while simultaneously working behind the scenes and out of the spotlight to build the promotional and technical infrastructure needed for "performances" to go without a hitch. On West, see Sherman, "Thomas Wade West."

73. "Sketch of the Mosquito Shore."

74. See, for example, Hackett, *Narrative of the Expedition*; Hippisley, *Narrative of the Expedition*.

75. An Officer Late in the Colombian Service, *Present State of Colombia*. On the ties between William Murray and the Latin American debt market, see Blake, *Disraeli*, 24–26; Flandreau, *Anthropologists in the Stock Exchange*, 87. On William Murray, see Zachs et al., "Murray Family."

76. Murray, Disraeli, and Powles would later formalize their association by founding together the *Representative*. Smiles, *Publisher and His Friends*, 252–54.

77. "More Loans!!!," *London Courier*, October 25, 1822.

78. "New Loans! Arrival Extraordinary," *London Courier*, October 26, 1822.

79. Verax, *A Letter to the Editor of the Quarterly Review*. Apparently, Verax was a pen name used by Strangeways. Douglas, *Journals and Reminiscences*, 96.

80. Gregor MacGregor to Don Victor Damian Saez, November 25, 1823, ESTADO,50,N.52(13), AGI.

81. To recap, one of the £2,000 100 bonds into which the £200,000 loan was divided could be acquired by paying an initial instalment of £15. Thus, the initial sale of all the scrips should have ensured a first payment of £30,000 for MacGregor's project.

82. Lowe, "Letter to the Rt. Hon. George Canning," 411.

83. William John Richardson, "To the Editor of the Public Ledger," *Public Ledger and Daily Advertiser*, January 26, 1824.

84. "MacGregor v. Lowe," *The Times*, April 23, 1824.

85. John Lowe to Nathan M. Rothschild, January 7, 1824, XI/112/71, RA.

86. John Lowe, "Poyais Loan of £200,000," *Public Ledger and Daily Advertiser*, January 15, 1823; John Lowe, "Poyais Loan of £200,000," *Scotsman*, January 29, 1823.

87. John Lowe, "The Subscribers to the Poyais Loan," *Morning Chronicle*, February 1, 1823; John Lowe, "The Subscribers to the Poyais Loan," *Morning Chronicle*, March 13, 1823.

88. "The Ship Kennersly Castle," *Oxford Journal*, January 25, 1823; A subscriber to the Poyais loan, "Extract from the Morning Herald of the 6th Inst.," *Caledonian Mercury*, February 15, 1823.

89. Hastie, *Narrative of a Voyage*, 2–3.

90. Alexander Arnott, "Poyais Loan," *Morning Post*, December 31, 1822.

91. Gregor MacGregor to Brigadier General Baron Tinto, April 7, 1823, CO 123/34, TNA.

92. Douglas, *Journals and Reminiscences*, 105; *Post-Office Annual Directory*, 290.

93. Douglas, *Journals and Reminiscences*, 116–19.

94. Great Britain War Office, *List of the Officers*, 40; Cannon, *Historical Record of the Twenty-Second*, 23–25.

95. Codd, *Proceedings of an Inquiry*, 100–105.

96. "Sir Gregor MacGregor's Settlements" (May 10, 1823), CO 123/34, TNA.
97. Douglas, *Journals and Reminiscences*, 85–120.
98. Hector Hall, "Preface" (Belize, September 30, 1823), 17, CO 123/34, TNA. James Douglas, the settlement's medical officer, equates a dollar to about four shillings and sixpence sterling. Douglas, *Journals and Reminiscences*, 116.
99. Hastie, *Narrative of a Voyage*, 5.
100. "Sir Gregor MacGregor's Settlements" (May 10, 1823), CO 123/34, TNA.
101. Hastie, *Narrative of a Voyage*, 8.
102. Hastie, *Narrative of a Voyage*, 8–9.
103. Douglas, *Journals and Reminiscences*, 111–12.
104. Douglas, *Journals and Reminiscences*, 102–3.
105. George Frederic to Alexander Murray, March 28, 1823, CO 123/34, TNA.
106. George Arthur to Jean-Louis Mallet, April 24, 1823, GBR/0115/RCMS 270/2, RCSL; Shaw, *Sir George Arthur*, 61–62.
107. On this regiment, see Wallace, *Regimental Chronicle*, 292.
108. Naylor, *Penny Ante Imperialism*, 97; Thomson, *Belize*, 41.
109. Naylor, *Penny Ante Imperialism*, 106.
110. Inhabitants of Honduras, *Defence of the Settlers of Honduras*, 40; Cundall, *Historic Jamaica*, 103.
111. William Bullock to the Magistrates and Pye, April 26, 1822, Meeting of Magistrates 1822–1823_16, BSRAS.
112. Burdon, *Archives of British Honduras*, Vol. 2, 272.
113. Edward Codd to Marshall Bennett, April 12, 1823, CO 123/34, TNA.
114. George Arthur to Bathurst, January 15, 1821, GBR/0115/RCMS 270/46_41, RCSL.
115. Marshall Bennett to George Frederic, April 26, 1823, CO 123/34, TNA.
116. Marshall Bennett and Geo. Westby to Edward Codd, May 13, 1823, CO 123/34, TNA.
117. James Douglas to Hector Hall, May 7, 1823, CO 123/34, TNA.
118. Hector Hall to Edward Codd, May 7, 1823, CO 123/34, TNA.
119. "Minutes of a Deposition" (Belize, May 28, 1823), Meeting of Magistrates 1822–1823, BSRAS.
120. "Minutes of a Deposition" (Belize, May 28, 1823), Meeting of Magistrates 1822–1823, BSRAS.
121. Thomas Pickstock, "Minutes of a Deposition" (Belize, May 31, 1823), Meeting of Magistrates 1822–1823, BSRAS.
122. Marshall Bennett and Thomas Pickstock, "Meeting of Magistrates" (Belize, June 5, 1823), Meeting of Magistrates 1822–1823, BSRAS.
123. Nicol Smith et al., "Deposition" (May 16, 1823), CO 123/34, TNA; Thomas Westcott and George Gouger, "Deposition" (May 16, 1823), CO 123/34, TNA.
124. Lloyd's of London, "Minutes of the Committee of Lloyd's" (London, 1823–1824), 177, CLC/B/148/A/001/MS31571/007, GL; "Public Meeting" (Belize, March 4, 1822), Meeting of Magistrates 1822–1823, BSRAS.
125. "The Following Is an Extract of a Letter Received at Lloyd's from Honduras," *The Times*, June 9, 1823; "The Following Is an Extract of a Letter Received at Lloyd's from Honduras, Dated 13th April," *Morning Post*, June 9, 1823.

Chapter 5

1. Gregor MacGregor to Brigadier General Baron Tinto, April 7, 1823, CO 123/34, TNA.
2. Hendriks, *Plain Narrative of Facts*, 9.
3. Ragatz, *Fall of the Planter Class*, 354–55.
4. Gregor MacGregor to Brigadier General Baron Tinto, April 7, 1823, CO 123/34, TNA.
5. The testimonies of settlers who landed in Poyais concur that Woodbine, who had officially been named vice cazique of Poyais by MacGregor, was not actually present onsite. In fact, he is identified as a British resident living in Cape Gracias a Dios in 1824. See George Woodbine, "Depositions Relating to His Late Majesty George Frederic Augustus" (Cape Gracias a Dios, March 10, 1824), CO 123/35, TNA; Hastie, *Narrative of a Voyage*.
6. Bingham, "Skeen v. M'Gregor," 242.
7. Gregor MacGregor to Brigadier General Baron Tinto, April 7, 1823, CO 123/34, TNA.
8. Codd, *Proceedings of an Inquiry*, 155; Eastment, *Wanstead Through the Ages*, 93–96.
9. "Poyais Loan," *Public Ledger and Daily Advertiser*, April 7, 1823. Publishing this article, in passing, certainly allowed Richardson to identify some of the other remaining Poyais backers.
10. The issue date is determined based on the missing coupons from the share certificates printed a few months later: "Poyais Share Certificate A501," 1823, Coins & Medals CIB.14660, BM.
11. Hendriks, *Plain Narrative of Facts*, 8–9.
12. Rafter, *Memoirs of Gregor McGregor*, 45.
13. Hendriks, *Plain Narrative of Facts*, 9.
14. Gregor MacGregor to Brigadier General Baron Tinto, April 7, 1823, CO 123/34, TNA.
15. "Government of Poyais-Council of State," *Morning Chronicle*, April 1, 1823.
16. Gregor MacGregor and Louis Dominique Février, "Dépôt et reconnaissance d'écritures d'un acte de concession S.S.P. fait par S.A.S. le Prince Grégor à la Compagnie coloniale française de la Nouvelle Neustrie" (Paris, August 9, 1825), MC/ET/LX/673, AN.
17. Duncan Phillips, "Silver Seal Box Reveals Tales of Fraud and Corruption," The Guilford Antiques & Fine Art Fair, April 20, 2012, http://www.antiquespr.com/uppdf/GUILDFORD%20FAIR%20SEAL%20BOX%20PRESS%20RELEASE%201.pdf.
18. Rubinstein, "End of 'Old Corruption,'" 72.
19. William John Richardson, "To the Editor of the Public Ledger," *Public Ledger and Daily Advertiser*, January 26, 1824.
20. Hendriks, *Plain Narrative of Facts*, 7.
21. Wetenhall James, *Course of the Exchange*, July 7, 1823.
22. Wetenhall James, *Course of the Exchange*, July 28, 1823, and August 8, 1823; Hendriks, *Plain Narrative of Facts*, 7.

23. Cope, "Stock Exchange Revisited," 7.

24. This conflict perhaps grew out of a pre-existing quarrel. The same groups had previously clashed in 1819 on whether options (contracts between two parties conferring on the buyer the right but not the obligation to buy or sell securities in the future in return for paying a premium), which were illegal at the time under British law, could be traded on the London Stock Exchange. See Neal, "London Stock Exchange in the First Age of Globalization," 8–9.

25. Neal, "London Stock Exchange in the First Age of Globalization," 8–10.

26. Committee for General Purposes of the London Stock Exchange, "Minute Book" (London, 1819–1823), 321–25, MS14600/009, GL.

27. Hendriks, *Plain Narrative of Facts*, 6–7.

28. William John Richardson et al. to Earl Bathurst, March 1824, CO 123/35, TNA.

29. On Thick, see "Obituary," *Gentleman's Magazine and Historical Chronicle*, October 1856. On Sowerby, see Woodcroft, "Gilman Sowerby," 818.

30. Studying the formation in the early nineteenth century of the U.S. banking system, which was essentially made up of independent corporations, Naomi Lamoreaux details how these institutions extended a large proportion of loans to their own directors or shareholders. A common and recognized practice, the allocation of funds by the directors of these banks to shareholders, others with close ties to the board or to themselves, was a strategy that gave these directors preferred access to the capital needed to grow their own parallel business activities. Purchasing stocks in a specific banking corporation thus acted as a targeted investment that made it possible to place funds in the diversified businesses of the bank's directors and to gain an indirect but preferred stake in the entrepreneurial activities of a given region or business consortium. See Lamoreaux, *Insider Lending*.

31. "The Following Is an Extract of a Letter Received at Lloyd's from Honduras," *The Times*, June 9, 1823; "The Following Is an Extract of a Letter Received at Lloyd's from Honduras, Dated 13th April," *Morning Post*, June 9, 1823.

32. William John Richardson, "To the Editor of the Times," *The Times*, June 10, 1823.

33. "(Advertisement)—The Skeene," *The Times*, June 11, 1823.

34. "Despatches of Skeene Arrived at Belize" (August 13, 1823), CO 123/34, TNA.

35. Bennett Marshall, Wright John, August John et al., "Meeting of Magistrates" (Belize, August 13, 1823), Meeting of Magistrates 1822–1823, BSRAS.

36. Marshall Bennett et al., "Meeting of Magistrates" (Belize, August 13, 1823), Meeting of Magistrates 1822–1823, BSRAS.

37. Marshall Bennett, Thomas Pickstock, and John Wright, "Meeting of Magistrates" (Belize, August 6, 1823), Meeting of Magistrates 1822–1823, BSRAS; "Public Meeting" (Belize, February 7, 1823), Meeting of Magistrates 1822–1823, BSRAS; Marshall Bennett, John Wright, John August, and David Betson, "Meeting of Magistrates" (Belize, July 24, 1823), Meeting of Magistrates 1822–1823, BSRAS; Marshall Bennett et al., "Meeting of Magistrates" (Belize, July 26, 1823), Meeting of Magistrates 1822–1823, BSRAS.

38. "Despatches of Skeene Arrived at Belize" (August 13, 1823), CO 123/34, TNA.

39. Marshall Bennett et al., "Meeting of Magistrates" (Belize, August 16, 1823), Meet-

ing of Magistrates 1822–1823, BSRAS; Marshall Bennett, John Wright, and Thomas Pickstock, "Meeting of Magistrates" (Belize, August 19, 1823), Meeting of Magistrates 1822–1823, BSRAS.

40. Codd, *Proceedings of an Inquiry*, 74–75.

41. Edward Irving to John Campbell, December 8, 1823, CO 123/35, TNA.

42. Which is what happened in fact, because Campbell passed the letter on to Superintendent Codd, which explains why the document turned up in a Colonial Office file containing a collection of correspondence forwarded by Codd to his London superiors: Edward Codd to Robert Wilmot-Horton, "Private," February 21, 1824, CO 123/35, TNA.

43. On Hendriks, see "Herman Hendriks," LBSD, accessed February 22, 2018, http://wwwdepts-live.ucl.ac.uk/lbs/person/view/21098; *Gentleman's Magazine and Historical Chronicle*. "Marriages." September 1821, 278; Jensen, *Last Colonials*, 77–78.

44. Hendriks, *Plain Narrative of Facts*, 8–9.

45. Madiou, *Histoire d'Haïti*, 318–20.

46. Hendriks, *Plain Narrative of Facts*, 9–10.

47. Gregor MacGregor, "General Bond for the Poyaisian Loan of 1823 for £300,000 Sterling" (1823), J 284/1823 19, ADD; Hendriks, *Plain Narrative of Facts*, 10.

48. Flandreau and Flores, "Bonds and Brands," 657.

49. Hendriks, *Plain Narrative of Facts*, 10, 24.

50. Wright, *Memoir of the Mosquito Territory*.

51. James Sool, "Narrative of All the Circumstances" (November 19, 1823), CO 123/34, TNA.

52. Burdon, *Archives of British Honduras*, Vol. 2, 279. On British Honduras trade in Central America, see Naylor, "British Commercial Relations with Central America."

53. George Frederic to Edward Codd, March 1, 1824, CO 123/35, TNA; George Frederic to Admiral Wright, March 1, 1824, CO 123/35, TNA.

54. "Proclamation of the King of the Mosquito Shore," *The Times*, September 1, 1823; "Proclamation of the King of the Mosquito Shore," *Hull Packet*, September 8, 1823.

55. Hippisley, *Acts of Oppression*; Mérilhou, *Précis pour le Général Sir Grégor Mac-Grégor*.

56. Edward Irving to John Campbell, December 8, 1823, CO 123/35, TNA.

57. On Thomas Irving, see Thomas Carlyle to Alexander Carlyle, "Thomas Carlyle to Alexander Carlyle," April 27, 1822, DOI: 10.1215/lt-18220427-TC-AC-01; CL 2:92–95, CLO; Thomas Carlyle to James Carlyle, "Thomas Carlyle to James Carlyle, the Elder," June 25, 1824, DOI: 10.1215/lt-18240625-TC-JCE-01; CL 3:96–97, CLO. On Gustavus Hippisley, see Hippisley, *Siege of Barcelona*.

58. Gregor MacGregor to Vicomte de Chateaubriand, November 25, 1823, P16108/227–230, AD; Gregor MacGregor to Don Victor Damian Saez, November 25, 1823, ESTADO,50,N.52(13), AGI.

59. On France's relationship with Latin American uprisings, see Robertson, *France and Latin-American Independence*, 253–95.

60. Ouvrard, *Mémoires de G.-J. Ouvrard*, 188–91. On Ouvrard, see Gille, *Histoire de la maison Rothschild*, 111. On Theodore I of Corsica, see Gasper, *Theodore von Neuhoff*.

61. On Dard's work defending the property of French émigrés, see Dard, *Biens des*

émigrés; Dard, *Opinion d'un jurisconsulte*. On his advocacy for French and Spanish colonial interests in the West Indies, see Dard, *Observations sur le droit de souveraineté de la France sur Saint-Domingue*.

62. Gregor MacGregor to Joseph Mérilhou, December 11, 1826, J 284/1826 185, ADD. On Mérilhou, see Becquart, "Joseph Mérilhou"; Sarrut and Saint-Edme, "Mérilhou, Joseph"; Robert and Cougny, "Mérilhou, Joseph."

63. Jean-François Lehuby and Louis Dominique Février, "Dépôt et reconnaissance d'écritures d'un acte de concession fait à Mr Odolant Desnos par la Compagnie coloniale de la Nouvelle Neustrie" (Paris, August 12, 1825), MC/ET/LX/673, AN; Gregor Mac-Gregor and Louis Dominique Février, "Dépôt et reconnaissance d'écritures d'un acte de concession S.S.P. fait par S.A.S. le Prince Grégor à la Compagnie Coloniale française de la Nouvelle Neustrie" (Paris, August 9, 1825), MC/ET/LX/673, AN.

64. Joseph Mérilhou, "Notes sur le procès Lehuby" (Paris, May 31, 1826), J 284/1826 159, ADD; Lehuby, *Procès contre la Compagnie de la Nouvelle-Neustrie*; Hippisley, *Acts of Oppression*.

65. Brown, "Gregor MacGregor," 46–47, 56–57.

66. Bennett, *General MacGregor*, 222.

67. "Public Dinner to Don Francisco Antonio Zea," *The Times*, July 11, 1822.

68. House of Commons, "Recognition of the Independence of South America-London, Petition For," June 15, 1824, HC Deb 15 June 1824 Vol 11 cc1344–406, Hansard.

69. "Poyais Share Certificate A501," 1823, Coins & Medals CIB.14660, BM.

70. On James Whiting, see Costeloe, *Bonds and Bondholders*, 6.

71. For an example of a similarly designed certificate, see "Colombian Loan Share Certificate A 7826," May 31, 1824, CLC/B/060/MS34613, GL.

72. "Poyais Share Certificate A501," 1823, Coins & Medals CIB.14660, BM. According to the departmental archivists contacted for this research, Achille Dutertre's minutes seem to contain no such document. See François-Nicolas-Achille Dutertre, "Minutes Notariales" (Boulogne-sur-Mer, 1823), 4 E 50/81, ADPC.

73. Gregor MacGregor, "General Bond for the Poyaisian Loand of 1823 for £300,000 Sterling" (1823), J 284/1823 19, ADD.

74. Gregg, *Gregor MacGregor*, 15–17.

75. "New Poyais Loan," *Saunders's News-Letter*, October 24, 1823.

76. Hendriks, *Plain Narrative of Facts*, 25. Based on three hundred thousand securities issued at £10.

77. "New Poyais Loan," *Saunders's News-Letter*, October 24, 1823.

78. Wetenhall James, *Course of the Exchange*, October 1823

79. "Mansion-House," *Morning Chronicle*, October 21, 1823; "Mansion-House—Poyais Settlers—More Cases," *The Times*, October 21, 1823.

80. Flandreau and Flores, "Bonds and Brands," 665.

81. Hastie, *Narrative of a Voyage*, 19–20.

82. Hastie, *Narrative of a Voyage*, 21–22.

83. "Poyais Emigrants," *The Times*, October 25, 1823.

84. On duels as a reputational tactic, see Bignon and Flandreau, "Economics of Bad-mouthing," 622; Simpson, "Dandelions on the Field of Honour."

85. "Mansion-House," *The Times*, October 29, 1823.

86. On the reputational impact of the press on the financial markets, see Bignon and Flandreau, "Price of Media Capture."

87. Marshall Bennett, Geo. Westby, and Edward Codd, "Poyais Settlement," *The Times*, September 1, 1823.

88. Hendriks, *Plain Narrative of Facts*, 10, 24; Low, *Belise Merchants Unmasked*, 3; Codd, *Proceedings of an Inquiry*, 143–45.

89. Low, *Belise Merchants Unmasked*, 42.

90. Scott, *Mary English*, 43–64, 83–87. Mary English's story is a fascinating one. Because of her knowledge of and ties to the networks of British mercenaries and Latin American revolutionaries, she was hired in 1822 as a commercial agent and sent to South America by the banking house of Barclay, Herring, and Richardson, which acted as the issuing bank for the Guatemala and Mexico loans of 1825.

91. Low, *Belise Merchants Unmasked*, 6–11.

92. According to Robert Naylor, these men formed a united group working in Bennett's interests: Naylor, "British Commercial Relations with Central America," 163.

93. William Gentle, "Meeting of Magistrates" (Belize, September 10, 1823), Meeting of Magistrates 1822–1823, BSRAS.

94. Low, *Belise Merchants Unmasked*, 58.

95. William John Richardson et al. to Earl Bathurst, March 1824, CO 123/35, TNA.

96. William John Richardson to Robert Wilmot-Horton, March 22, 1824, CO 123/35, TNA.

97. George Augustus Low to Edward Codd, May 24, 1824, CO 123/35, TNA.

98. "The King Versus Low George Augustine" (Belize, June 29, 1824), Grand Court Jun 1824 -Jun 1825, BSRAS.

99. On this topic, see Slapper and Kelly, *English Legal System*, 6.

100. On Low's gout, see Hall, *Falsehood Detected*, 39.

101. "The King Versus Low George Augustine" (Belize, June 30, 1824), Grand Court Jun 1824–Jun 1825, BSRAS.

102. "The King Versus Low George Augustine" (Belize, July 1, 1824), Grand Court Jun 1824–Jun 1825, BSRAS.

103. "The King Versus Low George Augustine" (Belize, July 1, 1824), Grand Court Jun 1824–Jun 1825, BSRAS.

104. On the criteria to be considered an inhabitant, see Burdon, *Archives of British Honduras*, Vol. 2, 202.

105. Edward Codd to Marshall Bennett, April 12, 1823, CO 123/34, TNA.

106. Codd, *Proceedings of an Inquiry*, iii, 5–6.

107. "The King Versus Low George Augustine" (Belize, July 2, 1824), Grand Court Jun 1824–Jun 1825, BSRAS.

108. "The King Versus Low George Augustine" (Belize, July 3, 1824), Grand Court Jun 1824–Jun 1825, BSRAS.

109. Hall, *Falsehood Detected*.

110. Hendriks, *Plain Narrative of Facts*, 15–16.

Notes to Chapter 5   239

111. Flandreau, "Sovereign States, Bondholders Committees, and the London Stock Exchange."

112. The Barnard Act banned stock jobbing and forward and options trading. See Banner, *Speculation*, 61–62; Neal, "London Stock Exchange in the First Age of Globalization," 8.

113. For example, in November 1823, Jasper Vander Sluys, a merchant banker in the City, brought a case before the Foreign Stock Market about a debt owed to him by one Teschmacher. After hearing both parties, the committee ruled in favor of Teschmacher and ordered Vander Sluys to pay him more than the amount demanded in the original request. See Committee of the Foreign Stock Market, "Minute Book" (London, 1823–1828), 91–92, MS14617/001, GL.

114. Polden, "Court of Chancery."

115. Dickens, *Bleak House*.

116. Taylor, *Boardroom Scandal*, 30–31.

117. Flandreau, "New Facts and Old Fictions," 675. For examples of disputes made public, in particular regarding the case of Poyais, see "To Our Country Cousins," *Morning Advertiser*, January 3, 1823; Mary Anne Lloyd, "To the Gentlemen of the Stock Exchange: Lines on the Poyais Bonds" (Lambeth, August 12, 1823), General Reference Collection 1872.a.1.(172), BL.

118. Stringham, "Emergence of the London Stock Exchange as a Self-Policing Club."

119. Committee of the Foreign Stock Market, "Minute Book" (London, 1823–1828), 279–82, MS14617/001, GL.

120. Dawson, *First Latin American Debt Crisis*, 22–28.

121. Committee of the Foreign Stock Market, "Minute Book" (London, 1823–1828), 76–78, MS14617/001, GL.

122. Committee of the Foreign Stock Market, "Minute Book" (London, 1823–1828), 94–95, MS14617/001, GL. On Richardson as a Colombian bondholder, see "Colombian Bonds," *Morning Chronicle*, September 17, 1823.

123. Committee of the Foreign Stock Market, "Minute Book" (London, 1823–1828), 96, MS14617/001, GL. On Cohen, see Kaplan, *Nathan Mayer Rothschild*, 8, 10, 25–26, 30.

124. Committee of the Foreign Stock Market, "Minute Book" (London, 1823–1828), 98–99, MS14617/001, GL.

125. Committee of the Foreign Stock Market, "Minute Book" (London, 1823–1828), 99, MS14617/001, GL.

126. Wetenhall appears to have been accused of a lack of impartiality, possibly money-driven, when deciding which securities to list in the *Course of the Exchange*. See Committee of the Foreign Stock Market, "Minute Book" (London, 1823–1828), 99, MS14617/001, GL.

127. Committee of the Foreign Stock Market, "Minute Book" (London, 1823–1828), 100, MS14617/001, GL.

128. Committee of the Foreign Stock Market, "Minute Book" (London, 1823–1828), 105, 108, 133–35, MS14617/001, GL.

129. Committee of the Foreign Stock Market, "Minute Book" (London, 1823–1828),

108, MS14617/001, GL. On Greek independence, the Greek loan, and Bowring, see Chatziioannou, "War, Crisis and Sovereign Loans"; Bartle, "Bowring and the Greek Loans"; Saint Clair, *That Greece Might Still Be Free*; Cunningham, "Philhellenes, Canning and Greek Independence."

130. Saint Clair, *That Greece Might Still Be Free*, 85.

131. Committee of the Foreign Stock Market, "Minute Book" (London, 1823–1828), 109, MS14617/001, GL.

132. "De Wintz v Hendriks," *Morning Chronicle*, November 11, 1824; Saint Clair, *That Greece Might Still Be Free*, 127–31.

133. Committee of the Foreign Stock Market, "Minute Book" (London, 1823–1828), 109, MS14617/001, GL.

134. Committee of the Foreign Stock Market, "Minute Book" (London, 1823–1828), 115, MS14617/001, GL.

135. Daniel Mocatta, "Greek Loan of £800,000 Stock" (London, February 19, 1824), 1890.c.6.(70.), BL.

136. Committee of the Foreign Stock Market, "Minute Book" (London, 1823–1828), 118–19, MS14617/001, GL.

137. Committee of the Foreign Stock Market, "Minute Book" (London, 1823–1828), 119–20, MS14617/001, GL.

138. "He objected to them & declared them to be spurious & not marketable." Committee of the Foreign Stock Market, "Minute Book" (London, 1823–1828), 185, MS14617/001, GL.

139. The existence of these bonds is mentioned in a short article published in the review of the International Bond & Share Society, which reported that two extremely rare bonds from the 1824 loan had been discovered at an auction sale. Photographs of these Poyais securities have also been located, but the resolution does not allow us to read the inscriptions in full. We can nevertheless decipher some of its signatures. In addition to that of MacGregor, we can find the signature of one Archibald Harny, who acted as the loan's contractor. Interests were to be paid directly at the latter's house, on Bartholomew Lane in the City of London. International Bond & Share Society, "'New' Poyais."

140. Committee of the Foreign Stock Market, "Minute Book" (London, 1823–1828), 186, MS14617/001, GL.

141. For the specific mention of Darien, see "An Account of the Poyais Scheme," *Canadian Magazine and Literary Repository*, October 1824, 291. This article is published in two parts. The reference to Darien appears in the first part. For the second part, please see "An Account of the Poyais Scheme," *Canadian Magazine and Literary Repository*, November 1824. The Darien scheme was a failed attempt, primarily backed by Scottish investors, to establish a colony in the Darién Gap on the Isthmus of Panama. For an account of this venture, see Watt, *Price of Scotland*. MacGregor and his agents generally did not make reference to the memory of the unfortunate Darien settlement when advertising for Poyais. Instead, it was MacGregor's adversaries who drew comparisons between Poyais and this infamous Central American episode in Scottish colonial history. During his time as a mercenary fighting for the Latin American republican cause, MacGregor appealed to a sense of Scottish history and made reference to the Darien scheme to recruit

foreign officers for his military campaigns near the Isthmus of Panama. Brown, "Inca, Sailor, Soldier, King," 53; Weatherhead, *Account of the Late Expedition Against the Isthmus of Darien*, 36.

142. On trading off the London Stock Exchange, albeit covering a later period, see Taylor, "Inside and Outside the London Stock Exchange."

Chapter 6

1. Kafka, *Das Schloss*.
2. Gregor MacGregor to Nicholas Vansittart, March 13, 1821, CO 137/152, TNA.
3. See, for example, Edward Codd, "Dispatch No4 Transmitting to Earl Bathurst the Imports and Exports for the Quarter Ending 31 Dec 1822" (Honduras, February 24, 1823), CO 123/34, TNA; George Arthur to Bathurst, January 19, 1816, CO 123/25, TNA.
4. Edward Codd to Earl Bathurst, June 20, 1823, CO 123/34, TNA.
5. George Arthur to Bathurst, January 15, 1821, GBR/0115/RCMS 270/46_41, RCSL.
6. Murray-Young, *Colonial Office*, 1–4.
7. Johnston, *British Emigration Policy*, 15.
8. See, for example, Robert Wilmot-Horton to George Arthur, July 30, 1821, R3_19, BSRAS; Robert Wilmot-Horton to Edward Codd, July 3, 1823, R3_03, BSRAS.
9. Richards, "Horton, Sir Robert John Wilmot-"; Lamont, "Robert Wilmot Horton and Liberal Toryism"; Murray-Young, *Colonial Office*, 47–83; Bashford and Chaplin, *New Worlds of Thomas Robert Malthus*, 209–15; Johnston, *British Emigration Policy*, 57–68.
10. Lamont, "Robert Wilmot Horton and Liberal Toryism," 196–97.
11. Wilmot-Horton, *West India Question*.
12. Lamont, "Robert Wilmot Horton and Liberal Toryism," 193–95; Ward, *British West Indian Slavery*.
13. House of Commons, "Abolition of Slavery," May 15, 1823, HC Deb 15 May 1823 vol 9 cc257–360, Hansard.
14. Robert Wilmot-Horton to George Arthur, September 22, 1821, R3_21, BSRAS.
15. Robert Wilmot-Horton to George Arthur, March 16, 1822, R3_39, BSRAS.
16. George Arthur, "Private," July 17, 1819, GBR/0115/RCMS 270/41, RCSL.
17. On the Tambora eruption and its global cultural, economic, and political consequences, see Wood, *Tambora*. On the Peterloo massacre, see Hernon, *Riot!*, 21–38.
18. House of Commons, "Reform of Parliament," July 1, 1819, HC Deb 01 July 1819 vol 40 cc1440–503, Hansard.
19. Bashford and Chaplin, *New Worlds of Thomas Robert Malthus*, 209. Original underlining.
20. Green, *Pauper Capital*, 6–7.
21. See, for example, Torrens, *Paper on the Means of Reducing the Poors Rates*.
22. Malthus, *Essay on the Principle of Population*, 1798, 24–25; Malthus, *Essay on the Principle of Population*, 1803; Malthus, "Population."
23. Jonsson, *Enlightenment's Frontier*.
24. House of Commons, "Emigration to the Cape of Good Hope" (House of Commons, July 12, 1819), HC Deb 12 July 1819 vol 40 cc1549–51, Hansard; Lamont, "Robert Wilmot Horton and Liberal Toryism," 88.

25. Gregor MacGregor to Nicholas Vansittart, March 13, 1821, CO 137/152, TNA.

26. Lamont, "Robert Wilmot Horton and Liberal Toryism," 88; Johnston, *British Emigration Policy*, 37–48.

27. Wilmot-Horton, *Letters Containing Observations on Colonial Policy*, 16–27; Johnston, *British Emigration Policy*, 63–64.

28. Wilmot-Horton, *Outline of a Plan of Emigration to Upper Canada*.

29. Select Committee on the Employment of the Poor in Ireland, *Report*; Select Committee on Emigration, *Report*.

30. Richards, "Horton, Sir Robert John Wilmot-," sec. Proponent of Emigration.

31. Semmel, *Rise of Free Trade Imperialism*, 105.

32. William Cobbett, "The Old Roman Plan, or, the Project for Getting Rid of the People," *Cobbett's Weekly Register*, April 9, 1825. Apparently, Cobbett did not oppose voluntary emigration in general but the way that the issue was instrumentalized by the government. See, for example, Cobbett, *Emigrant's Guide*. On Cobbett, see Rustin, "William Cobbett."

33. Wilmot-Horton, *Observations upon the Outline of a Plan of Emigration to Upper Canada*, 63–65.

34. Select Committee on Emigration, *Report*, 5.

35. Select Committee on Emigration, *Report*, 5; Johnston, *British Emigration Policy*, 9.

36. Gregor MacGregor to Nicholas Vansittart, March 13, 1821, CO 137/152, TNA.

37. Ward, *British West Indian Slavery*, 74.

38. Johnston, *British Emigration Policy*, 7–8.

39. Robert Wilmot-Horton to Edward Codd, July 3, 1823, R3_03, BSRAS. See also: Edward Codd to Robert Wilmot-Horton, December 22, 1823, CO 123/34, TNA; Robert Wilmot-Horton to Edward Codd, August 30, 1823, R3_159, BSRAS; Robert Wilmot-Horton to Edward Codd, October 31, 1823, R3_201, BSRAS.

40. William John Richardson et al. to Earl Bathurst, March 1824, CO 123/35, TNA; William John Richardson to Robert Wilmot-Horton, March 22, 1824, CO 123/35, TNA.

41. Robert Wilmot-Horton to Edward Codd, July 3, 1823, R3_03, BSRAS.

42. "The Following Is an Extract of a Letter Received at Lloyd's from Honduras," *The Times*, June 9, 1823.

43. "Public Meeting" (Belize, March 11, 1823), Meeting of Magistrates 1822–1823, BSRAS.

44. Edward Codd to Earl Bathurst, December 12, 1823, CO 123/34, TNA.

45. House of Commons, "Abolition of Slavery," May 15, 1823, HC Deb 15 May 1823 vol 9 cc257–360, Hansard. On Thomas Fowell Buxton, see Blouet, "Buxton, Sir Thomas Fowell."

46. Edward Codd to Earl Bathurst, December 12, 1823, CO 123/34, TNA.

47. Inhabitants of Honduras, *Defence of the Settlers of Honduras*, 12.

48. Edward Codd to Earl Bathurst, March 8, 1823, CO 123/34, TNA.

49. Robert Wilmot-Horton to Edward Codd, August 30, 1823, R3_159, BSRAS; Robert Wilmot-Horton to Edward Codd, October 31, 1823, R3_201, BSRAS.

50. For an anecdotal mention of Poyais, see, for example, House of Lords, "Settlement

[on] the Swan River," December 20, 1830, HL Deb 20 December 1830 vol 1 cc1345–9, Hansard.

51. "WE Are Extremely Glad to Perceive That MR. HUME Has 'Asked a Question' on the Subject of the POYAISIAN Emigration," *John Bull*, March 8, 1824; House of Commons, "Poyais Emigration," March 4, 1824, HC Deb 04 March 1824 vol 10 cc727–8, Hansard. To date, there is no evidence of a Poyais-style project for New Zealand. On Joseph Hume, see Chancellor, "Hume, Joseph."

52. Bartle, "Bowring and the Greek Loans," 62.

53. House of Commons, "Poyais Emigration," March 4, 1824, HC Deb 04 March 1824 vol 10 cc727–8, Hansard.

54. See, for example, "Poyais Emigrants," *Morning Post*, October 22, 1823. See also the following anonymous letter to warn investors: "Take Care of Your Pockets. Another Poyais Humbug" (July 1827), General Reference Collection 1881.c.16.(7.), BL.

55. House of Commons, "Poyais Emigration," March 4, 1824, HC Deb 04 March 1824 vol 10 cc727–8, Hansard.

56. House of Commons, "Petition of F. Jones Complaining of Country Bank Notes Not Being Paid in Gold," June 27, 1825, HC Deb 27 June 1825 vol 13 cc1382–400, Hansard; House of Commons, "The King of Oude," July 28, 1834, HC Deb 28 July 1834 vol 25 cc620–35, Hansard; House of Commons, "South Australian Colonization," July 29, 1834, HC Deb 29 July 1834 vol 25 cc700–11, Hansard.

57. Robert Wilmot-Horton, "Genl Codd's Subject of Enquiry" (December 9, 1824), CO 123/35, TNA.

58. While seemingly dishonest, Wilmot-Horton's reaction was similar to that of Earl Bathurst when faced with other colonial scandal. In her book, Kristen McKenzie reveals that the keen interest shown by nineteenth-century colonial officials in rumors of "deviant" behavior—notably homosexuality or adultery—and subsequent in-depth investigations reflected the wish of the Colonial and Foreign Offices to settle potential scandals internally and avoid informing the parliamentary opposition. McKenzie, *Imperial Underworld*.

59. Johnston, *British Emigration Policy*, 15.

Conclusion

1. "Police," *The Times*, December 10, 1824.

2. "An Announcement Was Made Yesterday at the Foreign Stock Exchange," *The Times*, April 1, 1825.

3. Edward Irving, "Poyais-an Advertisement," *The Times*, December 3, 1824; "Poyais Bonds—a Half-Yearly Dividend," *The Times*, December 3, 1824.

4. "The Money Market," *The Times*, May 7, 1825.

5. For a recent summary of the Latin American sovereign debt crisis, see Jackson, *Impunity and Capitalism*, chap. 6.

6. Whitefeather, *Handbook of Swindling*.

7. Hatt, "Parable of Poyais, Part III."

8. Levi, "On Microhistory," 97, 107.

9. See, for example, "Poyaisian Three Per Cent Consolidated Stock Certificate 37," 1827, author's collection; "Poyaisian New Three Per Cent Consolidated Stock Certificate 702," 1831, GD50/184/104/3, NRS.

10. Gregor MacGregor, "Plan of a Constitution for the Inhabitants and Settlers of the State of Indiada on the Indian Coast of Central America," 1828–1832, GD50/68, NRS; Gregor MacGregor, "Plan of a Constitution for the Inhabitants of the Indian Coast in Central America" (1837), GD50/68, NRS; MacGregor, *Constitution de la nation poyaisienne*; MacGregor, *Plan of a Constitution*. On the supposed backing by English financial markets of democratic regimes in the early nineteenth century, see Flandreau and Flores, "Bonds and Brands," 649–50.

11. Smeeton, *Doings in London*, 90.

12. "LONDEN Den 30 Augustus," *Rotterdamsche Courant*, September 4, 1823.

13. "Advertentie," *Groninger Courant*, June 3, 1834; "Advertentie," *Groninger Courant*, June 6, 1834.

14. "Money-Market and City Intelligence," *The Times*, November 11, 1835.

15. Zola, *L'argent*.

16. On the British Central American Land Company, see, for example, *Proposed Colony in the District of Black River*; Naylor, *Penny Ante Imperialism*, 212–133; Flandreau, *Anthropologists in the Stock Exchange*, 153–54."

17. MacGregor, *Exposición documentada*.

18. On the controversy surrounding MacGregor's final resting place, see Brown, "Gregor MacGregor," 66; Massi, "Gregor MacGregor."

19. Daniel Mocatta, "Greek Loan of £800,000 Stock" (London, February 19, 1824), 1890.c.6.(70.), BL.

20. Obert, "Charte de concession du territoire de Vera Paz"; Naylor, *Penny Ante Imperialism*, 121–33.

21. "Greek Loan—Dewitts v. Hendriks," *Evening Mail*, November 12, 1824.

22. Brière, *Haïti et la France*, 200–2001; Madiou, *Histoire d'Haïti*, 318–20; Hendriks, *Statement of Facts in Reference to the Formation of the Haytien Mining Company*.

23. Knight Bruce, "Richardson v. Larpent."

24. Burke, *Index to Burke's Dictionary of the Landed Gentry*, 371. Gustavus Hippisley published several poems in honor of his sister, Mrs. Richardson: Hippisley, *Hours of Idleness*.

25. Sorsby, "Mosquito Indian King George III," 399–402.

26. George Frederic to Edward Codd, March 8, 1824, CO 123/35, TNA. For a picture of the flag, see Clavel, *Créer un pays*, 322.

27. Peter Lelacheur et al., "Inquest" (Cape Gracias a Dios, March 10, 1824), CO 123/35, TNA; George Woodbine, "Depositions Relating to His Late Majesty George Frederic Augustus" (Cape Gracias a Dios, March 10, 1824), CO 123/35, TNA; George Woodbine to Edward Codd, March 11, 1824, CO 123/35, TNA.

28. Sorsby, "Mosquito Indian King George III," 400.

Bibliography

Archival Collections
AD   Archives diplomatiques, la Courneuve.
ADD   Archives départementales de la Dordogne, Périgueux.
ADPC   Archives départementales du Pas-de-Calais, Dainville.
AGFM   Archivos del General Francisco de Miranda, Caracas. http://www.franciscode
        miranda.org
AGI   Archivo General de Indias, Sevilla.
AN   Archives Nationales, Paris.
BL   British Library, London.
BM   British Museum, London.
BSRAS   Belize State Records and Archives Service, Belmopan.
CLO   Carlyle Letters Online. https://carlyleletters.dukeupress.edu
GL   Guildhall Library, London.
Hansard Hansard 1803–2005, London. https://api.parliament.uk/historic-hansard/index
        .html
JCBL   John Carter Brown Library, Providence.
JFSGRL Jamaican Family Search Genealogy Research Library, Kingston. http://www
        .jamaicanfamilysearch.com
LBGA   Lloyds Banking Group Archives, Edinburgh.
LBSD   Legacies of British Slave-ownership database, University College London.
        http://wwwdepts-live.ucl.ac.uk/lbs
LMA   London Metropolitan Archives, London.
MOA   Marsden Online Archive. http://marsdenarchive.otago.ac.nz
NPG   National Portrait Gallery, London.
NRS   National Records of Scotland, Edinburgh.
RA   Rothschild Archive, London.
RCSL   Royal Commonwealth Society Library, Cambridge.
SCRO   Staffordshire County Record Office, Stafford.
TNA   The National Archives, Kew.
TNYPL   The New York Public Library, New York.

Newspapers and Magazines
Aberdeen Journal
Aberdeen Press and Journal
Caledonian Mercury
Canadian Magazine and Literary Repository
Cobbett's Weekly Register
Course of the Exchange
Dublin Evening Post
Evening Mail
Gentleman's Magazine and Historical Chronicle
Groninger Courant
Honduras Gazette and Commercial Advertiser
Hull Packet
John Bull
Kentish Weekly Post or Canterbury Journal
Legal Observer
London Courier
London Gazette
Missionary Register
Morning Advertiser
Morning Chronicle
Morning Post
Newcastle Courant
Observer
Oxford Journal
Penny Magazine of the Society for the Diffusion of Useful Knowledge
Public Ledger and Daily Advertiser
Rotterdamsche Courant
Saunders's News-Letter
Scotsman
The Times

Works Cited
Adelman, Jeremy. "Independence in Latin America." In *The Oxford Handbook of Latin American History*, edited by Jose C. Moya, 153–80. Oxford University Press, 2010.
———. *Sovereignty and Revolution in the Iberian Atlantic*. Princeton University Press, 2006.
Alexander, Alexander. *The Life of Alexander Alexander*. Edited by John Howell. Vol. 1. 2 vols. Blackwood, 1830.
———. *The Life of Alexander Alexander*. Edited by John Howell. Vol. 2. 2 vols. Blackwood, 1830.
Allan, Victor. "The Prince of Poyais." *History Today* 2 (1952): 53–58.
Amazing Grace. Momentum Pictures, 2006.
An Officer Late in the Colombian Service. *The Present State of Colombia, by an Officer Late in the Colombian Service*. Murray, 1827.

Anderson, Jennifer L. *Mahogany: The Costs of Luxury in Early America.* Harvard University Press, 2012.

———. "Nature's Currency: The Atlantic Mahogany Trade and the Commodification of Nature in the Eighteenth Century." *Early American Studies: An Interdisciplinary Journal* 2, no. 1 (2004): 47–80.

Baeza, Andrés. *Contacts, Collisions and Relationships: Britons and Chileans in the Independence Era, 1806–1831.* Liverpool Latin American Studies 19. Liverpool University Press, 2019.

Ballade vom kleinen Soldaten. New Yorker Films, 1984.

Banner, Stuart. *Speculation: A History of the Elusive Line Between Gambling and Investment.* Oxford University Press, 2017.

Bard, Samuel A. *Waikna; or Adventures on the Mosquito-Shore.* Harper, 1855.

Barthes, Roland. *Mythologies.* Seuil, 1957.

Bartle, G. F. "Bowring and the Greek Loans of 1824 and 1825." *Balkan Studies* 3, no. 1 (January 1962): 61–74.

Bashford, Alison, and Joyce E. Chaplin. *The New Worlds of Thomas Robert Malthus: Rereading the Principle of Population.* Princeton University Press, 2016.

Bassi, Ernesto. *An Aqueous Territory: Sailor Geographies and New Granada's Transimperial Greater Caribbean World.* Duke University Press, 2017.

Bebbington, David William. *Evangelicalism in Modern Britain: A History from the 1730s to the 1980s.* Routledge, 1995.

Becquart, Noël. "Joseph Mérilhou." In *Cent portraits périgourdins*, edited by Les membres de la société historique et archéologique du Périgord, 132–33. Fanlac, 1980.

Belaubre, Christophe, Jordana Dym, and John Savage, eds. *Napoleon's Atlantic: The Impact of Napoleonic Empire in the Atlantic World.* Atlantic World, vol. 20. Brill, 2010.

Belisario, Isaac Mendes. *Sketches of Character, in Illustration of the Habits, Occupation, and Costume of the Negro Population in the Island of Jamaica, Drawn after Nature and in Lithography.* Published by the artist, 1837.

Belmonte, Kevin Charles. *William Wilberforce: A Hero for Humanity.* Zondervan, 2007.

Bennett, Charles E. *General MacGregor: Hero or Rogue?* Mid Nite Books, 2001.

Bennett Murray, Sonia. *The First Parish Register of Belize, 1794–1810, and the First Four Censuses, 1816–1826.* Clearfield, 2010.

———. *They Came to Belize, 1750–1810: Compiled from Records of Jamaica, the Mosquito Shore, and Belize at the British & Belize National Archives.* Clearfield, 2017.

Bentham, Jeremy. "Proposals for the Junction of the Two Seas, the Atlantic and the Pacific, by Means of a Joint-Stock Company, to Be Styled the Junctiona Company (1822)." In *The Works of Jeremy Bentham, Now First Collected*, edited by John Bowring, Vol. 8, 561–71. Tait, 1839.

Beraldi, Henri. *Les graveurs du XIXe siècle : guide de l'amateur d'estampes modernes.* Vol. 2. Conquet, 1885.

Berg, Maxine. "Sea Otters and Iron: A Global Microhistory of Value and Exchange at Nootka Sound, 1774–1792." *Past & Present* 242, Suppl. 14 (November 2019): 50–82.

Bergamin, André. *Gregor Macgregor.* July 2009. Super Interessante Magazine. https://www.flickr.com/photos/andrebergamin/3680943855

Bergeron, Louis. *Banquiers, négociants et manufacturiers parisiens du Directoire à l'Empire.* Les ré-impressions. EHESS, 2013.

———. *Les révolutions européennes et le partage du monde.* Le monde et son histoire. Laffont, 1972.

Bertrand, Romain, and Guillaume Calafat. "La microhistoire globale: affaire(s) à suivre." *Annales. Histoire, Sciences Sociales* 73, no. 1 (2018): 1–18.

Besseghini, Deborah. "The Weapons of Revolution: Global Merchants and the Arms Trade in South America (1808–1824)." *Journal of Evolutionary Studies in Business* 8, no. 1 (2023): 81–118.

Besseghini, Deborah, and Ander Permanyer-Ugartemendia. "The Hispanic World at War and the Global Transformation of Commerce. Global Merchants in Spanish America: Business, Networks and Independence (1800–1830)." *Journal of Evolutionary Studies in Business* 8, no. 1 (2023): 1–42.

Bethell, Leslie, ed. *The Cambridge History of Latin America.* Reprint. Vol. 3. Cambridge University Press, 2002.

———. "The Independence of Brazil." In *The Cambridge History of Latin America*, edited by Leslie Bethell, Reprint, Vol. 3, 157–96. Cambridge University Press, 2002.

Bignon, Vincent, and Marc Flandreau. "The Economics of Badmouthing: Libel Law and the Underworld of the Financial Press in France Before World War I." *Journal of Economic History* 71, no. 3 (September 2011): 616–53.

———. "The Price of Media Capture and the Debasement of the French Newspaper Industry During the Interwar." *Journal of Economic History* 74, no. 3 (September 2014): 799–830.

Bingham, Adrian. "The Digitization of Newspaper Archives: Opportunities and Challenges for Historians." *Twentieth Century British History* 21, no. 2 (June 2010): 225–31.

Bingham, Peregrine. "Skeen v. M'Gregor." In *Reports of Cases Argued and Determined in the Court of Common*, Vol. 1, 242. London: Strahan, 1823.

Blake, Robert. *Disraeli.* 4th ed. St. Martin's Press, 1967.

Blaufarb, Rafe. "The Western Question: The Geopolitics of Latin American Independence." *American Historical Review* 112, no. 3 (June 2007): 742–63.

Blaut, James M. "Environmentalism and Eurocentrism." *Geographical Review* 89, no. 3 (July 1999): 391–408.

Blouet, Olwyn M. "Buxton, Sir Thomas Fowell, First Baronet." In *Oxford Dictionary of National Biography*, edited by Brian Harrison. Oxford University Press, 2004. https://doi.org/10.1093/ref:odnb/4247

Bolivar, Simon. "Reply of a South American to a Gentleman of This Island (Jamaica)." In *Selected Writings of Bolivar*, by Vicente Lecuna, edited by Harold A. Bierck, translated by Lewis Bertrand, Vol. 1. Colonial Press, 1951.

Bolland, O. Nigel. "Systems of Domination After Slavery: The Control of Land and Labor in the British West Indies After 1838." *Comparative Studies in Society and History* 23, no. 4 (1981): 591–619.

———. *The Formation of a Colonial Society: Belize, From Conquest to Crown Colony.* Johns Hopkins University Press, 1977.

Bonvini, Alessandro. "«L'aratro e la spada». Gli esuli italiani oltre la frontiera argentina, 1855–1859." *Viaggiatori*, no. 2 (March 2018): 195–241.
Brière, Jean-François. *Haïti et la France 1804–1848. Le rêve brisé*. Karthala, 2008.
Broughton, E. C. *Memoirs of the 65th Regiment, 1st Battn. the New York & Lancaster Regt.* Clowes, 1914.
Brown, Matthew. *Adventuring Through Spanish Colonies: Simón Bolívar, Foreign Mercenaries and the Birth of New Nations*. Liverpool University Press, 2006.
———. "British Informal Empire and the Origins of Association Football in South America." *Soccer & Society* 16, no. 2–3 (May 2015): 169–82.
———. "Gregor MacGregor : Clansman, Conquistador and Coloniser on the Fringes of the British Empire." In *Colonial Lives Across the British Empire : Imperial Careering in the Long Nineteenth Century*, edited by David Lambert and Alan Lester, 32–57. Cambridge University Press, 2006.
———. "Inca, Sailor, Soldier, King: Gregor MacGregor and the Early Nineteenth-Century Caribbean." *Bulletin of Latin American Research*, no. 1 (2005): 44–70.
———, ed. *Informal Empire in Latin America: Culture, Commerce and Capital*. Blackwell, 2008.
———. "The Life of Alexander Alexander and the Spanish Atlantic, 1799–1822." In *Bridging the Early Modern Atlantic World: People, Products, and Practices on the Move*, edited by Caroline Williams, 203–22. Ashgate, 2009.
———. "Not Forging Nations but Foraging for Them: Uncertain Collective Identities in Gran Colombia." *Nations & Nationalism* 12, no. 2 (April 2006): 223–40.
Brown, Matthew, and Gabriel B. Paquette. "Between the Age of Atlantic Revolutions and the Age of Empire: Europe and Latin America in the Axial Decade of the 1820s." In *Connections After Colonialism: Europe and Latin America in the 1820s*, edited by Matthew Brown and Gabriel B. Paquette, 1–28. Atlantic Crossings. University of Alabama Press, 2013.
Bulmer-Thomas, Victor. *The Economic History of Latin America since Independence*. 2nd ed. Cambridge Latin American Studies 77. Cambridge University Press, 2003.
Burdon, John Alder, ed. *Archives of British Honduras*. Vol. 1. 3 vols. Sifton Praed, 1931.
———, ed. *Archives of British Honduras*. Vol. 2. 3 vols. Sifton Praed, 1934.
Burke, Edmund. "Speech on Divorce Bill (29 April 1771)." In *The Writings and Speeches of Edmund Burke*, edited by Paul Langford, Vol. 2, 357–59. Clarendon Press, 1981.
———. *Thoughts on the Prospect of a Regicide Peace in a Series of Letters*. Owen, 1796.
Burke, Sir Bernard. *Index to Burke's Dictionary of the Landed Gentry of Great Britain & Ireland*. Vol. 3. 3 vols. Colburn, 1853.
Burnaby, William. *Regulations for the Better Government of His Majesty's Subjects in the Bay of Honduras*. Edited by William Hunt. Gillet, 1809.
Bushnell, David. *The Santander Regime in Gran Colombia*. Greenwood Press, 1970.
Caballero, Jesús Díaz. "Incaísmo as the First Guiding Fiction in the Emergence of the Creole Nation in the United Provinces of Río de La Plata." *Journal of Latin American Cultural Studies* 17, no. 1 (2008): 1–22.
Campbell, Mavis Christine. *Becoming Belize: A History of an Outpost of Empire Searching for Identity, 1528–1823*. University of the West Indies Press, 2011.

Cannon, Richard. *Historical Record of the Twenty-Second, or the Cheshire Regiment of Foot: Containing an Account of the Formation of the Regiment in 1689, and of Its Subsequent Services to 1849*. Parker, Furnivall, & Parker, 1849.

"Cases in Which Alterations Have Been Made in Customs and Excise Duties, by a Treasury Order, Since 1800." In *Accounts and Papers 1831–1832 Relating to Customs and Excise, Imports and Exports, Shipping and Trade*, Vol. 7, 9. H.M. Stationery Office, 1832.

Cassis, Youssef. *Capitals of Capital: A History of International Financial Centres, 1780–2005*. Translated by Jacqueline Collier. Cambridge University Press, 2006.

Challandes, Jean-Philippe. "Les vaincus des archives: Réflexions sur le lien entre État-nation et mémoire collective à partir du cas brésilien (1839–1844)." In *Penser l'archive: histoires d'archives-archives d'histoire*, edited by Mauro Cerutti, Jean-François Fayet, and Michel Porret, 116–30. Histoire. Antipodes, 2006.

Chaloner and Fleming. *The Mahogany Tree*. Rockliff, 1850.

Chamberlain, Muriel Evelyn. *Pax Britannica? British Foreign Policy, 1789–1914*. Longman, 1988.

Chancellor, V. E. "Hume, Joseph (1777–1855)." In *Oxford Dictionary of National Biography*, edited by Brian Harrison. Oxford University Press, 2004. https://doi.org/10.1093/ref:odnb/14148

Chapman, Stanley D. *The Rise of Merchant Banking*. Allen & Unwin, 1984.

Chatziioannou, Maria Christina. "War, Crisis and Sovereign Loans: The Greek War of Independence and British Economic Expansion in the 1820s." *Historical Review/La Revue Historique* 10 (2013): 33–55.

Chicago, Judy. *The Dinner Party*. 1979. Mixed media. Brooklyn Museum.

Chippendale, Thomas. *The Gentleman and Cabinet-Maker's Director*. Printed for the author, 1754.

Clavel, Damian. *Créer un pays, le royaume de Poyais. Gregor MacGregor, emprunts d'État et fraude financière 1820–1824*. Les routes de l'histoire. Éditions Livreo-Alphil, 2022.

———. "The Rise and Fall of George Frederic Augustus II: The Central American, Caribbean, and Atlantic Life of a Miskitu King, 1805–1824." *Business History Review* 96, no. 3 (Autumn 2022): 525–58.

———. "What's in a Fraud? The Many Worlds of Gregor MacGregor, 1817–1824." *Enterprise & Society* 22, no. 4 (December 2021): 997–1036.

Cobbett, William. *The Emigrant's Guide in Ten Letters Addressed to the Tax-Payers of England*. Mills, Jowett, & Mills, 1829.

Codd, Edward. *Proceedings of an Inquiry and Investigation: Instituted by Major General Codd, His Majesty's Superintendent and Commander-in-Chief at Belize, Honduras, Relative to Poyais, &c. &c. &c.* Lawler & Quick, 1824.

"Code de commerce (1807)." In *Les archives de la révolution française*, 354–421. Micro Graphix, n.d.

Cohen, Deborah. "Love and Money in the Informal Empire: The British in Argentina, 1830–1930." *Past & Present* 245, no. 1 (November 2019): 79–115.

A Collection of All the Treaties of Peace, Alliance, and Commerce Between Great-Britain and Other Powers. Vol. 3. 3 vols. Debrett, 1785.

Colley, Linda. *The Gun, the Ship, and the Pen: Warfare, Constitutions and the Making of the Modern World*. Profile Books, 2022.
Colthart, James M. "Ellice, Edward." In *Dictionary of Canadian Biography*. Vol. 9. Université Laval/University of Toronto, 2003. https://www.biographi.ca/en/bio/ellice_edward_9E.html
Committee for General Purposes of the London Stock Exchange. *Rules and Regulations*. Couchman, 1812.
Connery, James. *An Essay on Charitable Economy, upon the Loan Bank System: Called on the Continent "Mont de Piété", That Is, the Mount, or Rather the Heap, for the Distribution of Charity: Being an Antidote to Counteract the Baneful Effects of Pawnbroking . . . : Dedicated, by Permission, to William Sharman Crawford*. Cumming, 1837.
Conzemius, Eduard. *Ethnographical Survey of the Miskito and Sumu Indians of Honduras and Nicaragua*. U.S. Government Printing Office, 1932.
———. "Les tribus indiennes de la Côte des Mosquitos." *Anthropos* 33, no. 5/6 (September 1938): 910–43.
Cook, Roger, and Tim Tate. "Gregor MacGregor: The Crown Prince of Never-Never Land." In *The Ten Greatest Conmen: True Stories of the World's Most Outrageous Scams*, 1–22. Blake, 2008.
Cope, S. R. "The Goldsmids and the Development of the London Money Market During the Napoleonic Wars." *Economica* 9, no. 34 (May 1942): 180–206.
———. "The Stock Exchange Revisited: A New Look at the Market in Securities in London in the Eighteenth Century." *Economica* 45, no. 177 (1978): 1–21.
Copland, Ian. "Christianity as an Arm of Empire: The Ambiguous Case of India Under the Company, c. 1813–1858." *Historical Journal* 49, no. 4 (December 2006): 1025–54.
Costeloe, Michael P. *Bonds and Bondholders: British Investors and Mexico's Foreign Debt, 1824–1888*. Praeger, 2003.
———. *Bubbles and Bonanzas: British Investors and Investments in Mexico, 1821–1860*. Lexington Books, 2011.
———. *La primera República Federal de México (1824-1835) : un estudio de los partidos políticos en el México independiente*. Seccion de obras de historia. Fondo de cultura económica, 1975.
Cot, Annie L. "Jeremy Bentham's Spanish American Utopia." In *Economic Development and Global Crisis: The Latin American Economy in Historical Perspective*, edited by José Luís Cardoso, Maria Cristina Marcuzzo, and María Eugenia Romero, 34–52. Routledge Studies in the History of Economics 161. Routledge, 2014.
Court of Common Council. *Report of the Proceedings in the Court of Common Council Relative to the Equitable Loan Bank Company*. 1825.
Cox, Gary W. *Marketing Sovereign Promises: Monopoly Brokerage and the Growth of the English State*. Cambridge University Press, 2016.
Culbertson, William Smith. *International Economic Policies: A Survey of the Economics of Diplomacy*. Appleton, 1925.
Cundall, Frank. *Historic Jamaica*. West India Committee, 1915.
Cunningham, Allan. "The Philhellenes, Canning and Greek Independence." *Middle Eastern Studies* 14, no. 2 (May 1978): 151–81.

Dard, Henri Jean Baptiste. *Biens des émigrés*. Le Normant, 1814.

———. *Observations sur le droit de souveraineté de la France sur Saint-Domingue et sur les droits des colons propriétaires de cette île*. Gide, 1823.

———. *Opinion d'un jurisconsulte, concernant la confiscation, la vente des biens des émigrés et la confirmation de la vente de ces biens par l'autorité royale*. Trouvé, 1821.

Davis, Madeleine. "The Marxism of the British New Left." *Journal of Political Ideologies* 11, no. 3 (October 2006): 335–58.

Davis, T. Frederick. "MacGregor's Invasion of Florida, 1817." *Florida Historical Society Quarterly* 7, no. 1 (July 1928): 2–71.

Dawson, Frank Griffith. "The Evacuation of the Mosquito Shore and the English Who Stayed Behind, 1786–1800." *The Americas* 55, no. 1 (July 1998): 63.

———. *The First Latin American Debt Crisis: The City of London and the 1822–25 Loan Bubble*. Yale University Press, 1990.

———. "William Pitt's Settlement at Black River on the Mosquito Shore: A Challenge to Spain in Central America, 1732–87." *Hispanic American Historical Review* 63, no. 4 (November 1983): 677–706.

Defence of the Principles of the Equitable Loan Bank, and Mont de Piété, Against the Attacks of the Meeting of Pawnbrokers. Robins, 1824.

Dempsey, Jessica. "Tracking Grizzly Bears in British Columbia's Environmental Politics." *Environment and Planning A: Economy and Space* 42, no. 5 (May 2010): 1138–56.

Dennis, Philip A., and Michael D. Olien. "Kingship Among the Miskito." *American Ethnologist* 11, no. 4 (November 1984): 718–37.

Dickens, Charles. *Bleak House*. Chapman & Hall, 1853.

Dod's Peerage, Baronetage and Knightage, Etc of Great Britain and Ireland. Simpkin, Marshall, Hamilton, Kent, 1915.

Douglas, James. *Journals and Reminiscences of James Douglas, M.D.* Edited by James (Junior) Douglas. Torch Press, 1910.

Draper, Nicholas. "The Rise of a New Planter Class? Some Countercurrents from British Guiana and Trinidad, 1807–33." *Atlantic Studies* 9, no. 1 (March 2012): 65–83.

Dumas, Alexandre. *Le capitaine Pamphile*. Dumont, 1839.

———. *Le capitaine Pamphile*. Calmann-Lévy, 1877.

Dunham, Jacob. *Journal of Voyages*. 1850.

Dziennik, Matthew P. "The Miskitu, Military Labour, and the San Juan Expedition of 1780." *Historical Journal* 61, no. 1 (March 2018): 155–79.

East, Robert A. "The Business Entrepreneur in a Changing Colonial Economy, 1763–1795." *Journal of Economic History* 6 (1946): 16–27.

Eastment, Winifred. *Wanstead Through the Ages*. 4th ed. Dawn Press, 1976.

Edgell, Zee. *Time and the River*. Caribbean Writers Series. Heinemann, 2007.

Edwards, Bryan. *Poyais: An Account of the British Settlements on the Musquito Shore*. COL, 1773.

Eichengreen, Barry, Asmaa Adel El-Ganainy, Rui Pedro Esteves, and Kris Mitchener. *In Defense of Public Debt*. Oxford University Press, 2021.

Ellen, Roy, and Holly Harris. "Introduction." In *Indigenous Environmental Knowledge and Its Transformations: Critical Anthropological Perspectives*, edited by Roy Ellen, Peter Parkes, and Alan Bicker, 1–31. Routledge, 2006.

Equitable Loan Bank Company. *Plan of the Company*. London, 1824.

"Extract from a Proclamation of Gregor MacGregor, Dated Head-Quarters, Amelia Island, June 30, 1817." *Niles' Weekly Register* 13, no. 22 (January 24, 1818): 350.

Fawcett, William. "The Public Gardens and Plantations of Jamaica." *Botanical Gazette* 24, no. 5 (November 1897): 345–69.

Fenn, M. J. "British Investment in South America and the Financial Crisis of 1825–1826." Master's thesis, University of Durham, 1969.

Ferguson, Mison, Phylicia Pelayo, and Nigel Encalada. *A History of Slavery & Emancipation in Belize*. ISCR and NICH, 2015.

Ferguson, Niall. "The Rise of the Rothschilds: The Family Firm as Multinational." In *The World of Private Banking*, edited by Youssef Cassis and Philip L. Cottrell, 1–30. Ashgate, 2009.

Finamore, Daniel. "'Pirate Water': Sailing to Belize in the Mahogany Trade." In *Maritime Empires: British Imperial Maritime Trade in the Nineteenth Century*, edited by David Killingray, Margarette Lincoln, and Nigel Rigby, 30–47. Boydell Press, 2004.

Flandreau, Marc. *Anthropologists in the Stock Exchange: A Financial History of Victorian Science*. University of Chicago Press, 2016.

———. "Pricing Moses Montefiore." *Capitalism: A Journal of History and Economics* 1, no. 1 (2019): 166–230.

———. "Sovereign States, Bondholders Committees, and the London Stock Exchange in the Nineteenth Century (1827–68): New Facts and Old Fictions." *Oxford Review of Economic Policy* 29, no. 4 (2013): 668–96.

Flandreau, Marc, and Juan H. Flores. "Bonds and Brands: Foundations of Sovereign Debt Markets, 1820–1830." *Journal of Economic History* 69, no. 3 (2009): 646–84.

Floyd, Troy S. *The Anglo-Spanish Struggle for Mosquitia*. University of New Mexico Press, 1967.

Fodor, Giorgio. "The Boom That Never Was? Latin American Loans in London 1822–1825." Discussion paper. Universita' degli studi-Dipartimento di economia, 2002.

Folkman, David I. *The Nicaragua Route*. University of Utah Press, 1972.

Foreign Office. *British and Foreign State Papers 1849–1850*. Vol. 38. Harrison, 1862.

Frankel, Tamar. *The Ponzi Scheme Puzzle: A History and Analysis of Con Artists and Victims*. Oxford University Press, 2012.

Friede, Juan. "La expedición de Mac-Gregor a Ríohacha—Año 1819." *Boletín Cultural y Bibliográfico* 10, no. 9 (1967): 69–85.

Fuligni, Bruno. *Royaumes d'aventure: Ils ont fondé leur propre État*. Les Arènes, 2016.

Gabbert, Wolfgang. "'God Save the King of the Mosquito Nation!' Indigenous Leaders on the Fringe of the Spanish Empire." *Ethnohistory* 63, no. 1 (January 2016): 71–93.

Gallagher, John, and Ronald Robinson. "The Imperialism of Free Trade." *Economic History Review*, New Series, 6, no. 1 (January 1953): 1–15.

Gambetta, Diego. *The Sicilian Mafia: The Business of Private Protection*. Harvard University Press, 1996.

García, Claudia. "Ambivalencia de las representaciones coloniales: líderes indios y zambos de la Costa de Mosquitos a fines del Siglo XVIII." *Revista de Indias* 67, no. 241 (December 2007): 673–94.

Gasper, Julia. *Theodore von Neuhoff, King of Corsica: The Man Behind the Legend.* University of Delaware Press, 2012.

Geggus, David Patrick, ed. *The Impact of the Haitian Revolution in the Atlantic World.* The Carolina Lowcountry and the Atlantic World. University of South Carolina Press, 2001.

Gehrenbeck, Lupe. *Gregor McGregor: Rey de los Mosquitos y otras obras.* Dramaturgia. Editorial Eclepsidra, 2018.

Ghobrial, John-Paul A. "Introduction: Seeing the World like a Microhistorian." *Past & Present* 242, Suppl. 14 (November 2019): 1–22.

———. "The Secret Life of Elias of Babylon and the Uses of Global Microhistory." *Past & Present* 222, no. 1 (February 2014): 51–93.

Gille, Bertrand. *Histoire de la maison Rothschild: des origines à 1848.* Vol. 1. 2 vols. Travaux de droit, d'économie, de sociologie et de sciences politiques 39. Droz, 1965.

Ginzburg, Carlo. *Ecstasies: Deciphering the Witches' Sabbath.* Pantheon Books, 1991.

———. "Microhistory and World History." In *The Cambridge World History*, edited by Jerry H. Bentley, Sanjay Subrahmanyam, and Merry E. Wiesner-Hanks, 446–73. Cambridge University Press, 2015.

———. "Morelli, Freud and Sherlock Holmes: Clues and Scientific Method." Translated by Anna Davin. *History Workshop*, no. 9 (1980): 5–36.

———. *The Cheese and the Worms : The Cosmos of a Sixteenth-Century Miller.* Translated by John Alfred Tedeschi and Anne C. Tedeschi. Penguin Books, 1982.

Goldgar, Anne. *Tulipmania: Money, Honor and Knowledge in the Dutch Golden Age.* University of Chicago Press, 2007.

Graham, Richard. *Independence in Latin America: Contrasts and Comparisons.* 3rd ed. Joe R. and Teresa Lozano Long Series in Latin American and Latino Art and Culture. University of Texas Press, 2013.

Great Britain War Office. *A List of the Officers of the Army and of the Corps of Royal Marines.* War Office, 1821.

Green, David R. *Pauper Capital: London and the Poor Law, 1790–1870.* Ashgate, 2010.

Gregg, Richard T. *Gregor MacGregor, Cazique of Poyais, 1786–1845 . . . or, Gregor MacGregor: On the Trail of the Gullible!* Scripophily Library 1. International Bond & Share Society, 1999.

Hackett, James. *Narrative of the Expedition Which Sailed from England in 1817, to Join the South American Patriots.* Murray, 1818.

Hagen, Victor Wolfgang von. "The Mosquito Coast of Honduras and Its Inhabitants." *Geographical Review* 30, no. 2 (April 1940): 238–59.

Hakewill, James. *A Picturesque Tour of the Island of Jamaica.* Hurst and Robinson, 1825.

Hall, Hector. *Falsehood Detected, or, A Reply to an Unfounded and Slanderous Publication, Entitled "The Belize Merchants Unmasked": With Some Characteristic Traits of the Author.* 1824.

Halperin Donghi, Tulio. *Revolución y guerra: formación de una élite dirigente en la Argentina criolla.* 2nd ed. Historia y cultura 16. Siglo Veintiuno Argentina, 2005.

Hamel, Jean-François. "Les uchronies fantômes." *Poétique* 144, no. 4 (2005): 429–41.
Hamilton, Alexander. "Report Relative to a Provision for the Support of Public Credit, [9 January 1790]." Founders Online. Accessed July 8, 2024. https://founders.archives.gov/documents/Hamilton/01-06-02-0076-0002-0001
Harper Fender, Ann. "Smuggling." In *The Oxford Encyclopedia of Economic History*, edited by Joel Mokyr, Vol. 1, 518–21. Oxford University Press, 2003.
Harris, Ron. *Industrializing English Law: Entrepreneurship and Business Organization, 1720–1844*. Political Economy of Institutions and Decisions. Cambridge University Press, 2000.
———. "Political Economy, Interest Groups, Legal Institutions, and the Repeal of the Bubble Act in 1825." *Economic History Review* 50, no. 4 (November 1997): 675–96.
———. "The Bubble Act: Its Passage and Its Effects on Business Organization." *Journal of Economic History* 54, no. 3 (1994): 610–27.
Hartzell, Caroline A. "Nation-State Crises in the Absence and Presence of Segment States: The Case of Nicaragua." *Ethnopolitics* 13, no. 1 (January 2014): 28–47.
Hasbrouck, Alfred. *Foreign Legionaries in the Liberation of Spanish South America*. Columbia University Press, 1928.
———. "Gregor McGregor and the Colonization of Poyais, Between 1820 and 1824." *Hispanic American Historical Review* 7, no. 4 (November 1927): 438–59.
Hastie, James. *Narrative of a Voyage in the Ship Kennersley Castle from Leith Roads to Poyais with Some Account of the Proceedings of the Workmen on Their Arrival at Black River, in That Territory, and of Their Subsequent Removal to Belize*. Printed for the author, 1823.
Hatt, Sam. "The Parable of Poyais, Part III." *The Emigre* (blog), October 2023. https://www.the-emigre.com/column/parable-of-poyais-3
Hayes, Cameron. *Elmyr de Hory, Fernand Legros and Real Lessard in the Republic of Poyais in 1969*. 2015. Oil on linen, 198 x 254 cm.
Head, David. *Privateers of the Americas: Spanish American Privateering from the United States in the Early Republic*. Early American Places. University of Georgia Press, 2015.
Hecht, Susanna B. *The Scramble for the Amazon and the "Lost Paradise" of Euclides Da Cunha*. University of Chicago Press, 2013.
Helms, Mary W. "Miskito Slaving and Culture Contact: Ethnicity and Opportunity in an Expanding Population." *Journal of Anthropological Research* 39, no. 2 (1983): 179–97.
———. "Of Kings and Contexts: Ethnohistorical Interpretations of Miskito Political Structure and Function." *American Ethnologist* 13, no. 3 (August 1986): 506–23.
———. "The Cultural Ecology of a Colonial Tribe." *Ethnology* 8, no. 1 (January 1969): 76–84.
Henderson, George. *An Account of the British Settlement of Honduras: Being a Brief View of Its Commercial and Agricultural Resources, Soil, Climate, Natural History, &c. To Which Are Added Sketches of the Manners and Customs of the Mosquito Indians, Preceded by the Journal of a Voyage to the Mosquito Shore . . .* Baldwin, 1809.
Henderson, John Alexander. *History of the Society of Advocates in Aberdeen*. University of Aberdeen, 1912.
Hendriks, Herman. *A Plain Narrative of Facts*. Couchman, 1824.
———. *A Statement of Facts in Reference to the Formation of the Haytien Mining Company, with Copy of the Original Grant, and Other Documents;* Wilson, 1827.

Hernon, Ian. *Riot! Civil Insurrection from Peterloo to the Present Day*. Pluto, 2006.
Hewitt, Elizabeth. *Speculative Fictions: Explaining the Economy in the Early United States*. Oxford Studies in American Literary History. Oxford University Press, 2020.
Hippisley, Gustavus Butler. *Acts of Oppression, Committed Under the Administration of M. de Villéle, Prime Minister of Charles X in the Years 1825–6. In a Series of Letters*. Miller, 1831.
———. *Hours of Idleness*. Printed for private circulation, 1865.
———. *The Siege of Barcelona, a Poem in Three Cantos*. 1842.
Hippisley, Gustavus Matthias. *A Narrative of the Expedition to the Rivers Orinoco and Apuré, in South America: Which Sailed from England in November 1817, and Joined the Patriotic Forces in Venezuela and Caráccas*. Murray, 1819.
Hobsbawm, Eric John. *The Age of Revolution 1789–1848*. Weidenfeld & Nicolson, 1962.
Hodgson, Robert. *Some Account of the Mosquito Territory*. Edited by Robert Hodgson. 2nd ed. Blackwood, 1822.
Holloway, Carson, ed. "Establishing the Public Faith: Hamilton's Report on Public Credit." In *Hamilton Versus Jefferson in the Washington Administration: Completing the Founding or Betraying the Founding?*, 9–37. Cambridge University Press, 2015.
The Honduras Almanack. Authority of the Legislative Assembly, 1828.
Hooker, William Jackson. *Journal of Botany*. Vol. 4. Longman, Orme, 1842.
Hopkins, A. G. "Informal Empire in Argentina: An Alternative View." *Journal of Latin American Studies* 26, no. 2 (1994): 469–84.
Hosler, Dorothy. "Ancient West Mexican Metallurgy: A Technological Chronology." *Journal of Field Archaeology* 15, no. 2 (1988): 191–217.
House of Commons. *Correspondence Respecting the Mosquito Territory. Presented to the House of Commons, July 3, 1848, in Pursuance of Their Address of April 3, 1848*. Harrison, 1848.
Humboldt, Alexander von. *Political Essay on the Kingdom of New Spain*. Translated by John Black. Longhan, Hurst, Rees, Orme, & Brown, 1811.
Humphreys, Robert Arthur. "British Merchants and South American Independence." In *Tradition and Revolt in Latin America and Other Essays*, 106–29. Columbia University Press, 1969.
———. *The Diplomatic History of British Honduras, 1638–1901*. Oxford University Press, 1961.
Huntington, Ellsworth. *Civilization and Climate*. 3rd ed. Yale University Press, 1948.
Iglesias-Rogers, Graciela. "The Hispanic-Anglosphere: Transnational Networks, Global Communities (Late 18th-20th Centuries)," 2017. https://hispanic-anglosphere.com/
Inhabitants of Honduras. *The Defence of the Settlers of Honduras Against the Unjust and Unfounded Representations of Colonel George Arthur, Late Superintendent of That Settlement*. Aikman, 1824.
International Bond & Share Society. "'New' Poyais." *Scripophily*, no. 78 (December 2008): 6.
Irving, Washington. *The Life and Voyages of Christopher Columbus*. Edited by John Harmon McElroy. The Complete Works of Washington Irving 11. Twayne, 1981.
Jackson, Trevor. *Impunity and Capitalism: The Afterlives of European Financial Crises, 1690–1830*. Cambridge University Press, 2022.

James, Preston E. "The Changing Patterns of Population in São Paulo State, Brazil." *Geographical Review* 28, no. 3 (1938): 353–62.

Jansen, Jan C. "Aliens in a Revolutionary World: Refugees, Migration Control and Subjecthood in the British Atlantic, 1790s–1820s." *Past & Present* 255, no. 1 (May 2022): 189–231.

Jasanoff, Maya. *The Dawn Watch: Joseph Conrad in a Global World*. Penguin Press, 2017.

Jefferys, Thomas. *A Complete Pilot for the West-Indies*. Laurie & Whittle, 1794.

———. *The West-India Atlas, or, A Compendious Description of the West-Indies*. Sayer & Bennett, 1771.

Jensen, Peta Gay. *The Last Colonials: The Story of Two European Families in Jamaica*. Radcliffe Press, 2005.

Johnston, H.J.M. *British Emigration Policy 1815–1830: Shoveling Out Paupers*. Clarendon Press, 1972.

Jones, Charles. "'Business Imperialism' and Argentina, 1875–1900: A Theoretical Note." *Journal of Latin American Studies* 12, no. 2 (1980): 437–44.

Jonsson, Fredrik Albritton. *Enlightenment's Frontier: The Scottish Highlands and the Origins of Environmentalism*. The Lewis Walpole Series in Eighteenth-Century Culture and History. Yale University Press, 2013.

Kafka, Franz. *Das Schloss*. Wolff, 1926.

Kalb, Courtenay de. "A Bibliography of the Mosquito Coast of Nicaragua." *Journal of the American Geographical Society of New York* 26, no. 1 (January 1894): 241–48.

Kaplan, Herbert H. *Nathan Mayer Rothschild and the Creation of a Dynasty: The Critical Years 1806–1816*. Stanford University Press, 2006.

Kaukiainen, Yrjö. "Shrinking the World: Improvements in the Speed of Information Transmission, c. 1820 1870." *European Review of Economic History* 5, no. 1 (April 2001): 1–28.

Kelly, Patrick. *Le cambiste universel, ou Traité complet des changes, monnaies, poids et mesures, de toutes les nations commerçantes et de leurs colonies*. Vol. 1. Bossange, 1823.

Khatri, Vikas. "Gregor MacGregor: Chief of Poyais." In *World Famous Crooks & Con Men*, 120–27. Pustak Mahal, 2011.

King, Emory. *Slavery in Belize: A Family Affair*. Tropical Books, 1999.

Klaus, Ian. *Forging Capitalism: Rogues, Swindlers, Frauds, and the Rise of Modern Finance*. Yale Series in Economic and Financial History. Yale University Press, 2014.

Klerman, Daniel. "Legal Fictions as Strategic Instruments." Working paper. USC Law School, September 16, 2013. http://dklerman.usc.edu/secure/documents/4/.KlermanandBakerAppsDE.pdf

Klose, Bernd. "Sind wir noch zu retten? : Charles Ponzi und sein legitimer Nachfolger: Bernard Madoff." *ZRFC: Risk, Fraud & Compliance ; Prävention und Aufdeckung in der Compliance-Organisation* 4, no. 2 (April 2009): 84–89.

Knight Bruce, J. L. "Richardson v. Larpent." In *Reports of Cases Decided in the Court of Chancery*, Vol. 2. Banks, Gould, 1843.

Kupperman, Karen Ordahl. *Providence Island, 1630–1641: The Other Puritan Colony*. Cambridge University Press, 1993.

Lambert, David, and Alan Lester, eds. *Colonial Lives Across the British Empire: Imperial Careering in the Long Nineteenth Century*. Cambridge University Press, 2006.

Lamont, Stephen Peter. "Robert Wilmot Horton and Liberal Toryism." PhD thesis, University of Nottingham, 2015.
Lamoreaux, Naomi R. *Insider Lending: Banks, Personal Connections, and Economic Development in Industrial New England*. NBER Series on Long-Term Factors in Economic Development. Cambridge University Press, 1996.
———. "Rethinking Microhistory: A Comment." *Journal of the Early Republic* 26, no. 4 (December 2006): 555–61.
Ledru-Rollin, Sulpicy, F. Roger, J.-A. Levesque, F. Noblet, Amable Boullanger, and Durand De Saint-Amand. "Messal C. Sturt." In *Journal du Palais: jurisprudence française*, Vol. 6, 721. Patris, 1838.
Lehuby, Jean-François. *Procès contre la Compagnie de la Nouvelle-Neustrie*. Boucher, 1826.
Lepler, Jessica M. *The Many Panics of 1837: People, Politics, and the Creation of a Transatlantic Financial Crisis*. Cambridge University Press, 2013.
Lester, V. Markham. *Victorian Insolvency: Bankruptcy, Imprisonment for Debt, and Company Winding-up in Nineteenth Century England*. Repr. Oxford Historical Monographs. Clarendon Press, 1999.
Levi, Giovanni. "Frail Frontiers?" Past & Present 242, Suppl. 14 (November 2019): 37–49.
———. "On Microhistory." In *New Perspectives on Historical Writing*, edited by Peter Burke, 93–113. Polity Press, 1991.
Liedtke, Rainer. "Modern Communication: The Information Network of N.M. Rothschild and Sons in Nineteenth-Century Europe." In *Finance and Modernization*, edited by Gerald D. Feldman and Peter Hertner, 155–61. Ashgate, 2008.
Livi-Bacci, Massimo. "The Depopulation of Hispanic America After the Conquest." *Population and Development Review* 32, no. 2 (June 2006): 199–232.
Llorca-Jaña, Manuel. "British Merchants in New Markets: The Case of Wylie and Hancock in Brazil and the River Plate, c. 1808–19." *Journal of Imperial and Commonwealth History* 42, no. 2 (March 2014): 215–38.
———. "Shaping Globalization: London's Merchant Bankers in the Early Nineteenth Century." *Business History Review* 88, no. 3 (September 2014): 469–95.
———. "The Economic Activities of a Global Merchant-Banker in Chile: Huth & Co. of London, 1820s-1850s." *Historia (Santiago)* 45, no. 2 (December 2012): 399–432.
Locard, Edmond. "The Analysis of Dust Traces. Part I." *American Journal of Police Science* 1, no. 3 (1930): 276–98.
López-Morell, Miguel A., and José M. O'Kean. "A Stable Network as a Source of Entrepreneurial Opportunities: The Rothschilds in Spain, 1835–1931." *Business History* 50, no. 2 (March 2008): 163–84.
Low, George Augustus. *The Belise Merchants Unmasked, or, A Review of Their Late Proceedings Against Poyais: From Information and Authentic Documents Gained on the Spot, During a Visit to Those Parts in the Months of August and September, 1823*. Maurice, 1824.
Lowe, John. "A Letter to the Rt. Hon. George Canning, MP on the Policy of Recognising the Independence of the South American States." In *The Pamphleteer* 21, no. 42 (1823): 401–13. London.
———. "Mr. John Lowe to the Marquess of Londonderry." In *Correspondence, Despatches*,

and Other Papers of Viscount Castlereagh, edited by Charles William Vane, Vol. 4, 476–82. Murray, 1853.

Lowe, Richard G. "American Seizure of Amelia Island." *Florida Historical Quarterly* 45, no. 1 (July 1966): 18–30.

MacGregor, Gregor. *Constitution de la nation poyaisienne dans l'Amérique Centrale.* Johnson, 1825.

———. *Exposición documentada que el General Mac-Gregor dirijió al Gobierno de Venezuela y resolución que a ella recayó.* Damiron, 1839.

———. *Plan of a Constitution for the Inhabitants of the Indian Coast in Central America, Commonly Called the Mosquito Shore.* Balfour & Jack, 1836.

Madden, Richard Robert. *A Twelvemonth's Residence in the West Indies, During the Transition from Slavery to Apprenticeship: With Incidental Notices of the State of Society, Prospects, and Natural Resources of Jamaica and Other Islands.* Vol. 2. 2 vols. Cochrane, 1835.

Madiou, Thomas. *Histoire d'Haïti.* Vol. 4. Éditions Henri Deschamps, 1826.

Magnússon, Sigurður Gylfi. "Far-Reaching Microhistory: The Use of Microhistorical Perspective in a Globalized World." *Rethinking History* 21, no. 3 (July 2017): 312–41.

Mahon, John K. "British Strategy and Southern Indians: War of 1812." *Florida Historical Quarterly* 44, no. 4 (April 1966): 285–302.

Malthus, Thomas Robert. *An Essay on the Principle of Population.* 2nd ed. Johnson, 1803.

———. *An Essay on the Principle of Population, as It Affects the Future Improvement of Society. With Remarks on the Speculations of Mr. Godwin, M. Condorcet and Other Writers.* Johnson, 1798.

———. "Population." In *Supplement to the Encyclopædia Britannica*, Vol. 6, 307–33. Constable, 1824.

Marichal, Carlos. *A Century of Debt Crises in Latin America: From Independence to the Great Depression, 1820–1930.* Princeton University Press, 1989.

———. "Historical Reflections on the Causes of Financial Crises: Official Investigations, Past and Present, 1873–2011." *Investigaciones de Historia Económica—Economic History Research* 10 (2014): 81–91.

Massi, Cindy. "Gregor MacGregor (1786–1845)." Find a Grave, April 1, 2016. https://fr.findagrave.com/memorial/160320089/gregor-macgregor

Mather, Cotton. *Some Considerations on the Bills of Credit Now Passing in New-England.* Harris & Allen, 1691.

Mathew, W. M. "The First Anglo-Peruvian Debt and Its Settlement, 1822–49." *Journal of Latin American Studies* 2, no. 1 (May 1970): 81–98.

McKay, George L. *Early American Currency.* Typophile Chap Books 10. Typophiles, 1944.

McKenzie, Kirsten. *Imperial Underworld: An Escaped Convict and the Transformation of the British Colonial Order.* Critical Perspectives on Empire. Cambridge University Press, 2016.

McSweeney, Kendra. "The Dugout Canoe Trade in Central America's Mosquitia: Approaching Rural Livelihoods Through Systems of Exchange." *Annals of the Association of American Geographers* 94, no. 3 (September 2004): 638–61.

Melville, Jennifer. "Lizars, William Home (1788–1859)." In *Oxford Dictionary of National*

Biography, edited by Brian Harrison. Oxford University Press, 2004. https://doi.org/10.1093/ref:odnb/16815

Mérilhou, Joseph. *Précis pour le Général Sir Grégor Mac-Grégor, Cacique de Poyais, dans l'Amérique centrale*. Porthmann, 1825.

Merle, Isabelle. "Les Subaltern Studies: Retour sur les principes fondateurs d'un projet historiographique de l'Inde coloniale." *Genèses* 3, no. 56 (2004): 131–47.

Metcalf, Alida C. *Go-Betweens and the Colonization of Brazil, 1500–1600*. University of Texas Press, 2005.

Mignolo, Walter D. *The Idea of Latin America*. Blackwell, 2009.

Millett, Nathaniel. "Law, Lineage, Gender, and the Lives of Enslaved Indigenous People on the Edge of the Nineteenth-Century Caribbean." *William and Mary Quarterly* 78, no. 4 (2021): 687–720.

———. *The Maroons of Prospect Bluff and Their Quest for Freedom in the Atlantic World*. University Press of Florida, 2015.

Moore, John H. "The Miskitu National Question in Nicaragua: Background to a Misunderstanding." *Science & Society* 50, no. 2 (July 1986): 132–47.

Morillo, Pablo. *Mémoires du général Morillo, comte de Carthagène, marquis de la Puerta, relatifs aux principaux événemens de ses campagnes en Amérique de 1815 à 1821*. Dufart, 1826.

Murray-Young, D. *The Colonial Office in the Early Nineteenth Century*. Uncorrected proof copy. Longmans, 1961.

Nars, Kari. *Swindling Billions: An Extraordinary History of the Great Money Fraudsters*. Marshall Cavendish Business, 2011.

Naylor, Robert Arthur. "British Commercial Relations with Central America, 1821–1851." PhD thesis Tulane University, 1969.

———. *Penny Ante Imperialism: The Mosquito Shore and the Bay of Honduras, 1600–1914: A Case Study in British Informal Empire*. Fairleigh Dickinson University Press, 1989.

———. "The Mahogany Trade as a Factor in the British Return to the Mosquito Shore in the Second Quarter of the Nineteenth Century." *Jamaican Historical Review* 7 (1967): 40–67.

Neal, Larry. "The Financial Crisis of 1825 and the Restructuring of the British Financial System." *Federal Reserve Bank of St. Louis Review* 80, no. 3 (May 1998): 53–76.

———. "The London Stock Exchange in the First Age of Globalization, 1801–1914." In *EHES Conference*. 2005.

———. *The Rise of Financial Capitalism: International Capital Markets in the Age of Reason*. Studies in Monetary and Financial History. Cambridge University Press, 1993.

The New Bankrupt Act, with an Explanation of the Difference Between the Old Acts and the New Act. Clarke, 1824.

Newson, Linda A. *The Cost of Conquest: Indian Decline in Honduras Under Spanish Rule*. Dellplain Latin American Studies 20. Westview Press, 1986.

Nicholls, Kit. "'All Abbotsford to an Acre of Poyais': Highlandry and the Revolutionary Atlantic." *European Romantic Review* 22, no. 6 (2011): 727–44.

Nicholson, Bob. "The Digital Turn." *Media History* 19, no. 1 (February 2013): 59–73.

Nogues-Marco, Pilar. "The Microeconomics of Bullionism: Arbitrage, Smuggling and Silver Outflows in Spain in the Early 18th Century." Working Papers in Economic History. Universidad Carlos III, June 2011. http://e-archivo.uc3m.es/handle/10016/11425

Noveck, Daniel. "Class, Culture, and the Miskito Indians: A Historical Perspective." *Dialectical Anthropology* 13, no. 1 (January 1988): 17–29.

Nugent, Maria. *Lady Nugent's Journal of Her Residence in Jamaica from 1801 to 1805*. Edited by Philip Wright. University of the West Indies, 2002.

Obert, Henri. "Charte de concession du territoire de Vera Paz accordé par le gouvernement de Guatemala à la compagnie commerciale et agricole des côtes orientales de l'Amérique centrale." In *Mémoire contenant un aperçu statistique de l'état de Guatemala: ainsi que des renseignements précis sur son commerce, son industrie, son sol, sa température, son climat, et tout ce qui est relatif à cet état*. Lesigne et cie, 1840.

Offen, Karl H. "British Logwood Extraction from the Mosquitia: The Origin of a Myth." *Hispanic American Historical Review* 80, no. 1 (2000): 113–35.

———. "Creating Mosquitia: Mapping Amerindian Spatial Practices in Eastern Central America, 1629–1779." *Journal of Historical Geography* 33, no. 2 (April 2007): 254–82.

———. "The Sambo and Tawira Miskitu: The Colonial Origins and Geography of Intra-Miskitu Differentiation in Eastern Nicaragua and Honduras." *Ethnohistory* 49, no. 2 (April 2002): 319–72.

Olien, Michael D. "E. G. Squier and the Miskito: Anthropological Scholarship and Political Propaganda." *Ethnohistory* 32, no. 2 (April 1985): 111–33.

———. "General, Governor, and Admiral: Three Miskito Lines of Succession." *Ethnohistory* 45, no. 2 (April 1998): 277–318.

———. "Micro/Macro-Level Linkages: Regional Political Structures on the Mosquito Coast, 1845–1864." *Ethnohistory* 34, no. 3 (July 1987): 256–87.

———. "The Miskito Kings and the Line of Succession." *Journal of Anthropological Research* 39, no. 2 (July 1983): 198–241.

Orain, Arnaud. *La politique du merveilleux: une autre histoire du système de Law (1695–1795)*. L'épreuve de l'histoire. Fayard, 2018.

O'Rourke, Kevin H. "The Worldwide Economic Impact of the French Revolutionary and Napoleonic Wars, 1793–1815." *Journal of Global History* 1, no. 1 (March 2006): 123–49.

Ouvrard, Gabriel-Julien. *Mémoires de G.-J. Ouvrard: sur sa vie et ses diverses opérations financières*. Moutardier, 1827.

Overton, J. H., and Ian Machin. "Pratt, Josiah (1768–1844)." In *Oxford Dictionary of National Biography*, edited by Brian Harrison. Oxford University Press, 2004. https://doi.org/10.1093/ref:odnb/22707

Owsley, Frank L. "Ambrister and Arbuthnot: Adventurers or Martyrs for British Honor?" *Journal of the Early Republic* 5, no. 3 (October 1985): 289–308.

Pagden, Anthony R. *Spanish Imperialism and the Political Imagination: Studies in European and Spanish-American Social and Political Theory, 1513–1830*. Yale University Press, 1990.

Paquette, Gabriel. "The Intellectual Context of British Diplomatic Recognition of the South American Republics, C. 1800–1830." *Journal of Transatlantic Studies* 2, no. 1 (Spring 2004): 75–95.

Parry, Clive, ed. "Convention Between Great Britain and Spain, Signed at London, 14 July 1786." In *The Consolidated Treaty Series*, Vol. 50, 47–51. Oceana, 1969.

Parton, James. *Life of Andrew Jackson*. Houghton, Mifflin, 1888.

Patalano, Christopher P. "Poyais: A Novella." Honors Theses, Wesleyan University, 2009. http://wesscholar.wesleyan.edu/etd_hon_theses/230

The Pawnbrokers' Reply to the Pretended Fair and Candid Statement of the Equitable Loan Bank Company. Tower, 1825.

Pepe, Guglielmo. *Relation des événements politiques et militaires qui ont eu lieu à Naples en 1820 et 1821, adressée à S. M. le Roi des Deux Siciles*. Chez les principaux libraires, 1822.

Pérez Morales, Edgardo. *No Limits to Their Sway: Cartagena's Privateers and the Masterless Caribbean in the Age of Revolutions*. Vanderbilt University Press, 2018.

Petley, Christer. "Rethinking the Fall of the Planter Class." *Atlantic Studies* 9, no. 1 (March 2012): 1–17.

Pim, Bedford, and Berthold Carl Seemann. *Dottings on the Roadside, in Panama, Nicaragua, and Mosquito*. Chapman & Hall, 1869.

Platt, Desmond Christopher Martin. "British Bondholders in Nineteenth Century Latin America: Injury and Remedy." In *Foreign Investment in Latin America: Cases and Attitudes*, edited by Marvin D. Bernstein, 81–102. Knopf, 1966.

———, ed. *Business Imperialism 1840–1930: An Inquiry Based on British Experience in Latin America*. Reprint. Clarendon Press, 1977.

———. "Further Objections to an 'Imperialism of Free Trade', 1830–60." *Economic History Review* 26, no. 1 (February 1973): 77–91.

———. "Introduction." In *Business Imperialism 1840–1930*, edited by Desmond Christopher Martin Platt, Reprint, 1–16. Clarendon Press, 1979.

———. "The Imperialism of Free Trade: Some Reservations." *Economic History Review*, 21, no. 2 (August 1968): 296–306.

Pluymers, Keith. "Atlantic Iron: Wood Scarcity and the Political Ecology of Early English Expansion." *William and Mary Quarterly* 73, no. 3 (July 2016): 389–426.

Pocahontas. Buena Vista Pictures, 1995.

Polden, Patrick. "The Court of Chancery, 1820–1875." In *The Oxford History of the Laws of England*, by William Cornish, J. Stuart Anderson, Ray Cocks, Michael Lobban, Patrick Polden, and Keith Smith, 646–92. Oxford University Press, 2010.

Post-Office Annual Directory. Schaw, 1822.

Potthast, Barbara. *Die Mosquitoküste im Spannungsfeld britischer und spanischer Politik 1502–1821*. Lateinamerikanische Forschungen 16. Böhlau, 1988.

Pouchepadass, Jacques. "Les Subaltern Studies ou la critique postcoloniale de la modernité." *L'Homme*, no. 156 (2000): 161–85.

Pratt, Josiah, ed. *The Works of the Right Reverend Father in God Ezekiel Hopkins, D.D.* Vol. 1. 4 vols. Seeley, 1809.

Pratt, Josiah, and John Henry Pratt. *Memoir of the Rev. Josiah Pratt, B.D.* Seeleys, 1849.

Prebble, John. *The King's Jaunt: George IV in Scotland, August 1822*. Birlinn, 2000.

Press, Steven. *Rogue Empires: Contracts and Conmen in Europe's Scramble for Africa*. Harvard University Press, 2017.

Pro Ruiz, Juan. "Figure du cacique, figure du caudillo: les langages de la construction nationale en Espagne et en Argentine, 1808–1930." *Genèses* 62, no. 1 (March 2006): 27–48.

Proposed Colony in the District of Black River on the Northern Coast of Central America . . . : Granted to the British Central American Land Company. Wilson, 1838.

Puga, Diego, and Daniel Trefler. "International Trade and Institutional Change: Medieval Venice's Response to Globalization." *Quarterly Journal of Economics* 129, no. 2 (May 2014): 753–821.
Rafter, Michael. *Memoirs of Gregor McGregor Comprising a Sketch of the Revolution in New Granada and Venezuela with Biographical Notices of Generals Miranda, Bolivar, Morillo and Horé and a Narrative of the Expeditions to Amelia Island, Porto Bello and Rio de La Hache Interspersed with Revolutionary Anecdotes.* Stockdale, 1820.
Ragatz, Lowell Joseph. *The Fall of the Planter Class in the British Caribbean, 1763–1833: A Study in Social and Economic History.* Century, 1928.
Ranston, Jackie. "Belisario: A Historical Biography of a Jamaican Jewish Artist." *Jamaque*, 2011. http://www.jamaquemagazine.com/arts-and-culture/26-belisario-a-historical-biography-of-a-jamaican-jewish-artist
Read, Jan. "'Independence or Death': British Adventurers in South America." *History Today* 25, no. 6 (June 1975): 381.
Reinhart, Carmen M., and Kenneth S. Rogoff. *This Time Is Different: Eight Centuries of Financial Folly.* Princeton University Press, 2009.
Remington, V. "Rochard, Simon Jacques (1788–1857)." In *Oxford Dictionary of National Biography*, edited by Brian Harrison. Oxford University Press, 2004. https://doi.org/10.1093/ref:odnb/23906
A Retired Pawnbroker. *An Examination of the Present Modes of Granting Temporary Loans on Pledges by Pawnbrokers and of Those Proposed by the London Equitable Loan Bank Company, as Far as They Are Calculated to Affect the Trader and Manufacturer with Small Capitals, and Others Requiring Occasional Advances: With a Few Remarks on the Objections Which Have Been Urged by Pawnbrokers and Others Against the Equitable Loan Bank.* Wilson, 1825.
Revels, Craig S. "Timber, Trade, and Transformation: A Historical Geography of Mahogany in Honduras." PhD thesis, Louisiana State University, 2002.
Richards, Eric. "Horton, Sir Robert John Wilmot-, Third Baronet." In *Oxford Dictionary of National Biography*, edited by Brian Harrison. Oxford: Oxford University Press, 2004. https://doi.org/10.1093/ref:odnb/13827
Richter, Daniel K. "To 'Clear the King's and Indians' Title': Seventeenth-Century Origins of North American Land Cession Treaties." In *Empire by Treaty: Negotiating European Expansion, 1600–1900*, edited by Saliha Belmessous, 45–77. Oxford University Press, 2015.
Richter, John Henry. *Belisario of Jamaica.* National Library of Jamaica, n.d.
Rippy, Fred J. *British Investments in Latin America, 1822–1949: A Case Study in the Operations of Private Enterprise in Retarded Regions.* University of Minnesota Press, 1959.
——. "Latin America and the British Investment 'Boom' of the 1820's." *Journal of Modern History* 19, no. 2 (June 1947): 122–29.
Robb, George. "Before Madoff and Ponzi: 19th-Century Business Frauds." *Phi Kappa Phi Forum* 92, no. 1 (Spring 2012): 7–9.
Robbins, Paul. *Political Ecology: A Critical Introduction.* 2nd ed. Wiley, 2012.
Robert, Adolphe, and Gaston Cougny, eds. "Mérilhou, Joseph." In *Dictionnaire des parlementaires français*, Vol. 4, 344–45. Bourloton, 1891.

Roberts, Orlando W. *Narratives of Voyages and Excursions on the East Coast and in the Interior of Central America.* Constable, 1827.

Robertson, William Spence. *France and Latin-American Independence.* Albert Shaw Lectures on Diplomatic History. Johns Hopkins University Press, 1939.

Rochat, Jean-Philippe. "La société anonyme en France (1807–1867): représentations et pratiques." PhD thesis, Université de Genève, 2014.

Rodríguez, Moises Enrique. *Freedom's Mercenaries: British Volunteers in the Wars of Independence of Latin America: Northern South America.* Vol. 1. 2 vols. Hamilton Books, 2006.

———. *Freedom's Mercenaries: British Volunteers in the Wars of Independence of Latin America: Southern South America.* Vol. 2. 2 vols. Hamilton Books, 2006.

———. "Gregor MacGregor: General, Privateer and Cazique." In *Freedom's Mercenaries: British Volunteers in the Wars of Independence of Latin America: Northern South America*, Vol. 1, 87–133. Hamilton Books, 2006.

Rothschild, Emma. "Economic History and Nationalism." *Capitalism: A Journal of History and Economics* 2, no. 1 (2021): 227–33.

———. *The Inner Life of Empires: An Eighteenth-Century History.* Princeton University Press, 2011.

Roughley, Thomas. *The Jamaica Planter's Guide; or, A System for Planting and Managing a Sugar Estate, or Other Plantations in That Island, and Throughout the British West Indies in General.* Longman, Hurst, Rees, Orme, & Brown, 1823.

Rubinstein, William D. "The End of 'Old Corruption' in Britain 1780–1860." *Past & Present*, no. 101 (November 1983): 55–86.

Rubinstein, William D., Michael Jolles, and Hilary L. Rubinstein, eds. *The Palgrave Dictionary of Anglo-Jewish History.* Palgrave Macmillan, 2011.

Rustin, Michael. "William Cobbett and the Invention of Popular Radical Journalism." *Soundings*, no. 1 (Autumn 1995): 139–55.

Ryden, David. "Does Decline Make Sense? The West Indian Economy and the Abolition of the Slave Trade." *Journal of Interdisciplinary History* 31, no. 3 (2001): 347–74.

Sabato, Hilda. *Republics of the New World: The Revolutionary Political Experiment in Nineteenth-Century Latin America.* Princeton University Press, 2018.

Safier, Neil. "Global Knowledge on the Move: Itineraries, Amerindian Narratives, and Deep Histories of Science." *Isis* 101, no. 1 (2010): 133–45.

Saint Clair, William. *That Greece Might Still Be Free: The Philhellenes in the War of Independence.* Open Book, 2008.

Sandage, Scott A. *Born Losers: A History of Failure in America.* Harvard University Press, 2005.

Sarna, David E. Y. *History of Greed: Financial Fraud from Tulip Mania to Bernie Madoff.* Wiley, 2010.

Sarrut, Germain, and B. Saint-Edme. "Mérilhou, Joseph." In *Biographie des hommes du jour*, Vol. 1, 139–49. Krabe, 1835.

Schnakenbourg, Eric. "Neutres et neutralité dans le monde antillais du XVIIIe siècle." *Bulletin de la Société d'Histoire de la Guadeloupe*, no. 174 (2016): 5–19.

Schorsch, Jonathan. "Sephardic Business: Early Modern Atlantic Style." *Jewish Quarterly Review* 100, no. 3 (2010): 483–503.

Scott, Drusilla. *Mary English: A Friend of Bolivar*. Book Guild, 1991.
Select Committee on Emigration. *The Report of the Select Committee on Emigration in 1826*. Murray, 1827.
Select Committee on the Employment of the Poor in Ireland. *Report from the Select Committee on the Employment of the Poor in Ireland: Ordered by the House of Commons, to Be Printed, 16 July, 1823*. 1823.
Semmel, Bernard. *The Rise of Free Trade Imperialism: Classical Political Economy, the Empire of Free Trade and Imperialism 1750–1850*. Cambridge University Press, 1970.
Sharpe, James. "History from Below." In *New Perspectives on Historical Writing*, edited by Peter Burke, 24–41. Polity Press, 1991.
Shaw, A.G.L. *Sir George Arthur, Bart., 1784–1854: Superintendent of British Honduras, Lieutenant-Governor of Van Diemen's Land and of Upper Canada, Governor of the Bombay Presidency*. Melbourne University Press, 1980.
Sherman, Susanne K. "Thomas Wade West, Theatrical Impressario, 1790–1799." *William and Mary Quarterly* 9, no. 1 (1952): 10–28.
Shimbo, Akiko. *Furniture-Makers and Consumers in England, 1754–1851: Design as Interaction*. The History of Retailing and Consumption. Routledge, 2015.
Simpson, Anthony. "Dandelions on the Field of Honour: Duelling, the Middle Classes, and the Law in Nineteenth-Century England." *Criminal Justice History* 9 (1988).
Sinclair, David. *The Land That Never Was: Sir Gregor MacGregor and the Most Audacious Fraud in History*. Review, 2003.
"A Sketch of the Mosquito Shore." *Quarterly Review* 28, no. 55 (October 1822): 157–61.
Slapper, Gary, and David Kelly. *The English Legal System*. 6th ed. Cavendish, 2003.
Smalligan, Laura M. "An Effigy for the Enslaved: Jonkonnu in Jamaica and Belisario's Sketches of Character." *Slavery & Abolition* 32, no. 4 (December 2011): 561–81.
Smeeton, George. *Doings in London: Or, Day and Night Scenes of the Frauds, Frolics, Manners, and Depravities of the Metropolis*. Hodgson, 1828.
Smiles, Samuel. *A Publisher and His Friends: Memoir and Correspondence of John Murray 1768–1843*. Murray, 1911.
Smits, Thomas. "Problems and Possibilities of Digital Newspaper and Periodical Archives." *Tijdschrift Voor Tijdschriftstudies*, no. 36 (December 2014): 139–46.
Sorsby, Karen. "Mosquito Indian King George III and the Scot Cacique Sir Gregor MacGregor, 1800–1825: The Kingdom of Poyais." In *Regards sur l'histoire de la Caraïbe: des Guyanes aux Grandes Antilles*, edited by Serge Mam-Lam-Fouck, Juan Gonzales Mendoza, Jacques Adélaïde-Merlande, Jacqueline Zonzon, and Rodolphe Alexandre, 385–402. Ibis rouge éditions, 2001.
Sorsby, William S. "Spanish Colonization of the Mosquito Coast, 1787–1800." *Revista de Historia de América*, no. 73/74 (January 1972): 145–53.
Spence, Clark C. *British Investments and the American Mining Frontier 1860–1901*. Vail-Ballou Press, 1958.
Springer, James Warren. "American Indians and the Law of Real Property in Colonial New England." *American Journal of Legal History* 30, no. 1 (1986): 25–58.
Squier, Ephraim G. *Honduras Interoceanic Railway: Preliminary Report*. Tubbs, Nesmith, & Teall, 1854.

———. *Information on the Coal Mines of the River Lempa, Republic of San Salvador, Central America.* Chiswick Press, 1856.

———. "Nicaragua." *Harper's New Monthly Magazine* 11, no. 66 (November 1855): 744–63.

———. *Nicaragua: Its People, Scenery, Monuments, and the Proposed Interoceanic Canal.* 2 vols. Appleton, 1852.

———. "Something About the Mosquitos." *Harper's New Monthly Magazine* 11, no. 64 (September 1855): 456–66.

———. *Tropical Fibres: Their Production and Economic Extraction.* Scribner, 1861.

Squier, Ephraim G., and E. H. Davis. *Ancient Monuments of the Mississippi Valley.* Smithsonian Contributions to Knowledge. Bartlett & Welford, 1848.

Stansifer, Charles Lee. "The Central American Career of E. George Squier." PhD thesis, Tulane University, 1959.

Stock, Eugene. *The History of the Church Missionary Society: Its Environment, Its Men and Its Work.* Church Missionary Society, 1899.

Stone, Irving. "British Long-Term Investment in Latin America, 1865–1913." *Business History Review* 42, no. 3 (1968): 311–39.

Stout, Peter F. *Nicaragua: Past, Present and Future.* Potter & Cie, 1859.

Strangeways, Thomas. *Sketch of the Mosquito Shore, Including the Territory of Poyais: Descriptive of the Country; with Some Information as to Its Production, the Best Mode of Culture, &c. . . . Chiefly Intended for the Use of Settlers.* Blackwood, 1822.

Stringham, Edward. "The Emergence of the London Stock Exchange as a Self-Policing Club." *Journal of Private Enterprise* 17, no. 2 (2002): 1–19.

Substance of the Debate in the House of Commons on the 15th May, 1823, on a Motion for the Mitigation and Gradual Abolition of Slavery Throughout the British Dominion. Ellerton & Henderson, 1823.

Summerhill, William Roderick. *Inglorious Revolution: Political Institutions, Sovereign Debt, and Financial Underdevelopment in Imperial Brazil.* Yale Series in Economic and Financial History. Yale University Press, 2015.

Taylor, Chris. *The Black Carib Wars: Freedom, Survival, and the Making of the Garifuna.* University Press of Mississippi, 2012.

Taylor, James. *Boardroom Scandal: The Criminalization of Company Fraud in Nineteenth-Century Britain.* Oxford University Press, 2013.

———. "Inside and Outside the London Stock Exchange: Stockbrokers and Speculation in Late Victorian Britain." *Enterprise & Society* 22, no. 3 (September 2021): 842–77.

Thomson, Peter. *Belize: A Concise History.* Macmillan Caribbean, 2004.

Tomkins, Stephen. *The Clapham Sect: How Wilberforce's Circle Transformed Britain.* Lion Books, 2010.

Tomz, Michael. *Reputation and International Cooperation: Sovereign Debt Across Three Centuries.* Princeton University Press, 2007.

Torrens, Major. *A Paper on the Means of Reducing the Poors Rates, and of Affording Effectual and Permanent Relief to the Labouring Classes.* 1817.

Trivellato, Francesca. "Is There a Future for Italian Microhistory in the Age of Global History?" *California Italian Studies* 2, no. 1 (January 2011).

Trouillot, Michel-Rolph. *Silencing the Past: Power and the Production of History*. Beacon Press, 1995.
Ugolini, Stefano. "The Origins of Swiss Wealth Management? Genevan Private Banking, 1800–1840." *Financial History Review*, March 2018, 1–22.
Uribe, Víctor M. "The Enigma of Latin American Independence: Analyses of the Last Ten Years." *Latin American Research Review* 32, no. 1 (1997): 236–55.
Vale, Brian. *Independence or Death! British Sailors and Brazilian Independence, 1822–25*. International Library of Historical Studies 5. Tauris Academic, 1996.
Verax. *A Letter to the Editor of the Quarterly Review for Oct. 1822 on a Review of Captain Strangeway's Sketch of the Mosquito Shore*. Gilbert, 1823.
Villiers, Marc de. "Une vente de terrain ou Gregor Mac Gregor, « Cacique des Poyais »." *Journal de la Société des Américanistes* 16, no. 1 (1924): 197–200.
Vittorino, Antonio. *Relaciones colombo-británicas de 1823 a 1825: según los documentos del Foreign Office*. Ediciones Uninorte, 1990.
Waddell, David Alan Gilmour. *British Honduras: A Historical and Contemporary Survey*. Oxford University Press, 1961.
———. "British Neutrality and Spanish-American Independence: The Problem of Foreign Enlistment." *Journal of Latin American Studies* 19, no. 1 (May 1987): 1–18.
Walker, J., R. Lea, and J. Nunn. *The Parliamentary Register; Or, History of the Proceedings and Debates of the House of Commons*. Vol. 1. 17 vols. Stockdale, 1802.
Wallace, Nesbit Willoughby. *A Regimental Chronicle and List of Officers of the 60th, or the King's Royal Rifle Corps, Formerly the 62nd, or the Royal American Regiment of Foot*. Harrison, 1879.
Walvin, James. *Slavery in Small Things: Slavery and Modern Cultural Habits*. Wiley Blackwell, 2017.
Wang, Hsiang-Hua, and Frederick N. Scatena. "Regeneration After Hurricane Disturbance of Big-Leaf and Hybrid Mahogany Plantations in Puerto Rico." In *Big-Leaf Mahogany: Genetics, Ecology, and Management*, edited by Ariel E. Lugo, Julio C. Figueroa, and Mildred Alayón, 237–60. Ecological Studies, Vol. 159. Springer, 2003.
Ward, J. R. *British West Indian Slavery, 1750–1834: The Process of Amelioration*. Clarendon Press, 1988.
Warsh, Molly A. "A Political Ecology in the Early Spanish Caribbean." *William and Mary Quarterly* 71, no. 4 (2014): 517–48.
Wasserman, Henry. "Hep! Hep!" In *Encyclopaedia Judaica*, edited by Michael Berenbaum and Fred Skolnik, 2nd ed., Vol. 8, 811–12. Macmillan Reference USA, 2007.
Wasserman, Henry, Simon R. Schwarzfuchs, and Vivian David Lipman. "Rothschild." In *Encyclopaedia Judaica*, edited by Michael Berenbaum and Fred Skolnik, 2nd ed., Vol. 17, 487–91. Macmillan Reference USA, 2007.
Watt, Douglas A. *The Price of Scotland: Darien, Union and the Wealth of the Nations*. Luath, 2006.
Weatherhead, W. Davidson. *An Account of the Late Expedition Against the Isthmus of Darien, Under the Command of Sir Gregor M'Gregor: Together with the Events Subsequent to the Recapture of Portobello, till the Release of the Prisoners from Panama; Remarks on

the Present State of the Patriot Cause, and on the Climate and Diseases of South America. Longman, Hurst, Rees, Orme, & Brown, 1821.

Wertime, Theodore A. "The Beginnings of Metallurgy: A New Look." *Science* 182, no. 4115 (1973): 875–87.

A West Indian. *No Colonies No Funds!!!* Wilson, 1826.

White, Richard. *Railroaded: The Transcontinentals and the Making of Modern America.* Norton, 2012.

———. *The Middle Ground: Indians, Empires, and Republics in the Great Lakes Region, 1650–1815.* Cambridge Studies in North American Indian History. Cambridge University Press, 1991.

Whitefeather, Barabbas. *The Handbook of Swindling.* Edited by John Jackdaw. Chapman & Hall, 1839.

Wilberforce, William. *An Appeal to the Religion, Justice, and Humanity of the Inhabitants of the British Empire: In Behalf of the Negro Slaves in the West Indies.* Hatchard, 1823.

Williams, Eric Eustace. *Capitalism & Slavery.* University of North Carolina Press, 1944.

Wilmot-Horton, Robert. *Letters Containing Observations on Colonial Policy.* Cunningham, 1839.

———. *Observations upon the Outline of a Plan of Emigration to Upper Canada.* Clowes, 1823.

———. *Outline of a Plan of Emigration to Upper Canada.* Warr, 1823.

———. *The West India Question Practically Considered.* 2nd ed. Murray, 1826.

Winters, Jeffrey A. *Oligarchy.* Cambridge University Press, 2011.

Wood, Gillen D'Arcy. *Tambora: The Eruption That Changed the World.* Princeton University Press, 2014.

Woodcroft, Bennet. "Gilman Sowerby 13th April 1825." In *Titles of Patents of Invention*, Vol. 2. Eyre & Spottiswoode, 1854.

Wright, J. Leitch, Jr. "A Note on the First Seminole War as Seen by the Indians, Negroes, and Their British Advisers." *Journal of Southern History* 34, no. 4 (November 1968): 565–75.

Wright, John. *Memoir of the Mosquito Territory, as Respecting the Voluntary Cession of It to the Crown of Great Britain.* Hatchard, 1808.

Young, Neil, and Crazy Horse. *Cortez the Killer.* Zuma. Reprise, 1975.

Zachs, William, Peter Isaac, Angus Fraser, and William Lister. "Murray Family." In *Oxford Dictionary of National Biography*, edited by Brian Harrison. Oxford University Press, 2004. https://doi.org/10.1093/ref:odnb/64907

Zaugg, Roberto. "Le crachoir chinois du roi." Translated by Antoine Heudre. *Annales. Histoire, Sciences Sociales* 73, no. 1 (2018): 119–59.

Zola, Émile. *L'argent.* Bibliothèque Charpentier, 1891.

Index

Page numbers in *italics* refer to illustrations.

Adoboli, Kweku, 7
Albion (ship), 145, 146, *147*, 148, 151, 157, 159, 174, 207, 208
Alexander, Alexander, 73
Alexander, George, 142, 159
Allan, Victor, 8–9
Ambrister, Robert Christie, 79
Amelia Island, 75–80, 82, 84, 90, 149, 195
Anderson, Grace Tucker, 44, 47–48
aniline, 31
An Appeal to the Religion, Justice, and Humanity of the Inhabitants of the British Empire (Wilberforce), 60, 178
Arbuthnot, Alexander, 79
Arenas, Baron, 140
Arismendi, Juan Batista, 75–76
Arnott, Alexander, 117, 126
Arnott, John Alexander, 117
Arthur, Elizabeth, 57
Arthur, George, 52–72, 88, 131–35, 162, 177, 179–81, 188, 196
August, S., 43
Aury, Jean-Louis, 67, 69, 70, 78, 82–83, 88, 100, 133
Austria, 100, 109, 113, 168, 169
Aux Cayes, Haiti, 80–82

Balcarres, Alexander Lindsay, earl of, 63
Bard, Samuel (pseud. of Ephraim G. Squier), 24
Baring, Alexander, 106
Barnard Act (1734), 164
Barthes, Roland, 9
Bathurst, Henry Bathurst, Earl, 56, 132, 133, 159, 176–78, 186, 189
Battle of Boyacá (1819), 89
Battle of St. George's Caye (1798), 41, 59
Battle of San Juan (1780), 34
Beckford family, 97
Belgrano, Manuel, 92
Belisario, Isaac Mendes, 111, *112*, 113
Belisario, Jacob, 111, 113, 145
Belize. *See* British Honduras
The Belise Merchants Unmasked (Low), 158–62
Bennett, Marshall, 43–47, 50, 54–56, 132–35, 143, 144, 155–59, 161–63, 188
Bentham, Jeremy, 68, 169
Berbice, 97
Bertall, Charles Albert d'Arnoux, 5, *6*
Betson, David, 43
bills of exchange, 104

269

Black River, 21, 28, 38, 85, 126, *129*;
    continuing British presence at, 39;
    evacuation of, 40, 64; Miskitu links to,
    35; Pitt's settlement at, 30; shortages
    in, 131; in slave trade, 34, 40, 57
Blackstone, William, 160
Blackwood, William, 118
Bleak House (Dickens), 165
Boggs, William, 85
Bolívar, Simón, 14, 78, 81, 91, 139, 145, 150, 166, 198, 204
Bolland, Nigel, 42
Bowen, Frederick, 45–46
Bowen, Mansfield, 57
Bowring, John, 169, 170
Boyer, Jean-Pierre, 145, 207
Braena, Count, 140
Brazil, 97, 100
British Central American Land Company, 206
British Honduras (Belize), 18, 23, *35*;
    British-Miskitu links in, 64–66, 68;
    legal system of, 44–46, 50, 51, 53–55, 158–61, 175, 181, 187; magistrates in, 45–57; natural resources of, 30, 39–40, 49, 52, 56–59, 66, 122, 132, 133, 144, 174, 180, 196; as oligarchy, 41–43, 47, 48, 51, 53–54, 56, 61, 158, 163, 175, 186; Poyais settlers' evacuation to, 131, 135, 142, 143, 154, 157, 170; Poyais's failure linked to, 156, 162, 170; settlement of, 18, 19, 23, 27, 40, 41, 122, 196; slavery in, 40, 44, 59–60, 132, 177, 179–80, 188; soil conditions in, 31; tensions in, 69, 83, 131
British West Indies, 56, 86, 96–97, 99, 101, 103, 114, 118, 201; MacGregor's links to, 138; slavery in, 60, 178, 185; sugar trade in, 178
Brown, Manfield W., 43
Brown, Matthew, 9–10, 16, 91, 150
Bubble Act (1720), 104
Bullock, William, 132
Burke, Edmund, 61
Burnaby, William, 45

Burnaby Code, 45, 55
Buxton, Thomas Fowell, 188
Byron, George Gordon Byron, Baron, 123, 169, 178

Campbell, John, 144–45
Canning, George, 118, 178
Castaign, James, 108
The Castle (Kafka), 176
Castlereagh, Robert Stewart, Viscount, 114, 118
cedar, 28, 32
Challandes, Jean-Philippe, 211n32
Chancery, Court of, 165
Chateaubriand, François René de, 149
Chevalier, Michel, 209n5
Chile, 2, 4, 12, 15, 107, 110, 141, 197
Chippendale, Thomas, 31
Clarke, George, 152
Clementi (governor), 66, 70
Cobbett, William, 181, 184
Codd, Edward, 131, 132, 133, 159, 161–62, 177, 187–89, 208
Codrington family, 97
Cohen, Joseph, 167, 168
Colombia, 2, 73, 114, 118, 175; bonds issued by, 15, 107, 109, 152, 123, 141, 152, 165–67, 197; British trade treaty with, 108; independence movement in, 124, 137, 151
Colonial Office, 176–78, 186, 188–89, 191, 192
Colquhoun, James, 43
Columbus, Christopher, 26, 28
Compagnie de la Nouvelle-Neustrie, 150
Congress of Cariaco (1817), 81
Congress of Cúcuta (1821), 73, 89, 90, 166
Congress of Vienna (1814–15), 87
Contra rebellion, 25
Cortés, Hernán, 38
cotton, 95
Course of the Exchange, 108, 115, 126, 140, 154, 167–73
Craig, Charles, 43
Crouch, Henry, 128
Cuba, 97

Dard, Henri, 149–50
Darien scheme, 173
Davison, George, 134
Demerara, 97
Denmark, 107
de Wintz, Count, 169, 170, 207
Díaz Caballero, Jesús, 92
Dickens, Charles, 165
Disraeli, Benjamin, 123
Dos de Mayo Uprising (1808), 41
Douglas, James, 127–28, 130, 133, 135
Dragan, Mr. (bondholder), 230n46
Dumas, Alexandre, *père*, 5, 6, 193
Dunham, Jacob, 65, 66
Dutertre, Achille, 152

Earnee (admiral), 66
East, Robert, 87
East India Company, 221n45
Edgell, Zee, 44
Edward Augustus, Duke of Kent and Strathearn, 76, 90
Ellice, Edward, 50
encomienda system, 33
English, James Towers, 157
English, Mary, 157
epidemics, 33
Equitable Loan Bank Company, 104–5
Essay on the Principle of Population (Malthus), 182
Essequibo, 97
Estrada, Baron, 140
Evans, Charles, 43
Evans, William, 170

Falsehood Detected (Hector Hall), 163
Ferdinand VII, king of Spain, 14, 149
financial crisis of 2008, 193–94
Flandreau, Marc, 164
Floyd, Troy, 23
Foreign Stock Market, 143; disputed transactions on, 164–65, 166–67; executive committee of, 1, 18, 20, 164–65, 167–71, 173, 175, 192, 195, 204–6; Latin American securities traded on, 141, 151; offerings regulated by, 13, 20, 141–42, 168; origins of, 141; Poyais bonds delisted by, 1, 5, 18, 173, 175, 192; Poyais bonds traded on, 154, 164, 166–67, 170–71, *174*, 198
Frain, Thomas, 43
France, 61; British trade with, 103; Caribbean colonies of, 97; Dutch alliance with, 39–40; Haitian independence recognized by, 207; North American campaign of, 32–33; royalists' flight from, 149–50; Spanish peace treaty with, 41; war reparations paid by, 106
France, Alexander, 45
Frazer, Hugh, 124
French Revolution, 61, 67, 150, 199
Fry, Joseph, 155
Fry and Chapman (banking house), 155
furniture, 30, 31, 128

Gallagher, John, 16
Galveston Island, 78–79
Garbo, Greta, 9
Gatmore (Scottish migrant), 96
Gentle, William, 43, 158
George Frederic, king of the Miskitu, 13, 27, 38, 50, 133; abolition resisted by, 66–67; ascent to the throne of, 64–65; as British-Miskitu go-between, 63–64, 71, 196; death of, 208; drinking habits of, 18, 23, 72, 208; Gordon esteemed by, 83, 88; growing ambitions of, 69–70, 200–201; lumber resources and, 68, 85; MacGregor resented by, 130; Miskitu independence sought by, 53; Poyais land grant from, 21, 23, 42, 43, 51, 70–74, 83–86, 122, 124, 128, 145, 146, 196, 201; Poyais land grant rescinded by, 148, 156, 199, 204
George I, king of the Miskitu, 34, 38
George II, king of the Miskitu, 38, 63, 66, 68
George IV, king of Great Britain, 121

Gibraltar, 39, 177
Gibson (captain), 134
Gibson, George, 43, 46
Goldsmid, Asher, 110
gold standard, 99
Gordon, James David Roy, 82, 83, 84–89, 100, 103, 128, 133, 138
Graham, William, 166
Great Britain: anti-slavery movement in, 56–60, 66–72, 106, 131–32, 162, 163, 178, 188, 196; Colombia recognized by, 108; emigration policies of, 20; empire of, 15–17, 53, 97, 203; Miskitu links to, 36, 39
Greece, 165–66, 168–70, 173, 175, 203
Gregg, Richard, 152
Guatemala, 168

Haiti, 67, 80, 82, 145, 207
Hakewill, James, 94
Hall, Hector, 126–31, 137, 140, 148, 157, 163
Hall, William, 43
Hamilton, Alexander, 12
Hamilton, Mark Kerr, 54, 55
Harny, Archibald, 240n139
Harris, Ron, 105
Hasbrouck, Alfred, 8–9
Hastie, James, 128, 129–30, 135, 154, 155
Head, David, 78
Hedgcock, Thomas, 117, 130, 206
Helms, Mary, 25, 36
Henderson, George, 58
Hendriks, Herman, 145, 151, 152, 154, 156, 164, 165, 207
Henri Christophe, king of Haiti, 82
Hep-Hep riots (1819), 86
Herrera, José Manuel de, 78
Herring, Charles, 166
Herring, Graham, and Powles (banking house), 109
Hey, William, 60
Hibbert family, 97
Higson, Thomas, 89, 94–99, 101, 138
Hill, John Emmons, 44

Hill, Louise, 44
Hippisley, Gustavus, 149, 207
Hippisley, Jane-Augusta, 207
Hodgson, Robert, 34
Honduras Packet (ship), 115–17, 126, 127, 128, 130, 137, 142–45, 154, 157–58, 164, 174, 206
Hope & Co., 106
Hosmore (captain), 83, 85, 89
Humboldt, Alexander von, 107
Hume, Joseph, 169, 182, 184, 189, 190, 191
Hunt, William, 219n8
Huntington, Ellsworth, 24
Hyde, George, 50–51
Hyde, James, 43, 47, 50–51
Hyslop, Maxwell, 80–81, 138, 145
Hyslop, Wellwood, 80–81, 138, 145

Iles, Thomas, 43, 47–48
Incas, 92
Inglis, John, 50–51
Ionian Islands, 177
ironwork, 34
Irving, Edward, 144–45, 149
Irving, Thomas, 149

Jackson, Andrew, 79, 80
Jamaica, 53, 56, 57, 86, 123; George Frederic's teenage years in, 63, 64, 65, 69; land access limited in, 42; liquidity troubles in, 99; MacGregor's trip to, 80–81; sarsaparilla trade in, 32; sugar trade in, 95–98, 111, 113; trees of, 31; U.S. trade with, 96–97
James, Preston, 40–41
Jefferys, Thomas, 71
Jerrold, Douglas William, 193
Johnson, P., 142, 159
Jonsson, Fredrik Albritton, 182
Johnston, H.J.M., 191
joint-stock companies, 104–6, 136
Jones (agent of Herring, Graham, and Powles), 166, 167
Jones, Thomas Howell, 205

Joseph Bonaparte, king of Spain, 14, 41
Josephs, Edward, 165, 171, 173

Kafka, Franz, 176
Kennersley Castle (ship), 117, 125–29, 134, 142–45, 154, 157–58, 164, 174
Kerviel, Jérôme, 7
King, Emory, 220n24
The King v. Low George Augustine (1824), 159–61
Klerman, Daniel, 109

Lake Nicaragua, 34; canal project envisioned for, 68, 118, 120
Lamoreaux, Naomi, 142
Law, William, 134
Lawrie, James, 38
legal fictions, 109–10, 123–24
Legge, William, 57
Lehuby, Jean-François, 150
Lelacheur, Pierre, 208
Levi, Giovanni, 204
Lewis and Clark, 38
Liverpool, Robert Banks, 2d earl of Liverpool, 107–8
Lizars, William Home, 121
Lloyd's of London, 114, 135, 142, 143, 188
logwood, 31, 39, 41
Lombard, Alexandre, 225n55
London Philhellenic Committee, 169, 170, 206–7
London Stock Exchange, 164; Committee for General Purposes of, 121–22; Latin American bonds issued on, 15, 106–7; Poyais bonds issued on, 4, 115, 117, 122, 140–41, 168, *174*, 198; securities lightly regulated by, 108, 109, 197
Louriottes, Andreas, 169, 170
Louis XVI, king of France, 169
Low, George Augustus, 157–60, 180, 186
Lowe, John, 1, 122, 140, 151; Latin America markets coveted by, 114, 118; MacGregor abandoned by, 126, 137, 156; Ogilvie's agreement with, 113–15;

self-dealing by, 124–25, 136, 138–39, 148
Lustig, Victor, 8

MacGregor, Gregor, *4*, *120*; archival sources on, 11–12; battered reputation of, 1–2, 190, 204; confidence of, 137; conventional view of, 2, 4, 8–9, 10, 18, 194; criticisms of, 135, 151, 198–99; Dard's support for, 150; egotism of, 21, 135; death of, 206; fictional and satirical treatments of, 6–7, 204–5; financing options for, 104–7, 151; fraud imputed to, 154, 156; Lowe criticized by, 124–25, 126; as mercenary, 75–83, 100, 103, 196; military commitments abandoned by, 91; as monarch, 21, 139–40, 198, 199; naïveté of, 203; Poyais colonization plans of, 86–99, 101; Poyais land grant to, 21, 23, 42, 43, 51, 70–74, 83–86, 122, 124, 128, 145, 146, 196, 201; reputational risks borne by, 122; revisionist views of, 9–10, 195; Scottish emigration encouraged by, 185; Strangeways's praise of, 121; John Wright enlisted by, 146
MacGregor, Jane, 100, 102
MacGregor, Josepha, 139, 206
MacGregor, Rob Roy, 121
Madoff, Bernard, 7–8
mahogany trade, 23, 41, 98, 104, 118, 129, 132, 180; British Honduras magistrates in, 49–50; financing of, 41, 47; importance of, 30–31; limits on, 27, 35, 40, 52; oligarchy linked to, 43, 50, 53, 174, 196; in Poyais development plans, 95–96; seasonality of, 34, 40, 46–47; slavery linked to, 32, 35, 42, 196
Malitzin (La Malinche), 38
Malta, 169, 177
Malthus, Thomas, 123, 181, 182, 184
Margarita Island, 73, 76, 77, 84, 89–90
Mayangna (Sumu) people, 28, 32
Meighan, Edward, 43
Mérilhou, Joseph, 150, 152

Index

Metcalf, Alida, 38
Metternich, Klemenz Wenzel von, 169
Mexican Eagle (ship), 133, 134, 157
Mexico, 2, 78, 82,168
Middle Ground (White), 27, 33
Miranda, Francisco de, 76, 90, 91, 92
Miskitu people, 28; British links to, 36, 39; mahogany harvested by, 35; in slave trade, 32; tribute paid to, 33–34, 36
Mocatta, Aaron, 113
Mocatta, Abraham, 110
Mocatta, Daniel, 110–11, 113, 114, 140, 141, 142, 170, 206
Monroe, James, 82
Montefiore, Abraham, 141
Montefiore, Horatio, 140–41
Morillo, Pablo, 81
Moskitia, 16–17, 20–28, 29, 37, 73, 74; academic interest in, 25; illegal-logging raids in, 40; Indigenous peoples in, 28, 127, 128; mahogany resources in, 31, 111; map of, 119; political economy of, 51; royal arbitration in, 62; transatlantic links of, 26; Spanish jurisdiction over, 122
Moss, John, 54
Mount Tambora eruption (1815), 181
Murray (captain), 83, 85, 89
Murray, John, 122, 123
Murray-Young, Douglas, 177

Napoleon Bonaparte, emperor of the French, 13–14, 224n18
Napoleonic Wars, 2, 9, 87, 96; British economy buffeted by, 99, 118, 181, 182; economic and political upheaval linked to, 101, 103; independence movements ignited by, 67
Nariño, Antonio, 75
Navigation Act (1818), 96
Naylor, Robert, 26–27
Netherlands, 97
Neuhoff, Théodore-Antoine, baron de, 149
New Granada, 81, 89

Newson, Linda, 25, 36
Newte, Thomas, 80, 82, 88, 103
Nicaragua, 24; independence of, 26
Nicholson, G., 142, 159
Nugent, Maria, 63

Odier, Charles, 225n55
Offen, Karl, 31
Ogilvie, George, 103
Ogilvie, James, 104, 114, 115, 122, 124, 138; MacGregor's fund raising aided by, 106–7, 110, 117, 197; mercantile background of, 103; Mocatta's proposal rejected by, 113, 140; Poyais project abandoned by, 126, 137, 156, 198; as shipper, 117, 126, 128
Ogilvie, Jean-Jacques, 103, 138
Olien, Michael, 25
Orellana, Baron, 140
Orlandos, Jean, 169, 170
Osburn, Thomas, 46
Outline of a Plan of Emigration to Upper Canada (Wilmot-Horton), 182
Ouvrard, Gabriel-Julien, 149

Paslow, Thomas, 43, 47, 135
Paya people, 28, 32, 36, 67, 70, 92
Peace of Basel (1795), 41
Peggy (Honduran slave), 57, 58
Pepe, Guglielmo, 113
Perceval, Spencer, 76, 90
Perring, John, 114
Perring, Shaw, Barber & Co., 114, 115, 117, 138, 139, 146, 152
Peru, 2, 4, 12, 15, 107, 109, 110, 141, 155, 197
Peterloo Massacre (1819), 181
Pétion, Alexandre, 80
Piar, Manuel, 75
Pickstock, Thomas, 43, 134, 157, 159, 161–63
Pictet, Louis, 225n55
Pitt, William, the Elder, 30, 31
Pluymers, Keith, 219n3
Pocahontas, 38

Political Essay on the Kingdom of New Spain (Humboldt), 107
polygamy, 36, 39, 62
Ponzi, Charles, 8
Poor Laws, 181, 182
Porto Bello, 81–82, 86, 88, 91, 95, 150, 195
Potthast, Barbara, 26
Powles, John Diston, 123, 166
Poyais, *3, 22, 93, 119, 129*; as American Indigenous project, 16–17; bonds issued for, 4–5, 7, 13, 19, 20, 114–15, *116,* 124–25, 136–46, 151–52, *153,* 154, 156–57, 163–66, 170–71, *172,* 173–75, 192, 204–6; as bulwark against U.S. expansion, 185; cargo confiscated from, 144, 148–50, 157, 159, 163, 174, 175, 180, 186; changing rationale for, 74, 92, 99, 101; coat of arms of, 95–96, *120,* 121; Colonial Office and, 176–77; conventional views of, 2, 5, 8–12, 18, 73, 194; criticisms of, 151, 156, 193, 205; deteriorating conditions in, 131; emigration from, 131–35, 137, 142, 144, 154, 162–63; land grant for, 21, 23, 42, 43, 51, 70–74, 83–86, 122, 124, 128, 145, 146, 196, 201; mahogany trade linked to, 95, 98, 101, 103–4; mercenaries linked to, 91, 94; military plans for, 74, 84, 90, 99, 149; neutrality of, 92, 96–98, 101, 103–4, 197; political status of, 97–98, 109–10, 149, 154, 197, 199, 204; promotional guide to, 118, 122–23; repercussions of, 17, 191, 206; settlers and cargo sent to, 117, 125–30, 143–46, *147,* 148, 157, 158–59, 161, 198, 199; sugar trade linked to, 96, 138, 145
Pratt, Josiah, 59–60
Prince (City of London Common Councillor), 154–56
Providence Island Company, 30
Prussia, 7, 106, 169
Pye, Allen Hampden, 131

Rafter, Michael, 102
Rama people, 28, 32, 36, 64

Reis, Josiah, 230n46
Ricardo, David, 141
Ricardo, Jacob, 141
Rich, Robert, duke of Warwick, 30
Richards, Eric, 184
Richardson, John William (bondholder), 167
Richardson, William John (Poyais agent), 138–43, 145, 146, 151–59, 163, 174, 180, 186, 190, 199, 207
Rio de la Hacha, 75, 82, 86, 88, 91, 95, 102, 150, 195
Robert Charles Frederic, king of the Miskitu, 63, 131, 206, 208
Roberts, Orlando, 65, 68, 69, 85
Robinson (general), 66, 67, 68–70, 134–35
Robinson, Ronald, 16
Rochard, Simon Jacques, 121
Rodrígues, Moises Enrique, 9–10
Rothschild, Carl, 113
Rothschild, Nathan Mayer, 113, 114, 141, 167; Lowe hired by, 125; MacGregor's overtures to, 86–90, 94–95, 98–100, 197; Prussian loan managed by, 106
Roughley, Thomas, 85–86
Rubinstein, William, 140
rum production, 97
Russia, 7, 107, 109, 146, 169

Sacagawea, 38
Sáez, Victor Damián, 149
Saint Helena, 177
St. Lucia, 97
Sambo-Miskitu people, 28, 36, 38
Sandinista uprising, 25
San Martín, José de, 14, 90
Santander, Francisco de Paula, 14, 91, 167
sarsaparilla, 27, 30, 32, 34, 68, 98
Schneidler, Mr. (bondholder), 230n46
Scotland, 11, 100, 102–3, 182
Scott, Walter, 123
Second Carib War (1797), 70
Seminoles, 79
Serra, Giuseppe, 230n46

Shaw, Nathan, 114
Shepherd, Peter, 64
Sinclair, David, 8–9
Skeene (ship), 138, 143–44, 148, 157, 174, 188
slave trade, 35, 40, 47, 66–67; abolition of, 42, 56–57, 60, 97, 99, 101, 178, 188; of Africans, 32, 34; of Indigenous Americans, 32, 34, 36, 57–58, 60, 66–67, 69, 82, 132, 163, 179, 183, 196; in Jamaica, 96, 97; mahogany trade linked to, 32, 43, 44, 58–59, 132, 162
smallpox, 33
smuggling, 97
Sorsby, William, 23
sovereign debt, 106, 109, 135–36
Sowerby, James William, 142, 156, 159
Spain: empire of, 1–2, 13–14, 30, 33–35, 39–41, 72, 97, 114, 122, 181, 195, 203; Miskitu links to, 25, 26, 28, 30; uprisings against, 15
Spong, Francis Mellite, 113
Springer, James Warren, 38
Sproat, George, 45
Sproat v. France (1822), 45
Squier, Ephraim G. (pseud. Samuel Bard), 24
Stephen, regent of the Miskitu, 64–65, 66, 68
Strangeways, Thomas, 118, 120–21, 122, 123, 125, 126, 129, 146
sugar trade, 26, 58, 60, 80, 106, 145; in Jamaica, 95–98, 111, 113
Sumu (Mayangna) people, 28, 32
Symons (bondholder), 171

Tawira-Miskitu people, 28, 36, 38
Tempest, Luttrell, 38–39
textiles, 31, 32, 181
Thick, James, 142, 159
Thomas, Mr. (Lowe's claimee), 230n46
Time and the River (Edgell), 44
Tobago, 97
Treaty of London (1786), 39–40, 41, 50, 52, 74
Treaty of Paris (1763), 41
Treaty of Paris (1783), 39
Treaty of Tordesillas (1494), 30
Treaty of Versailles (1783), 39, 41
Trinidad, 97
turtle shells, 27, 30, 32, 65

Vander Sluys, Jasper, 239n113
Van Diemen's Land, 131, 132
Vansittart, Nicholas, 90, 91, 96, 176, 182–83
Venezuela, 11, 73, 76, 89, 91, 206
von Hagen, Victor, 23

Waikna (Squier), 24
Walsh, William, 157
Walvin, James, 58
War of Jenkins' Ear (1739–48), 30
War of the Spanish Succession (1701–1714), 98
Warren, Samuel, 83, 85, 89
West, Thomas Wade, 232n72
Westby, George, 132, 133, 156, 157
Westcott, Thomas, 140
Wetenhall, James, 108–9, 115, 140, 141–42, 167, 168, 170–71, 173
White, Richard, 27, 32–33
Whiting, James, 152
Wilberforce, William, 57, 58, 60–61, 66, 106, 121–22, 131, 163, 178, 179–80, 196
Willer (captain), 161
Williams, Charles, 5, 6
Williams, Lewis Evans, 50
Wilmot-Horton, Robert, 20, 55–56, 159, 177–91, 202
Woodbine, George, 79–80, 82, 83, 86, 92, 138
Wright, John (British naval officer), 146, 148, 208
Wright, John W. (Belizean magistrate), 43, 44, 47, 49, 157, 159, 160–63, 188
Wright & Young (wholesaler), 45, 47, 49

Young, John, 49

Zea, Antonio Francisco, 109, 151, 166, 167
Zola, Émile, 205
Zwinger (investor), 171

The authorized representative in the EU for product safety and compliance is:
Mare Nostrum Group
B.V Doelen 72
4831 GR Breda
The Netherlands

www.ingramcontent.com/pod-product-compliance
Lightning Source LLC
Chambersburg PA
CBHW031801220426
43662CB00007B/483